GLOBAL LATIN/O AMERICAS
Frederick Luis Aldama and Lourdes Torres, Series Editors

Sponsored Migration

The State and Puerto Rican Postwar Migration to the United States

Edgardo Meléndez

THE OHIO STATE UNIVERSITY PRESS
COLUMBUS

Copyright © 2017 by The Ohio State University.
All rights reserved.

Library of Congress Cataloging-in-Publication Data
Names: Meléndez, Edgardo, author.
Title: Sponsored migration : the state and Puerto Rican postwar migration to the United States / Edgardo Meléndez.
Other titles: Global Latin/o Americas.
Description: Columbus : The Ohio State University Press, [2017] | Series: Global Latin/o Americas | Includes bibliographical references and index.
Identifiers: LCCN 2017009221 | ISBN 9780814213414 (cloth ; alk. paper) | ISBN 0814213413 (cloth ; alk. paper)
Subjects: LCSH: Puerto Ricans—United States—Migrations. | Puerto Ricans—United States—Politics and government. | Puerto Ricans—United States—Social conditions. | Migrant labor—United States. | Puerto Rico—Colonial influence. | Puerto Rico—Politics and government—1898–1952. | Puerto Rico—Politics and government—1952–1998. | United States—Politics and government—1933–1953.
Classification: LCC E184.P85 M45 2017 | DDC 305.868/7295073—dc23
LC record available at https://lccn.loc.gov/2017009221

Cover design by Christian Fuenfhausen
Text design by Juliet Williams
Type set in Adobe Minion Pro and Myriad Pro

Cover image: AGPR, Photographic Archives, *Colección Departamento de Instrucción Pública* (Department of Education Collection). Photo by Charles Rotkin.

♾ The paper used in this publication meets the minimum requirements of the American National Standard for Information Sciences—Permanence of Paper for Printed Library Materials. ANSI Z39.48–1992.

9 8 7 6 5 4 3 2 1

CONTENTS

List of Illustrations — vii

Acknowledgments — ix

Abbreviations — xiii

INTRODUCTION Migration in the Periphery of Empire — 1

CHAPTER 1 Puerto Rican Migration and the Colonial State — 25

CHAPTER 2 "Neither Encouraging nor Discouraging": The Making of Puerto Rico's Migration Policy — 49

CHAPTER 3 Puerto Ricans as Domestic Workers and the Farm Placement Program — 72

CHAPTER 4 There Ain't No Buses from San Juan to the Bronx: Postwar Migration and Air Transportation — 93

CHAPTER 5 "Every Puerto Rican a Potential Migrant": Migrant Education and the English Language Issue — 122

CHAPTER 6 The Beets of Wrath: Migration Policy and Migrant Discontent in Michigan, 1950 — 159

CHAPTER 7 Puerto Ricans as Migratory Labor, the State as a Labor Contractor — 186

Notes — 215

Bibliography — 243

Index — 255

ILLUSTRATIONS

TABLES

1	Arrivals to and departures from Puerto Rico, 1950–60	115
2	Number of visitors to Puerto Rico, 1946–65	115
3	Hotel registrations in San Juan by origin, 1950–65	116
4	Top eight hotel registrations in San Juan, by U.S. states origin, 1955–65	117
5	Air traffic movement in Puerto Rico, 1956–61, by category	119
6	Net yearly migration, 1947–48 to 1960–61, by fiscal year	202
7	BEM job placements in the United States, by fiscal year	203
8	Puerto Rico farm placements in the United States, by state and selected fiscal years	204
9	Total service requests in Migration Division, by fiscal year	207

FIGURES

Figures appear in a gallery following page 148.

1   Cover, DIVEDCO booklet *Emigración*

2   Farmworkers in front of BEM office ready to depart, circa 1953

3   Ad in Arecibo bar announcing airfares to New York, Sept. 1946

4   Ad in Arecibo bar announcing airfares to New York, Sept. 1946 (close-up)

5   Aerial view of Isla Grande Airport, March 1948

6   Aerial view of the International Airport at Isla Verde, Carolina, Puerto Rico, after inauguration

7   Pan Am building at Isla Grande Airport in San Juan, August 1946

8   Main lobby at the International Airport after inauguration in 1955

9   Passengers and mother and child boarding unscheduled flight by Waterman Airlines at Isla Grande Airport in San Juan, July 1946

10 Farmworkers at Isla Grande Airport ready to depart, circa 1953

11 Farmworkers on their way to the United States in unscheduled airline, Salinas, Puerto Rico, July 1946

12 Governors Averel Harriman of New York and Luis Muñoz Marín of Puerto Rico at the tenth anniversary of the Migration Division in New York City, 1958

13 Farmworkers arriving at farm housing, circa 1953

14 Puerto Rican functionaries visiting farmworkers at camp, no date

15 English lesson from *Semana,* November 14, 1960

16 "Our Holocaust: United States—Puerto Rico, 204 Deaths" (editorial cartoon by Filardi)

ACKNOWLEDGMENTS

THIS BOOK is about Puerto Rican migration to the United States. I argue that migration is an integral part of the island's history since 1898, that is, since the United States took over Puerto Rico as a consequence of the War of 1898 with Spain. Moreover, the book focuses specifically on the role that the Puerto Rican government played in the process of migration in the postwar period, particularly during the years between 1947 and 1960. These years represent the "big wave" of Puerto Rican migration during the twentieth century.

I am a political scientist by training. When asked why a political scientist is engaged in the study of migration, a realm usually left to sociologists and anthropologists, I usually respond that this subject is one of the most important political phenomena in twentieth-century Puerto Rico. U.S. and Puerto Rican government functionaries espoused migration as an alternative to what they perceived was the island's most significant problem: overpopulation. Puerto Rican migration to the United States is directly related to U.S. colonial policies on the island, including the granting of citizenship to its residents in 1917. It is best understood as a colonial migration—that is, within the context and framework of U.S. colonialism and citizenship in Puerto Rico during the twentieth century. This should make the topic of Puerto Rican migration to the United States an eminently political subject for research and study.

Migration was also an integral part of Puerto Rican politics in the 1940s and in later years, as is widely discussed in the book. Furthermore, migration *policy*—a central topic in this study—reflects an issue of importance for the government's decision-making process and the political leadership that managed it at the time (the Popular Democratic Party, or PPD). Migration and migration policy were also at the center of the process of reform of the Puerto Rican government during the late 1940s. As argued throughout the book, migration was as important for PPD and U.S. policy makers as was economic policy and the island's political status issue at that time. The book also focuses on the implementation of the government's migration policy. One of the book's goals is to provide an understanding of the profound impact that migration had on Puerto Rican society in areas like education and air transportation, subjects which have remained unexplored until today. The book also points to areas where Puerto Rico's migration policy influenced the development of Puerto Rican communities in the United States with programs like farm placement for agricultural workers and institutions like the Migration Division.

Like all other academic texts, this book has benefitted from the support and assistance of many people. I am most grateful to all of them. Many of the primary documents used in this book come from the Archivo General de Puerto Rico (AGPR—Puerto Rico's General Archives) in San Juan. Numerous individuals helped me during my research at the AGPR. My deepest thanks go particularly to archivist Pedro Roig, whose knowledge and devotion to his work made my time here as productive as it could be. María Isabel Rodríguez, archivist of the AGPR photographic collection, facilitated finding most of the photos included in the book.

I also carried out research at the Library and Archives of the Center for Puerto Rican Studies (Centro), housed in Hunter College–CUNY in New York City. My heartfelt gratitude to senior archivist Pedro Juan Hernández, whose knowledge of the archives furthered my research there. Also to librarian Félix Rivera, as well as to all the other members of the Centro Library, for supporting my work there.

Many days I have spent using the resources—particularly the invaluable collection of newspapers, government reports, and books—of the Colección Puertorriqueña (the Puerto Rican Collection) in the General Library of the University of Puerto Rico at Río Piedras. My thanks to all of those there who have helped me throughout the years in this and other research projects, particularly to its director, María Ordoñez. My appreciation also to the staff of the Fundación Luis Muñoz Marín in San Juan, who provided assistance in using its premier collection of documents, and particularly to the director of the documents section, Julio Quirós.

The research for this book began many years ago while I was still in the Department of Political Science at the University of Puerto Rico. I would like to acknowledge the School of Social Sciences and the department for supporting the initial research and writing for this book with a sabbatical leave. The research and writing for most of this book was done while at Hunter College, where I have been a faculty member since 2009. The administration here has always supported my work for this book. My gratitude to President Jennifer Raab and particularly to Provost Vita Rabinowitz for granting me the support and resources to advance this project. I would like to recognize also the support given to me by the School of Arts and Sciences and the Department of Africana and Puerto Rican/Latino Studies at Hunter College. Also at Hunter College, the Center for Puerto Rican Studies (Centro) has provided significant support to my research and invaluable editorial assistance since I came here. I am indebted to Centro copy editor Ryan Morgan, who had the patience and perseverance to read and edit the initial version of the manuscript.

My gratitude to several colleagues and friends who have supported me all through the duration of this book project by reading chapters of the book, either in the previous or current version of the manuscript, or by sharing ideas that benefitted the book through multiple conversations about my undertaking. Special thanks to my dear friend and colleague Angel Israel Rivera Ortiz, who read most of the latest version of the manuscript and helped me to clarify the text and many ideas. Others who provided guidance and support throughout include Edwin Meléndez, Carlos Vargas, José Cruz, Pedro Cabán, Ismael García, Victor Torres, Jorge Duany, and Xavier Totti.

I would like to acknowledge the anonymous reviewers of the manuscript for the Ohio State University Press. Their thoughtful comments and observations of the manuscript have contributed to a more discerning and insightful book.

Finally, I would like to thank the editor-in-chief of the Ohio State University Press, Kristen Elias Rowley, and the editors of the OSUP Global Latin/o Americas series for believing in this book and for supporting it throughout its publication process. I also want to express my gratitude to Taralee Cyphers and Rebecca S. Bender for their work in editing and revising the manuscript.

ABBREVIATIONS

MOST OF the primary documents used in this book come from Puerto Rico's General Archives (Archivo General de Puerto Rico; to be abbreviated as AGPR), particularly from the Governor's Office File (Fondo Oficina del Gobernador; to be abbreviated as FOG). In endnotes, the full reference to this source, particularly for the fund I used the most (Tarea 96-20) (e.g., AGPR, Fondo Oficina del Gobernador, tarea 9620, box xxx), will be quoted as AGPR, FOG 96-20, xxx.

Another important source of documents used in this book comes from the archives of the Luis Muñoz Marín Foundation (Archivo de la Fundación Luis Muñoz Marín; to be abbreviated as AFLMM). A full reference from this source—for example, AFLMM, Section IV, Series 2, Subseries 9, Department of Labor, Folder 277, doc. 23—will be quoted as AFLMM IV:2, Sub. 9, folder 277, doc. 23.

Other abbreviations used throughout the book are as follows:

BEM: Bureau of Employment and Migration, Puerto Rico Department of Labor

Comm. Labor: Commissioner of Labor

EDA: Economic Development Administration, or Fomento

FPP: Farm Placement Program

GPR: Government of Puerto Rico

OGPRUS: Office of the Government of Puerto Rico in the United States, Center for Puerto Rican Studies Library and Archives

PPD: Partido Popular Democrático (Popular Democratic Party)

USES: United States Employment Service

INTRODUCTION

Migration in the Periphery of Empire

IT IS QUITE significant that in the years close to the commemoration of the centennial of the Jones Act and the grant of U.S. citizenship to Puerto Ricans by Congress in 1917, most news regarding Puerto Rico in the local, U.S., and global media is related to the worst economic crisis the island has experienced since the 1930s. While Puerto Ricans argue about the turmoil created by the Puerto Rican government's seemingly unpayable public debt and its related financial crisis, the second news item widely debated in the local media is the continued discussion regarding the increasing number of Puerto Ricans leaving the island for the United States as a result of this economic situation. According to academic and government reports, Puerto Rican migration in the twenty-first century is comparable in terms of volume and magnitude to the one experienced during the period of the "great wave of migration" from the late 1940s to the early 1960s. At that time, an average of forty thousand people left the island for the United States; in 2014 the net migration was estimated to be sixty-four thousand.[1] In the United States, news regarding Puerto Rico is dominated by the same two issues: the economic collapse of the island and its related fiscal crisis, and the continued and increasing migration of Puerto Ricans to the U.S. mainland.[2]

This is not Puerto Rico's first economic crisis since the United States occupied the territory in 1898, nor is it the first time Puerto Ricans have moved to the U.S. mainland in large numbers as a consequence of economic turmoil on the island. But to fully comprehend the issue of Puerto Rican migration to the United States, one must understand the complexities of U.S. rule in Puerto Rico ever since the island was taken as war booty at the end of the Spanish-American War. In 1901 the U.S. Supreme Court declared Puerto Rico to be an "unincorporated territory," a novel legal and political category in more than one hundred years of U.S. territorial expansion and incorporation. This declaration legitimized the U.S. colonial regime implanted on the island by Congress in 1900. In 1917 Congress granted U.S. citizenship to Puerto Ricans. One of the most important consequences of this act was to uphold the unrestricted entry of Puerto Ricans to the United States. Thus, colonialism, citizenship, and migration are interrelated elements of the Puerto Rican experience and have been important in shaping the lives of Puerto Ricans—whether on the island or on the U.S. mainland—since 1898.

Migration to the United States has been an integral part of the history of Puerto Ricans since the beginning of the twentieth century. The civilian colonial government established by the United States in 1900 through the Foraker Act promoted migration as a mechanism to solve what colonial administrators concluded was the island's major problem: overpopulation. Migration to the United States increased significantly after the grant of citizenship in 1917. From the late 1940s to the early 1960s, over half a million Puerto Ricans migrated to the United States. By 2006, more than half of all Puerto Ricans lived on the U.S. mainland. Puerto Rican migration is characterized by the movement of citizens from a U.S. unincorporated (i.e., colonial) territory to the main jurisdictional boundaries of the American polity. Puerto Rican migration to the United States therefore needs to be understood as a *colonial migration,* that is, within the context of U.S. colonialism and citizenship in Puerto Rico.

One important aspect of this experience is the very active role that the government of Puerto Rico played in this process from the late 1940s to the mid-1970s. While the governments of many nation-states in the late twentieth century—like many in Latin America and the Caribbean—have engaged in the promotion of migration and in the incorporation of their citizens in the host society, what is peculiar to the Puerto Rican experience is that Puerto Rico is an unincorporated territory of the United States, not an independent nation-state, and Puerto Ricans are U.S. citizens. The Puerto Rican migration experience is particular, then, in that it presents a case where the government of a non-nation-state was engaged in promoting the migration and incorporation of its people to the metropolis of which they are technically citizens. To achieve its goals of organizing migration, Puerto Rico's government formulated and implemented its own migration policy.

Puerto Rico's migration policy was influenced by the ideas and policies adopted by civic and political institutions in the United States—particularly in New York City—toward Puerto Rican migrants, as well as by actions and ideas of U.S. and Puerto Rican policy makers managing Puerto Rico's affairs. The Puerto Rican government played an important role in the social and political incorporation of its migrants in the United States as part of its migration project. The policies and practices of Puerto Rico's government—the creation of the Bureau of Employment and Migration (BEM) in San Juan, the Migration Division in the United States, and the Farm Placement Program (FPP), for example—are crucial factors in understanding migration from Puerto Rico and Puerto Rican incorporation and community formation in the United States in the postwar period.

The Puerto Rican migration experience must be included in the study of the long and complex history of migrations to the United States. Recent major studies of the American migration experience do not pay due attention to the study of a colonial migration to the United States.[3] One reason for this situation is that the Puerto Rican experience poses a set of questions that are not easy to answer, and this may lead to its exclusion from more comprehensive studies of U.S. migrations: Are Puerto Ricans internal migrants or are they immigrants? Are they traditional immigrants or transnational migrants? What is the role played by U.S. citizenship and colonialism in the migration of Puerto Ricans to the United States? If Puerto Ricans are U.S. citizens, why did the government of Puerto Rico have to play a role in their incorporation in the United States? In other words, the Puerto Rican migration experience does not fit with the traditional perspectives applied to the study of migrations to the United States.

THE STUDY OF PUERTO RICO'S MIGRATION POLICY

This book will focus on the role that Puerto Rico's government played in the migration experience of Puerto Ricans, particularly in the development of its migration policy and its specific actions to promote the incorporation of Puerto Rican migrants in the United States during 1940s and 1950s, the period displaying the largest migration wave in the twentieth century. The study of Puerto Rico's migration policy has not been extensive so far, although it was an important element of the Puerto Rican migration experience, as the central chapters of this book will maintain. I depart from previous studies of Puerto Rican migration policy, particularly from theories that seek to explain migration policy as a reaction to the individual decisions of migrants to relocate abroad, or that suggest that migration policy is simply a consequence of socioeconomic structural processes.

The former perspective—migration policy as a reaction to the spontaneous migration of individuals—was the official policy of the Puerto Rican government since the enactment of the 1947 migration law. This perspective was disseminated in the academic arena by Clarence Senior, an adviser to Puerto Rico's government on issues of migration and director of the Puerto Rican Department of Labor's Migration Division for many years. During and after his work with the Puerto Rican government, Senior wrote extensively trying to explain Puerto Rican migration to the U.S. public, always maintaining the Puerto Rican government's view that "the government neither encourages nor discourages migration." Following a traditional push and pull theory of migration, Senior argued that Puerto Rico's migration was caused by the island's overpopulation and lack of jobs, which forced individuals to move to the United States, where jobs were available. The government's migration policy came as a reaction to the abuses by labor contractors or to aid individuals who migrated on their own in their insertion in the new society—that is, to manage the two migrant flows from the island: individual migrants and organized migration.[4] Senior contended that the strong reaction in the United States to the entry of Puerto Ricans after 1947 was due to racism and a traditional antagonism toward immigrants. In that sense, he argued, Puerto Rican migration followed the traditional pattern of incorporation of previous immigrants.[5]

In reaction to this official view of migration presented by the Puerto Rican government, a structural perspective on Puerto Rican migration emerged in the 1970s spearheaded by the work of the newly created Centro de Estudios Puertorriqueños (Center for Puerto Rican Studies) in New York City. That perspective was particularly related to the works of two scholars directly linked to Centro, director Frank Bonilla and researcher Ricardo Campos. This structural, neo-Marxist approach was first presented in the groundbreaking *Labor Migration under Capitalism: The Puerto Rican Experience*, produced by Centro's History Task Force.[6] The book posed a very critical review of the official perspective on migration, arguing that Puerto Rican migration—like all contemporary migrations—had to be understood as a consequence of the process of capitalist accumulation at a global level. Puerto Rican migration thus represented the movement of labor from one area of capitalist accumulation to another. Historical peculiarities of the Puerto Rican case—like colonialism—had to be incorporated into this analysis, but the Puerto Rican experience followed the rules of labor migration under the structure of world capitalist accumulation. In the book, only a few cursory remarks are made on the role of the Puerto Rican government in the management of the island's migration. It can be deduced from this analysis that politics and state policies, including migration policy, follow the dictates of capitalism.

Bonilla and Campos expanded the perspective introduced in *Labor Migration* for many years. They nonetheless maintained the perspective on migration advanced in the book and paid little attention to the role that the Puerto Rican government played in the management of the island's migration.[7] I share Bonilla and Campos's view in explaining migration by structural forces, but I think that it is still very important to include the role played by the colonial state in the organization and management of Puerto Rican migration to the United States. Migration was not a creation of the Puerto Rican colonial state, of course. However, once it was deemed a "problem" that had to be dealt with, the colonial state played a very important role in the lives of migrants by encouraging and organizing migration, expanding the air transportation infrastructure to facilitate the movement of migrants, carrying a process of migrant selectivity, channeling them into specific locations in the United States, becoming an intermediary between laborers and contractors, facilitating their incorporation in the United States, taking their defense in labor disputes with American employers, and even confronting the federal government in defending the rights of Puerto Ricans as U.S. citizens to be treated as domestic labor with preferential access for jobs before alien workers. By focusing on the structural forces that promote migration, this perspective has placed a very limited emphasis on the important role played by the Puerto Rican government in this process.

The only work that until now has focused on the formulation of Puerto Rico's migration policy is historian Michael Lapp's excellent 1991 doctoral dissertation on the Migration Division in New York. Lapp's study provides the most comprehensive study of Puerto Rico's migration policy to date.[8] It is, nevertheless, limited by a lack of examination of primary documents from archival sources in Puerto Rico that render a different perspective on the formulation of migration policy and the political factors that influenced this process. Furthermore, by arguing that migration policy in the late 1940s was the result of "technocratic" imperatives and policy makers, Lapp presents an inaccurate view not only as to why migration policy was formulated but also on who formulated it. By focusing on the creation and programs of the Migration Division in New York, Lapp overstates the role of Senior.[9] For the most part, he overlooks the workings of the Department of Labor's BEM, to which the Migration Division was subordinated and which organized and directed the movement of workers from Puerto Rico to the United States; the Division took care of migrants once they were in the United States, but always under the directives of the San Juan office. In neglecting this point, Lapp implies that the formulation of migration policy was not an important policy issue to the rising governing party, the Popular Democratic Party (Partido Popular Democrático—PPD). I will sustain in later chapters that migration was indeed a fundamental issue for the PPD and its main leader, Luis Muñoz Marín. It was Muñoz Marín and his inner circle (which did not include Senior) who debated, formulated, and implemented the government's migration policy. Puerto Rico's migration policy was originally formulated and later implemented by the Commissioner of Labor, Fernando Sierra Berdecía. For Muñoz Marín and the PPD, migration was as fundamental a government issue as economic development and the island's political status issue. In fact, I will argue throughout the book that these three policy areas were directly related to one another.

PUERTO RICAN MIGRATION AND TRANSNATIONALISM

International migration is a central phenomenon of the expansion of the global economy and of recent changes in the relationships between states. Transnational migrations—where immigrants maintain social, economic, and political relationships with the home country—are an important element of modern global migration studies.[10] A key element of the transnational phenomenon is the role played by the homeland state in the promotion of migration and in the incorporation of its citizens in the host society.[11] Thus, one important aspect of the migration projects of these homeland states involves the elaboration and implementation of migration policies. Eva Ostergaard-Nielsen emphasizes the importance of migration policies by sending states: "Migration policy stands out as a policy area because it is a transnational issue which spans the borders between states, blurs the distinction between domestic and foreign policy, goes to the heart of the two-way relationship of obligations and rights between state and citizens."[12] If Ostergaard-Nielsen is right, if migration policy is a clear sign of a transnational issue by a nation-state, then how to explain the fact that the Puerto Rican government, a U.S. colonial state, elaborated and sustained a migration policy to promote the migration and incorporation of Puerto Ricans—technically U.S. citizens—to the United States? Even if the Puerto Rican migration experience is not considered as transnational, it resembles aspects that are proposed in the literature on political transnationalism with regard to the issue of migration policy and the role of the state in managing migration.[13]

Although the Puerto Rican case has been excluded from the comparative analysis of major scholars using the transnational perspective, some scholars have argued that the Puerto Rican experience should be studied as a transnational case even though Puerto Rico is not a nation-state and Puerto Ricans are U.S. citizens. Well-known anthropologist Jorge Duany, for example, contends that even if the Puerto Rican case is characterized as a colonial migration, it can be understood as a transnational one.[14] Other scholars have also argued that Puerto Rican migration and community formation in the United States must be understood as a transnational experience.[15] The Puerto Rican case has been compared to other experiences of Latin American transnationalism in the United States.[16]

In *Puerto Rican Nation on the Move,* Duany emphasizes the importance of migration for Puerto Ricans and the linkages between the island and its diaspora in the United States. He also studies the role of the Puerto Rican government in the promotion and management of migration to the United States.[17] But Duany avoids the question of why the Puerto Rican government had to engage in such a peculiar role. Furthermore, he follows Lapp's argument that Puerto Rico's migration policy was mostly designed by Senior,[18] a mistaken notion that, as I have just argued, has important historical and analytical connotations. In later writings, including his excellent *Blurred Borders,* Duany has expanded his framework of study of Puerto Rican migration. He has compared Puerto Rican migration to the Dominican and Cuban transnational migrations to the United States, arguing that the former is an example of "colonial transnationalism." Making comparisons to the experience of other transnational countries, Duany points to the role the Puerto Rican government played in migration, calling it a "transnational colonial state."[19]

But even after Duany's very incisive examination of Puerto Rican migration, his work still raises an important question: can a migration of citizens from a colonial territory to the metropolitan homeland be considered as transnational?[20] The argument made by Duany and other scholars to define the Puerto Rican experience as a transnational one is that although Puerto Ricans do cross social, economic, and cultural borders, they do not cross national political boundaries. Are Puerto Ricans transnational migrants? Not in the sense that they have to cross international borders, which is the widely accepted definition in this field. But neither can they be considered as traditional internal migrants to the United States. For Puerto Rican policy makers, the island migrants, although U.S. citizens, were moving to the United States from an "ethnologically different" society, like the European immigrants before them. The goal of easing their incorporation and assimilation into American society was one of the reasons that justified the Puerto Rican government's migration policy.[21]

How, though, can the migration of citizens from a colonial territory parallel a transnational migration, which is supposed to involve relations between nation-states and the movement of peoples from one state to another as immigrants? As I have argued elsewhere,[22] while it is true that some significant political aspects discussed by the transnational perspective are similar to the Puerto Rican experience, this unusual condition needs to be explained as a consequence of Puerto Rico's and Puerto Ricans' constitutional and political positioning on the periphery of American empire. The transnational paradigm was not developed to understand colonial migrations; there are several factors that limit the full application of the transnational framework to the understanding of colonial migrations like Puerto Rico's (citizenship and free entry to the metropolis is one). Nevertheless, these scholars are right in pointing out that the Puerto Rican case does resemble a transnational migration in many ways. It certainly does in the role played by the colonial state in the migration experience of Puerto Ricans.

On the other hand, the role played by the colonial state in Puerto Rican migration makes this experience very different from any other internal migration in the United States. If Puerto Ricans are to be considered as internal migrants, why did Puerto Rico's government take upon itself the role to protect its migrants in the United States and to facilitate their incorporation into American society and polity? As U.S. citizens, were not they already incorporated into the American polity? If Puerto Rican migration is to be regarded as an internal migration, then it has no parallel with other internal migrations in the United States. There is no evidence that state governments played a major role in the migration process or in the protection of their migrants elsewhere in the United States, taking actions to facilitate their social, economic, political, and cultural incorporation outside of their jurisdictions.

The role of the Puerto Rican colonial state in migration also raises questions regarding the nature of the Puerto Rican colonial state within the American polity and the nature of U.S. citizenship for Puerto Ricans. The particular arrangement of the Puerto Rican colonial state within the U.S. polity (as one representing the peoples of an unincorporated territory) and the distinct construct of U.S. citizenship for Puerto Ricans (as one diminished by the colonial territory and formulated early in the twentieth century based on the notion that these subjects were "alien" to the American polity) made them appear foreign to the United States not only culturally but also politically, thus making the Puerto Rican migration experience look like a transnational one in many ways.

I agree with Duany and others that the Puerto Rican migration experience has many attributes similar to those of transnational migrations, particularly with aspects related to political transnationalism. But characterizing it as "colonial transnationalism" does not provide a fuller understanding of this migration experience. Puerto Ricans do not move from one nation-state to another, so there is no need to acquire the host state citizenship and all that this entails in terms of incorporation, identity, and so on. There is no need for dual citizenship and all that implies in terms of relationship with the home state. There are no obstacles to returning since the homeland territory is under the jurisdiction and sovereignty of the metropolitan state, which explains the much noticed back and forth or circular migration among Puerto Ricans. While Duany underscores the transnational nature of Puerto Rican migration, one with a colonial character, I rather emphasize the colonial nature of Puerto Rican migration, one that because of the specific context of U.S. colonialism in Puerto Rico seems like a transnational migration. It is a migration that has been shaped by a specific kind of U.S. citizenship that, according to the Supreme Court in *Balzac v. the People of Porto Rico,* is limited by the colonial territory where Puerto Ricans live—a diminished and problematic metropolitan citizenship, but one that has allowed Puerto Ricans to enter the U.S. territory with no legal obstacles. This is something that transnational migrants do not experience.

Puerto Rican migration to the United States seems like a transnational migration largely due the particular construction of U.S. colonialism in Puerto Rico. The territory was defined by congressional acts and by the Supreme Court in the Insular Cases as "foreign in a domestic sense" to the United States (the unincorporated territory), a status that has persisted even after Congress granted citizenship to Puerto Ricans in 1917. The widespread notion among the American elite that Puerto Ricans were "alien" to the United States due to their ethnic and cultural characteristics and their presumed low level of civilization provided the basis for defining the territory as unincorporated and outside the boundaries of the American polity. This territorial status allowed the exclusion of Puerto Ricans from citizenship for many years. But even after Puerto Ricans became citizens, the idea that they were somehow alien to the United States remained an integral notion to the character of the citizenship that they were granted in 1917.[23] Although other historical factors have to be considered as well, citizenship allowed Puerto Ricans unrestricted access to the U.S. mainland. But even as citizens, Puerto Ricans moving to the United States were regarded for many decades as alien or foreign in character and nature to the United States and not as full members of the American polity.[24]

U.S. EMPIRE STUDIES AND PUERTO RICAN MIGRATION

I argue in this book that Puerto Rican migration to the United States has to be understood as a colonial migration—that is, as a migration of U.S. citizens coming from a colonial (unincorporated) territory of the United States, which highlights the importance of understanding the relationship between U.S. colonialism, citizenship and migration in the Puerto Rican experience. Herein lies what might be the most important contribution of studying Puerto Rican migration to the United States: it is the most significant case of a migration of citizens from the colonial periphery of overseas territories to the U.S. mainland.[25]

Puerto Ricans and Puerto Rico occupy a liminal position within the American polity. Puerto Ricans are U.S. citizens who, because of their linguistic and cultural characteristics, are seen as foreigners in the United States. Although citizens, their territory is still defined as "foreign in a domestic sense," according to a U.S. Supreme Court 1901 ruling. Their migration to the U.S. mainland reflects this confounding status. This might be why American academia in the postwar period was not capable of understanding the character of this migration and of the new migrants, placing their experience within the traditional framework of European migrations and concluding repeatedly that they were destined to fail in their incorporation to American society, contrary to the experience of previous "traditional immigrants."[26] Today, scholars trying to place the Puerto Rican experience within the transnational framework face a similar analytical predicament: although Puerto Rican migration presents some elements that resemble a transnational migration, it does not fit adequately within a perspective that focuses on the movement of immigrants from one nation-state to another.

Given that the framework of this book seeks to understand migration within the context of U.S. colonialism and citizenship in Puerto Rico, this book benefits from and seeks to expand the literature on U.S. empire. The hundredth anniversary of U.S. colonialism in the Caribbean and the Pacific after the Spanish-American War of 1898 and later the war in Iraq expanded the interest and the introspection of studying the United States as an empire. The works of distinguished scholars like William Appleman Williams and Walter LaFeber, among many others, point to the notable tradition of studying the American imperial venture.[27] However, the emphasis of these scholars was mostly on "U.S. imperialism," that is, a focus on the economic, political, and military expansion of the United States outside its borders. They mostly centered on the study of U.S. diplomacy and followed either the parameters of traditional history or Marxism, with its heavy emphasis on economic interests and the exploitation of colonies or neocolonies.[28] But beginning in the 1990s, a new generation of U.S. scholars began to examine other factors in the character of U.S. empire: race, gender, class, and culture, among others. They also began to accentuate U.S. empire from the inside, that is, on the consequences of empire for American society.

The work that is usually cited in the resurgence of studying U.S. empire is *Cultures of United States Imperialism*, a volume edited by Amy Kaplan and Donald Pease.[29] The book questioned the myth of "American exceptionalism," that is, that contrary to the European great powers, the United States never became an empire. It also aimed at putting culture in its widest sense (race, gender, identity, etc.) at the center of studies of U.S. empire. Furthermore, the book challenged the distinction between the foreign and the domestic as two separate fields of inquiry in studies of American society and focused on the consequences of empire back home.[30] But, ironically, in a book devoted to "cultures of imperialism," there is no essay devoted to Puerto Rico or to Puerto Ricans in the United States. In addition, in a book dedicated to analyzing the relationship between the "domestic" and the "foreign," there is no inquiry regarding colonial migrations, that is, the movement of people from the colonial periphery to the metropolitan territory as a consequence of the imperial venture.[31]

A more recent and significant contribution to the study of U.S. empire is the volume edited by Alfred W. McCoy and Fransciso Scarano, *Colonial Crucible: Empire in the Making of the Modern American State*. Like Kaplan and Pease, they question the idea of American imperial exceptionalism and the separation between the foreign and the domestic in U.S. affairs. The basic aim of the book is to present the consequences of empire on American society, politics, state formation, and economics. The authors point to a continuum between territorial expansion at home and overseas colonial expansion, between empire inside and empire outside the borders of the American polity.[32] Notwithstanding the greater inclusion of inquiry on the consequences of empire than the Kaplan and Pease volume, the McCoy and Scarano book does not deal with one of the most visible consequences of empire for both the colonized and the metropolitan societies, with one relationship that clearly connects the two ends of the imperial divide and eclipses the divide between the foreign and the domestic in empire: the movement of people from the colonial periphery to the metropolitan territory.

In the last two decades, several scholars have applied the perspective of U.S. empire studies to the research on Puerto Rico and its relationship with the United States, including the construction and development of the colonial state in the first half of the twentieth century and its relationship to U.S.

imperial policies;[33] comparative studies of U.S. colonialism in Puerto Rico and the Philippines,[34] and also of U.S. colonial policies throughout the American "imperial archipelago";[35] the reproductive policies imposed on Puerto Rican women by colonial structures and metropolitan private institutions;[36] and the relationship between education and empire in Puerto Rico.[37] The McCoy and Scarano volume includes essays on the consequences of U.S. empire in Puerto Rico in such areas as justice and law enforcement, education, militarization, citizenship, and national identity.[38]

One area of particular interest in the study of American empire has been the field of legal studies, particularly in the Supreme Court decisions known as the Insular Cases. The role played by the Supreme Court in the rationalization and legitimization of the U.S. imperial presence in Puerto Rico has been carefully studied by several scholars.[39] The status of Puerto Rico and Puerto Ricans in the American polity played an important role in the Insular Cases. Related to the latter, as it is also connected to U.S. colonialism in Puerto Rico, is the issue of American citizenship for Puerto Ricans. In this area, historians and legal scholars have examined the nature of this particular manifestation of citizenship and its relationship to U.S. colonialism in Puerto Rico.[40]

With few notable exceptions, the field of U.S. empire studies has not adequately examined the subject of migration from the colonial periphery to the United States.[41] Recently, several Filipino scholars have provided excellent accounts of the relationship between the construction of a colonial regime in the Philippines and the migration and incorporation of Filipinos in the United States.[42] In the Puerto Rican case, Robert McGreevy has focused on the relationship between U.S. empire and Puerto Rican migration to the United States.[43] This book seeks to expand on these studies of the American empire and its consequences abroad and at home, particularly as it relates to the topic of empire and colonial migrations. It sustains the importance of examining the relationship between U.S. colonialism and citizenship in Puerto Rico in order to provide a more comprehensive framework for the study of Puerto Rican migration to the United States.

MIGRATION, COLONIALISM, AND CITIZENSHIP IN THE PERIPHERY OF EMPIRE

The creation of a colonial periphery by the United States after it took over the island in 1898 is crucial to understanding Puerto Rican migration to U.S. mainland. Through congressional laws, executive policies, and Supreme Court decisions, the American state created a colonial periphery that subordinated

Puerto Rico and its people economically and politically and excluded the territory in important political and constitutional areas of the American polity. In 1900 Congress implemented a colonial government on the island under the Foraker Act, an act deemed legal and constitutional by the Supreme Court in *Downes v. Bidwell* (1901) under the legal guise of the unincorporated territory. In 1917, the U.S. Congress granted Puerto Ricans a citizenship that came to be defined by the colonial relationship between Puerto Rico and the United States according to the Supreme Court in *Balzac v. the People of Porto Rico* (1922).

The issue of migration has been an important element of how the U.S. citizenship of Puerto Ricans was defined and redefined throughout the twentieth century. After the United States took over the island in 1898, exclusion from citizenship for the new colonial subjects was at the center of congressional acts approved for Puerto Rico (the Treaty of Paris of 1898, the Foraker Act of 1900) and U.S. Supreme Court decisions, most importantly in *Downes v. Bidwell*. One reason for this exclusion was the fear among many U.S. policy makers that granting citizenship to the new colonial subjects would allow their unrestricted entry to the United States.

Under Article IX of the Treaty of Paris, Filipinos and Puerto Ricans ("the natives of the islands") were excluded from both U.S. and Spanish citizenship, although *Peninsulares* (those born in Spain) retained their Spanish citizenship (and thus could become U.S. citizens through naturalization). In his influential report to Secretary of War Elihu Root on guidelines to a U.S. colonial policy, Charles Magoon argued that exclusion from citizenship could prevent the new colonial subjects from entering the United States.[44] Senator Foraker included a clause making Puerto Ricans U.S. citizens in the first draft of his bill to create a colonial government in Puerto Rico in 1900. He later declared that he withdrew this clause from the bill in reaction to the strong opposition it generated; opponents argued that citizenship could imply "incorporation" of the territory to the United States and also limit congressional powers in ruling the newly conquered territories.[45] The April 1900 Foraker Act excluded Puerto Ricans from U.S. citizenship and declared them to be "citizens of Porto Rico" (the name of the island was also changed).

Exclusion from citizenship was also at the center of a Supreme Court ruling that justified U.S. colonialism and became the basis for the Insular Cases: *Downes v. Bidwell*. The opinions presented by Justices Henry Brown and Edward White were very influential in shaping U.S. policy toward the new territories. Although these two opinions differed greatly in important matters, there were nevertheless two issues where both were in agreement: the right of the United States to conquer foreign territories as a necessary means to become a great power and the exclusion from the American polity of the peoples of the newly conquered territories.[46] For both Brown and White, the exclusion of the new colonial subjects was justified by the ideas that they were alien in nature to the American polity and that they had no right to become members of the nation.

Justice Brown believed that the "power to acquire territory" would be curtailed if the United States was forced to incorporate these "savage" and "uncivilized" peoples as citizens. Congress would not accept the annexation of foreign territory if "its inhabitants, however foreign they may be to our habits, traditions, and modes of life, shall become at once citizens of the United States." He argued that the newly conquered territories differed from those previously annexed not only in terms of territorial contiguity but also on the differences in race and culture of its inhabitants (the latter territories had been settled by whites). According to Brown, the peoples of the newly acquired territories would have their "natural rights" (life, freedoms, property) protected but not their "artificial" or "residual rights" (like the rights of citizenship and suffrage, and others "which are peculiar to Anglo-Saxon jurisprudence"). It was only after warning about the nefarious consequences of incorporating alien peoples into the union that Brown's opinion stated its well-known ruling that "the island of Porto Rico is a territory appurtenant and belonging to the United States, but not a part of the United States."[47]

Justice White argued that the central question in this case was this: "Had Porto Rico, at the time of the passage of the act in question, been incorporated into and become an integral part of the United States?" Like Brown, he argued that the right to conquer territory would be invalidated if its alien population was incorporated as citizens by "the immediate bestowal of citizenship on those absolutely unfit to receive it." White affirmed "how unwarranted is the principle of immediate incorporation," stating that it was inconceivable that a treaty "by a mere cession can incorporate an alien people in to the United States without the express or implied approval of Congress." His opinion concluded that "while in an international sense Porto Rico was not a foreign country, since it was subject to the sovereignty of and was owned by the United States, *it was foreign to the United States in a domestic sense,* because the island had not been incorporated into the United States, but was merely appurtenant thereto as a possession."[48] Out of this opinion the doctrine of the unincorporated territory became part of U.S. jurisprudence; it has shaped the status of Puerto Rico and Puerto Ricans within and without the American polity ever since.

Downes v. Bidwell said nothing about curtailing the entry of Puerto Ricans to the U.S. mainland. The U.S. government tried to control the entry of Puerto

Ricans and Filipinos to the United States when it extended in 1902 the regulations of the 1891 immigration law to the inhabitants of these islands. On the basis of this interpretation of the law, the commissioner of immigration detained a Puerto Rican woman—Isabel González—and prevented her from entering New York by arguing that she would become a "public charge," as established in the 1891 law. González not only fought the charge but argued that as a Puerto Rican, a U.S. subject living "under the jurisdiction of the United States," she was a U.S. citizen. The U.S. government contended that it could prevent Puerto Ricans and Filipinos from entering the United States by declaring them as "aliens by birth and race" that could be excluded under the Chinese Exclusions laws approved by Congress and sustained by the Supreme Court.[49] In 1904 the Supreme Court ruled in *Gonzales v. Williams* that Puerto Ricans, although not citizens, could enter the United States freely since they were not alien immigrants as the U.S. government argued in that case.[50] After this decision, Puerto Ricans and Filipinos were acknowledged as U.S. "nationals" by the American government.

Puerto Ricans became U.S. citizens on April 1917 after a decade of debate within different sectors of the government. In 1916, Congress approved two Jones Acts, one for the Philippines and one for Puerto Rico. For Filipinos, it began a long transition toward independence during which they remained U.S. nationals. For Puerto Ricans, it entailed U.S. citizenship.[51] After this congressional act, several U.S.-appointed judges on the island ruled that this grant of citizenship had incorporated Puerto Rico to the United States and that all constitutional rights must apply in the territory. In *Balzac v. the People of Porto Rico*, the Supreme Court—in a unanimous ruling written by Chief Justice William Howard Taft in 1922—ruled that the people living in an unincorporated territory do not enjoy all the rights guaranteed to U.S. citizens: "It is *locality* that is determinative of the application of the Constitution in such matters as judicial procedure, and *not the status of the people* who live in it." Another important ruling in *Balzac* was the affirmation that the granting of citizenship to inhabitants of an unincorporated territory by itself was not a sign of its incorporation into the Union, as it had been prior to 1898. Taft reiterated one of Brown's arguments used to deny citizenship and incorporation to territories like Puerto Rico and the Philippines: territorial contiguity and the opportunity to be settled by whites. Race and cultural difference still remained important elements in denying incorporation and thus future statehood to the colonial territories.[52]

Balzac presented another important pronouncement that often goes unnoticed when this ruling is discussed: that moving to the "U.S. proper" was the most important additional right that Puerto Ricans would enjoy as U.S. citizens, and that once there they could "enjoy every right of any other citizen of the United States, civil, social and political. A citizen of the Philippines must be naturalized before he can settle and vote in this country."[53] *Balzac* affirms that the still-colonial subjects in the unincorporated territory would have their constitutional rights and membership in the American polity limited by Congress even though they were now citizens. That is, the restrictions imposed by the unincorporated territory on the constitutional rights of the colonial subjects remained as ruled in *Downes*. Puerto Rico and Puerto Ricans still remained "foreign in a domestic sense." On the other hand, what was intrinsically new in *Balzac* with regard to constitutional rights, as Taft stated twice, was the idea that Puerto Ricans, as citizens, could now have access to full political and civil constitutional rights when they moved within the rightful borders of the American polity.

The Filipino and Puerto Rican migration experiences in the United States share some similar elements, at least until 1917: both groups were defined as "alien" to the U.S. polity immediately after the U.S. occupation of their territories, and both were excluded from U.S. citizenship and defined as U.S. nationals for a time. The right of Puerto Ricans and Filipinos to enter the United States freely had been acknowledged in *Gonzales v. Williams*. After Congress approved a Jones Act for each territory (for the Philippines in 1916 and for Puerto Rico in 1917), their respective paths in relation to the United States differed greatly: under the Jones Act for the Philippines, Filipinos remained as U.S. nationals, and their migration to the U.S. territory would be restricted in later decades. After the Tydings-McDuffie Act of 1934, Congress imposed extremely restrictive quotas to the Philippines, essentially ending Filipino migration to the United States at that time; furthermore, repatriation was forced on Filipinos living in the United States. As Paul Kramer has argued, in their efforts to stop Filipino migration to the United States, American nativists played a significant role in getting Congress to grant independence to the Philippines in some undefined future; while not granting immediate independence to their country, this act made Filipinos "aliens within the U.S. Empire."[54] In *Balzac*, the U.S. Supreme Court underscored the right of U.S. citizens from the unincorporated territories to freely enter the U.S. territory.[55] In *Balzac*, as in *Gonzales*, the debate on the nature of U.S. citizenship for Puerto Ricans was related to their right to enter the U.S. mainland, that is, to migration. After 1917 migration from the colonial territories would be linked to the citizenship status of the colonial subjects. For all practical purposes, citizenship eventually became a requisite for migration from the U.S. colonial periphery to the metropolitan territory.

Filipino migration to the United States was greatly curtailed in the 1930s, while Puerto Rican migration increased after the 1920s. The end of World War II also marked different paths for both nationalities: while the Philippines was granted independence by the United States in 1946, Puerto Rico remained a U.S. colonial territory. On the other hand, the end of the war marked the beginning of a great wave of migration from Puerto Rico to the U.S. mainland. While Filipinos and Puerto Ricans moved to the United States as colonial subjects, since 1917 Puerto Ricans have migrated as colonial citizens. The fact that Puerto Ricans were U.S. citizens might be why the same forces in Congress—represented by Senator Millard Tydings—that pushed for the independence of the Philippines in the 1930s failed in their attempt to do the same with Puerto Rico (in 1936 Tydings submitted a bill for Puerto Rico's independence).

If Puerto Ricans' new citizenship did not extend to their full incorporation as members of the American polity, why, then, were they made citizens? According to José Cabranes, it was to guarantee the U.S. presence on the island and to secure U.S. strategic interests in the Caribbean, as well as to prevent any future demand for independence at a moment when separatist fervor was on the rise.[56] For Efrén Rivera Ramos, citizenship was "imposed" on Puerto Ricans not to free these colonials subjects from colonialism but, to the contrary, to maintain colonialism on the island. To him, citizenship became the most important means of maintaining U.S. hegemony (in the Gramscian sense) in Puerto Rico.[57]

The two Jones Acts for the Philippines and Puerto Rico might also be seen as a formal shift in U.S. imperial policy from creating a formal empire to creating one of an informal character—that is, from the goal of owning and controlling overseas colonies in the mold of European powers to a more indirect form of economic, political, and military domination over foreign countries. During this period, U.S. invasions of Caribbean and Central American countries reflected the new emphasis on gunboat diplomacy. There was never a complete agreement within the American elite on having colonial territories as the best means of projecting American economic, political, and military power abroad. Elihu Root, the architect of U.S. imperial policy as secretary of war, always opposed direct control of overseas territories; he also opposed the granting of citizenship to Puerto Ricans. In the coming decades, the United States took over other overseas territories through purchase or as spoils of World War II in the Caribbean and the Pacific. Many became unincorporated territories, and in all of these except for one, their populations became U.S. citizens, following the Puerto Rican model. All of these unincorporated territories were small islands with strategic value and relatively small populations. Puerto Rico would be the largest and most populated of all of them.[58]

POSTWAR MIGRATION AND THE MEANING OF U.S. CITIZENSHIP IN PUERTO RICO

U.S. citizenship has impacted all areas of Puerto Rican society—political, economic, social, cultural, and ideological—but perhaps none more than migration. If migration was fundamental in the transformation of Puerto Rican society after the end of World War II, then the transformative element of this citizenship for thousands of Puerto Ricans in their daily life has been felt nowhere more than in their right to migrate to the United States in search for jobs when none were available on the island. Citizenship guaranteed their right to free movement within the borders of the American nation-state. If economic and social factors might explain the causes of Puerto Rican migration to the United States, it is Puerto Rico's political relationship with the United States and Puerto Ricans' U.S. citizenship that explains the *direction* and the *nature* of their migration: the movement from a U.S. colonial territory to the metropolitan mainland by colonial subjects who happened to be U.S. citizens.

The colonial or territorial nature of U.S. citizenship in Puerto Rico influenced the way Puerto Ricans migrated to the United States and the way they were incorporated into American society. It also influenced the manner in which the Puerto Rican government intervened in the organization of migration to the United States. Perhaps nothing reflects this more than the constant efforts of Puerto Rico's government after 1947 to have federal agencies and U.S. agricultural employers recognize Puerto Rican farmworkers as domestic labor with preference on employment over foreign labor. Although they were U.S. citizens, for many years the federal government treated Puerto Ricans as alien labor along with Mexicans and West Indians. The meaning of "foreign in a domestic sense"—as Puerto Rico was declared to be in *Downes v. Bidwell*—extended outside the legal-constitutional and political realm: for several decades after the end of World War II, Puerto Ricans were treated as "foreign in a domestic sense" in the American labor market mostly because they came from a territory that had been defined as foreign to the U.S. constitutionally and politically and also because they looked foreign to the United States culturally and ethnically. Puerto Rico's government had to lobby the U.S. government intensely in order to have it recognize Puerto Rican workers as U.S. citizens so they could have preferential treatment before foreign labor in agricultural jobs.

After the end of World War II, the PPD leadership and government moved away from advocating independence for Puerto Rico and into a discourse of closer political and economic relations with the United States. In this process, the PPD had to reinterpret its notion of the meaning of U.S. citizenship for Puerto Ricans: it was heralded as the strongest bond of "permanent union" with the United States in the Commonwealth Constitution in 1952. Migration played a part in redefining the meaning of citizenship for the poor and the working classes in Puerto Rico. The Puerto Rican masses had begun to use this citizenship right after the end of World War II in a different way than the elite: for them, a significant meaning of citizenship at that moment was their right to move to the U.S. mainland in search for jobs. It was the massive and rapid entry of Puerto Ricans to the city that created the "Puerto Rican problem" in New York in 1947, forcing Puerto Rico's government to face this issue and later to formulate its migration policy. U.S. citizenship provided Puerto Ricans with the right to move freely to the United States and later gave the island government the tools to ease their incorporation into American society.

THE COLONIAL STATE AND PUERTO RICAN POSTWAR MIGRATION

As Taft stated in *Balzac,* to enjoy full citizenship rights, Puerto Ricans would have to move to "the United States proper." And so they did, not necessarily looking to enhance their citizenship rights but in search of jobs that were not available in Puerto Rico. Citizenship had not changed the economic structure of the island, and the number of Puerto Ricans moving to the United States in search of jobs increased rapidly after 1917. Although they were now citizens, many sectors in the U.S. mainland—from policy makers to employers to landlords to white workers—still regarded Puerto Ricans moving to the United States as "citizens of Porto Rico," that is, as culturally, racially, and politically alien or foreign to the United States, as colonial subjects that came from a territory that was still not part of the United States, and not as full members of the nation.[59]

Despite the Americanization policies implemented during the first forty years of American rule on the island, the maintenance of linguistic and cultural differences in Puerto Rico preserved a Puerto Rican national identity that manifested itself in the political arena. The economic and political crisis of colonialism in the 1930s was accompanied by a growing sense of cultural and political nationalism in Puerto Rico. This growing nationalism in a sense culminated in the cultural and political aspects that characterized the creation of the Commonwealth in 1952 as an autonomous political and cultural structure under U.S. sovereignty.

Although it was within a U.S. colonial state, the Puerto Rican government became the representative of Puerto Ricans during the 1940s, particularly after the electoral victory of the PPD in 1940, the election of Muñoz Marín as the first elected governor of the island in 1948, and the creation of the Commonwealth in 1952. All of these changes and reforms to the colonial structure were sought and supported by the majority of Puerto Ricans and legitimized through successive elections. Its electoral hegemony and the U.S.-supported reforms in the 1940s and 1950s allowed the PPD-led colonial government in Puerto Rico to assert a "relative autonomy" over local economic, political, and policy areas, including migration. The Puerto Rican government—even before the Commonwealth status was created in 1952—became the organizer and sponsor of migration to the United States as a mechanism to provide stability to the colonial regime in Puerto Rico as well as to legitimize its own political authority. In doing so, the Puerto Rican government assumed the representation and protection of Puerto Rican migrants in the United States and strove to facilitate their incorporation in the U.S. mainland. The Puerto Rican government extended its reach to and established government structures on the U.S. mainland to provide services to its migrants and to facilitate their incorporation in the American polity simply because at the time no other state structure cared for them. Since Puerto Ricans' U.S. citizenship did not imply de facto inclusion or full membership in the American polity, for several decades the Puerto Rican government assumed the task of promoting incorporation and providing representation for many island migrants in the United States.

This book focuses on the formulation and implementation of Puerto Rico's migration policy in the postwar period. Migration became an important issue for U.S. and Puerto Rican policy makers after the end of World War II. Migration policy required a relatively vast space of action for the Puerto Rican government during this period. It involved the promotion and organization of migration through bureaucratic agencies like the BEM in San Juan and the Migration Division in the United States, both under the umbrella of the Labor Department. It also necessitated reaching other areas of Puerto Rican life, like education, air transportation and infrastructure, population control policy, tourism, and economic planning. Furthermore, Puerto Rican migration policy and politics cannot be divorced from what is traditionally understood as politics in Puerto Rico, usually seen from the perspective of the island's political status, that is, its relationship with the United States. By the late 1940s and early 1950s, migration politics *was* status politics as the migration issue took a central position in the status debate at this time for Puerto Rican and U.S. policy makers.

There are two issues regarding the book's topic and perspective that call for further elaboration. First, this book focuses on the formulation and implementation of the Puerto Rican government's migration policy, and hence its institutional focal point. I am in no way proposing or advocating a state-centric approach exclusively to the study of migration or denying agency to migrants in defining the Puerto Rican migration experience. Policy issues deal with the actions and the ideas that guide such behavior by the state, in this case Puerto Rico's government. As such, the book must focus on (colonial) state action in the specific field of migration. By concentrating on this heretofore underappreciated perspective, I am not denying migrant agency. On the contrary, my argument throughout the book is that once this mass migration was set in motion spurred by aggregate individual actions, Puerto Rico's government intervened to manage, organize, and regulate this flow of people to the United States. The reasons for this course of action are the substance of this book. Puerto Rico's government decided to take a more active role in migration only after the mass movement of Puerto Ricans to New York City beginning in 1946 produced the "Puerto Rican problem" there. It was people moving on their own to the U.S. mainland (what government officials called "individual migrants") that led the government to take action to provide a modern air transportation infrastructure, to use the public school system to organize and regulate migration, and to try to ease the incorporation of its migrants in the U.S. mainland through the Migration Division. It was migrant discontent in the beet fields of Michigan in 1950 that led Puerto Rico's government to revise and streamline its migration policy guidelines for decades to come. All these events are examined in the book. I do pay attention to the institutional factors that influenced this migration (e.g., Puerto Rico's political relationship with the United States, U.S. citizenship, political actors and interests on the island and the U.S. mainland, etc.) that very often are absent from the history and analysis of Puerto Rican migration to the United States. There are many good accounts on the Puerto Rican migrant experience in the United States, but there is none that exclusively examines the formulation and implementation of the Puerto Rican government's migration policy.[60] This is one of the contributions of this book.

Second, the book discusses the transnational perspective on migration in this introduction, but it does not provide an account or advance the theory of transnationalism. The main issue of interest and its primary focus is the role played by Puerto Rico's government in Puerto Rican migration to the United States. The perspective or theory of transnationalism is addressed here because of the prevalence of that perspective in contemporary accounts of Puerto Rican migration, particularly by authors who point to the role played by Puerto Rico's government in migration after World War II. Instead I see Puerto Rican migration as a colonial migration that is defined by the particular construction of Puerto Rico as a colonial territory (the unincorporated territory) and the particular construction of Puerto Ricans as (colonial) citizens. It is because of these factors the Puerto Rican migration experience has shown elements similar to those cited commonly in the literature of political transnationalism.

As in any academic field, the theories of transnationalism, transnational migration, and transnational politics have engendered more than a few debates. Particularly significant are the debate related to the meaning and scope of transnationalism and transnational migration and the debate regarding the spaces where transnationalism is supposed to occur, whether it is defined by the actions and borders of the nation-state or by the social fields created by the actions and behavior of the immigrants themselves. Although these and other debates are significant for the field of transnationalism, they do not have any bearing on the arguments made in this book. While transnationalism as an analytical approach may inform some of the debates on Puerto Rican migration in recent decades, I take a different approach that focuses on the institutional policies implemented by the Puerto Rican government and the political and ideological underpinnings that support them.

WHAT'S AHEAD

Chapter 1 elaborates on how the role played by Puerto Rico's government in migration after 1945 was related to the increased relative autonomy of the colonial state during this period. It traces the role played by Puerto Rico's government in migration to the early years of U.S. rule on the island and pays particular attention to how migration was discussed by U.S. and Puerto Rican policy makers during World War II. The chapter explores how policy makers' perception during the first half of the twentieth century that the island's major social problem was overpopulation led them to advance migration as a solution to this important issue. It also examines how migration was linked to discussions of the island's political status during the 1940s.

Chapter 2 analyzes the making of Puerto Rico's migration policy in 1947, paying particular attention to how the Puerto Rican government took the issue of migration to the United States seriously only after the "Puerto Rican problem" campaign erupted in New York City that year. The chapter studies the role played by Commissioner of Labor Fernando Sierra Berdecía in the formulation of the government's migration policy and discusses why the official government policy—to neither encourage nor discourage migration—concealed a more active participation of the government in the management of migration. It also reviews the debates held in Puerto Rico on population control and migration during the 1940s and examines the experience faced by Puerto Rican migrants in Chicago in 1946, a precursor to the "Puerto Rican problem" in New York City and the 1947 migration law.

Chapter 3 explains how the Puerto Rican government after 1947 lobbied U.S. employers and the federal government to have island workers considered as domestic labor and given preference over foreign labor, particularly in agricultural work. This analysis shows how Puerto Rico's government used U.S. citizenship to promote its own interests and those of its migrants when facing federal government agencies and U.S. employers. The chapter also analyzes the political and ideological foundations and workings of the Farm Placement Program (FPP), the best example of an organized migration by the Puerto Rican government. In addition, it explores how, even when the government's migration policy was directed at promoting migration to the United States, it continued to consider possible migration plans to Latin America.

Chapter 4 examines the Puerto Rican government's actions to provide cheap and safe air transportation for island migrants going to the United States. The government intervened with the federal government and air carriers to ensure that reasonable fares and safe travel conditions were provided. The chapter analyzes an issue that presented a real threat to the government's migration program: the high number of air crashes from 1947 to 1952. Furthermore, I dispute here the widely accepted idea that tourism was the central factor explaining the growth of air transportation in the postwar period. Instead, I argue that migration is what led the Puerto Rican government to expand the island's airport infrastructure, to lobby the federal government to increase the number of air carriers flying to the island, and to pressure major airlines to lower their airfares in Puerto Rico.

In chapter 5, I examine the connection between education policy and migration in the 1940s and 1950s, particularly regarding the teaching of English in public schools and the use of the public school system by the government to promote and encourage migration to the United States. The intensification of English language education in public schools after the early 1950s, an issue that had been closely related to the policy of Americanization implemented in earlier decades by the colonial government, is directly associated to the government's migration policy. Education became part of Puerto Rico's migration policy as migration affected all areas of Puerto Rican life and the government sought to make "every Puerto Rican a potential migrant."

Chapter 6 discusses the upheaval and discontent of Puerto Rican workers in the sugar beet fields of Michigan in the summer of 1950. This event represents the first major incident of Puerto Rican migrant discontent in the United States and also shows how the Puerto Rican government intervened in labor disputes involving its workers and U.S. agricultural interests. The Michigan incident was the first major challenge to the government's migration policy, both on the island and the U.S. mainland, and had important implications for its implementations afterwards. The Michigan episode is also relevant because it links migration to the island's political status issue. Defending the Michigan sugar beet growers was Congressman Fred L. Crawford, then the Puerto Rican government's best ally in Congress and a strong supporter of Puerto Rican migration to the United States and of Commonwealth status. The chapter also looks at how U.S. sugar politics—particularly those represented by sugar beet producers like the ones in Michigan—influenced Puerto Rican economic and political affairs after 1898, including migration.

By 1950, Puerto Rican farmworkers were already part of that class of exploited agricultural workers in the United States known as migratory labor. This was in part a consequence of the Puerto Rican government's migration policy and programs, particularly through the FPP. Chapter 7 analyzes the status of Puerto Rican farmworkers as migratory labor in the United States and the role played by Puerto Rico's government as a labor contractor, that is, as a provider of labor to U.S. agricultural interests. In studying this subject, I explain why Puerto Ricans were hired to work in U.S. farms even when, in many instances, they were more expensive than foreign or domestic labor, and why the FPP—central to the government's migration policy by then—lasted for three decades. The chapter also examines how the Puerto Rican government provided labor to U.S. employers through the Migration Division's employment program.

CHAPTER 1

Puerto Rican Migration and the Colonial State

A CRUCIAL ASPECT of the Puerto Rican migration experience to the United States in the postwar period is the central role played by the island government in the process of organizing the movement of its people. In this process, although the government of Puerto Rico formulated and implemented its own migration policy, it did so while accepting the boundaries of its colonial subordination to the United States. Its migration policy was influenced not only by what was happening in Puerto Rico, but also by the way its migrants were received in the metropolitan society. Puerto Rico's migration policy in the late 1940s has to be understood within the perspective of what U.S. and Puerto Rican government functionaries defined as the "Puerto Rican problem," both on the island and in the United States. Government functionaries believed that migration was the best solution to overpopulation, which was considered one of Puerto Rico's most important policy problems. State officials had been engaged with this issue from the very early days of the U.S. regime in Puerto Rico.

The making of Puerto Rico's migration policy in the late forties cannot be seen only as a long-thought-out and well-planned Malthusian alternative to the island's perceived overpopulation problem by the state officials, particularly by those represented in the PPD.[1] Other important factors need to be considered in order to have a more comprehensive analysis of the Puerto Rican migration experience. First, since the very first days of the American colonial government in Puerto Rico, state officials have seen migration as an alternative to overpopulation, believed to be one of Puerto Rico's major social and economic problems. Second, although many Puerto Rican government officials in the postwar period shared this idea, representatives of the federal government and other U.S. institutions and North American advisors to the Puerto Rican government were influential in promoting migration as a serious alternative to the island's economic plight. And third, the historical context in which migration policy was elaborated is extremely important in its definition: Puerto Rican policy makers in the late 1940s formulated a migration policy only after the massive migration of Puerto Ricans to New York City became a political issue there, with the ensuing negative response by the city's government representatives and media—what became known there as "the Puerto Rican problem."

The first part of this chapter elaborates on the concept of the relative autonomy of the colonial state in Puerto Rico to explain the role played by the Puerto Rican government in migration. I will argue that migration policy—like economic policy—was one major area where the colonial government achieved certain autonomy in the management of local affairs. The second part of this chapter explores how since the beginning of U.S. rule in Puerto Rico, leading government officials—many appointed by the U.S. government until 1948—began to advance migration as a solution to the problem of overpopulation. The chapter discusses migration policies and programs from the early days of the twentieth century to the 1940s. It argues that some important migration policies implemented by the popularly elected PPD government during the late 1940s had already been executed by previous governments.

MIGRATION AND THE RELATIVE AUTONOMY OF THE COLONIAL STATE

At the heart of this book is an examination of the role that the government of Puerto Rico played in the encouragement and organization of Puerto Rican migration to the United States. If the colonial status of Puerto Rico and the status of Puerto Ricans as citizens made the unrestricted movement of islanders to the U.S. mainland possible, the concrete manifestation of this process after 1945 significantly involved the colonial state in Puerto Rico. Like colonialism and citizenship, and closely related to the two, the colonial state is also a manifestation of U.S. rule in Puerto Rico.

In the last few years, renewed interest in the manifestations of U.S. empire abroad has brought attention to this peculiar state formation. McCoy, Scarano, and Johnson, for example, conceive the colonial state as a structure within what they call the American "imperial state."[2] Recent interest in the workings of colonial states in U.S. empire is related to another important issue in the imperial dynamic: the role of local elites in maintaining colonialism in their territories.[3] In *American Empire and the Politics of Meaning*, Go examines how the U.S. co-opted but also accommodated the interests of local elites in its colonial regimes in the Philippines and Puerto Rico, and how these elites participated in the management of the colonial state.[4] In his study of U.S. colonialism in the Philippines, Kramer conceives the colonial state as a "new inclusionary formation" that works to accommodate the local "elite's desire for power and recognition."[5] Although scholars studying the Puerto Rican experience have examined the role of the colonial state on the island and the role of local elites in its management, they have not related the latter to the issue of migration. The increased role played by the Puerto Rican government in the late 1940s in managing migration to the U.S. mainland has to be related to its increased relative autonomy in local affairs and vice versa: migration was significant in increasing the colonial state's management of local affairs in Puerto Rico.

The Colonial State in Puerto Rico

Although the U.S. government had previous experience in colonial administration with annexed territories such as those taken in the Mexican-American War, the experience in the overseas territories acquired in 1898 was quite different. The latter would not be settled by Euro-Americans and would not be incorporated into the nation as states. Thus, not only did the ideological and judicial justifications for colonial subordination have to be distinct from those applied in the annexed territories, but the structures of their colonial governments had to be different as well. Using the experience of previous European colonial powers, as well as its own experience in the annexed territories, the United States created colonial states in Puerto Rico, the Philippines, and the other overseas territories in order to sustain its colonial rule there.

Go asserts that in order to maintain its rule over the Philippines, the United States "had to construct a colonial state—a political institution that was geographically distant and juridically distinct from, but subordinate to, the metropolitan government."[6] Go argues that this experience was something new for U.S. state functionaries; American colonial administrators

> had to construct and administer a political, juridical, and economic system separate from the metropolitan state. Simply put, U.S. colonial rule of the Philippines demanded something that the Americans had not yet perfected in their prior experience: an overseas colonial state. Two interrelated process had to unfold in the Philippines: colonial state building and colonial governance.[7]

As in the Philippines, the process of colonial state building and colonial governance in Puerto Rico were interrelated. Building the colonial state implied colonial rule on the island. More important yet, both processes required the co-optation and cooperation of local elites.

Although during the first half of the twentieth century the colonial state in Puerto Rico was administered by a cadre of American colonial functionaries appointed by the federal government, this structure always included the participation of local elites in positions within the executive and legislative branches of colonial government. The Foraker Act, for example, allowed for a party system that provided a resemblance of democratic ruling and political participation—although limited—within a colonial context.[8] The election of the PPD in 1940, the appointment of New Deal reformist governor Rexford G. Tugwell, and the reformulation of colonial policies in the aftermath of World War II illustrate how the metropolitan state allowed more participation of local elites in the governing of the colonial state during this period. This imperial detachment from direct colonial governance responded to increasing nationalism and desire for participation among Puerto Ricans and the needs of a changing global system where the United States now played a hegemonic role. The process of increased participation of local elites in the management of the colonial state culminated with the creation of the Commonwealth in 1952.

While the position of Puerto Ricans changed within the American polity when they became citizens in 1917, the status of Puerto Rico as an unincorporated territory and the major structures of the colonial state did not. The major reforms to the colonial state by the Jones Act were the creation of a fully elected senate and the provision to allow the still presidentially appointed governor to name all except two of the cabinet members (previously appointed by the U.S. president). That is, colonial state building and colonial governance in Puerto Rico did not change with the new status of Puerto Ricans as U.S. citizens. The main functions, workings, and structures of the colonial state remained the same during the first half of the twentieth century, as Pedro

Cabán has argued. He contends that the colonial state "was set up to administer the colony, promote economic growth, preserve political stability, and legitimize colonial rule." Furthermore, Cabán asserts that "its functions have changed as the colonial state has gained relative autonomy to mediate the content and direction of social and economic change."[9] Although always subordinated to the metropolitan state, the colonial state nevertheless functioned as a contested space for conflicts and accommodations between local elites and between the elites and the U.S. government.

Throughout its several incarnations (1900-1917, 1917-1952, 1952 to present), the colonial state has played an important role not only in governing the territory but also in maintaining the stability of the colonial regime and thus in sustaining U.S. hegemony in Puerto Rico. The move toward allowing more autonomy to local forces in Puerto Rico during the late 1940s responded to the increasing demands for reforms (up to and including independence) in Puerto Rico as well as to the new global responsibilities of the United States as a hegemonic power in the postwar period. To retain a colonial outpost in the Caribbean—one of U.S. citizens, no less—seemed hypocritical at a time when the United States was moving to reshape the international order by supporting the independence of European colonial territories. The very first act of the U.S. government after consenting to the Commonwealth status for Puerto Rico in 1952 was to have the United Nations declare that Puerto Ricans had exercised their right to self-determination and that Puerto Rico had thus ended its colonial subordination to the United States.

The intervention of the Puerto Rican government in migration coincided with those U.S. policies seeking to enhance self-government for Puerto Ricans. The management of migration must be understood as an integral element of the increased autonomy of the Puerto Rican colonial state in overseeing local affairs in Puerto Rico in the postwar period. For U.S. and Puerto Rican policy makers, migration—understood as the outflow of surplus population from the island—was intertwined with the increased autonomy in local economic and political affairs by providing stability in these two areas of colonial governance. Furthermore, as indicated by the negative reactions in New York City and elsewhere to the entry of Puerto Ricans in the postwar period, for many U.S. policy makers Puerto Rican migration to the U.S. mainland was a policy question that should be managed by the Puerto Rican government. If, as understood by U.S. and Puerto Rican decision makers, migration was a means of providing social, political, and economic stability to the colonial regime in Puerto Rico at a crucial juncture in time for the American government, then by managing migration, the Puerto Rican government played an important role in maintaining U.S. rule on the island.

The Colonial State's Relative Autonomy in Migration

In the early 1970s, a new generation of Puerto Rican scholars began to redefine the study of Puerto Rican history and economic and political development, particularly the changes that Puerto Rico experienced during the 1930s and 1940s. This is understandable, given the importance of that period for the creation of the Commonwealth in 1952 and the era of economic growth spurred under Operation Bootstrap. It was also the period that established the PPD's political hegemony and thus ushered in the economic and political developments of the 1950s.

One of several concepts that gained particular acceptance during this process of reconceptualization of Puerto Rican history was the notion of the relative autonomy of the colonial state in Puerto Rico.[10] The idea of the relative autonomy of the state was, of course, widely discussed in Europe and the United States regarding the development of the modern liberal welfare state. In Puerto Rico, the idea of the relative autonomy of the colonial state was an attempt to understand the transformations occurring on the island since the 1930s, particularly the political and economic reforms of the 1940s. The concept of the relative autonomy of the state was used to understand the greater role played by the colonial government in economic development and economic policy and how the Commonwealth's supposed autonomy in local affairs was used to sustain and maintain U.S. colonial rule in Puerto Rico.

Dietz applied the concept of "relative state autonomy" to explain the so-called ideological transformation of the PPD economic program, from one emphasizing reforms and populism in the early 1940s with policies like state-owned industries, land reform, and workers' rights to one set on providing incentives to foreign (i.e., U.S.) capital as the basis of economic development by the end of that decade. He argued that the colonial state assumed a relative autonomy with regard to the established elite in response to the economic and social crisis of the 1930s. The reforms implemented by the colonial state under the leadership of the PPD and Governor Tugwell provided the basis for the social, economic, and political stability that made the creation of the Commonwealth possible. But these reforms could not surpass the limits imposed by Puerto Rico's colonial relationship with the United States.[11] The process of reforms in Puerto Rico that began in the mid-1930s was promoted both by those local forces that coalesced in the PPD and by the metropolitan state. That is, the relative autonomy enjoyed by the colonial state that allowed the PPD to have a more influential role in public policy was something that was not only acceptable but was indeed promoted by the dominant sectors of the metropolitan state. As Dietz and others have argued before, the autonomy enjoyed then by the colonial state was always relative within the constraints imposed by the colonial subordination of Puerto Rico to the United States.

Missing from this analysis is the relevance of migration in this period and the role that the colonial state played in this experience. I would like to claim once again the use of the concept of the relative autonomy of the colonial state in order to understand not only the role that the colonial state played in migration, but also what migration meant in terms of policy making in the process of reforming the colonial state. Several scholars have argued that the colonial state used its relative autonomy in economic affairs to promote economic growth and maintain the stability of the colonial regime. This relative autonomy in economic affairs was recognized by the metropolitan state as part of its reforms of the colonial relationship with Puerto Rico.[12]

The colonial state developed another area of relative autonomy in the realm of migration. As in the economic arena, migration was a sphere where the metropolitan state allowed a certain autonomy for a policy issue that was deemed local and of a relative interest to U.S. policy makers, but not one that required their immediate intervention. In the economic area, the colonial state—before and after the Commonwealth—used the colonial relationship with the United States to attract U.S. corporations to the island with local tax exemption, exemption from federal wage laws, a common market and currency with the metropolitan state, and the political and constitutional presence of the United States in the territory as the final arbiter in case of any conflict with the local authorities. In the area of migration, the colonial state was encouraged by federal, state, and private institutions in the United States to assume an active role in the regulation and control of migration from Puerto Rico to the United States. As the representative of colonial citizens, the Puerto Rican government acted and had a direct presence on U.S. soil, something that no national state could openly do.

To manage its economic and industrialization policy, the colonial state created government bureaucratic institutions, like the Economic Development Administration (Fomento), that negotiated with U.S. corporations and the federal government over the conditions under which American capital would invest on the island. Likewise, to manage migration, the colonial government created its own bureaucratic institutions, such as the Bureau of Employment and Migration (BEM) in San Juan and the Migration Division in New York. As in the area of economic development, where the colonial government created its particular policy (the Industrial Incentives Act, better known as Operation Bootstrap), the Puerto Rican government also formulated and implemented its own migration policy (both, by the way, approved in 1947). The BEM opened offices throughout the island to organize and regulate migration and was supported in this mission by municipal mayors. The island government used the Department of Education, its largest bureaucracy, to "advise" and "orient" "prospective migrants." To manage the affairs of its migrants in the United States, Puerto Rico's government established migration offices in dozens of cities there, extending its bureaucratic and political reach well beyond its territorial and constitutional boundaries.

Like in the economic realm, the autonomy enjoyed by the colonial state in migration was also relative to what was allowed by the colonial relationship and by the metropolitan state. As happened with economic policy, Puerto Rico's migration policy was constrained by the limits imposed by the colonial relationship with the United States. For many years, even after the implementation of its migration law in 1947, Puerto Rican policy makers attempted to carry out migration plans to Latin America, plans that were repeatedly rejected by U.S. government officials and thus never accomplished. That is, the direction of the flow of Puerto Rican migration to the United States was determined not only by U.S. citizenship but also by the limits imposed by Puerto Rico's colonial subordination. Migration to the United States thus imposed a set of policy goals, like facilitating the incorporation of Puerto Rican migrants in the metropolitan territory and society, a job that private and state institutions in the United States were demanding that the Puerto Rican government should assume. Indeed, U.S. citizenship facilitated Puerto Rican migration to the United States, but it was the nature of that citizenship as a colonial one, along with the cultural and ethnic makeup of the island migrants, that presented obstacles and imposed limitations to their full incorporation in the United States.

The role played by the Puerto Rican government in organizing migration and in facilitating the incorporation of its migrants in the United States reflects the ambiguities of the colonial relationship with the United States. If indeed the status of Puerto Ricans as citizens and the status of Puerto Rico as a U.S. colonial territory facilitated migration to the United States and made possible the intervention of the Puerto Rican government there, it was precisely because of the status of Puerto Ricans as colonial subjects that the colonial state had to intervene in order to advance and ease their incorporation in the U.S. mainland.

Because of its character as a colonial state, the Puerto Rican government was limited in what it could do in terms of protecting and representing its "citizens" in the United States. The Puerto Rican government had to secure protection and services for its migrants from private and state institutions, always acknowledging their institutional and political jurisdictions and spheres of influence and power. That is what happened in New York City after the anti–Puerto Rican campaign emerged in 1947 and, later, elsewhere in the United States where the Puerto Rican government established its presence in representation of Puerto Rican migrants. And that is why Puerto Rico's migration policy followed very closely the recommendations made by private and public institutions in the United States in how to deal with Puerto Rican migrants, from the creation of the BEM in San Juan, to screening and selecting migrant prospects and channeling them away from New York City, to the creation of the Migration Division in New York in order to facilitate their incorporation and assimilation in the United States. In doing this, the Puerto Rican government followed the traditional perspectives of U.S. institutions in dealing with immigrants, that is, to facilitate their incorporation and assimilation into American life. But these were different times and Puerto Ricans were different migrants, and the institutions that had previously facilitated the incorporation of European immigrants—the dominant political parties, the church, unions, Tammany Hall, and so on—were not there to do the same for these migrants. This role was assumed by the Puerto Rican government for nearly two decades.

Although it is important to recognize that this autonomy in managing migration to the United States was relative—that is, one limited by Puerto Rico's colonial relationship to the United States—one should not minimize or downplay the role that the Puerto Rican government played in the representation and protection of its "citizens" in the U.S. mainland. The Puerto Rican government regulated the hiring of workers by U.S. employers with government-approved contracts. It lobbied and pressured the federal government to protect and give priority to Puerto Rican agricultural workers over alien workers based on their rights as citizens. It regulated and lobbied the federal government for safe air transportation for Puerto Ricans moving to the United States, and lobbied the U.S. government to allow major airlines to fly to Puerto Rico to satisfy the needs for air transportation and eventually opening air routes to many major U.S. cities. It mediated labor conflicts between Puerto Rican migrants and U.S. employers—the 1950 sugar beet strike in Michigan is a noteworthy example—not only to protect the farmworkers but also to assure mainland employers of the Puerto Rican workers' and government's reliability. It became the representative of New York Puerto Ricans for notable private city institutions like the Welfare Council and for the political establishment, in the form of the Mayor's Committee on Puerto Rican Affairs. It got involved in New York City politics in 1949 by campaigning and mobilizing against Congressman Vito Marcantonio and in support of Mayor William O'Dwyer.

In Puerto Rico, the government used its bureaucratic institutions, like the Departments of Labor and Education, to advise and organize the flow of migrants to the United States, be it as individual migrants (those moving to the U.S. mainland on their own) or in organized migration (mostly farmworkers going under a government-approved contract to work in U.S. farms). The Department of Labor's BEM created a vast government superstructure to oversee and regulate the flow of people to the U.S. mainland. In order to fulfill its goals in the United States, the government of Puerto Rico developed an impressive bureaucracy after it opened its Migration Office in New York in 1948. It later became the Migration Division, with main offices in New York City, Chicago, and the Lake Erie region, and by 1958–59, field offices in Boston; Hartford, Connecticut; Rochester, Middletown, and Riverhead in New York; Keyport and Camden in New Jersey; and Hamburg, Pennsylvania (these would grow in numbers in the 1960s).

MIGRATION AND THE "PUERTO RICAN PROBLEM" IN PUERTO RICO

In the second part of this chapter, I will examine how Puerto Rico's government dealt with migration from 1900 to the mid-1940s. The colonial government promoted the organized migration of workers under labor contracts to Hawaii and other countries in Latin America starting in 1900, and migration to the United States became an alternative during World War I. After 1917, when Puerto Ricans were granted U.S. citizenship, the migration of individuals to the United States increased, particularly to New York City. During this period, there were attempts by the Puerto Rican government to regulate migration due to the abuses experienced by island workers. Local and federal government officials tried to foster migration to the United States and other places like Panama during World War II, plans that faced many obstacles. Migration was also a metropolitan objective inasmuch as North American advisers and U.S. federal government institutions favored migration as a mechanism to alleviate the island's social and economic plight and thus provide stability to the colonial regime.

Contract Labor, Individual Migrants, and Migration Policy Before World War II

Most of the U.S.-appointed colonial functionaries since 1900 understood Puerto Rico's main problem to be a lack of resources, a lack of capital and industries, and overpopulation.[13] Migration was seen as an alternative to the island's overpopulation problem. In the first report by a U.S.-appointed governor, Charles Allen favored the migration of Puerto Rican laborers to Hawaii, Cuba, and the Dominican Republic. Noting that "these emigrants comprise the least desirable elements of this people," he argued that "the emigration of these people can do no great harm to the island. . . . Porto Rico has plenty of laborers and poor people generally."[14] In 1915 Arthur Yeager, the colonial governor who oversaw the grant of citizenship to Puerto Ricans, ascertained that "undoubtedly the fundamental cause [of poverty] is the enormous population." He argued that "the only really effective remedy is the transfer of large numbers of Porto Ricans to some other region."[15] He proposed a project to colonize the Dominican Republic by Puerto Rican laborers.

An important mechanism through which the colonial state intended to lower the surplus labor on the island since the time of Governor Allen was the use of contract labor. Thousands of Puerto Rican workers went to work under labor contracts to places like Hawaii, Cuba, and the Dominican Republic in the first years of the twentieth century, mostly in the sugar industry. Nearly three thousand workers went to work under contract to Hawaii; their experience there was an important reference regarding migration for other workers and for the government as well.[16] As the Puerto Rican press reported, many laborers returned dissatisfied with the working and living conditions in Hawaii. In 1903, a report by Puerto Rico's commissioner of labor sustained the complaints raised by Puerto Rican laborers on the contract violations, abuses, harsh living conditions, and discrimination suffered in Hawaii.[17]

Other contract labor expeditions to Cuba, the Dominican Republic, and Mexico during the first two decades of the twentieth century were not very successful, either. The complaints were similar to those of previous experiences in Hawaii. In several instances, workers abandoned their jobs and had to be repatriated back to Puerto Rico, as when the Puerto Rican legislature funded for the repatriation of Puerto Rican workers from Mexico in 1911.[18] As a consequence of these experiences, Puerto Rico's Labor Bureau felt that these expeditions had to be regulated; it concluded in a 1914 report: "If selected Porto Rican laborers could be sent in small groups to Cuba or Santo Domingo, protected by proper contracts in which the government of Porto Rico is a party, such emigration might be advisable."[19] This was precisely the intent of the 1919 emigration law approved by the Puerto Rican legislature to protect Puerto Rican migrant workers, not only for their benefit but also as a means of allowing the continuance of migration flows.

The 1919 law, the island's first legislation to regulate migration, established an important precedent that would be followed by the migration law approved in 1947. This law authorized the commissioner of agriculture and labor to intervene "in all matters concerning the emigration of laborers from Porto Rico"; it allowed this institution to "regulate such propositions, promises, conditions or offers made to native laborers in cases of emigration; to procure, subscribe and enforce such contracts" between Puerto Rican laborers and any U.S. or foreign contractors. Furthermore, it states that the insular government "shall have no obligation in any emigration to protect or enforce the rights of such persons as shall leave this country, unless the contracts entered into and between emigrants and the State contracting them shall have been approved by the Commissioner of Agriculture and Labor."[20] Nevertheless, its effectiveness was never proven since the intensity of hiring Puerto Ricans under labor contracts decreased in the 1920s and the Puerto Rican government proved incapable of enforcing the law, as shown by a 1926 investigation into the abuses suffered by Puerto Rican migrants in Arizona.[21]

World War I had an important impact on the character of Puerto Rican migration to the United States. In 1917 the Jones Act made Puerto Ricans U.S. citizens, one of the reasons for the increase in the movement of people from the island. Although Puerto Ricans had enjoyed free access to the U.S. mainland since 1898, migration during this period was not very significant; it increased dramatically after 1917.[22] Furthermore, some U.S. colonial functionaries saw Puerto Ricans as a source of (cheap) labor that could satisfy the manpower needs created by the conflict in Europe.[23] Around thirteen thousand Puerto Ricans were employed by 1918 in war-related industries in the United States, in places such as New Orleans; Wilmington, North Carolina; Brunswick and Savannah, Georgia; and Charleston, South Carolina. As in previous experiences, contract violations and abuses were common complaints of migrants; according to newspaper and government reports, ninety-three men died on these projects during several months from 1918 to 1919.[24]

After the war ended, U.S. colonial functionaries kept insisting on the need to encourage migration from Puerto Rico to the United States in order to reduce overpopulation on the island and to provide cheap labor to U.S. industries. For example, the 1926 annual report of the Bureau of Insular Affairs, the U.S. bureaucracy in charge of Puerto Rican affairs, noted the negative attitude of Puerto Ricans toward migration, particularly to the United States due to its different environment, but stated that "the surplus people of Porto Rico have an unusual opportunity in the United States" and could migrate "if once encouraged to do so."[25]

Some Puerto Rican functionaries were concerned with labor contract expeditions; they were particularly worried by the abuses experienced by migrants going to the U.S. mainland. They called for a greater supervision by the Puerto Rican government, as was reflected in a 1927 report by the interim chief of the island's Labor Bureau. The report questioned the viability of contract labor expeditions organized by private interests and argued that "it would be best to facilitate a voluntary migration." It concluded with a request to the Employment Bureau of the Department of Agriculture and Employment to enter into agreements with its counterparts in the United States "as a means to obtain knowledge of the places where labor is needed and that the latter be selected . . . so that they go directly to the appropriate places, contributing this way to lower in an intelligent and methodical way the surplus population of the country."[26]

In the 1920s, individual, or "spontaneous," migration replaced labor contract migration as the dominant form of labor migration from Puerto Rico to the United States. This migration was represented by the movement of Puerto Ricans on their own to the United States, most particularly to New York City. By 1930 Puerto Rican officials acknowledged that most of Puerto Rico's migration was made of "voluntary" migrants moving to the United States.[27] This form of migration fueled the dramatic increase of Puerto Ricans living in the United States after the 1920s: in 1920 there were 11,811 Puerto Ricans living on the mainland, increasing to 52,774 by 1930 and to 69,967 by 1940.[28] Most migrants headed toward New York City, where, as Sánchez-Korrol so aptly put it, the Puerto Rican conglomerate developed from "colonia to community" in the 1930s and early 1940s.[29]

World War II and Puerto Rican Migration Policy

The war years (1940–1945) were years of debate regarding Puerto Rico's population problem and the migration of workers. Various U.S. functionaries in Puerto Rico and the mainland generally saw Puerto Ricans as an available pool of cheap labor accessible for wartime-related activities. But island government functionaries, including Governor Tugwell and some PPD leaders, were generally more cautious about sending out large numbers of workers to the U.S. mainland. Metropolitan interests would, of course, prevail, and thousands of Puerto Rican laborers were recruited to satisfy the needs of the American industries in a time of war. The War Manpower Commission (WMC) became the best example of the American government's action in recruiting Puerto Rican labor for mainland labor needs. But although most government functionaries agreed that migration was a good alternative to deal with the overpopulation problem, there was no consensus among U.S. and Puerto Rican policy makers on how to proceed. For example, there was disagreement about whether the government should be involved in a mass planned migration or encourage migration of individuals only. Furthermore, issues of race, culture, and the status of Puerto Ricans as U.S. citizens influenced how these plans were conceived.

In 1939 Admiral William Leahy was appointed governor of Puerto Rico by President Franklin D. Roosevelt, signaling Puerto Rico's increasing military importance for the U.S. government. In 1940 Leahy and U.S. functionaries began to consider the possibility of an expedition of Puerto Rican workers to work in the Panama Canal Zone. The Panama plan is a good example of how U.S. policy makers viewed the role that Puerto Rican labor could play for U.S. economic and military interests during World War II. It also shows the problems faced by the Puerto Rican government in organizing labor migrations during the war period, the place of colonial citizens within broader U.S. global interests, and how issues of race and citizenship intersected for Puerto Ricans at that time.

In a letter to Leahy on April 8, 1940, Atherton Lee, from the U.S. Department of Agriculture in Puerto Rico, proposed a plan to send Puerto Rican workers to Panama. On a visit there, he consulted with the American ambassador on the use of Puerto Ricans to satisfy the Panama Canal Zone's increasing labor needs; because of their status as U.S. citizens, the ambassador "felt that Puerto Ricans should have the advantage over other West Indians in such employment." Lee added that during a visit to Panama, President Roosevelt "had expressed the opinion that American citizens exclusively should be employed in the new construction work in the Canal Zone. It seemed to me that this may have been a result of one of your conversations with the President." Puerto Ricans, he pointed out, would be acceptable to the Panama government, which "was not particularly pleased with the importation of further West Indians," worried that the entrance of so many black workers could have "a great influence on the racial characters of the people of Panama." Lee discarded other migration projects to Colombia, Venezuela, and Ecuador for several reasons, including the possibility they might be "at considerable expense to the Federal Government. The Canal Zone seems to have the best opportunities for any mass migration from Puerto Rico."[30]

For U.S. colonial functionaries, sending Puerto Ricans to the Panama Canal Zone would also address the population problem on the island. In a letter to Harold Ickes, U.S. secretary of the interior, Leahy argued that

> in view of the heavy overpopulation of Puerto Rico this would appear to be a critical time to press upon the War Department the desirability of utilizing Puerto Rico's excess labor population for work on the Canal Zone, and by

doing so to relieve to some small extent the unemployment situation which now exists here.³¹

On May 21, C. S. Ridley, governor of the Panama Canal Zone, informed Leahy that he had received authorization for the recruitment of Puerto Ricans to work in Panama and submitted a plan that included specific conditions to be enclosed in a labor contract.³²

But there were some apprehensions from functionaries in Puerto Rico about the idea. In a June 6 letter to Carlos Gallardo, Puerto Rico's executive secretary, Atherton Lee dismissed his objections to the migration of Puerto Ricans to Panama, reasoning that if "properly organized" and if the events that led to the disastrous migration to Hawaii could be avoided, there should be no reason for this project to fail. He concluded that "the easiest solution for the crowded population conditions would be an intelligent migration" and Panama "can be made a first step in such a migration."³³ Other Puerto Rican functionaries also raised doubts regarding the proposal to send Puerto Rican laborers to Panama. Labor Secretary Prudencio Rivera Martínez questioned the proposed labor contract, declaring that under the conditions of the contract, the Panama Canal people would not be able to recruit in the United States. But even after the contract was modified to include his concerns, the secretary of labor asserted that the "prevailing conditions" in the Panama Canal Zone should be investigated by representatives of the Puerto Rican government before any agreement was made or any worker sent there.³⁴

Other war-related obstacles prevented the Panama proposal from coming to fruition. Brigadier General E. L. Daley complained to Leahy in October 1940 that he lacked labor to complete required military constructions in Puerto Rico in time; he requested some thirty thousand laborers, maintaining that the current twenty thousand were insufficient.³⁵ Another critical issue was the transportation of workers to Panama. Leahy had suggested the use of military vehicles for this purpose. But on October 25, U.S. Secretary of War Henry L. Stimson denied this petition, saying that the military needed their transportation vehicles for purposes related to the war.³⁶

The idea to send Puerto Rican workers to the Panama Canal Zone came to an end due to war-related events, the improvement in the economic conditions in Puerto Rico during the war, and continued concerns among island government functionaries on how island workers would be treated there and what their working and living conditions would be. In a February 1941 report on his visit to Panama, William D. López, acting commissioner of labor, complained that salaries there were too low for Puerto Ricans and that they would be treated as other "foreign" workers and not as U.S. citizens.³⁷ The Canal Zone governor complained to Puerto Rico's governor, Guy J. Swope, that worker transportation to Panama and lower wages were two main obstacles to the proposal. After insisting that López's suggestion for higher wages for Puerto Ricans was unfeasible since they would have to raise wages for other "tropical workers," he concluded that "there is little prospect of obtaining desirable employees for our work from Puerto Rico in the immediate future."[38] Swope replied that the employment situation in Puerto Rico had improved dramatically due to military projects and the construction of the navy base in Vieques and that lower salaries on the Panama Canal Zone were not an incentive for Puerto Rican workers to go there since unemployment on the island had decreased, there was a lack of skilled workers, and higher salaries in construction had propelled an increase in other areas.[39]

Although the proposal to send workers to Panama went no further, migration continued to be a preoccupation for U.S. and Puerto Rican policy makers. Several proposals to send Puerto Ricans to Latin American countries were discussed by government officials in the United States and Puerto Rico during the war period. As on previous occasions, island functionaries raised concerns regarding these proposals for planned migrations. In April 1942, U.S. newspapers reported on a proposal to send five hundred thousand Puerto Ricans to colonization projects in undisclosed Latin American countries. The proposal raised some concerns, primarily about the adaptation of Puerto Ricans to working conditions in a foreign place and the cost to the government of such an endeavor. Also considered was the issue that "Puerto Ricans are American citizens. If the government should sponsor their emigration to foreign soil, the fact that they went on their own volition would not relieve us of moral responsibility for their future welfare."[40]

In late May 1942, an *El Mundo* editorial commented on a proposition under consideration by the U.S. State Department's Office of the Coordinator of Inter-American Affairs to send Puerto Rican workers to Brazil and Venezuela. The newspaper complained that although the proposal had been under discussion for several months in Washington and Latin American capitals, Puerto Rico "has not yet had the occasion to even know properly the basis and orientations of the migration proposed."[41] In December 1942, it became public that Puerto Rico's Land Authority was considering buying five hundred thousand acres of land in the Dominican Republic to distribute to Puerto Ricans moving there.[42]

Another proposal for a planned migration to Venezuela was explored by island functionaries in 1945. Following a petition by Governor Tugwell, Carlos Chardón, then director of the Institute of Tropical Agriculture and better known for the Chardón Plan of 1935, traveled to Venezuela to study the possibility of sending Puerto Rican workers there. Like previous Puerto Ricans officials, Chardón raised questions regarding the idea of a planned migration to this country. He reported that the problem with Puerto Rican emigration was that "Puerto Ricans have no emigration tradition; they love their country and their people too much to take risks going abroad." He concluded that if there was to be a planned migration, it should be "on individual basis," sending only workers with the adequate skills.[43]

U.S. government officials also expressed their opposition to the Venezuela migration plan. In a report to the secretary of state from the U.S. embassy in Caracas, Frank Corrigan quoted Chardón's negative response to the plan; he also stated that even though the idea was supported by Venezuela's ambassador in Washington and by Abe Fortas, under secretary of the interior, it was opposed by Governor Tugwell and had been ignored by the Venezuelan government. Furthermore, Corrigan mentioned other negative aspects of the colonization plan already named by previous reports and proposed that the State Department give no further consideration to this plan.[44]

Beginning in 1942, officials in the United States and Puerto Rico began to discuss planned migrations to the U.S. mainland. One of the earliest proposals comes from the minutes of a meeting between two Puerto Rican officials (Jaime Bagué and Commissioner of Labor Santiago Iglesias Jr.) and four North American functionaries on December 26, 1942. The meeting was called to "discuss problems associated with the migration of Puerto Ricans to the U.S. during the present emergency both in order to satisfy labor needs in the States and to relieve the pressure of overpopulation in Puerto Rico." The committee concluded that "migration should be on an individual basis and that settlement into strictly Puerto Rican communities . . . should be automatically discouraged." Two important issues raised in this meeting were the racial composition and the selection of the migrants. Regarding race, the committee report stated "that only white workers should be encouraged to migrate to Southern states although this policy should not be formally incorporated in any statements or documents." The report added that "good selection in Puerto Rico and adequate supervision in the States was considered indispensable to any successful migration program." It also reported that migration should be encouraged without worrying "whether the migrants will secure permanent or only temporary jobs" and that at the present only "only younger, single, skilled workers whether proficient in agriculture or industry" should be encouraged to migrate.[45]

In early October 1942, *El Mundo* editorialized in favor of a planned migration to the United States and rejected an earlier proposal to take Puerto Rican workers to Brazil on the basis that they were not prepared for the harsh work on rubber plantations; it argued that a well-planned and well-organized migration, with a careful selection of workers, would be effective and valuable for the island.[46] Days later, Resident Commissioner Bolívar Pagán was informed that the U.S. House of Representatives would consider a bill to facilitate the hiring of Puerto Rican workers on the mainland. Puerto Rico's Chamber of Commerce also favored the migration of workers to the mainland to alleviate unemployment and misery on the island.[47] Later that month, several members of congress gave their support to a measure that would finance the transport of Puerto Rican workers, thus allowing their employment on the mainland.[48]

In October 1942, Iglesias Jr. reported to Tugwell on his trip to Washington to discuss Puerto Rico's "labor problem." There he met with numerous government officials interested in island affairs, including Interior Secretary Harold Ickes and War Projects Administration Commissioner Malcolm Miller. Iglesias traveled to Washington for another round of meetings in November 1942.[49] In mid-December he announced an agreement that would facilitate the emigration of twenty thousand Puerto Rican workers to the mainland. Transportation of an estimated one thousand workers per month would be provided by the army and navy, as conditions allowed. Iglesias also announced that the government of Puerto Rico would not sanction the transfer of workers to Brazil and Venezuela, arguing that it was a risky proposition and that the government was concentrating on sending workers to the United States, which "assures absolute guarantees for the Puerto Rican worker."[50]

In December 1942, the War Department agreed to transport from 800 to 1,500 workers to the mainland. The U.S. Employment Service (USES) was asked to coordinate recruitment with island functionaries. As recommended in previous government reports on migration, the government was to select workers based on several qualifications: workers were required to have a working knowledge of English, a "nest egg" of from $75 to $100, and the skills demanded by mainland employers. Some 1,030 workers were recruited. The program was ended after six months, however, and the WMC decided to have employers carry out their own recruitment of workers through labor contractors. Clarence Senior reported the major employers and the number of workers recruited as follows: Baltimore and Ohio Railroad, 1,038; Campbell Soup Co., 488; Huff Canning Co., 338; and Utah Copper Co., 200.[51] In March 1943, George H. Cross, of the U.S. Human Resources Commission, met in Puerto Rico with federal and local functionaries and representatives of the labor movement to discuss a migration plan to the United States. According to him, the federal government would establish a recruitment center and pay for the transportation to the mainland, wages, health services, and transportation back to the island.[52]

According to Edwin Maldonado, the policy change in favor of recruitment of Puerto Rican labor was due to several reasons, including the decrease of Mexican *bracero* labor in the United States during this time and—perhaps the most important reason, according to him—the pressure by congressional sources, mostly the Senate Committee on Territories and Insular Possessions, to hire Puerto Ricans and not aliens for war-related jobs.[53] Nevertheless, the recruitment of Puerto Rican laborers during the war raised some apprehensions in the United States. A significant issue with Puerto Ricans was precisely their status as citizens, which prevented their return to the island once their contract expired, as many U.S. government functionaries and employers demanded.[54] The latter considered Puerto Ricans unreliable, breaking their contracts and leaving for other destinations, and often favored the contract of "domestic" workers before "foreign labor." But many U.S. policy makers believed that hiring Puerto Ricans provided a safety valve for the island's unemployment and was in the United States' best interests, politically and economically.[55] The WMC ceased its recruiting program in Puerto Rico in June 1944, after Congress voted to deny the necessary funds for its campaign on the island. According to Senior, "Congressmen are reported to have objected to bringing Puerto Ricans on the grounds that they could not be sent back home after the need for them had ended."[56] As stated by Maldonado, the WMC blamed Puerto Ricans for the program's failure, arguing that 60 percent of workers abandoned their jobs before the end of the contract, only 25 percent completed their contracts, and just 15 percent returned to Puerto Rico.[57]

Puerto Rican government functionaries also had some reservations about the recruitment of labor on the island. Governor Tugwell favored the recruitment of island workers for war-related needs on the mainland but "was skeptical of the success of large scale labor importation programs."[58] Commissioner of Labor Manuel A. Pérez was also apprehensive of planned migration. He favored individual migration and restraint on the part of government in playing any role in the recruitment of labor for the United States, as he stated in a memo to Tugwell dated February 1945. According to him, the "Department has had a bad experience with the group of workers who emigrated to the States during the last two years" to work at the Baltimore and Ohio Railroad Co., the Huff and Campbell companies, and the Calco Chemical Co. There were numerous complaints and "discontent prevailed among the workers." He alluded to the example of the Calco Chemical Co. in Brooklyn, where 72 out of 104 workers broke their contracts and left; the other companies had an even worse experience. Pérez concluded that the government should not encourage these migrations unless "we could plan these migrations very carefully, making the proper selection of the workers according to their skill and that steps be taken to insure that they would not have difficulties on account of the language, food, etc."[59] It was precisely against this background of labor recruitment during the last years of the war that the Puerto Rican government functionaries began to debate the issue of migration immediately after the war.

Migration and Puerto Rico's Political Status

The end of the war was a time of debates in Puerto Rico and the United States regarding the political future of the island. The PPD won the 1944 elections by a landslide, but it was internally divided regarding its option for the island's political status. Pro-independence forces within the PPD wanted to push this alternative in the United States. During 1945 and 1946, Muñoz Marín himself was revising his ideas about Puerto Rico's political future, moving away from a weak support for independence to some form of autonomous government with a continued economic and political relationship with the United States. In 1946 Muñoz Marín expelled the *independentistas* from the party, which allowed him and the party to support a status of self-government in autonomy with the United States, what later came to be the Estado Libre Asociado (or Commonwealth, in English).[60]

Winds of change were also strengthening in the United States regarding Puerto Rico. In 1946 President Truman appointed Jesús T. Piñero as the first Puerto Rican governor of the island. In 1948 the people of Puerto Rico elected their governor for the first time after Congress approved this measure. The huge electoral victory by Muñoz Marín and the PPD in 1948 facilitated their push in Washington for further reforms to the political status of the island. In 1950 Congress approved Law 600, which allowed Puerto Ricans to write their own constitution and led to the creation of Commonwealth status in 1952.

This was the context in which Puerto Rican migration to the United States became a "problem" for the PPD government. The point to be made here— and which shall be elaborated further in later chapters—is that the issue of migration was always present in the discussions of Puerto Rico's political and economic future during this period. To support this argument, I would like to mention three reports from Washington that were important in this deliberation. Scholars who study the evolution of Puerto Rico's political status concur on the importance of these reports to debates in Puerto Rico and the United States on the subject.[61] The reports spoke of the deplorable economic conditions the island suffered and presented some suggestions for the reform of its government and its relationship to the United States. They questioned the viability of independence for Puerto Rico, rejected statehood as an alternative that was not feasible for the island and that would be turned down in the United States, and suggested some form of self-government for Puerto Ricans. What no scholar of the island's political status question ever mentions is that these reports also discussed the issue of migration when analyzing the economic and political future of Puerto Rico.

The first report, the 1943 U.S. Senate Committee on Territories and Insular Affairs' report on the problems facing Puerto Rico, tried to define the "Puerto Rican problem" in a wider perspective regarding U.S. global, national, and regional interests. It argued that the "the Puerto Rican problem"

> transcends national life; it unavoidably injects itself into the wider field of international relations, an undeniable fact which we cannot afford to ignore. The Caribbean zone has recently become of unusual mutual interest to the United States and England and the policies which will be necessarily adopted in any event will affect Puerto Rico to a large extent. . . . It must be considered from three aspects: (a) The viewpoint of the island, (b) the viewpoint of the Nation, and lastly, (c) the international viewpoint.

According to the committee, among the most important issues facing Puerto Rico were overpopulation, lack of arable land, emigration, a high birth rate, agriculture, and need of new industries. With regard to the issue of migration, the report stated:

> Unlike the problem of arable land, which cannot be solved emigration can be accomplished if there would be a determined effort on the part of the Federal Government to that end. Left to the individual or to the local insular government, it will never be accomplished.[62]

The second report, produced by the House Committee on Insular Affairs in 1945, was the conclusion of an investigation of political, economic, and social affairs in Puerto Rico. The inquiry carried its own political agenda, since it was used by congressional Republicans to examine and criticize Tugwell's government on the island. Migration of Puerto Ricans was one of the issues addressed in its conclusions. It stated that in view "of the fact that there appears to be no immediate complete solution to the current chronic problems of Puerto Rico arising because of the lack of natural resources and the congestion of population there, the subcommittee feels that a wise and prudent program of emigration might be helpful." The report goes on to propose migration to Latin America, where some countries reported a need for labor. It advises a migration of one million persons, or half the island's population at the time, so that "there would be a sharp increase in the island's living standards, unemployment would end, and United States taxpayers would be relieved of the heavy annual relief burden." The report added that Puerto Ricans and their government "have been cool toward emigration in the past and might be so again. The island's past experiences have not been favorable although it is the feeling of the subcommittee that wise and adequate planning could overcome obstacles that are now objectionable to Puerto Ricans." It suggests that with the support of the U.S. secretary of interior and Puerto Rican leaders, "such a plan could be worked out successfully" to the benefit both of the United States and the island.[63]

The third report was produced by the U.S. Tariff Commission and came to be known in Puerto Rico as the Dorfman Report (in reference to its chief economist, Ben Dorfman). The commission was asked by Congress to examine the economic and political consequences of independence, statehood, and self-government for the island. Like the two previous congressional reports already mentioned, the Dorfman Report recommended self-government for Puerto Rico accompanied by new U.S. policies to help the island's economy.[64]

According to Muñoz Marín's biographer and historian Carmelo Rosario Natal, the Dorfman Report, along with Muñoz Marín's conversations with leaders in Washington, had a great impact on the leader's thought regarding the island's political status. Relevant to his new thinking was the negative economic impact independence would have on the island, according to Rosario Natal. Publication of the Dorfman Report in March 1946 preceded the now-famous writings by Muñoz Marín in *El Mundo,* generally known as *nuevos caminos hacia viejos objetivos* (new paths to old goals). In these articles, the PPD leader presented his arguments against independence and statehood and proposed a "third way" to solve Puerto Rico's colonial status: self-government with the United States.[65] This was precisely what some policy makers in the United States and congressional reports were saying. The Dorfman Report also recommended migration as one of its major conclusions.

While the Dorfman Report's conclusions regarding the island's political status received the most attention in Puerto Rico (the report rejected both independence and statehood on political and economic grounds), it was received differently on the U.S. mainland. For example, the *New York Times* headline on the report read: "Ask million people leave Puerto Rico: Tariff experts say this and not change in island's status offers the only economic hope." The article asserts that Puerto Rico would suffer economically under any of the political status options that were considered (independence, statehood, or dominion). It then adds: "The Commission's economists reached the conclusion that only the emigration of 1,000,000 people and a sharp diminution in the birth rate among those remaining would permit the island even to approach economic self-support." After reviewing the disadvantages of the three status alternatives, the news report indicated that although emigration in itself would not solve the island's economic problem, it "would make a solution possible." If Puerto Rico was not able to control its population, maintaining a minimum standard of living "will be contingent upon their receiving a substantial and very likely an ever-increasing, measure of outside aid."[66]

It is also worthwhile to point out how a prelude to this report was embraced a year earlier in Puerto Rico. The Tariff Commission study had been commissioned by the Senate Committee on Territories and Insular Affairs at the request of Senator Millard Tydings, who, in 1945, submitted another of his bills for the independence of Puerto Rico. In April 1945, Dorfman presented some of the report's findings to the Senate committee, arguing that all status alternatives had economic disadvantages for the island, although he acknowledged that Puerto Rico's relationship to the United States had been on the whole beneficial. He questioned the idea (under discussion by the Puerto Rican policy makers and scholars then) that measures like population control, industrialization, and increases in health and education standards alone would remedy the island's dismal economic situation. Dorfman advanced the Tariff Commission's conclusions that a "large-scale emigration from the island, amounting to between 750,000 to 1,000,000 persons, would not of itself assure a solution of the island's major economic problems, but would merely make a solution possible."[67] The report added that past Puerto Rican experiences with emigration had been unsuccessful and that "any new emigration program would clearly have no possibility of success unless it were carefully planned under competent and honest auspices and unless it were adequately financed." It then presented one of the findings repeated throughout the report: "As long as Puerto Rico remains in its present political relation to the United States, however, Puerto Ricans are legally free to move to the mainland without restriction." On the other hand, Puerto Rican emigration to the United States "would be restricted under the proposed independence alternative."[68]

It is very important to notice here that although throughout the war period U.S. and Puerto Rican policy makers debated the idea of migration, there was really no consensus regarding its character (if it should be on an individual basis or a mass planned migration) or its direction (whether it should be directed to Latin America or to the U.S. mainland). For example, the three congressional reports discussed earlier recommended migration—but not necessarily to the United States; these usually suggested that Puerto Rican migration would be directed to Latin America or the Caribbean. By the summer of 1947, Puerto Rican policy makers would be debating not whether to promote migration but where to direct it: to allow the continuation of migration to the U.S. mainland or to direct it to Latin America. But by the time U.S. and Puerto Rican policy makers came to discuss the issue, Puerto Rican migration was already moving in one direction: to the United States. It was decided by the Puerto Rican masses, not the government. Puerto Rico's migration policy simply followed the footsteps of migrants.

CHAPTER 2

"Neither Encouraging nor Discouraging"

The Making of Puerto Rico's Migration Policy

A MASSIVE MOVEMENT of people from Puerto Rico to the United States—mainly to New York City—began by the end of the war, promoted by the end of the war blockade, cheaper air transportation, and the need for cheap labor in mainland industries and spurred by the deepening economic crisis on the island. In August 1946, Puerto Rico's first native-appointed governor, Jesús T. Piñero, declared in New York that one of his priorities was to the deal with "the situation of approximately three hundred fifty thousand Puerto Ricans living in New York." Decision makers in Puerto Rico and New York City were concerned about the "problems" created by the massive entrance of Puerto Ricans to the city.[1] It would take almost a year for the Puerto Rican government to adopt some concrete steps in dealing with the migration of Puerto Ricans to New York. Meanwhile, the most rabid anti–Puerto Rican campaign in the United States began in New York City by early 1947.[2] It became known in the United States and Puerto Rico as the "Puerto Rican problem."

The Puerto Rican government's migration policy, enacted into law in December 1947, was a reaction to the "Puerto Rican problem" in New York City. It was after this racist anti–Puerto Rican campaign that the island government formulated and implemented its policy to organize and promote migration to the United States. Some of the most important aspects of the government's migration policy came as a response to the public debate generated by this event: its attempt to control and regulate the labor flow to the

United States, the channeling of migrants outside New York City, the opening of the Migration Division in New York City, the teaching of English to prospective migrants, and the process of screening and selecting potential migrants in Puerto Rico, among other policies.

The rapid and massive entry of Puerto Ricans to New York City in the immediate postwar period reflects a crucial dilemma in the relationship between the United States and its colonial territory and subjects. One important feature of the "Puerto Rican problem" debate in New York was the call by several institutions, including the report by the New York Welfare Committee on Puerto Ricans and by representatives of the Puerto Rican government, for the U.S. federal government to get involved in the regulation of the mass movement of islanders to the U.S. mainland. The federal government did not attend to this call for obvious reasons: Puerto Ricans are technically U.S. citizens, and the federal government could not intervene in the movement of citizens from one area of the United States to another. When nativists reacted to the presence of Filipinos in western states in the 1920s and 1930s, they forced the federal government to intervene to stop migration from the Philippines since Filipinos were U.S. nationals, not citizens.[3] Given the inability of any government entity in the United States—federal, state, or city—to stop or regulate Puerto Rican migration, the Puerto Rican government assumed the organization of migration from Puerto Rico to the United States. The Puerto Rican government, with the consent and support of social and political institutions in New York (a predominant receiving destination for island migrants), also assumed responsibility for the incorporation of Puerto Ricans in U.S. mainland society in the postwar years. Even though the colonial state had engaged in the management of migration since the U.S. occupation, several elements were needed for this more encompassing management role: a revised policy, a new philosophy, and new bureaucratic institutions.

The first section of this chapter reviews the government's ideas on how to control population growth and its relationship with migration policy. In the absence of a concrete program for population control, by the late 1940s the Puerto Rican government espoused migration as the main mechanism to control overpopulation. The chapter later examines several factors that influenced the making of Puerto Rico's migration policy in 1947. It presents an analysis of the first newsworthy postwar experience of Puerto Rican migrants—in Chicago, during early 1947—and how the island government responded. After examining the "Puerto Rican problem" in New York City, the chapter follows with a discussion on how the issue of migration to the United States and elsewhere was debated by island government functionaries and advisers. The creation of the governor's Advisory Committee on Migration at the height of the "Puerto Rican problem" campaign signaled the beginning of a process that led to the formulation of a migration policy by the end of 1947.

The chapter concludes with a discussion of how migration policy was formulated, particularly the important role played in that process by the commissioner of labor, Fernando Sierra Berdecía. It also examines how the government's migration policy main discourse—that the government did not encourage or discourage migration—not only tried to address the worries of U.S. government and private institutions concerned with the entry of island migrants, but also concealed the government's active participation in the movement of its people into the United States.

MIGRATION AND POPULATION CONTROL

Since the 1920s, birth control programs were discussed in Puerto Rico as a mechanism to control population growth, and there were repeated attempts to implement these programs on the island. According to Briggs, a group of "modernizers"—who saw in birth control policies a means to advance Puerto Rico's economic and social modernization and development—made their voices heard in the 1940s. For modernizers, overpopulation was the cause of Puerto Rican poverty; it was a problem that needed to be solved in order to move the island forward.[4] This was the position assumed by the PPD leadership in the mid-1940s. Like many others, Muñoz Marín believed that overpopulation was the most important problem facing Puerto Rico then. He was nevertheless reluctant to propose population control programs as a remedy to the problem. Instead, he emphasized the "battle of production" as a solution to overpopulation—that is, economic modernization and growth would in time lead to a decrease in population.[5] Although many PPD leaders favored birth control programs, their government did not officially promote the practice, probably due to fear of opposition from the Catholic Church and nationalists.[6]

An example of how overpopulation and migration became an important issue of public debate at this time is the public forum sponsored by the Public Health Association of Puerto Rico, held on July 18 and 19, 1946, titled "Puerto Rico's Population Problem." Its conclusions, published later that year, listed possible solutions to the "population problem": education, migration, birth control, economic improvement, industrial and agricultural development, and population redistribution. It concluded by noting the general agreement among the participants that none of the solutions were themselves sufficient to solve the problem, and that it would take a combination of some or all of them to affect the situation.⁷ In his introduction to this publication, Muñoz Marín stated that "this population problem is possibly the most serious one that our people confront [since] it affects practically all the other great problems of Puerto Rico."⁸ Although Muñoz Marín was initially hesitant to support any specific solution to the population problem, particularly if it meant supporting birth control programs, by 1947 the government had adopted migration as the best solution to solve Puerto Rico's population problem.⁹

On the issue of migration, the major debate was between Clarence Senior and Salvador Tió (an important PPD intellectual). Senior presented his view of migration, later published in his *Puerto Rican Emigration*: migration might be an immediate alternative, but it was not the solution to the island's population problem. He saw in organized mass migration a sign of defeat in facing the island's economic and social problems, a policy too costly and extremely difficult to carry out. Tió assumed a different position, arguing that migration would be the "cheapest" solution to the population problem. The dilemma for him was between "emigration or hunger," and migration would allow other social and economic measures to succeed. He proposed migration to South America, where the best conditions for an organized mass migration of Puerto Ricans prevailed.¹⁰ Similarly, Teodoro Moscoso, Economic Development Administration (EDA) director, argued that without "a vast program of emigration to more promising lands, coupled with an intense program of industrialization and birth control, Puerto Rico's greatest problem will never be resolved."¹¹

The government's reluctance to promote birth control programs meant that migration became the main mechanism to control the island's overpopulation. According to Senior some years later, migration was "contributing greatly to the reduction of population pressures in Puerto Rico. It is the only means, short of widespread death, of directly reducing the present population. That such reduction is needed to give the industrial, agricultural, educational, and other reconstruction programs a chance to work seems clear."¹² Population expert Kingsley Davis characterized Puerto Rico as a "crowded island," the result "of an extremely rapid population growth." He stated that without emigration, the island's population density would have been even higher and concluded: "Emigration has been Puerto Rico's demographic escape valve."¹³

Puerto Rico's postwar government became seriously involved with the management of migration for the first time in late 1946. Surprisingly, this involvement began with labor issues arising in Chicago. This situation prompted the first examination of the question of migration in the postwar period and was the first in a series of events that led to the making of Puerto Rico's migration policy in late 1947.

CHICAGO

In December 1946, a group of Puerto Rican and progressive students from the University of Chicago released a preliminary report on the conditions of Puerto Rican workers in Chicago. It criticized the working and living conditions of nearly 300 women employed as domestic workers in the Chicago area and that of fifty males working at the Chicago Hardware Foundry Co. According to the report, these workers were hired under contract by the Castle, Barton and Associates (CBA) Employment Agency, and the working contracts were approved by the Puerto Rican Department of Labor. However, workers were hired under conditions that violated the department's own regulations. They complained that the department did not supervise the working conditions stipulated by the contract. They also stated that on a visit to the Chicago Hardware Foundry, the commissioner of labor, Manuel A. Pérez, was able to examine their poor working conditions and did nothing to improve them. Pérez responded that the workers had signed the contract voluntarily and that the department would intervene only in case of contract violations. Both domestic and foundry workers complained that the transportation costs were higher than the standard rate, that they received wages lower than the standard rate in Chicago, and that they had extreme deductions taken from their paychecks. Foundry workers complained of inadequate working and living conditions and that they had no health or unemployment benefits.[14]

One of the students protesting laborers' poor conditions was Muna (Munita) Muñoz Lee, Muñoz Marín's daughter. Writing to her father, Muñoz Lee stated that both students and workers were interested in having him study the situation, since "if don Luis [Muñoz Marín] knew [about the situation] this would not happen; he is the only person that defends us." Muñoz Lee explained that the group was not opposed, in principle, to migration as a means to solve Puerto Rico's economic problem; however, the existing migration system, comprising exploitative contracts, did not protect workers' rights. She insisted that the employment of Puerto Rican migrants had generated resentment among U.S. mainland workers because Puerto Ricans were hired at lower wages.[15]

In a letter to Muñoz Marín, Pérez insisted that "the actions of these kids, well intentioned as they might be, could obstruct these emigration projects that were beginning to develop very satisfactorily."[16] In a letter to Muñoz Lee, Pérez demanded to see all the evidence of their accusations and challenged the group to provide information on better jobs and better contracts available to Puerto Ricans in the Chicago area. This, he maintained—and not protest— would be a better contribution to his department's efforts to reduced unemployment and misery in Puerto Rico. He also questioned the group's criticism of an investigation carried out by the Illinois Department of Labor, which upheld the employer's side; he called it official and objective.[17]

In his reply to an editorial in *El Imparcial,* which also published the students' report, Pérez asserted that it is better to have a second-rate job than no job at all, and that those who protested were doing a disservice to Puerto Rico. He maintained that his department had no resources to supervise these contracts, that it had no part in the elaboration of contracts, that workers signed contracts voluntarily, and that the department's function was to guarantee that the contracts followed the law and provided satisfactory working and living conditions. He disregarded the workers' complaints of low salaries by saying that they were nonskilled workers who could not expect high salaries. Regarding the foundry workers' charges of exaggerated deductions by the employer, Pérez replied that if after all the legal deductions—including remittances to family back home—they had little, "Whose fault is it?" He added, "In Puerto Rico they do not have even the opportunity to cover their expenses." He argued that the workers were advised by his department of the working and living conditions they would face in the United States before leaving the island. Pérez insisted that these workers' expeditions were not organized by the government and that many migrants left for the United States on their own, without even the minimum of protection offered by a contract. He complained that if protests continued, the department would not be able to find workers any contracts, and they would be forced to search for jobs without a contract or stay in Puerto Rico living "in misery and hopelessness."[18]

This lack of solidarity with migrant workers' plight was out of step with a political party that still claimed to defend the masses. Furthermore, Pérez strongly believed that migration was an individual's decision and that the government should in no way intervene in the movement of people to the United States, most particularly in terms of organizing mass migration.[19] Just a few months after the Chicago incident, Pérez—an appointee of Governor Tugwell—was replaced as commissioner of labor by Fernando Sierra Berdecía.

The Chicago situation was more serious than Pérez acknowledged: two investigations by Puerto Rican government officials confirmed the complaints presented by workers and in the students' report. The first investigation was carried out by Carmen Isales, of the Department of Health's Division of Public Welfare. Her report to Muñoz Marín presented the evidence that Pérez had defiantly requested from the students. Isales was not against migration; her report's objective was "that mistakes be corrected to prevent that emigrations in the future have those undesired results that this one had." Isales's letter to Muñoz Marín presented the best political rationale for a conscious and managed migration by the government: migration should "become one of the most feasible means to solve our [population] problem" but must be managed correctly "since the mistakes that are made affect fundamentally the hegemony of the party. The frustrated worker that returns to the country without having achieved his ambitions is a seed of discontent and distrust for the party." Isales questioned the contract approved by the Department of Labor and asserted that the working conditions for these migrants were "completely undesirable in terms of wages and working conditions."[20]

While Isales's report contained the same conclusions as the university students' reports, her findings were more extensive. With the support of the Chicago YWCA, she confirmed the allegations made by many domestic workers. Isales also confirmed the allegations by foundry workers that the company was making excessive and illegal deductions from their salaries, while the migrants remained without access to social and medical services.[21] Isales's preliminary report presented a severe critique of the Puerto Rican Department of Labor, accusing it of betraying the interests of island migrants. She argued that the department pressured the workers to comply with the contract even if the working and living conditions were not those promised by the agency. She questioned how the department could support a contract for workers if, in the words of a CBA representative, it "wasn't worth the paper it was written on." The report interrogated its support for a contract that stipulated for salaries below regional standards. Also, the department was criticized for not providing any support to those domestic workers who had abandoned their jobs due to the unsatisfactory working conditions and contract violations. Regarding the foundry workers, Isales questioned how the department could approve their employment in an industry that did not provide decent working and living conditions. She concluded that Puerto Rican workers in Chicago were abandoned without any help or support from the Puerto Rican government or any other public agency.[22]

A second examination of the Chicago situation was entrusted by Muñoz Marín to Vicente Géigel Polanco, president of the Senate's Labor Committee and an outstanding PPD leader who was behind much of the PPD's social legislation. His investigation reaffirmed all of the conclusions of the students' and Isales's reports. Géigel Polanco proposed a better selection of workers and stricter regulations concerning their recruitment, concluding: "If we are able to channel the emigration of workers in a more effective way we will do a great service to Puerto Rico by reducing unemployment in the Island."[23] Based on Géigel Polanco's report, the legislature approved Law 89 in May 1947, granting powers to the Department of Labor to oversee the hiring of workers under contract to the United States and to regulate and approve all contracts. It also proclaimed that no worker would be protected by the government of Puerto Rico unless the contract had been approved by the department. All foreign employers would be forced to inform the department of their intention to hire workers in Puerto Rico.[24]

But the greatest push for what became Puerto Rico's 1947 migration policy came from outside Puerto Rico. It came from events happening in New York City. Here and in Puerto Rico it became known as the "Puerto Rican problem."

THE PUERTO RICAN PROBLEM IN NEW YORK CITY

From conservative tabloids to the liberal *New York Times*, an adverse public campaign against the entry of Puerto Ricans emerged in the city's media in 1947. This campaign concentrated on a number of "problems" posed by the entrance of the new migrants to the city: housing overcrowding, unemployment, crime, illnesses, and particularly this group's lack of capacity to assimilate to the new society. News articles emphasized the "tropical" character of these people, their inclination to go into welfare, and their ignorance of the English language. One issue of concern was the rapid and growing numbers of Puerto Ricans coming to the city; another was the support given by Puerto Ricans to Congressman Vito Marcantonio (a political issue that worried both the city's and the Puerto Rican governments).[25]

The "Puerto Rican problem" began in earnest in early February, when the New York tabloid *PM* began a series on Puerto Ricans in the city. It argued that in the previous six months, some fifty thousand Puerto Ricans had entered the city. Calling it "the first airborne migration of history," the report compared Puerto Ricans to the depression "Okies" that roamed the Southwest during the thirties (immortalized in John Steinbeck's *Grapes of Wrath*). The newspaper criticized the Puerto Rican government for not controlling this massive exodus of people and publicized the complaints by the city's welfare and service agencies said to be overwhelmed by the sheer numbers of migrants. It announced the formation of a New York Welfare Council committee to study the disconcerting situation created by and facing Puerto Ricans in the city. New York government officials deplored the problem Puerto Ricans presented for adaptation and assimilation: they came from a different culture and spoke a different language, were mostly unskilled laborers, moved to overcrowded areas, and had no traditions in basic health and education standards.[26] These ideas are, in a nutshell, the basic elements of what became known as the "Puerto Rican problem" in New York City. The issue took on a new perspective when the prestigious *New York Times* also reported on the situation of

Puerto Ricans in the city, particularly their substandard living conditions in El Barrio, claiming that their numbers reached three hundred fifty thousand.[27]

Meanwhile, the island's resident commissioner, Antonio Fernós-Isern, announced in New York the government's intention to open a "recolonization" program to supervise migration to the mainland. One office would be opened in San Juan to advise prospective migrants and another one in New York to help them in their adaptation to the city. He emphasized the need for migrants to relocate outside New York City. The news report indicated that "Dr. Fernós elaborated his plan after consultation with New York's welfare agencies, which took place last fall."[28]

By late May, another actor in the "Puerto Rican problem" campaign in New York entered the fray. The *New York World Telegram* launched a series on Puerto Ricans in the city, mostly reiterating the issues already presented to the public. One segment of the series paid attention to the relationship of Puerto Ricans to Marcantonio, whose district included the Puerto Rican El Barrio. The report indicated that there was no tangible evidence that he was financing Puerto Rican migration for his own electoral purposes, as was proclaimed by his opponents. It also confirmed city government functionaries' assertions that Puerto Ricans were not (yet) a "problem."[29]

The campaign took a new turn with a series by the *New York Times* in August, this one more virulent than the previous one. It began by estimating the numbers of Puerto Ricans in the city at an astronomic six hundred thousand and reported the public hysteria created by the avalanche of newcomers. The report stated that this "situation is causing New York City authorities increasing concern because of the housing, health and other problems involved." It characterized migrants as "ill and destitute," moving to overcrowded neighborhoods and causing problems in areas such as health and crime. It cited government officials declaring that Puerto Ricans constituted a welfare problem: "Within a day or two after arrival many migrants seek assistance from the City Welfare Department." Relief rolls were said to have increased dramatically with the arrival of Puerto Ricans and some charged that "many of the migrants continue on relief while they return to Puerto Rico." Furthermore, as citizens, Puerto Ricans had no difficulty registering to vote, which meant that Marcantonio—by then a "persona non grata" in New York and American politics—"has been able to benefit by the extra registration."[30]

The "Puerto Rican problem" became a national issue in the United States, as reflected in the publication of several articles in noted magazines with nationwide circulation. In late March, *Newsweek* reported that island migrants were reaching the city at a rate of eight thousand per month and that one out of twenty-two New Yorkers was then a Puerto Rican. In August, *Time* published an article provocatively titled "Sugar-Bowl Migrants," characterizing Puerto Ricans as "the 1947 version of the Okies" and asserting that their migration to the United States "was at flood tide." The article argued that the "Okies were mainly California's problem. The problem of Puerto Ricans is chiefly New York's." It criticized the Puerto Rican government for not doing enough to control the migrant tide.[31]

The 1947 "Puerto Rican problem" campaign lasted until the end of the year. By that time, Puerto Rico's government had formulated its migration policy. But the Puerto Rican government's counterattack to the "Puerto Rican problem" began in August. The government's ad hoc Migration Advisory Committee was meeting regularly to decide on measures to counter the situation. The government also decided to use the American media to defend their positions. An example is the well-known letter to the *New York Times* by Fernós-Isern, where he called Puerto Rico's economic and political situation a "national responsibility" and argued that Puerto Rican migration was necessary for the island's well-being.[32]

Also, Puerto Rican government functionaries announced in early August 1947 that Columbia University would conduct a "survey" of Puerto Rican migrants in New York to assess their situation there and make recommendations to solve the "problem." By commissioning Columbia University, the Puerto Rican government was trying to appease public opinion in New York City by hiring one of its outstanding academic institutions to carry out a "scientific" study of Puerto Ricans there. The study's conclusions were welcomed by the Puerto Rican government: Puerto Ricans went to New York looking for jobs, not welfare; their socioeconomic characteristics were higher than the general standards in Puerto Rico; and their numbers had not surpassed two hundred thousand in New York City. The so-called Puerto Rican Study later became *The Puerto Rican Journey*, written by C. Wright Mills, Senior, and Rose K. Goldsen.[33]

As acknowledged by José Monserrat, director of the Migration Division in the United States for many years, the "Puerto Rican problem" in New York City had a major impact on how Puerto Rican and U.S. policy makers viewed Puerto Rican migration afterward and played a determining role in the formulation of Puerto Rico's migration policy.[34]

EXAMINING MIGRATION IN 1947

As migration became an issue of debate in the Puerto Rican media and in government circles, policy recommendations began to emerge from within several government entities. For example, Julio Machuca, from the Department of Labor, included an analysis of "emigration under a scientific basis" in a policy paper submitted to government leaders on the situation of the working class in Puerto Rico. Emigration—a solution to Puerto Rico's biggest problem, overpopulation—had to be planned; workers should be given adequate preparation and receiving destinations carefully studied. Machuca proposed emigration to Latin America as the best alternative.[35]

An ardent promoter of migration as a solution to Puerto Rico's economic woes was Don O'Connor, an economic adviser at Puerto Rico's Office in Washington. In a March 1947 policy paper, O'Connor argued that a "guided and encouraged removal and relocation" program was the only rational alternative to the island's population pressure and that, "whatever the unpleasant connotations and implications are, the advocacy of seeking jobs elsewhere than in Puerto Rico is a counsel of necessity." He concluded by calling for an effective public policy to improve the island's ills, arguing that "voluntary removal and relocation guided and initially underwritten by government should serve to ameliorate the prospective conditions of life in Puerto Rico."[36]

O'Connor expanded his ideas on a "guided" migration in another paper, claiming that the "fear of political repercussions is proper" and that these would occur if "relocation" of migrants concentrated in one area, like New York City; he proposed that migration be diverted to several places in the United States. "But," he added, "repercussions, local and national, are a part of any significant program. They might be lessened if emphasis is given to the long history of internal migration" in the United States. Common elements like American citizenship should be stressed to diminish opposition in the mainland. O'Connor also suggested that the migration of women should be encouraged as a means of reducing population growth, if "public opinion permits": "The most assured way to reduce population, as Ireland did, is to remove the child-bearers to this mainland."[37]

O'Connor also proposed a plan for the relocation of Puerto Ricans to the Dominican Republic. In exchange for the free entry of Dominican goods to Puerto Rico, the Dominican government would agree to allow the resettlement of six hundred thousand Puerto Ricans over a period of ten years. The plan included a $40 million loan to buy some 2.5 million acres and to provide transportation costs. O'Connor's plan was vetoed by the U.S. State Department.[38]

O'Connor presented another plan for the resettlement of Puerto Rican farmers in Venezuela, in which this government would provide three million acres for the settlement and would allow the immigration of twenty thousand "certified" Puerto Rican farmers a year, up to a net total of five hundred thousand; Puerto Rican settlers would become Venezuelan citizens after seven years of residence. The U.S. government would create a Resettlement Corporation that would "prepare, select and certify" Puerto Ricans for immigration to Venezuela. It would also provide a $50 million loan to the corporation for transportation, housing, and infrastructure costs and to finance professional services. O'Connor's proposal found resistance in Puerto Rico and the United States.[39] Nevertheless, his plans for emigration programs to the Dominican Republic and Venezuela would be discussed in the coming weeks by the government's Emigration Advisory Committee.

By the autumn of 1947, another perspective on migration was published in Puerto Rico. This was the highly circulated *Puerto Rican Emigration* by Clarence Senior, director of the Social Science Research Center at the University of Puerto Rico and later director of the Migration Division in New York. This work is regarded by many as highly significant in delineating Puerto Rico's migration policy during this time—a misguided view, as will be clarified later in this chapter. For now, I would like to summarize some of Senior's most important findings in *Puerto Rican Emigration*. Senior proposed emigration within a broader program of economic and social development and not as a comprehensive solution to Puerto Rico's overpopulation problem. He argued that migration "can make a contribution *only* if it is part of a broad program of population adjustment. . . . Raising levels of living, education, planned parenthood and emigration are all inter-related and must be advanced vigorously."[40]

The first part of the publication is devoted to a study of past Puerto Rican migrations to the United States; the second part examines concrete plans for Puerto Rican "colonization" projects in Latin America. No concrete program of migration to the United States is discussed. Senior argued that in confronting Puerto Rico's "desperate" situation, emigration "must be pushed intensively, with enthusiasm, initiative and imagination but also with balanced judgment. . . . Emigration must be organized." Like O'Connor and other government functionaries before him, he proposed that migrants must be selected, and conditions of migration—including the places of reception—must be carefully considered. Although he acknowledged that "migration to the continental United States seems to offer the best immediate opportunities," migration plans to Latin America "should not be neglected."[41]

Perhaps the most often quoted recommendation of Senior's work was his proposal to create an "Emigration Office," usually understood as the precursor idea to the Migration Office in New York.[42] But in fact, the idea of an emigration office pertaining to migration to the United States was not extensively discussed in Senior's report, nor were its functions and objectives detailed. It is not evident that Senior was proposing the institution that would be created months later. Furthermore, Senior presented the idea for an emigration office while reviewing "colonization" plans for Puerto Ricans in Latin America, although in the conclusions he proposed that the office could also deal with migration to the United States. The office—to be attached to the Governor's Office—would report on "any definite possibilities for colonization with a specific program, including direct costs" and should gather information "on jobs and settlement possibilities in Latin America." Colonization projects in Latin America should be carefully considered, since "migration for settlement may offer far greater possibilities for 'export' of men and women."[43] Senior proposed a migration program to Venezuela as a possible alternative.

The idea that Senior played an influential role in the formulation of Puerto Rico's migration policy, including in the creation of the Migration Division, needs to be questioned. The ideas he presented in his emigration report might have had some influence in the debates held at the Governor's Advisory Committee on Migration, of which he was a member. But the idea to create a government office in charge of migration had been already presented in the debates related to the "Puerto Rican problem" in New York. Furthermore, Senior was never a member of the small circle of policy makers close to Muñoz Marín that formulated public policy in Puerto Rico at the time. Commissioner of Labor Sierra Berdecía was, and he played a central role in the formulation and implementation of the government's migration policy for several decades.

DEBATING POLICY: THE MIGRATION ADVISORY COMMITTEE

The creation of the Migration Advisory Committee by Governor Piñero at the height of the "Puerto Rican problem" in July 1947 signaled the government's acknowledgment of the need to develop a course of action to define a policy regarding Puerto Rican migration. Acting governor Juan A. Pons asserted in the letter creating the committee, "I think the moment has come to begin to make decisions that serve as guide to a program of migration." The "aspects of the problem" that required "careful consideration" were "encouragement and aid that must be provided by the Insular Government; the extent and direction of the program; areas that must be considered to provide good opportunities for employment; if the Federal government should be approached regarding a colonization program, or if we should limit ourselves to what can be done through our own effort even if it is on a smaller scale." The government officials appointed to the committee were Governor's Assistant Daisy D. Reck, Planning Director Rafael Picó, EDA's Moscoso, Secretary of Education

Mariano Villaronga, Ramón Colón Torres, Senior, and Géigel Polanco. The committee was presided over by Sierra Berdecía and met for the first time on July 21.[44]

Minutes of the first two meetings were not found in archival research. But related correspondence indicates that some of the issues discussed in the first meeting included the migration of female domestic workers to the United States and plans for migration to Brazil and Venezuela.[45] The committee's third meeting was held on August 18, and the "Puerto Rican problem" in New York was extensively discussed: "copies of reprints from New York newspapers, concerning Puerto Rican immigrants, were distributed to the members." Correspondence between Dr. Raymond Crist and Picó concerning migration to Venezuela was discussed. A report by "the Sub-committee of Long Range Emigration"—which recommended that the governor request the U.S. government to study the possibility of Puerto Rican migration to Brazil—was reviewed. Senior presented a report on his conversations with Brazilian officials regarding their economic development programs. A subcommittee of Sierra Berdecía, Senior, and Rafael Fernández García was created to discuss with Fernós-Isern the feasibility of talks with U.S. government officials regarding Puerto Rican migration to Venezuela.[46]

The committee's fourth meeting was held in late August. Fernández García and Senior reported on their meeting with Fernós-Isern, "who has been spending a considerable amount of time and energy in Washington on problems arising from Puerto Rican emigration to the United States and has been discussing possible emigration to other places with government officials." The "most important projects under discussion in Washington" were (1) the possibility of "mixing" Puerto Ricans with some four hundred thousand displaced persons from Europe if they were to be relocated in the Americas, (2) the plan to provide free trade to the Dominican Republic in exchange for admission of Puerto Rican farmers (the O'Connor plan), and (3) colonization plans in Venezuela. The first and second projects had been discussed at the State Department, the third at undisclosed Washington circles. Fernández García recommended that Fernós-Isern gave some thought to colonization plans in Brazil. Finally, "it was voted to arrange for an appointment with the Governor, Senator Muñoz Marín and Dr. Fernós to discuss further activities of the Committee."[47]

The fifth committee meeting, held on September 11, was an important one that included the participation of Piñero, Muñoz Marín, Sierra Berdecía, Géigel Polanco, Senior, Francisco Collazo (Department of Education), Reck, Moscoso, and Picó, among others. The presence of Muñoz Marín, Piñero, and other top government officials denoted the significance of this meeting:

a course of action was required. Fernós-Isern indicated that the possibility of mixing Puerto Ricans with displaced persons from Europe, specifically in Venezuela, was discussed at the State Department. Several objections were raised to this proposal; the committee agreed that although talks with Washington might be held on this issue, "it would be highly undesirable to try to mix the two groups in the actual colonization efforts." Piñero disclosed that representatives of the Dutch government had conveyed their willingness to accept Puerto Rican workers in the banana plantations of Surinam and in the oil refineries of Curaçao.

Piñero also shared that the government of the Dominican Republic had expressed its disposition to accept Puerto Rican farmers and had offered one hundred thousand acres to be distributed in family farms of one hundred acres each. Muñoz Marín questioned the viability of Puerto Rican families working such vast farms and also was concerned with the costs of such a venture to the Puerto Rican government. The committee agreed that "in spite of the dictatorship, the Dominican possibilities should be carefully investigated," although several objections were raised concerning this government's policy of accepting only "white" Puerto Ricans, and a small number at that. Finally, Muñoz Marín "raised the question of the need for the immediate organization of an Emigration office," as recommended in Senior's "Puerto Rican Emigration" report. The committee agreed to have Sierra Berdecía draft a plan that "after consultation with Senators Géigel Polanco, Muñoz Marín and Governor Piñero would be presented to the Executive Council" at its next meeting.[48]

What is the meaning of these discussions held by the Migration Advisory Committee? First of all, the incorporation of Muñoz Marín and Piñero into the last meeting denoted the urgency of developing a course of action to deal with the issue of Puerto Rican migration to the United States. Second, most committee discussions centered on migration plans to Latin America and not to the United States. It appears that Puerto Rican government officials intended to defuse the "Puerto Rican problem" by directing migration away from the U.S. mainland. Finally, it is evident that no specific course of action was taken during these meetings. It could be assumed that the committee could not come to a decision then as to a particular policy.

By the end of the summer of 1947, the Puerto Rican government realized the significance of the migration problem for its future economic and political reform programs. The very existence of the governor's Migration Advisory Committee, as well as the debates that ensued within it, signaled a shift in the direction of the government's attention on the topic: while in early August the government was still arguing that Puerto Rican migration was a "national" issue for the United States that required federal attention and action,[49] by September, the focus had shifted to a more active stance on the problem. By the end of December, the government approved its migration policy. It was formulated by Commissioner of Labor Sierra Berdecía.

FERNANDO SIERRA BERDECÍA AND PUERTO RICO'S MIGRATION POLICY

On June 30, 1947, Piñero appointed Sierra Berdecía commissioner of labor. He was a loyal PPD member and government functionary, and a close ally of Muñoz Marín, with whom he shared many experiences (he was a journalist and a writer, had lived in the United States, and was attracted to leftist ideals in his youth). Like Muñoz Marín, Sierra Berdecía had been an *independentista* in the Liberal Party; he followed him in forming the PPD in 1938, and he would eventually abandon independence as a goal and support the creation of Commonwealth status.[50] His designation as commissioner of labor represented a new chapter in Puerto Rico's migration history: he became the architect of the government's postwar migration policy. After a two-month journey throughout the United States, Sierra Berdecía's late 1947 report to the governor provided the framework for the government's migration policy as established in the Migration Law of December 1947. By the end of the year, the department's team in charge of migration was in place, with the appointment of Petroamérica Pagán de Colón as director of the BEM.[51] This bureau—along with the Migration Division in the United States, the Farm Placement Program, and the campaign to have Puerto Ricans declared domestic labor in the United States—carried Sierra Berdecía's intellectual signature. It is clear that no other government functionary influenced the government's migration policy as he did as commissioner of labor from 1947 to 1960—the heyday of not only the Commonwealth status and Operation Bootstrap but also of Puerto Rican migration to the United States.[52]

Most of organized labor in Puerto Rico welcomed Sierra Berdecía's appointment as commissioner of labor. His previous tenure at the Minimum Wage Board and the Labor Relations Board had made him sympathetic to labor demands and needs.[53] His philosophy for guiding the department was based on his belief that the state in Puerto Rico had historically guaranteed basic rights for labor, like organizing and negotiation of contracts, and that the PPD government had recognized the rights of workers to jobs and decent wages. So, there was no reason why workers should follow dangerous demagogues who wanted them to go "from justice to the area of privileges." According to Sierra Berdecía, the primary function of his department was to promote industrial peace among employers and workers through collective bargaining and the implementation of laws protecting workers."54

How did migration fit in this scheme presented by Sierra Berdecía? He argued that the government's labor policy was fourfold. It needed "to create jobs through the promotion of new industries and other programs," "to maintain industrial peace through the promotion of better employer-labor relations" by enforcing labor laws, and "to establish social security programs" to protect unemployed workers. Finally, the department was to "take advantage of available employment opportunities by a well-planned placement program in Puerto Rico itself designed to fill each vacant job with the workers best suited to it and by a search for jobs in other parts of the nation."55 Migration, by reducing unemployment on the island, would be an important element in the promotion of "industrial peace" in Puerto Rico. Since the "promotion of new industries" through the government's economic development program (Operation Bootstrap) failed to create the necessary number of jobs to reduce unemployment and promote the desired industrial peace, the migration of workers to the United States grew in importance for the PPD government.

THE MAKING OF PUERTO RICO'S MIGRATION POLICY

At the end of September 1947—after the last meeting of the governor's Advisory Committee on Migration—Sierra Berdecía began a journey of nearly two months in the United States devoted to the investigation of the "Puerto Rican problem" on the mainland. He visited those states in which Puerto Ricans were settling and working in agriculture, services, and industry. Having the island's commissioner of labor away for nearly two months reflected the top priority given to this issue by the government. Puerto Rico's new migration law came out from Sierra Berdecía's journey in the United States. His report to governor Piñero—"Migration of Puerto Rican Workers to the United States"— became the blueprint for the migration law. This document is without any doubt the most important text on the definition of Puerto Rico's migration policy.

Before leaving for the United States, Sierra Berdecía advanced several norms the Department of Labor would follow in supervising the employment of Puerto Rican workers in the United States. It would provide information and its expertise to workers regarding "all the possibilities of jobs or employment that could exist in Puerto Rico, in the United States or in any country of South America where the workers wish to move voluntarily in search for better means of life." The norms to be followed by the department were to ensure (1) provision of the labor force required for Puerto Rican industry, (2) that Puerto Rican workers would migrate only to areas where there was a real demand for labor, (3) that they would receive the same salary for the same work as workers in the area, and (4) that they would accept union organizing in industries where such institutions were prevalent.[56] Such norms became part of Puerto Rico's migration policy.

After taking part in a conference for state and federal labor officials in North Carolina on September 23, Sierra Berdecía visited farms employing Puerto Rican farmworkers in Pennsylvania and New Jersey, investigated the situation of female domestic workers in Chicago and Philadelphia, and met with city officials in New York City.[57] On October 28, he joined a conference devoted to the situation of island children in city schools with officials from the city's Education Department, teachers, and Puerto Rican representatives. Social integration and lack of English proficiency were the main issues discussed at the meeting. Sierra Berdecía insisted that the island's school system had "not been created with a perspective to prepare Puerto Ricans to emigrate in search of better opportunities." He asserted that as long as this migrant flow could not be prevented, "a plan will be created to help them with an aim to eliminate in all we can the inevitable conflicts of adaptation and readjustment to the new environment."[58]

The day after participating in this conference, Sierra Berdecía announced in New York that on his return to Puerto Rico, he would recommend "radical changes in the management of Puerto Ricans that migrate to the continental United States before they leave San Juan." Adding that the articles in the New York City press (referring to the "Puerto Rican problem") had induced him to take an interest in their situation, the commissioner insisted that "we believe that we should get into this migratory movement. . . . It is our obligation to try to give [migrants] some guide for them to adjust." He also claimed that Mayor O'Dwyer had offered his cooperation to improve the migrants' conditions in the city and that he would recommend the creation of an Identification Office in New York to deal with the readjustment problems of Puerto Ricans there.[59]

Sierra Berdecía subsequently traveled to Washington, DC, to discuss with government, labor, and employment officials, as well as representatives of private institutions, the possibilities of finding jobs for Puerto Ricans on the mainland. Among others, he met with U.S. Labor Secretary L. B. Schwellembach to discuss possibilities for Puerto Ricans' employment on the mainland.[60] Sierra Berdecía maintained that his meetings with people directly involved with Puerto Rican migrants had given him "an invaluable aid for the planning of the Insular government's program." He insisted that Puerto Rican migration to the United States had to be approached from two perspectives: (1) migrants should leave Puerto Rico well aware of working and living conditions on the mainland and with some vocational training and (2) the communities in which they settled must understand the migrants' backgrounds and help them adjust to the new environment.[61]

On his return to Puerto Rico, Sierra Berdecía announced in a press conference the results of his two-month investigation of the situation of Puerto Ricans in the United States. He declared that the problems faced by island migrants in New York City were "problems of adjustment to a foreign environment" and reflected the same obstacles faced by all previous immigrants arriving in the city. He praised the Puerto Rican community in New York City for its honest work, for building a decent living in a different and difficult environment, and for making a great contribution to the economic welfare of the city.[62] Days later, the local press reported that Sierra Berdecía was holding periodic meetings with Piñero, Muñoz Marín, and Fernós-Isern on how to confront the problems facing Puerto Ricans in New York City and how to increase their possibilities of success there.[63]

Sierra Berdecía submitted his report to governor Piñero on November 17, 1947. Its recommendations would be transferred—almost word by word—to the new migration law to be approved in December. The report concentrated on the situation of female domestic workers in Philadelphia and Chicago, the prospects for employment of agricultural workers, and the situation of Puerto Ricans in New York City. It highlighted the encouraging possibilities for the employment of Puerto Ricans in agriculture since the suspension of the U.S. government program for hiring foreign agricultural workers from Jamaica and Mexico, and it suggested that workers could be mobilized for seasonal work on the mainland during the sugar industry's *tiempo muerto* (dead season) (9–12).[64]

Sierra Berdecía devoted a long section of his report to the situation of Puerto Ricans in New York City. He observed that migration there had led to a widespread campaign in the city press "clearly aimed at achieving one way or the other that this migration be restricted." He mentioned his talks with representatives of many city government and private institutions concerned with the situation of Puerto Ricans, including Mayor O'Dwyer and Commissioner of Welfare Franklyn Fielding. According to Sierra Berdecía, the "problems that Puerto Ricans residing there confront are the typical problems of the groups that migrate to societies ethnologically different" (13). He contended that the greatest problem faced by Puerto Ricans in New York City was their lack of English proficiency, which "makes it impossible for them to get quickly in contact with the city agencies, private or public, that exist to solve the social problems" of city residents (14). The commissioner proclaimed that O'Dwyer and Fielding considered the "Puerto Rican problem" as one of education and not of "relief." He concluded that the three areas in which Puerto Ricans faced an "adjustment problem" were education, welfare, and employment (17).

The conclusions and recommendations of Sierra Berdecía's report were the most significant part of this report and became an integral part of the Puerto Rican government's migration policy. The report elucidated what would become the government's migration policy central aspect:

> A more active participation of the Government of Puerto Rico is necessary in this spontaneous migration of Puerto Ricans. We think that the government's policy should be that of neither encouraging nor discouraging the migration of Puerto Rican workers; but once it is spontaneously and freely initiated, it is the government's duty and it must be its policy to provide the best help and orientation so that migrants know beforehand the problems of adjustment that they will confront and that they can confront and solve them with the greatest success, reducing to a minimum the natural difficulties that every migratory movement faces. (18)

It must be Puerto Rico's government "public policy" to cooperate with government agencies in those areas where Puerto Ricans decide to work or settle. The government's involvement should cover two areas: (1) in Puerto Rico itself, where prospective migrants should be provided with the necessary information regarding U.S. working conditions, social and climatic environment, living and housing conditions, and so on, and (2) in migrants' settlement sites in the United States, where the Puerto Rican government should cooperate with state and local governments and private agencies for the "fastest and most efficient adjustment to the life of the community in which they will work or live" (19).

Sierra Berdecía's report recommended the elimination of the Identification Service in New York (ascribed to Puerto Rico's Office in Washington) and the reorganization of the department's Employment Service Office in order to create the Bureau of Employment and Migration within the Department of Labor. The bureau would administer all legislation regulating private employment agencies and the hiring of workers migrating to the United States or any other country. Among its functions would be (1) coordinating with federal and state employment agencies to obtain information regarding the demand for labor in the United States, (2) gathering information of prospective migrants to New York City and other areas, (3) providing information to migrants on the conditions they would face on the mainland, (4) opening and maintaining an information center for those interested in migrating, and (5) keeping an Identification Service center to provide official identifications to those wishing to migrate. Furthermore, the bureau would offer the necessary information to Puerto Ricans interested in working in the United States, whether they were hired by private, federal, or state employment agencies or moved to the U.S. mainland on their own. The bureau would also cooperate with all employers interested in hiring Puerto Rican workers: it would maintain contact between employment specialists and Puerto Ricans workers in the sectors of agriculture, industry, and domestic service for cooperation in the solution of any grievances. Finally, the bureau would maintain a record of migration (18–22).

The other important recommendation of Sierra Berdecía's report was to open an "office" in New York that would function

> as a contact agency between Puerto Ricans that go to reside in that city and government agencies from the city, the state, and the Nation, and private institutions of social welfare; with jurisdiction in the problems of adjustment that recently arrived Puerto Ricans confront there, giving these all kinds of cooperation in their effort to adapt to the new environment. (20–21)

This office would focus on the areas of education, welfare, and employment. The commissioner ended by stating that these recommendations were presented and approved by the mayor of New York and the city's Department of Welfare, among other institutions and personalities (22).[65]

PUERTO RICO'S MIGRATION LAW

On November 28, the Senate had approved a bill determining the government's policy henceforth regarding migration of Puerto Rican workers to the United States. Essentially institutionalized by the bill were the recommendations of Sierra Berdecía's report. First of all, the bill established what became the leading discourse of the Puerto Rican government's migration policy: that it did not "encourage nor discourage" the migration of Puerto Rican workers to the United States or any other country, but that it understood as its duty to orient those workers who chose to migrate to the conditions and "problems of adjustment" found in an "ethnically different environment." It also states that since Puerto Ricans migrated to the United States in an exercise of their right as citizens, and that such voluntary migration had caused some problems in New York as result of adjustment problems, the government assumed its duty to orient these migrants and to cooperate with federal, state, and private agencies interested in attenuating the problems of adjustment that such migration could cause. This cooperation would respect the jurisdiction of these agencies and aim to provide means of contact between the migrants and the agencies. The government's function of orientation and guidance would follow the principles enumerated in Sierra Berdecía's report. The bill created the BEM and established its functions and responsibilities, as specified in Sierra Berdecía's report.[66] Law 25, better known today as Puerto Rico's migration law, was approved on December 5, 1947.[67] Besides institutionalizing the recommendations of Sierra Berdecía's report, the law revised previous legislation regarding the Department of Labor to create the BEM and to open an office by this agency in New York City.

At the center of Puerto Rico's migration policy was the position that the government would neither "encourage nor discourage" migration. This policy statement ran contrary to all the actions that were taken by the government in the following decades, a period during which it not only encouraged the migration of Puerto Ricans to the United States but also facilitated and organized it. As Sierra Berdecía acknowledged years later, the government's policy of "not encouraging" migration to the United States was part of its "public relations" campaign to prevent opposition to Puerto Rican migration in the United States. Commenting on a proposal by O'Connor to create a public agency to finance transportation for migrant workers to the United States, Sierra Berdecía opposed the idea, arguing that "the change in the government's policy of 'not encouraging nor discouraging migration' for another of openly encouraging it could create very serious opposition and obstacles from the American communities where Puerto Ricans settle." This could "seriously delay if not permanently obstruct the employment program of Puerto Rican workers in the United States, which we are developing under the most desirable public relations in the Mainland."[68] But even a staunch supporter of the PPD government like A. W. Maldonado would recognize years later that this policy of "neutrality" on the issue of migration was contradicted by the government's actions:

> If birth control clinics and outreach programs were not possible [for population control], the only obvious alternative was massive migration. But Muñoz and the *Populares*' attitude toward migration was the same as toward birth control: neutrality—to neither discourage nor promote it.... But when a government makes it easy as possible for its people to migrate, when it trains them, gives instructions in new living conditions, provides basic English classes, battles the airlines to keep the fares low, and establishes employ-

ment offices at their destination, isn't it in effect sponsoring a policy that encourages migration?[69]

The idea that the Puerto Rican government was neutral in the migration of Puerto Ricans to the United States was a reaction to the "Puerto Rican problem" in New York City and elsewhere in the United States. The government argued for decades that although Puerto Ricans were migrating on their own, the government was helping them in their "adjustment" to the United States so that they would not become a "problem" there. Nevertheless, as Maldonado pointed out, there was no hiding the fact that the Puerto Rican government was promoting migration as a state policy, whether directly or indirectly.

CHAPTER 3

Puerto Ricans as Domestic Workers and the Farm Placement Program

THE PUERTO RICAN government's approval of the migration law in December 1947 signaled its intent to advance organized migration as a solution to the perceived major problem of the island: overpopulation. Once the decision for this policy was made, the government began to explore programs and ideas that could facilitate the movement of people out of Puerto Rico. This issue became an important part of the government's policies and its day-to-day affairs even though concerns like economic development and status politics dominated the government's public agenda and the public's attention.

This chapter discusses the Puerto Rican government's actions to advance the employment of Puerto Rican labor in the United States. Many U.S. employers preferred foreign workers who could be deported after their work was complete. The Puerto Rican government intervened with federal agencies and agricultural employers in the United States to encourage them to use Puerto Ricans workers. The government's claim was based on the status of Puerto Ricans as "domestic labor," with preferential treatment over foreign workers. The notion rested, of course, on their U.S. citizenship. The debate on Puerto Ricans as domestic labor illustrates how the privileges of citizenship—like having priority over alien labor—was not a given for these colonial citizens.

The chapter also discusses the Puerto Rican Farm Placement Program (FPP; also known as the Farm Labor Program), one of the most significant projects of Puerto Rico's migration policy. This program illustrates the role of the colonial government as a provider of labor to U.S. agricultural employers and places the government at the center of the movement of labor from the island to the U.S. mainland. The FPP remains the best example of an organized migration by the Puerto Rican government. But this program was also based on the notion that these migrants required special protection from the Puerto Rican government because, as a consequence of their racial and cultural characteristics and their place of origin, they were not acknowledged as U.S. citizens with a right to work and settle in the U.S. mainland.

Lastly, the chapter addresses the government's migration plans to Latin America. Although migration to the United States became the accepted course of action after 1947, the Puerto Rican government kept exploring other possible migration sites for Puerto Ricans, specifically countries in Latin America. This should be understood, among other things, as an attempt by policy makers to deal with the continuing "Puerto Rican problem" in the United States. But U.S. government institutions like the State Department constantly opposed these proposals of planned migrations to Latin America because it would have involved the mass movement of U.S. citizens to foreign countries. This is one more instance where U.S. citizenship largely oriented the migration of Puerto Ricans to the United States.

By examining the issue of Puerto Ricans as domestic labor and the FPP, one can understand more clearly the role played by the Puerto Rican government in migration and how it used citizenship as a tool to move forward its migration policy. This topic can also illuminate how U.S. citizenship for Puerto Ricans on the island or in the U.S. mainland was reexamined in postwar Puerto Rico.

PUERTO RICANS AS DOMESTIC LABOR

The government of Puerto Rico began to foster the orderly migration of Puerto Ricans to the United States after approving the migration law in December 1947. The government's FPP was aimed at not only selecting workers in Puerto Rico but also placing them where labor was needed. Island policy makers sought to move Puerto Rican migrants away from New York City and place workers in areas where they would be welcomed. But as President Harry Truman's Commission on Migratory Labor concluded, there was ambivalence among many American employers and some U.S. policy makers regarding Puerto Ricans: they were accepted as workers to satisfy immediate labor demands in agriculture, but they were not accepted as community members. Many employers were reluctant to hire Puerto Ricans because, as U.S.

citizens, they could not be deported at the end of their contract and were not as docile a labor force as foreign workers.[1] For many years, Puerto Ricans were characterized by U.S. government officials and employers as "foreign workers" and had to compete with Mexican and West Indian labor for jobs in American agriculture. This situation became an important obstacle in the Puerto Rican government's effort to promote migration to the United States.

The issue of Puerto Ricans being accepted as domestic labor in the United States places U.S. citizenship in the middle of the island's migration debate. Some scholars argue that while citizenship is not the only thing that distinguishes Puerto Ricans from other "immigrants" in the United States, it is the one advantage Puerto Ricans have when it comes to their entry and incorporation into American society.[2] But citizenship was not immediately acknowledged for these migrants, either from agricultural employers who preferred foreign noncitizen workers or from the federal government agencies in charge of supplying labor to U.S. farms. For Puerto Ricans at this time, citizenship was a contested area, one that had to be fought for in order to have spaces open for them to work in the United States. The colonial nature of Puerto Ricans' U.S. citizenship became a central issue in the migration project. Puerto Rico's status as "foreign in a domestic sense" applied to Puerto Rican labor as well: although citizens, these subjects were deemed by U.S. employers and by the federal government as foreign to the domestic labor market.[3] The colonial state assumed the representation and protection of its "citizens" in the United States, confronting labor-related agencies within the metropolitan state with the right of these subjects to have job priority on the mainland as U.S. citizens.

The confusing positioning of Puerto Ricans regarding U.S. citizenship became evident in the report by President Truman's Commission on Migratory Labor. It acknowledged that

> Puerto Ricans are U.S. citizens and that from *the standpoint of citizenship*, it is inappropriate to discuss Puerto Ricans in a chapter dealing with contract aliens. However . . . since they now find themselves in competition with alien labor, there is obviously a functional relationship which requires their being considered in this context.

After examining the Puerto Rican government's policies on migration and the reasons for the U.S. Bureau of Employment defining them as domestic labor in 1949, the report indicates another peculiarity of Puerto Rican labor migration to the United States. Because Puerto Ricans are citizens, their employment "does not require negotiation of work contracts or prior certification of labor shortage" as alien labor does. It then adds that, nevertheless, "in its desire to protect *its citizens* as much as possible, the Puerto Rican government has insisted on both work contracts and certification of labor needs before approving recruitment of *its people*. The Puerto Rican work contract is negotiated between farm employers on the mainland and the Puerto Rican Department of Labor," as other foreign government do.[4] The report acknowledged that even though Puerto Rican farmworkers were U.S. citizens, they were still treated as alien workers and that, furthermore, in order to minimize the hardships they faced on the U.S. mainland, the Puerto Rican government took care of "its citizens" like the Mexican government did: by requiring a contract, by negotiating directly with employers, and by requiring a certification of labor needs in order to authorize the movement of labor to the United States.

By 1950, Puerto Rican farmworkers were already part of the class of agricultural workers in the United States known as "migratory farmworkers," in large measure due to the policies of the Puerto Rican government under the FPP. In 1940, there were about one million domestic migrant workers, a figure that decreased during the war as the number of alien workers increased. After the end of World War II, according to President Truman's Commission on Migratory Labor, the number of migrant workers increased again to one million, out of which "domestic migrants represent only about one half. The other half is made up of approximately 100,000 Mexicans legally under contract, a relatively small number of British West Indians and Puerto Ricans, and by far the most important, illegal Mexican workers who in recent years have amounted to an estimated 400,000."[5] The commission, like other agencies of the U.S. government dealing with the management of the agricultural labor force, had trouble acknowledging Puerto Ricans as part of the domestic labor force, even though one of its recommendations was to have them recognized as such, with preference over foreign labor.

Puerto Ricans were in a disadvantaged position compared to foreign workers when the war ended since one "of the outstanding features of the wartime labor program was the neglect of Puerto Rico," according to President Truman's commission. The reason for the neglect of Puerto Ricans during this period "was the reluctance of farm employers to accept Puerto Ricans." According to statements made during hearings by the president of a Florida growers association, "The vast difference between the Bahama Island labor and the domestic, including Puerto Rican, is that labor transported from the Bahama Islands can be diverted and sent home if it does not work, which cannot be done in the instance of labor from domestic United States or Puerto Rico."[6] According to the president's commission, the "demand for migratory workers is thus essentially twofold: to be ready to go to work when needed; to be gone when not needed."[7] As U.S. citizens, Puerto Rican workers presented a dilemma to the farmers and their communities who did not want them to stay.

By 1947, Congress had ended the recruitment of foreign workers under a federal program to assist American agriculture. The Puerto Rican government lobbied the Division of Territories and Island Possessions of the U.S. Department of the Interior in vain to have the program reinstated and applied once again to Puerto Rico. Division officials nevertheless encouraged the Puerto Rican government to develop their own migration program to the mainland to alleviate the unemployment problem on the island.[8] Raymond Barr, chief of the division's Caribbean branch, suggested sending Puerto Ricans workers to California, where there was a dire need of farm labor, and recommended that the Puerto Rican government make direct arrangements with the farmers' associations and visit the farms to examine the working conditions there.[9]

Puerto Rican policy makers consistently complained about the refusal of U.S. government agencies and agricultural employers to give priority to Puerto Rican workers over foreign workers, citing it as a major impediment to the success of their migration program.[10] On February 10, 1949, Sierra Berdecía's intense lobbying efforts resulted in an agreement with the director of the Bureau of Employment Security, Robert Goodwin, to have the U.S. Department of Labor declare Puerto Ricans part of the U.S. domestic labor force with preference over foreign workers. The agreement stipulated that the movement of island workers to the United States would be through the U.S. Employment Service (USES). U.S. employers were required to request workers from their local USES office; if the office certified that no local workers were available, the request would be sent to the Puerto Rico office, which would do the screening and preselection of workers to be hired by the U.S. employer. This agreement specified that Puerto Rican workers would go only where there was a certified need for labor, that they would not displace local workers, and that their wages would be the prevalent ones in the area—that is, that they would not depress wages in the United States.[11] However, the agreement was not strongly binding for the federal agency, demanding only that U.S. employers be advised that there was Puerto Rican labor available if they desired it, and allowing employers to hire foreign labor if hiring Puerto Ricans caused them "undue hardships."[12]

The Puerto Rican government had to keep lobbying U.S. agencies for many years after the 1949 agreement in order to protect Puerto Rican workers against foreign competition for jobs in the United States. This is evidenced in an August 1949 memo from Sierra Berdecía to Governor Muñoz Marín, where he commented on a bill to empower the Federal Security Administration to coordinate the contracting of foreign labor in order to supplement domestic labor in the United States. He questioned the bill's alleged purpose, arguing that the "use of foreign workers who are already in the United States results in discrimination against domestic workers particularly Puerto Ricans who are classed as domestic workers." He suggested that the term "domestic labor" "be defined . . . to include those workers in the mainland as well in the territories and possessions on the United States [sic]." Sierra Berdecía charged that "not enough of an effort has been made to secure domestic labor of which there is an abundant supply in Puerto Rico."[13]

On October 21, 1949, Resident Commissioner Fernós-Isern, along with labor advisors Alan Perl and Estella Draper, met with USES officials in Washington to discuss the issue of West Indians competing for jobs with Puerto Rican workers in the Northeast. The Puerto Rican delegation expressed their dissatisfaction with the number of Puerto Ricans employed in relation to the high number of foreign workers contracted that year. USES officials stated that the resistance to hiring Puerto Rican workers was due to the employers' reluctance to have a labor contract—which other domestic workers did not have—and the need to advance transportation expenses to island workers, as required by the island government. According to Draper's memo, USES director Robert Goodwin stated that "congressional opinion was that the Puerto Ricans might stay in this country and create an unemployment problem, and therefore foreign workers should be allowed in." Fernós-Isern explained that Puerto Ricans on the island or the mainland were U.S. citizens who needed protection. He advanced his intention to convince the New York congressional delegation to favor "a policy of excluding foreign workers in favor of Puerto Ricans. He would explain to the congressmen that Puerto Ricans will migrate to New York City, unless other sections of the country are opened up to them."[14]

In January 1950, another Puerto Rican delegation composed by Perl, Draper, and José Cabranes, from New York's Migration Office, met in Washington with USES officials and representatives of agricultural employers. All farm interests present there defended the use of imported labor. According to Draper, Perl indicated that the Puerto Rican government was "willing to negotiate the contract to fit the need of employers in particular areas. (Despite this invitation, not one single member approached us at the end of the meeting)." Draper concluded that "it was the unanimous opinion of the group that the use of foreign labor should be continued," giving USES "ample justification for the use of foreign workers and resisting any attempts to place Puerto Rican labor."[15] Perl's assessment of the meeting was harsher, calling it a "disgusting spectacle . . . a regular love-fest with all the employers cheering the performance of the USES and ending up saying we love you, we love you, we love you." He proposed taking a more active approach, including lobbying members of Congress to put pressure on Labor Secretary Tobin, getting support from American labor unions, and encouraging the governor of Puerto Rico to be more active on this issue.[16]

The judgment of USES by the Puerto Rican functionaries was in agreement with the conclusions presented by Truman's Commission on Migratory Labor. Its report reasoned that the displacement of domestic labor by foreign workers could be reduced or even eliminated

> by separating the employment service function for domestic workers from the administrative responsibilities for contracting and importing foreign labor. When the agency which certifies a labor shortage also is the agency which fills that shortage by importation, it is much too easy to offset an ineffective recruiting and placement job at home by importing more workers from abroad.[17]

USES director Goodwin rejected the accusations of conflict of interest raised by the commission's report, arguing that the needs of agribusiness had to be taken into consideration and that foreign labor fulfilled a demand for labor in American agriculture.[18] The influence of big agribusiness on U.S. labor policy and its reluctance to restrain the use of foreign labor is reflected in the fact the even after the president's Commission on Migratory Labor urged ending the use of alien labor, Congress did not put an end to this practice.[19]

Despite a 1950 memo from Labor Secretary Tobin insisting on the need to hire island workers, opposition to the use of Puerto Rican labor by U.S. labor agencies and agricultural employers continued. The memo itself was confusing. Tobin maintained that USES must give preference to domestic labor when possible, but added: "If and when domestic workers on the continent are insufficient to meet agricultural needs, preference should be given to the use of our citizens from Puerto Rico."[20] Puerto Ricans were again differentiated from other "domestic workers."

Perl's advice for U.S. policy makers to pressure Tobin on the use of Puerto Rican labor was apparently followed. For example, Raymond M. Hilliard, chairman of the Mayor's Advisory Committee on Puerto Rican Affairs in New York City, questioned Tobin regarding why West Indians were still employed in agricultural jobs when large number of Puerto Rican citizens on the island and the mainland—particularly in New York City—were unemployed. "The fact that 90% of migrating Puerto Ricans locate in the City of New York compels our interest in this matter," he stated.[21] In April 1950, efforts by the Puerto Rican government led to an agreement by the U.S. Department of Labor and the state of New York to bar the use of West Indian labor in that state; the agreement explicitly benefitted Puerto Rican workers.[22]

The aggressive campaign by the Puerto Rican government to procure employment for its migrants in American agriculture raised concerns among several groups. Some labor organizers declared Puerto Ricans to be aliens displacing the domestic African American agricultural workers, while others accused the Puerto Rican government of racism for its campaign to substitute Puerto Ricans for West Indian labor.[23] Sierra Berdecía justified the latter policy on the basis that West Indians depressed wages for American workers, and that Puerto Ricans should work in the United States as a right of citizenship. He contended that admitting foreign workers "is not only an invasion of the rights of citizens but also the perpetuation of a serious American unemployment problem.[24]

Citizenship became instrumental in the government's migration policy after it began framing Puerto Ricans' status as domestic labor as a right of their U.S. citizenship. The fact that U.S. federal and state agencies and employers refused to recognize Puerto Ricans as citizens or acknowledge their right to work as domestic labor with preference over foreign labor led the Puerto Rican government to fight these institutions for the recognition of these migrants as U.S. citizens. Puerto Ricans' U.S. citizenship did not automatically guarantee them access to the U.S. labor market; citizenship was not a given, but something that had to be sustained and affirmed in the United States, in this case by the Puerto Rican government. If the U.S. citizenship of Puerto Ricans is a colonial or territorial citizenship that was constructed during several decades by U.S. congressional legislation, Supreme Court decisions, and executive polices, then by 1950, the colonial state was immersed in the process of using and redefining the meaning of that citizenship for Puerto Ricans to make policy and to extend the rights of Puerto Ricans as U.S. citizens on the mainland. The PPD, which years earlier had briefly supported Puerto Rico's independence, was now compelled to use American citizenship as an important tool to make migration possible, particularly after migration became an integral part of its social and economic development program. Once migration and Operation Bootstrap became central policies of the PPD government in 1947, U.S. citizenship became essential to the projects of modernization and state control. Citizenship was the fundamental basis for the Commonwealth constitution approved in 1952. The capacity to have Puerto Ricans move to the United States and the making of migration as a state policy certainly played a role in this new perspective by the PPD.

Correspondence between Sierra Berdecía and Tobin shows how the Puerto Rican government insisted that the U.S. government give priority to

Puerto Rican labor. Sierra Berdecía expressed his concern about statements by Tobin regarding the employment of Puerto Ricans only if they were on the mainland. He insisted that "Puerto Ricans as American citizens are entitled to every right that citizenship confers them regardless of whether they live in San Francisco, New York, Boston or San Juan." Sierra Berdecía indicated that "although it has never been our idea to displace foreign workers, we do not want to be displaced ourselves" and argued that if twenty thousand West Indians working in the United States were replaced by "American citizens living in Puerto Rico, .285 per cent of the United States unemployment situation in this Island would be alleviated."[25] Tobin replied to Sierra Berdecía that his statement was only to reaffirm that island workers in the United States "are entitled to the same rights and privileges accorded to any other citizens," and that such differentiation did not constitute a "distinction as to degree of citizenship status." He affirmed, however, that "it is desirable to concentrate on job placement of unemployed workers within the State before turning to distant sources for filling requirements."[26]

In September 1950, Congress created the U.S. Bureau of Employment Security with the passing of the Wagner-Peyser Act. The bureau's functions were extended to the island after the Puerto Rican legislature approved its local implementation in December. In February 1951, the Puerto Rico Employment Service, affiliated with USES, was created by the island government. The extension of the Wagner-Peyser Act to Puerto Rico, which Sierra Berdecía called "the most important event in the Employment and Migration Bureau during the fiscal year 1950-51,"[27] no doubt was the result of, among other things, the lobbying and political maneuvers of the Puerto Rican government during the previous two years. This law provided Puerto Rico with federal funds to operate the Bureau of Employment and Security (BES) within the Bureau of Employment and Migration (BEM). Consequently, the BEM was divided into two separate programs: BES and the newly restructured Migration Division, financed with funds from the Puerto Rican government. As Joseph Monserrat stated, the Wagner-Peyser Act "expands Puerto Rico's job market to areas beyond the island and it clearly established that Puerto Rico's work force is part of the U.S. domestic labor force."[28] The act incorporated Puerto Rico into the national employment system and the labor interstate clearance system. It allowed the employment of foreign workers only when domestic labor was unavailable, as established by the U.S. Department of Labor. As part of USES, local state offices were urged to hire Puerto Rican workers when there was a certifiable need of labor. Because of these efforts, according to Sierra Berdecía immediately after the act was approved, "our Employment and Migration Bureau is receiving an increasing number of orders for agricultural workers."[29]

As the statistics for the Farm Placement Program indicate, the number of Puerto Ricans working in agriculture increased dramatically after 1952.

Nevertheless, the Puerto Rican government had to continue lobbying in the United States to convince federal labor agencies to enforce the priority employment of Puerto Rican workers. This was true even after the approval of the Wagner-Peyser Act, and even after the report by President Truman's Commission on Migratory Labor, which recommended in its conclusions that when facing labor needs, "preference be given to citizens of the offshore possessions of the United States, such as Hawaii and Puerto Rico,"[30] given the continued preference for alien labor by agricultural employers. This issue came to the fore again when, in the spring of 1951, Congress began to discuss the Ellender-Poage bill that allowed the use of Mexican *braceros* and undocumented workers in American agriculture. This bill not only reflected the power of agribusiness in U.S. politics but also openly contradicted the recommendations of Truman's Commission on Migratory Labor.[31] In May 1951, Sierra Berdecía met with Goodwin, who had been recently appointed by President Truman to assess the manpower needs during the war, to urge him to enforce the employment of Puerto Ricans based on the fact that they were U.S. citizens and Puerto Rico was the only region in the United States with a declared surplus of labor.[32]

Still, by 1952, Secretary of Labor Tobin was hesitant to defend the use of Puerto Rican labor in American agriculture. In a letter to Hubert Humphrey from the Senate Labor Committee during hearings on the status of migratory labor in the United States, Tobin noted that several factors prevented further use of Puerto Rican labor on the continent, including the island's distance from agricultural areas where labor was needed, the difference in language, and the limitations imposed by the government of Puerto Rico on the recruitment of island labor through its labor contract.[33] During a previous Senate hearing Senior, director of the Migration Division, had urged the approval of strict limitations on the use of alien labor in the United States, arguing that as U.S. citizens, Puerto Ricans must have preference over foreign labor.[34] Discrimination against the use of Puerto Rican labor in agriculture continued through the 1950s. For example, in 1958, the commissioner of labor from New Jersey, Carl Holdeman, complained to then secretary of labor James P. Mitchell that West Indian labor was still used instead of available Puerto Rican labor. The reason for this was that farmers could exploit West Indians more openly, while Puerto Ricans were protected by a contract secured by the Puerto Rican government.[35]

Even after the Wagner-Peyser Act led to the restructuring of the Bureau of Employment and Migration, the Puerto Rican government kept its bureaucratic institutions in charge of implementing its migration policy intact. The reason for this, according to Sierra Berdecía, was that even though the Wagner-Peyser Act declared Puerto Rican workers to be part of the American domestic labor force, Puerto Ricans were different from other American workers and required aid and protection when moving to the United States in search for jobs. For him, Puerto Rico's BES involved a different function from that in the United States: it

> involves such work as providing special information to migrant workers from Puerto Rico to the mainland to assist them in facing new situations in an environment which is ethnologically different. It aims to reduce to a minimum those natural problems of adjustment for the individual and for the community to which he goes.[36]

Sierra Berdecía reaffirmed his government's policy of playing an important role in the migration process of Puerto Ricans due to the fact that these were considered as foreign to the United States, not only culturally and linguistically but also in citizenship rights.

THE BUREAU OF EMPLOYMENT AND MIGRATION AND THE FARM PLACEMENT PROGRAM

Puerto Rico's 1947 migration law expanded already established policies of the Puerto Rican government, like oversight over labor contracts and the maintenance of offices in the U.S. mainland. What had changed was the perspective on Puerto Rican migration to the United States and the correspondent bureaucratic structures created to deal with that migration. In his report to the governor that led to the 1947 migration law, Sierra Berdecía argued that there were two separate and distinct migration flows from Puerto Rico to the United States: migration of individuals going to the U.S. mainland on their own, like the one causing the "Puerto Rican problem" in New York City during the summer of 1947, and organized contract migration going mostly to provide cheap labor to U.S. agriculture.[37] The two flows had distinct social bases and destinations: the former had largely a urban character (as *The Puerto Rican Journey* indicated years later) and went mostly to urban areas like New York City, while the latter came from rural agricultural areas and searched for jobs in U.S. farms, mostly in the Northeast. The goal of the new migration law was to regulate migration so that it would be not only a continuous and organized movement of people away from the island but also one that would satisfy the needs of U.S. employers and cause the least problems for the adaptation of the migrant workers as well as for their U.S. communities.

To fulfill this goal, the law created two separate but interrelated bureaucratic structures within the Department of Labor: the Bureau of Employment and Migration in San Juan and the Migration Office in New York (later to become the Migration Division). The former was in charge of managing the recruitment and selection of workers going mostly to U.S. agricultural jobs, while the latter dealt with the migrants' needs and adaptation for those already in the United States. In short, BEM organized the movement of contract labor while the Migration Office addressed issues related largely to individual migration. Most scholars studying the government's role in migration have focused on the Migration Division following Lapp's influential study, reproducing the mistaken notion that the Migration Division and Senior were crucial in making Puerto Rico's migration policy. Migration policy was made in San Juan by Sierra Berdecía and a few other policy makers close to the center of power, Muñoz Marín. This was never truer than in the workings of the Farm Placement Program (FPP), managed by BEM in San Juan under the direction of Petroamérica Pagán de Colón and the supervision of the commissioner of labor. This was the agency in charge of recruiting, selecting, and then directing migrant workers from Puerto Rico's rural areas to farms in the United States. Initially, it regulated the contract labor agencies recruiting farmworkers on the island, but it later expanded its functions to enter into agreements directly with U.S. farmers employing Puerto Ricans.[38]

BEM's goals and procedures followed the guidelines of the 1947 migration law.[39] Its rationale was to aid the labor surplus population in finding jobs, whether in Puerto Rico or in the United States. Migration to the United States became an important outlet for the unemployed in Puerto Rico, particularly those from rural areas. First by regulating labor contractors and making sure farmworkers left the island with a labor contract approved by the government, and then by taking over the negotiation of contracts directly with U.S. employers, BEM sought to provide a regulated and reliable source of labor for U.S. agriculture. Additionally, the protection of farm labor by Puerto Rico's government made it possible for Puerto Rican farmworkers to look at migration to "the North" as a worthwhile endeavor, one that was protected by their government.[40]

The name itself—Bureau of Employment and Migration—pointed to the close relationship that existed in the minds of Puerto Rican policy makers between providing employment for island workers and migration to the United States: after a few years of operation, most of the job placements by BEM were in the United States. As several migration policy makers used to say, the FPP was the other side of Operation Bootstrap, the PPD's economic development program.[41] Furthermore, BEM was in full agreement with the broader goal established by Sierra Berdecía when he took over the Department of Labor: to provide "industrial peace" in Puerto Rico by managing the relationship between labor, the state, and capital (be it in Puerto Rico or in the United States).[42]

In his first report to the governor after BEM was created, Sierra Berdecía justified the FPP on the basis of a surplus labor from the sugar cane industry in Puerto Rico (particularly during the *tiempo muerto*—the dead season— when there was no harvest and no jobs) and the need for agricultural labor in the United States; Puerto Rican farmworkers would be employed in those areas where they were needed instead of foreign workers. In its first year of operation, the commissioner of labor boasted that "for the first time in the history of agricultural labor in the continent, a minimum guaranteed period of employment of 160 hours for every four week period was included in the contract for Puerto Ricans." Other achievements were the placement of laborers in the Midwest and the Northeast regions of the United States, and the opening of a migration office in Chicago.[43] Migration officials liked to point out the benefits of this program, particularly its economic impact on the island as a consequence of the remittances sent to the island by migrants and the impact on the unemployment rate and related social issues (education, social services, etc.) on the government's finances.[44]

One of the most important achievements for the BEM and the Department of Labor was the acceptance of a labor contract by both workers and U.S. employers. The required labor contract for migrants going to work in the United States was implemented in September 1947, months before the approval of Puerto Rico's migration law in December. Puerto Rican migration policy makers liked to boast that the Puerto Rican farmworkers' contract was the best one protecting migratory labor in the United States.[45] Migratory labor in the United States was laxly regulated throughout the first half of the twentieth century by a diverse set of federal and state laws and policies, usually in favor of farmers to the detriment of laborers. The latter composed a complex and diverse force, including the government-regulated Mexican *bracero* program, West Indian contract labor, undocumented Mexican workers, and the diverse domestic labor force largely consisting of U.S. peoples of color.[46] Puerto Ricans were particular in their membership as domestic labor in the migratory labor economy: they were the only domestic group openly protected by state (in this case, a U.S. territory) government contract, quite like the labor contracts protecting foreign labor from Mexico and the West Indies. Most of the central aspects of the Puerto Rican labor contract were similar to the contracts required by the Mexican and West Indian governments allowing their workers to come to the United States in terms of regulating wages and working conditions, transportation costs, and so on.[47] In this sense, Puerto Ricans were "foreign in a domestic sense" to the U.S. agricultural labor system in the same way that the U.S. Supreme Court had declared Puerto Rico to be in relationship to the United States in *Downes v. Bidwell*.

BEM director Pagán de Colón stated in her review of the FPP that both state and federal employment services and agricultural employers were strongly opposed to the contract enforced by the Puerto Rican government, arguing that as U.S. citizens they had no need for a formal contract as required for foreign workers (like the *bracero* program). She argued that U.S. laws did not protect agricultural workers and that, in addition, her department held "that the Puerto Rican worker is in a disadvantage with regards to local workers because of the difference in language, their ignorance of the traditions of work and housing, and for a lack of knowledge on the resources that communities have to benefit its citizens."[48] While claiming preference for Puerto Ricans as U.S. citizens over foreign workers, Department of Labor officials argued that they nevertheless required special attention in the United States because they were treated like foreign workers due to their different culture and language and their lack of knowledge and connection to U.S. culture, habits, language, laws, and social traditions. They contended that island workers were citizens of a different kind that needed the protection of Puerto Rico's government because there was no state structure in the United States to protect them and guarantee their rights as U.S. citizens.[49] That is, Puerto Rico's colonial state had to fight the metropolitan state over meanings of citizenship for Puerto Ricans.

According to Monserrat, the demise of FPP in the late 1970s was due to both the election of the New Progressive Party in Puerto Rico, whose pro-statehood ideology refused to sustain any kind of migration program, and to the strong opposition by U.S. farmers to employing Puerto Rican workers as domestic labor with preference over foreign labor. In 1976, apple farmers in the Northeast refused to hire Puerto Rican farmworkers on the basis that the contract required by the Puerto Rican government was too onerous for them and U.S. Department of Labor regulations prevented them from hiring cheaper foreign labor. Federal courts supported the claims of the apple growers and put a de facto end to Puerto Rico's FPP; Puerto Ricans' U.S. citizenship no longer provided them with preferential treatment over foreign labor.[50]

In its first year of operation, the BEM had four field offices in Puerto Rico and two main offices in San Juan and New York, with an additional office in Chicago. It enforced a contract between workers and employers guaranteeing not only minimum hours of work but also wages, transportation costs, living and working conditions, workmen's compensation, and a prohibition of any kind of discrimination.[51] During FPP's history, BEM never allowed the legal hiring of Puerto Rican workers in the South due to the region's widespread racism.[52] Another important part of the contract was that Puerto Rican workers would earn the prevalent wage in the region, that is, no higher but not less than the wages earned by the established workers in any specific area. This stipulation, as reported by Truman's Commission on Migratory Labor, was similar to other "foreign labor agreements."[53] This policy, along with the ones requiring that Puerto Rican workers would go where there was a certified need for workers and that they would support unions where they existed, was an attempt to prevent conflicts with U.S. organized labor in those regions where island workers migrated to work.[54] As in many other instances, Puerto Ricans were not included in the determination of a domestic labor shortage in American agriculture; like foreign labor, they would be called to fill the labor shortage of domestic workers.[55] Furthermore, Sierra Berdecía concluded in his first-year report that "for the first time, the Bureau was faced with the necessity of itself doing the recruitment which was carried on the year before by private employment agents."[56] That is, in order to guarantee an organized and selective process of migration, BEM assumed the role played before by private labor contractors, whose lack of selectivity and protection of workers in the United States had caused many problems for the workers and for the government.[57] The Puerto Rican government, then, became a labor contractor—an intermediary between the Puerto Rican worker and the U.S. agricultural employer. (This subject will be discussed further in chapter 7.)

During its first year of operations, the bureau placed 11,820 workers in jobs in Puerto Rico and the United States. While the overwhelming majority of the 6,024 placements in Puerto Rico were in industrial jobs (satisfying the labor needs of Fomento manufacturing plants), most of the 5,796 jobs found in the United States were in agriculture, a pattern that would not change in decades to come. The annual report stated that the net migration from Puerto Rico to the United States that year was 33,053; in other words, most Puerto Ricans going to the United States were individual migrants. The report also made note of the counseling services and warnings given to this group as they moved to the U.S. mainland.[58]

The Farm Placement Program came to be the most complex and important of BEM's programs in Puerto Rico, which included industrial and agricultural employment on the island, workers' compensation and arbitration (including the regulation of wages by specific industries), and unemployment benefits, among others.[59] By 1950, the recruitment process was carried out in twenty-eight offices working on the registration and orientation of workers. The bureau also carried out a coordinated media and publicity program to advise farmworkers not to migrate on their own, to avoid dishonest contractors and travel agencies, and to refrain from engaging in farm labor in the United States if they were not up to that kind of work.[60] According to Sierra Berdecía, the department's 1951 records showed "abundant proof . . . that workers were recruited from agricultural areas and not from larger metropolitan districts."[61]

In 1950, almost two-thirds of BEM's job placements were for jobs in the United States: by this time, migration was considered the best means for reducing agricultural unemployment on the island. For the fiscal year 1951–52 there were 424,797 visits to local offices in Puerto Rico, with 42,420 new job applications; in addition, some 24,331 people were interviewed for employment in the Migration Division in the United States. The total number of placements made in Puerto Rico that year was 12,263, out of which 11,457 were in nonagricultural jobs, a reflection of the growing impact of Operation Bootstrap on the island. On the other hand, 12,491 agricultural workers from the island went to the United States under the FPP, and 8,108 were placed by the Migration Division on the mainland.[62]

The FPP continued to grow in the coming years and decades, reaching its peak in the late 1960s when close to twenty thousand farmworkers would go to U.S. farms yearly under the auspices of the program. According to estimates by Monserrat, from 1948 to 1990, some 427,604 Puerto Rican migrant workers were recruited and placed in agricultural jobs in the United States under the FPP.[63] This program had an important impact on the development of Puerto Rican communities in the United States, as Pagán de Colón claimed, by procuring "job opportunities in areas outside of New York" and was also helpful to the island by finding "job opportunities for residents of the rural areas in Puerto Rico."[64] The farmworkers moved to the United States by the government's program were crucial in the making of Puerto Rican communities in places like Chicago, Philadelphia, Hartford, and many other cities around the Northeast.[65] The emergence and development of these communities was influenced by the migration of rural workers, overwhelmingly male, mostly unskilled and uneducated, with limited or no urban background, going first to do farmwork and then moving to urban areas in search of better jobs. Recruitment of prospective farmworker migrants in Puerto Rico's rural areas also had a significant impact on the social and economic development of these regions.[66]

Many agricultural employers in the United States resented the contract and the intervention of the Puerto Rican government, particularly small farmers who could not afford the costs related to the government contract. In order to avoid the illegal hiring of workers by labor contractors and farmers, the Department of Labor entered directly into labor agreements with U.S. agricultural employers, particularly with farm cooperatives or associations. Where these associations were nonexistent, the Puerto Rican government encouraged their formation to collectively guarantee fulfilling the requirements of the labor contract. Several farm cooperatives and associations were created in those states where Puerto Rican farmworkers became an important source of labor, including New Jersey, Pennsylvania, Massachusetts, and New York.[67]

By the early 1950s, a growing number of farmers in the Northeast began to depend on Puerto Rican labor to harvest their crops due to the reduction of domestic and foreign labor available at the time. Pagán de Colón indicates that in 1948, 2,382 Puerto Rican farmworkers were hired by just four U.S. employers; by 1951 some 11,725 Puerto Ricans were providing their services to thirty-six U.S. farmers and by 1954, 14,153 island workers were laboring for ninety-six U.S. farmers.[68] But there was another reason for the increased hiring of island farmworkers: the reliability of the Puerto Rican labor force guaranteed by the Puerto Rican government. The contract benefitted both parties, not only the workers; some of the most important contracts were supervised by Governor Muñoz Marín directly and guaranteed a reliable and screened labor force with stipulated labor costs.[69] By the early 1950s, federal and local functionaries agreed that the Puerto Rican government's migration program could provide jobs for some one hundred thousand Puerto Rican workers in the United States; they acknowledged that migration would be the best solution to solve the local unemployment problem and provide the needed labor in U.S. agricultural enterprises.[70]

MIGRATION PLANS TO LATIN AMERICA

After the approval of the December 1947 migration law, the accepted idea was to organize the migration of Puerto Ricans to the United States. Still, even after specific programs were implemented to coordinate and encourage migration to the mainland, island government officials considered the idea of advocating migration and colonization projects in Latin America. Although none of these projects was ever realized, the discussion around them nevertheless proves the government's interest in redirecting migration away from the United States. There are several plausible explanations for this position. Migration to Latin America could be seen as a mechanism to reduce the outflow to the mainland and thus prevent the emergence or recurrence of "Puerto

Rican problem" campaigns in areas where Puerto Ricans settled. This situation hurt the image of the Puerto Rican government in the United States and in Puerto Rico; it also hindered the entrance of new migrants to the mainland. Furthermore, during this time there was still opposition by some sectors in the United States to the continued entrance of Puerto Ricans.[71]

Latin America was seen by some Puerto Rican decision makers as an outlet where the government could promote the outflow of the island's excess labor force. Although migration to the United States was the official policy, some inside the government still questioned its merits. There were legitimate concerns with the adaptability of Puerto Ricans to American society in terms of culture, language, climate, and ideas. Some PPD leaders believed that Latin American societies would be more compatible for the adaptation of island migrants, while questioning migration to the United States based on the cultural and linguistic rejection faced by islanders on the U.S. mainland, along with the acute experiences of racism, prejudice, and discrimination. They also decried the status of Puerto Ricans in the United States as "second-class citizens."[72]

During the summer and fall of 1947, several proposals to allow the migration of Puerto Rican workers and families to the Dominican Republic and Venezuela were discussed by top government officials, including the governor's Migration Advisory Committee. There was opposition to these migration projects to Latin America from U.S. government functionaries, based on economic and political considerations. For H. Rex Lee, from the Department of Interior, migration to Latin American countries "seems to us to offer very little hope because of the many diplomatic and political factors involved. However, we agree with you that the whole subject should be explored thoroughly." Lee captured the prevailing sentiment for U.S. policy makers when he argued that

> it seems to us that the most hope lies in sending workers to the continent under a plan which would take them to cities, other than New York City, where there are job opportunities, and where there are reasonable chances for their integration into community life.[73]

Although consideration of these migration plans to Latin America by island government officials continued well into the mid-1950s, none of the plans ever materialized and migration to the United States remained the government's policy. One crucial reason for not implementing migration plans to Latin America was the opposition of the U.S. government. The colonial government could not implement these plans on its own. The major reason U.S.

government officials rejected the idea was, of course, because Puerto Ricans were U.S. citizens. The possible diplomatic entanglements of having U.S. citizens colonizing lands in postwar Latin America was simply too much trouble. This is one more example of how colonialism and citizenship determined the trend of Puerto Rican migration in just one direction: to the United States. But it also shows how Puerto Rican functionaries assumed the "relative autonomy" of the colonial state in the area of migration and how they kept pushing the limits of the colonial relationship with the United States by discussing emigration plans with Latin American governments.

Brazil was the country that received the sharpest attention from Puerto Rican government officials as a potential site for migration and colonization by island labor. In August 1946, *El Mundo* revealed that Brazilian representatives had expressed interest in receiving workers from Puerto Rico.[74] A year later, economic advisor Donald O'Connor informed government officials of a proposal to develop the San Francisco River Valley in Brazil; he hoped that "some arrangement for admitting Puerto Rican farmers can probably be effected."[75] In early January 1949, geographer Earl Parker Hanson, responding to a request made by the recently elected governor Muñoz Marín, submitted a proposal for the study of a planned migration program to Brazil, specifically in the San Francisco River Valley and the Amazon area. Hanson asserted that "the fact that U.S. capital and technology are themselves beginning to flow into the expanding economies of Latin America will eventually mean that Puerto Rican emigration will flow in the same direction."[76] Ventura Barnes, an adviser to the Planning Board, supported Hanson's proposal to send Puerto Ricans to the San Francisco River Valley, whose future development he characterized as "a kind of TVA [Tennessee Valley Authority]." Barnes proposed that the Puerto Rican Land Authority could buy vast tracts of land that could serve "as outlet to the tremendous population excess that we actually experience." He also supported the idea of sending migrants to the Amazon Basin. He concluded that the situation required "an educational development to forge in the minds of Puerto Rican generations the idea of migration" to more prosperous places that could sustain them.[77] Planning Board president Rafael Picó called Hanson and Barnes' support for this proposal "a bit too optimistic," although he added that "it is worthy to study all the possibilities, no matter how remote the solution is, to our awful population problem." At this time, Governor Muñoz Marín was very interested in the realization of this study by Hanson.[78] Puerto Rican and Brazilian officials also discussed a possible colonization plan for the State of Pará during the summer of 1949. Sierra Berdecía supported examining the idea but insisted on maintaining the government's strict guidelines for sending migrants to other places. During this time, the governor was still pushing for the realization of Hanson's study; financing it seems to have been the major obstacle.[79]

Despite the attention given to these proposals by top decision makers, other officials questioned the validity of the Brazilian migration plans. Attached to Hanson's proposal mentioned earlier are some typed notes that are very critical of this plan. The unknown author noted that the population required by the Brazil project would remove a very productive labor sector from the island and that the operation would be very costly to the island government; the notes further cautioned about migrant adaptation to the new environment and a lower standard of living and salaries than in the United States. The detractor warned that any "discontent that could emerge in the emigrant class could be used and exploited as a political weapon by the opposition" and argued that the current migration program by the Department of Labor "is approaching the problem in a realistic way."[80] The Brazilian colonization plan was also questioned by O'Connor, who argued that the costs of transportation and family settlement were too high and that migration to the United States and population control measures "appear to be more economical, more feasible, more constructive and more desirable."[81]

In 1951, Fomento director Teodoro Moscoso began to seriously consider renewed suggestions by Brazilian officials for a Puerto Rican colonization program in their country. He convinced Muñoz Marín to send Fomento's Rafael Fernández García to Brazil to study the possibilities of such a plan. After meeting with Brazilian government officials, including advisers to President Getulio Vargas, Fernández García found the "ideal" place in an area south of Sao Paulo along the Ribeira River and close to the Bay of Cananeia, where he envisioned a well-developed Puerto Rican colony of three hundred thousand. He drafted a sixteen-point plan stipulating that Brazil would provide some six thousand square kilometers of land while Puerto Rico would finance the transportation costs of migrants and administer the colony. The total cost of the project for Puerto Rico would be $100 million over a ten-year period. Two events prevented the project from further consideration: Muñoz Marín was too occupied in the political debate that led to the creation of the Commonwealth in 1952, and President Vargas was later removed from power in August 1954 by a military coup.[82] Another colonization plan to Brazil was presented in 1954 by Brazilian senator Assis Chateaubriand. News accounts reported that the government of Puerto Rico was discussing the details of implementing such a plan with the Brazilian government.[83] As with earlier colonization plans in Brazil, Chateaubriand's plan was not implemented.

Other Latin American countries were also considered by Puerto Rican decision makers as sites for possible migration and colonization by Puerto

Ricans. By late 1947, *El Mundo* revealed that Venezuela's consul in Puerto Rico announced that a high-level government delegation would visit Puerto Rico in search of an agreement with the island government. Venezuela was particularly interested in sugar cane workers, who could get year-round work on Venezuelan plantations. In February 1948, Venezuela's consul met with Governor Piñero and Muñoz Marín to discuss a concrete migration plan. The Venezuelan project envisioned the entrance of five million migrants during a twenty-year period. No agreement was reached, nor was any Puerto Rican worker ever sent to Venezuela by the island government.[84]

Surinam was also among the sites considered by Puerto Rican officials for a colonization project. In March 1947, several members of the island's House of Representatives submitted a resolution supporting a plan wherein the United States would buy the territory of Dutch Guiana (Suriname) and establish a Puerto Rican colony there. The idea was advanced by the Foreign Policy Association in the United States (which also proposed granting the island its independence). By the summer of 1948, the idea of a colonization and emigration program to Surinam was still under consideration by the Puerto Rican government; it was also an idea supported by the Caribbean Commission.[85] In March 1955, a government delegation from Costa Rica visited Puerto Rico to discuss the possible migration of Puerto Rican farmers to the Central American country. After meetings with Puerto Rican government officials, both parties agreed that an island delegation would visit Costa Rica to have further discussions on the project. But increasing opposition in Costa Rica and among Puerto Ricans detained the project.[86]

CHAPTER 4

There Ain't No Buses from San Juan to the Bronx

Postwar Migration and Air Transportation

PUERTO RICAN postwar migration is the first airborne migration in American history: this notion is a staple of most textbooks and studies dealing with Puerto Rican migration. Today, notions like *la guagua aérea* (the airbus) or the more scholarly concepts of the "commuter nation" or "the nation on the move" reflect the commonly accepted idea that moving by air from Puerto Rico to the United States is a common, safe, and affordable practice.[1] All indicate that air transportation allowed in the past and sustains today the massive movement of people between Puerto Rico and the United States. Although the study of the Puerto Rican experience in the United States has grown in quantity and quality during the last four decades, the issue of air transportation in the migration process has not been addressed. Even scholars focusing on Puerto Rican migration policy have paid no attention to the role played by the colonial state in this important policy area.

The increased regulation of air transportation, particularly to ensure greater flight safety, the entry of major airlines into the profitable Puerto Rican air space with scheduled flights, and the expansion and modernization of the air transportation infrastructure—including a modern international airport—were all areas where the Puerto Rican government intervened significantly to ensure the fastest and safest movement of people out of the island. That is, the modern, safe, and regular air transportation system that emerged in postwar Puerto Rico needs to be linked to the migration process experienced by Puerto Ricans in that period, as well as to the government's migration policy.

The Puerto Rican government—including the prominent participation of Governor Muñoz Marín—became concerned with the issue of air transportation after it took a more active approach in the management of migration in late 1947. Providing stable and safe air transportation for the tens of thousands of Puerto Ricans who decided to migrate on their own or through government programs every year became an important policy issue for the government. Securing safe air transportation became part of the government's agenda after numerous air accidents took place in the late forties, most of them linked to the "non-scheduled" or "irregular" airlines that provided the bulk of air transportation at that time. Air transportation emerged as one of the domains where the Puerto Rican government assumed greater responsibilities.

But air transportation in Puerto Rico reflects the dilemmas of the government's relative autonomy in a colonial context. Air transportation in all of the U.S. territory is in the jurisdiction of the federal government; the Puerto Rican government had no legally binding jurisdiction on this matter. This is another area where the colonial government had to lobby the federal government to implement policies that would further facilitate the movement of people out of the island. If migration is understood as a mechanism to further social and economic stability in the territory, the government's intervention to expand air transportation infrastructure and services is one more example where the colonial state was furthering U.S. rule on the island. In those areas where the colonial government did not require the extensive intervention of the federal government, like the construction of the international airport, it took the initiative to advance this project on its own.

This chapter examines the actions of the Puerto Rican government to influence the regulation of air transportation in Puerto Rico and to provide a more efficient movement of migrant labor to the United States. It looks at the role played by the government in the air transportation of workers. The government intervened to reduce the high number of air crashes that were negatively affecting the public's notion of air travel, it took the initiative to construct a modern and efficient airport to handle the increasing number of flights and passenger cargo, and it strove to assure the safe travel of island migrants to the mainland. This chapter also questions and debunks the widely accepted idea that tourism was the factor propelling the modernization and expansion of the island's air transportation system and infrastructure in the postwar period.

By March 1949, the Puerto Rican Labor Department had established a set of requirements for the transportation of workers from Puerto Rico to the

United States. These included the care and handling of passengers, like the number of workers delivered per day, as specified by the labor contract and the employer; the services provided to passengers during flights or delays, including food and water; and the provision of flight insurance acceptable to the department. There were also guidelines for carrier service, including that all planes had to have approval of the federal air transportation regulatory agencies (like the Civil Aeronautics Board [CAB] and the Puerto Rico Transportation Authority [TA]) and adequate facilities for the transport of workers; that workers had to be delivered at the specific site determined by employers; and that the carrier company had to post a bond of at least $50,000 with the contractor.[2]

AIR TRANSPORTATION OF LABOR

In its seminal work on Puerto Rican migration, the Centro History Task Force's *Labor Migration under Capitalism* set the basis for future migration studies by defining Puerto Rican migration as a labor migration. However, this text was silent on the role played by the Puerto Rican government in this process. Furthermore, although the book called for the study of migration as a movement of labor from one underdeveloped region to a more advanced one, no attention was paid to how the actual movement of people was carried out. That is, neither Centro's nor any other later study of Puerto Rican migration has so far focused on the transportation of labor from Puerto Rico to the United States.

Air transportation became an essential issue in hiring Puerto Rican laborers in the United States, not only in terms of the overall costs for this labor force but also regarding their availability and reliability. Air transportation in general has reduced the costs involved in hiring workers from faraway places for employers in the advanced economies of the postwar period, as Button and Vega argue. They postulate that as air transportation becomes cheaper and more reliable, it lowers the costs for the movement of labor and increases its mobility.[3] Air transportation not only allowed Puerto Ricans to move to the United States relatively cheaply and quickly but also made the idea of migration itself more acceptable, including specific patterns of migration like return migration and circular migration so characteristic of—but not unique to—the Puerto Rican experience. What Button and Vega do not consider is the role played by the state in this process through its regulations and policies. The Puerto Rican government was instrumental in making air transportation cheaper, safer, and more reliable in order to satisfy the needs of U.S. employers and jobs for Puerto Rican workers.

In his study of the "economic aspects" of migration, Belton Fleisher tackles the question of why migration of Puerto Ricans increased dramatically after 1945 and not in the 1920s, when U.S. immigration quotas created a vast need for cheap labor in the United States, particularly in agriculture. He argues that Puerto Rican workers were worse off in 1945 than in the 1920s as a consequence of the decline of the sugar industry and a rapid population growth that increased the labor force, in conjunction with an increasing urbanization of the population. These factors increased the pool of people inclined to migrate, which corresponded with a growing need for labor in the United States. Fleisher adds a second determining factor in explaining why Puerto Ricans decided to migrate after 1945: the increasing availability of air transportation along with declining airfare costs. He contends that there was a bottleneck in transportation before 1945, when transportation out of the island was limited due to the war and the highly restricted air transportation system. After the war, surplus airplanes and pilots allowed the nonscheduled charter airlines to expand. This coupled with the entry of major airlines and lower airfares meant the number of people leaving the island by air increased dramatically. Fleisher also discusses the nature of the flow of air travelers on the island, whether it was mainly of mainland tourists or migrants. He concludes that the seasonal behavior of air transportation was related to migration flows and airfare costs. Fleisher points out two factors that influenced what he calls the migration "costs" for the prospective migrant: increased information regarding migration and cheaper transportation.[4] What Fleisher fails to mention is that these two variables used to explain the potential costs of migration for likely migrants were influenced and employed by the Puerto Rican government to promote migration.

In his 1953 article on the economic links between Puerto Rico and the United States, Walton Hamilton called upon the Puerto Rican government to focus on three significant policy issues: population control, migration, and industrial development. Migration was central to the other two: by reducing population pressure and the labor market, it allowed those staying on the island to have better jobs and incomes. For Hamilton, transportation was essential to the migration of Puerto Ricans to the United States: he explained, "If migration is to provide a safety valve, passage must be available, reliable, and cheap—and Puerto Rico must consciously strive to make it so." Hamilton saw "the movement of people" as an essential instrument of policy, an important "bridge" between Puerto Rico and the United States. "It is impossible to think of an item in the government's far-reaching and forward-looking program which for its realization does not demand access to adequate, inexpensive, reliable, and economical means of carriage," he wrote. Air transportation became an indispensable tool in the movement of Puerto Ricans to the United States, the most efficient and effective means to achieve mass migration: "Between the island and mainland, the railroad does not run; automobiles, whether of modern design or ancient vintage, are not available; and as the Governor [Muñoz Marín] paraphrased Kipling, 'There ain't no buses running from the Bronx to Mayagüez.'" While ocean transportation was most desirable for the movement of goods, air transportation was the best and most reliable means of moving massive amounts of people. Hamilton acknowledged that "the government of Puerto Rico has been engaged in a struggle to secure to its people adequate and reliable air transport at rates they can afford to pay."[5]

In effect, the Puerto Rican government urged the federal government to implement measures to provide a greater air transportation system for Puerto Rico immediately after the end of World War II. In July 1948, Governor Piñero filed a complaint with the CAB demanding the expansion of air transportation in Puerto Rico. The complaint supported Eastern's petition to operate along the profitable New York–San Juan route; until then, Pan Am was the only major airline allowed to operate flights on that route. The Puerto Rican government argued that this situation was limiting the air transportation services on the island, curtailing competition and thus allowing Pan Am to maintain high-priced airfares. The complaint contended that Puerto Ricans had a right to cheap air transportation to the U.S. mainland, something equivalent to ground transportation between the continental states.[6]

In reaction to this complaint, the CAB held hearings in San Juan on the island's air transportation needs. In February 1949, Puerto Rico's governor and other top functionaries deposed before CAB representative William Madden. According to a news report, all government representatives agreed on three issues that required a greater and cheaper air transportation system: agriculture, migration, and industrialization. Muñoz Marín argued that although Puerto Ricans are U.S. citizens, Puerto Rico occupies a "precise position within the American federal system and the economy of the United States." The fact that the island is miles away from the U.S. mainland presents a "peculiar situation . . . a hurdle that must be overcome or defeated." Puerto Rico's situation is quite different from that of any other state in the continental United States, where land transportation can satisfy economic links. If Puerto Ricans were to be on an equal basis with other U.S. citizens, then their transportation needs had to be adequately addressed. For the governor, "the airplane provides the safe and cheap service that the train, buses, trucks, and passenger cars provide to other citizens of the United States." Air transportation was vital to the island's economic development and continued economic links with the United States, including migration. Muñoz Marín framed the demand for air transportation services between the island and the U.S. mainland within the framework of the rights of Puerto Ricans as U.S. citizens: "What more natural thing that people move from where the jobs are scarce to where they abound? And Puerto Ricans have as much a right as citizens of any state in the Union to be able to move to places where there are new job opportunities." Referring to the nonscheduled air carriers, he pointed out that among Puerto Rico's air transportation needs was a good "second class" system that should be adequate "in matters of security"; in the previous year, the CAB had imposed stricter regulations on their flights to the island. Conscious of the security concerns with these air carriers, linked to several deadly accidents during that time, the governor asserted that these companies "have made in the past a valuable service to Puerto Rico." Although these carriers should comply with the same safety regulations as other airlines, their "pioneering work" in linking the island to the continental U.S. "should not be lost." He also insisted that the "first class" system of air transportation between the island and the mainland needed to be expanded, referring to the scheduled carrier service provided by the major airlines. For Muñoz Marín, new developments in air transportation should provide a more efficient linkage between Puerto Rico and the United States. "Puerto Rico's future rests heavily on the economy, efficiency, and breadth of facilities for air transportation."[7]

The CAB announced its response to the complaint by the Puerto Rican government later that year. Not only did the agency maintain restrictions of nonscheduled airlines flying to Puerto Rico but it also rejected Eastern's petition to fly the New York–San Juan route. In reaction to this action, the Puerto Rican government filed a petition with the CAB in May 1949 demanding reforms to improve the "highly inadequate" air transportation services between the island and the U.S. mainland. It demanded that "another certified airline besides Pan Am" be allowed to have regular direct flights between Puerto Rico and New York, Washington, and Baltimore; that Pan Am be allowed to have direct flights to Puerto Rico from the latter two cities; and that smaller airlines with cheaper airfares be allowed to fly between New York and San Juan. The government's petition claimed that Puerto Rico "is not getting from Pan Am the quality air service that is justified by the significance of the island's air traffic, nor the quality of the regular service that is required by Puerto Rico in view of its complete dependence on air service."[8]

In response to the Puerto Rican petition, the report by CAB's Madden in March 1950 sustained its previous conclusions. The government countered that Madden's recommendations "fail to provide a passenger service at low cost. Therefore, Puerto Rico would have no assurance of receiving low-cost air service for migrants and middle-income passengers, which according to the same examiner is 'vital to the welfare of the island.'" The government's claim argued that the CAB should give Puerto Rico a different treatment than the rest of the nation, arguing that the island's insular condition was not the same as that of the states. The CAB opposed the government's petition for a low-airfare airline due to its implications in the American domestic market for the major regular airlines. Pan Am was strongly opposed to the Puerto Rican position. The Puerto Rican government argued that the proliferation of nonscheduled airlines in the Puerto Rican market was a reaction to Pan Am's inadequate service and high airfares.[9]

Muñoz Marín reiterated the same argument to the CAB chairman, Oswald Ryan, in August 1950. The transportation needs of Puerto Rico increased in the postwar period due to greater economic production, tourism, and, particularly, migration. The governor declared that "the whole economy of Puerto Rico, indeed the very continuance of its existence, is at the mercy of its external transportation facilities—sea and air." After recalling the German submarine blockade that almost starved Puerto Rico during the war years, he reminded Ryan that the circumstances had not changed dramatically in the Cold War era as a consequence of Puerto Rico's strategic position in the Caribbean:

> Of overwhelming importance is the air transportation link between the United States mainland and Puerto Rico in the carriage of people. . . . [I]t is in this field more than in any other that Puerto Rico can make its contribution to an integrated all-out American emergency effort.

The governor claimed that the island's surplus labor could satisfy U.S. labor needs in the face of the Korean War. For him, in an era of increased migration from the island, "air transportation is the only satisfactory method of effecting a movement of people between Puerto Rico and continental United States."[10]

One year earlier, Resident Commissioner Fernós-Isern pled before the House Merchant Marine and Fisheries Committee for the CAB to expand the air and sea transportation system in Puerto Rico: "Low-cost air carriage and dependable and alert regular air carriage are indispensable to the people of Puerto Rico. And they have not, on a satisfactory basis had either the one of the other." He emphasized the importance of air transportation for Puerto Rican migration to the United States: "It is expected that this movement of people will continue for several years. If it does, it will have to be largely by airplane." He also pointed out that most air transportation of passengers at the time was done by nonscheduled airlines that provided cheap airfare but "operated with too few efforts at enforcement of proper safety precautions."[11] The numbers provided by the resident commissioner on the flow of air passengers indicated the importance of air transportation for migration even then and predicted what was to come after 1950. Some 144,455 persons came to Puerto Rico by air from January 1945 to June 1948, while 231,542 departed by air in the same period.[12] The high number of departures indicated the rising importance of air travel for Puerto Rican migration. As Fernós-Isern stated in the *New York Times* in 1950: "The masses must move by air or they must stay at home unemployed."[13]

The CAB eventually accepted the wishes of the Puerto Rican government to improve air transportation services on the island, leading to an increase in the number of flights and to lower airfares.[14] All of this was in great measure made possible by the constant lobbying and efforts of the Puerto Rican government.

THE BATTLE FOR THE PUERTO RICAN SKY: REGULAR VERSUS NONSCHEDULED AIRLINES

The air transportation system in Puerto Rico before World War II was basically similar to what Dierikx describes as the modern means of connecting the colonial metropolis with its territories. He argues that during the 1930s, the airplane provided a more efficient and fast means of transportation for European colonial administrators, businessmen, military personnel, and tourists.[15] The same thing could be said about Puerto Rico; flying was limited to those categories mentioned above and the affluent on the island since very few Puerto Ricans could afford the cost of a plane ticket. To the overwhelming majority of Puerto Ricans, moving to the U.S. mainland implied going by sea transport. Pan Am's first flight to Puerto Rico from Miami was in 1929; by 1940, it had just four weekly flights on this route.[16]

The end of the war created a huge market for used warplanes; most of these were sold to independent companies that fueled the nonscheduled charter flights market. Many national governments created their own publicly owned airlines; others, like the United States, promoted and gave extensive benefits to their own major private airlines. After an end-of-war decrease in production, big airplane manufacturers like Boeing and McDonnell Douglas found a very profitable niche in selling modern airplanes to the major airlines providing regularly scheduled flights. Leading the pack of U.S. airlines expanding their services and fleets was Pan Am, which was extending its global reach with many international routes, including the Caribbean and Puerto Rico. The number of air passengers increased dramatically in the postwar period, from 2.5 million in 1940 to 8.2 million in 1945, 27.3 million in 1950, and 68 million in 1955.[17]

In 1945 only nine scheduled airlines provided air service to Puerto Rico and the Caribbean. By 1955, eight scheduled airlines flew to Puerto Rico, including Pan Am, Eastern, Delta, Southern, Air France, and Iberia; five nonscheduled airlines also provided service to Puerto Rico at that time.[18] Pan Am and Eastern took the lion's share of the Puerto Rican market after 1950. Soon after, Puerto Rico became one of the most profitable routes for Eastern, and the New York–San Juan route became one of Pan Am's "busiest north-south routes." By 1952, Pan Am had seventy weekly flights on this route. In 1948, Pan Am had offered one of its first "tourist" rates worldwide in its New York–San Juan route, lowering the fare from $133 to $75.[19]

On July 1, 1946, Pan Am made its first nonstop flight from New York to San Juan. The four-engine DC-4 took some eight hours to make the route, and the lowest-priced ticket cost $130; this was also the first flight of Pan Am's daily schedule.[20] On March 27, 1950, Eastern made history in Puerto Rico's air transportation system with the first nonstop flight by jet from New York to San Juan. The plane, aptly named "The Puerto Rican," made the flight in five hours and forty-one minutes. Passengers included Vincent Impelliteri, mayor of New York City, who went to Puerto Rico to celebrate the historic event and to meet with the top echelons of the Puerto Rican government.[21] New York City became the most important destination for air travelers coming from Puerto Rico, which was no coincidence: its Puerto Rican settlement was the largest in the United States.

The *New York Times* declared 1950 as "the best year for the airlines" worldwide; the next year it claimed that 1951 was "the best year in their history" for U.S. commercial airlines.[22] Much of this success was attributed to the expansion of tourism after the war. Puerto Rico benefitted from the expansion of both winter and summer tourism to the Caribbean. Tourist traffic to Puerto Rico, for example, increased from 77,457 in 1949–50 to 85,954 in 1950–51.[23] Tourism was a factor in explaining the increase in air travel to and from Puerto Rico, no doubt. But I will argue in the following sections that the expansion of air travel in Puerto Rico, the increase in the number of airlines and flights to and from the island, the modernization of the airport, and the reduction in airfares was not due to an increase in tourism but to the dramatic rise in migration after the war.

The number of nonscheduled airlines increased after the war when the U.S. government sold its huge supply of warplanes to private investors and former war pilots. As the major U.S. airlines controlled regularly scheduled flights, including the lucrative overseas market, the nonscheduled airlines expanded in the domestic market and the overseas territories. The nonscheduled airlines were not regulated as strictly as the regular scheduled airlines and were not included in international agreements regulating global air transportation. They were not allowed to cater to individual passengers like the major airlines, and they had to depend on flights chartered by specific groups or travel agencies.[24] The increase in the number of these airlines increased CAB oversight in their services. For example, in October 1947, the CAB suspended forty-two nonscheduled airlines in the United States, including some flying to Puerto Rico, for failure to comply with federal regulations.[25]

Nonscheduled airlines provided most of the air transportation after the war ended, just as thousands of Puerto Ricans began to move to the United States in search of jobs. According to a CAB report, these airlines came to the island after 1945 to serve "a large backlog of prospective passengers who were unable to obtain transportation whether by boat or by the regular service of Pan American. The demand for space was so great that these nonscheduled carriers had no difficulty filling their aircraft at the same rates charged by Pan American." The number of flights increased after these carriers began making flights to and from Puerto Rico.[26] Another observer described the status of air transportation in Puerto Rico around 1945 in the same terms, asserting that Puerto Rico "was badly served" by Pan Am: "Rates were very high, schedules were inconvenient and not lived up to; and accommodations were bad and hard to get. There was in Puerto Rico a backlog of passengers for whom it would have taken months to find seats." Nonscheduled carriers entered into the Puerto Rican market offering more flights and cheaper airfares. The Puerto Rican government intervened in 1946 to prevent the CAB from grounding these carriers in Puerto Rico. In 1948 it requested the CAB to certify several nonscheduled carriers so they could compete with Pan Am and provide cheaper fares and more flights out of the island.[27] By 1950, the rhetoric coming from Puerto Rican government officials began to change. That year, Fernós-Isern publicly criticized Pan Am's service and airfares in Puerto Rico. Writing after a spate of air crashes by nonscheduled airlines that shocked the Puerto Rican and American public, he argued that the entry and dominance of these carriers in the Puerto Rican market was due to Pan Am's resistance to providing a larger number of flights and cheaper fares.[28]

After 1947, major airlines like Pan Am and Eastern saw an opportunity to expand their markets in Puerto Rico. But their expansion came not because of their low fares and competitive advantage in free market competition with nonscheduled airlines, but in large part as a result of the intervention of the Puerto Rican government in its attempt to deal with one of its most pressing issues in one of its most important public policies: air security. The high number of casualties caused by air crashes rocked public opinion in Puerto Rico, particularly when migration to the United States was on the rise. Safety in air transportation became a major issue of the Puerto Rican government's migration policy.

AIR CRASHES AND AIR TRANSPORTATION SAFETY

On July 13, 1947, a DC-3 carrying thirty-three passengers and a crew of three crashed in the vicinity of Melbourne, Florida, at 4:30 in the morning. Twenty-two Puerto Rican passengers were killed, thirteen survived; they were all living in the New York City area and were going back to visit or return to the island. The flight left from Newark to Miami, with a refueling stop in Augusta, Georgia, on its way to San Juan. A travel agency in New York catering to Puerto Ricans had chartered the nonscheduled flight. It was the deadliest air tragedy in Puerto Rico's history to that point. *El Imparcial* reported "shocking and moving scenes of grief" at the Isla Grande Airport in San Juan among the relatives waiting to pick up their loved ones that morning. Similar scenes of despair and grief were reported by the Puerto Rican daily from the relatives of the dead in New York.[29]

The grief caused by the accident in Puerto Rico turned into rage when news reached the island that the flight was overweight. Puerto Rico's Senate initiated an investigation of the accident, and Fernós-Isern went to Melbourne to learn more. The CAB and the Civil Aeronautics Administration (CAA) also began investigations. The arrival of the bodies in San Juan was described as the most "tragic and painful" event ever witnessed on the island. A riot erupted when the police tried in vain the prevent the relatives of the dead from seeing and identifying the remains of their loved ones.[30] *El Imparcial* questioned why there was no oversight on flights to and from Puerto Rico and called for an investigation of the nonscheduled airlines, particularly along the New York-San Juan route.[31] A federal investigation concluded that the causes for the accident were the overweight plane and overworked and unrested pilots. In addition, a U.S. Senate investigator concluded that the lax maintenance of the airplane was a threat to the security of the passengers.[32]

Six months after the Melbourne accident, another air crash perturbed the Puerto Rican public. On January 7, 1948, the day after the Three Kings Day celebration, another C-47 converted into a DC-3 crashed in the marshes of Savannah, Georgia, killing fifteen Puerto Ricans on their way to the island from Newark. As on the Melbourne flight, most of the Puerto Rican passengers were from the New York area. Out of the twenty-six passengers, seventeen died in the crash, including the pilot. This time, the airplane was owned by Coastal Airways, from Teterboro, New Jersey; most of the tickets had been sold by Manuel Casiano's travel agency in the Bronx, who had chartered the flight to Coastal. The CAA announced that it would undergo an investigation into the causes of the crash, as did a U.S. Senate subcommittee on air safety and regulation. An *El Mundo* editorial called on the Puerto Rican government to pressure the federal government to determine the specific causes of the crash and to enforce more strict regulation of nonscheduled chartered flights.[33]

The plane that crashed in Savannah was carrying five more passengers than regulations allowed. While *El Mundo*'s front page that day was dominated by the news of the crash, two other headlines announced that 300 workers were going to Lorain, Ohio, under the government's migration program and that Muñoz Marín was receiving Venezuela's consul in Puerto Rico to discuss migration plans to that country.[34] The CAB denounced Coastal Airways for numerous safety infractions and noted that the CAA had not acted on them, nor had it reported these infractions to the Puerto Rican government. The U.S. Senate investigator on air safety reported that irregular nonscheduled airlines did not have to go through the more stringent safety regulations that scheduled airlines faced.[35]

During the CAB's hearings on the accident, the copilot confirmed earlier reports by survivors that the two engines had stopped working before the airplane fell. He also mentioned that the Puerto Rican passengers did not understand the safety warnings given by the English-speaking crew, which could not speak Spanish. The president of Coastal Airlines admitted that he did not have any permits to fly into San Juan but that since he had never been stopped, he presumed that he could do it. He argued that any mechanical problem with the aircraft was the pilot's responsibility and that any extra passengers above those allowed by regulations were the responsibility of the travel agency that chartered the plane. Casiano replied that his responsibility was to take the passengers to the plane, and did not include the aircraft's safety; he acknowledged that he paid from $2,000 to $2,200 per charter plane (so, any extra passengers would add to his profit margin). The CAB stated that it had no idea why the two engines failed at the same time.[36]

The Savannah air crash was not the only accident in 1948 involving Puerto Rican passengers. There was a series of air accidents and crashes in that year. On May 28, 1948, a World Airways four-engine Boeing flying from San Juan to New York experienced a forced landing on the outskirts of the Baltimore airport due to the bad weather conditions.[37] Another close call happened on the night of October 4 on another nonscheduled flight from Teterboro,

New Jersey, to Miami en route to San Juan. The pilot, also the owner of New England Air Express Company, decided to emergency land the plane on a Bahamas beach near Nassau when he realized he was off course to the Miami airport. The plane, which carried "nineteen Puerto Rican farmhands, who were booked by Puerto Rico World Airways, a travel agency," was the company's only aircraft.[38]

The year 1948, which had begun in tragedy with the Savannah air crash, ended with another calamity. On the night of December 28, another DC-3 disappeared into the night as it emitted an emergency call at 4:13 a.m.; it had left the San Juan airport at 10 p.m. the night before. Like the ones involved in earlier crashes, this Airborne Transport airplane was on a nonscheduled flight from San Juan to New York via Miami. It carried thirty passengers, twenty-seven of them Puerto Ricans on their way back to the New York area after spending the Christmas holidays on the island. Thus began "one of the biggest air search operations since the end of the war," involving over fifty airplanes from the navy, the coast guard, and the air force, plus scores of smaller private planes. The search extended one thousand miles from Miami in all directions. The airline's representative on the island declared that the plane was inspected and authorized to fly by West Indies Air Service, a company of private mechanics used by nonscheduled airlines to certify their planes; he also asserted that the plane was making its first flight after spending two months under repairs.[39] The usually calm *El Mundo* requested an investigation by federal and local authorities on nonscheduled flights, noting that all except one of the recurring air tragedies in the last years were on these chartered planes. It claimed that Puerto Ricans were fed up with the claims by the island government that it was taking all possible measures to safeguard lives on flights from San Juan to New York.[40] On July 18, 1949, the CAB closed its investigation into the Airborne Transport tragedy, stating that it would reopen the case if the remains of the airplane were ever discovered; its final report indicated that the tragic flight did not fulfill the requirements to operate when it departed from San Juan.[41]

On the night of June 7, 1949, a C-46 airplane owned by Strato Freight crashed in Punta Salinas, in the municipality of Toa Baja, west of San Juan. The cargo aircraft converted into a passenger plane left the San Juan airport at 12:21 a.m. and sent a distress signal at 12:23 a.m. Of the eighty-one persons aboard, fifty-three—all of them Puerto Ricans—died in the accident, making it the worst air accident in Puerto Rican history to date. Passengers and crew members acknowledged that there were only sixty-five seats, so the nineteen children aboard had to sit on their parents' laps, and several adult passengers sat on boxes or stood up during the short flight. Crew members later declared that there were not enough life vests for all the people aboard. The CAB reported that Strato Freight was allowed to fly from New York and Pennsylvania to San Juan and that no violations had been reported against the company; it was also allowed to fly both cargo and passengers using the same plane. As usual, the CAB announced its routine investigation into this air crash. It reported that the flight manifesto was false, understating its total weight.[42]

In Puerto Rico, Muñoz Marín ordered an exhaustive investigation of the tragedy to be led by the attorney general, also stating his direct involvement in the process. In Washington, Congressman Marcantonio requested an investigation of the crash on the House floor.[43] On June 10, Marcantonio made public a CAB secret report on the tragedy, which detailed the irregularities and federal violations incurred by Strato, including submitting a false report on the cargo and passenger weight. That same day, the governor ordered the TA to carry out exhaustive checks on any plane departing from Puerto Rico, while the Justice Department opened an investigation on the generalized practice by travel agencies of overselling plane tickets for a single flight. On June 16, the governor approved an insular regulation requiring all nonscheduled flights flying to and from the island to be approved by the TA.[44]

On July 14, the CAA "invoked its most dramatic authority to ground the airplanes of Strato Freight." It suspended the airline for thirty days and requested that the CAB put the company out of business permanently, stating that the plane that crashed on June 7 was overloaded and its flap was not working properly. Other charges included the use of overworked pilots, carrying passengers on planes certified only for cargo, and recording incorrect weights and balance data in the flight manifests for previous flights on the same route. The CAA stated that this company "manifests an attitude of indifference for the safety of others and a disregard of the civil air regulations."[45] During the CAB hearings on the Punta Salinas tragedy, the flight's copilot declared that the crew had been informed by West Indies Aviation Services that one of the engines was defective. The copilot also acknowledged what survivors had declared earlier, that smoke was coming from one of the engines even before the airplane took off. The CAB's final report on the Punta Salinas air crash declared engine failure and overload as the causes of the accident. The CAB charged Strato Freight with negligence and revoked its license to operate in October 1949.[46]

On June 9, *El Imparcial* published two editorials: one on the Punta Salinas tragedy and another on the problems facing Puerto Rican migrants in the United States. Its editorial the next day complained about the lack of regulations on travel agencies selling overbooked flights on charter airlines; these agencies had been involved in all of the air crashes to that point.[47] It would take *El Imparcial* and many others in Puerto Rico one more tragedy to confirm the relationship between the recurring air crashes and the expanding volume of migration to the United States, and for the Puerto Rican government to take a more active role in the regulation of nonscheduled airlines. On June 5, 1950, a C-46 plane owned by the nonscheduled Westair Lines crashed on the Florida coast, killing twenty-eight passengers, all of them Puerto Ricans. The plane had been chartered by the Michigan Field Corporation, the Michigan sugar beet producers' association, taking sixty-one Puerto Rican farmworkers under a contract approved by the Puerto Rican government. (This incident will be discussed further in chapter 6.) The CAA had previously requested that the CAB suspend Westair from flying passengers, charging the airline with gross negligence on safety regulations. After the Florida accident, *El Imparcial* editorialized that the real cause of the accident was the government's migration policy. This time it was impossible to avoid making the connection between migration and the air crashes, as well as noting the role the Puerto Rican government played in this exodus of people. As a consequence of this accident, government officials—headed by Muñoz Marín—engaged in more active and aggressive lobbying of the federal air transportation agencies in advocating the entry of the two major regular-schedule airlines, Pan Am and Eastern, into the Puerto Rican market. A new era of air transportation in Puerto Rico had begun.

The expansion of the two major airlines into the Puerto Rican market did not eliminate the nonscheduled airlines' movement of Puerto Ricans to the United States. The Puerto Rican government allowed the continued service of nonscheduled companies in Puerto Rico in order to maintain cheap airfares and facilitate a greater movement of people to the U.S. mainland. Furthermore, the fact that the two regular-schedule airlines increased their share of the air transportation market in Puerto Rico did not eradicate air accidents. For example, on March 11, 1952, a Holy Friday, a Pan Am DC-4 carrying sixty-two passengers and five crew members crashed immediately after taking off in San Juan, killing fifty-two people, most of them Puerto Ricans returning to their homes in the New York area. Even though the pilot had requested emergency measures before landing the plane because of engine trouble, the aircraft was allowed to return to New York, having been certified by Pan Am mechanics. Two engines failed immediately after takeoff, causing the plane to crash in the outskirts of the San Juan harbor, where a shocked multitude watched the latest air tragedy in Puerto Rico. After announcing a routine investigation, a CAB representative declared that the agency had increased its manpower in San Juan due to the high number of accidents on the island. From July 1947 to the Pan Am crash in 1952, 204 persons died in airplane disasters in Puerto Rico.[48] From January 1 to April 15, 1952, there were five crashes by U.S. airlines worldwide, with 118 dead; Puerto Rico's Holy Friday crash was the deadliest of them all. All five planes were from major, scheduled U.S. airlines; during that period, ironically, no nonscheduled plane had crashed.[49] By 1956, of the twenty-seven air accidents with more than fifty dead in the world, two had happened in Puerto Rico.[50]

Puerto Rican migration might be the first airborne migration to the United States, but it came with a price. This is a lesson that should not be forgotten because this, too, is part of Puerto Rico's migration history.

AIRFARES

Cheap airfares became an important issue in the government's project of moving people away from the island to work in the United States. In his response to Pan Am's claim that its $75 "tourist" fare was the cheapest it could offer, Fernós-Isern insisted that "the great masses of people moved at present belong to income classes which cannot afford to pay this $75 rate. They must have cheaper transportation if they are to find work in the mainland."[51] The Puerto Rican government had to actively engage with federal regulators and airlines—both scheduled and nonscheduled—in the determination of airfares. Its officials argued that cheap airfares were fundamental in allowing the greatest number of people to move off the island to the United States, a process that had significant benefits for both the Puerto Rican and the American economies.

The Puerto Rican government became directly involved in the negotiation of agreements with airlines regarding schedules and airfares. Many of these agreements where overseen by BEM director Pagán de Colón, who coordinated the government's migration programs. For example, a 1949 letter from a Pan Am representative to Muñoz Marín stated that after a discussion with Pagán de Colón, the airline offered bigger planes for the San Juan to New York route and that these "will be made available" to the BEM "for their exclusive use on a charter basis." The total flight cost was $3,600, or approximately $57 per passenger.[52] Pagán de Colón was also in constant communication with the Puerto Rico's TA making sure nonscheduled carriers were checked for compliance with safety measures and government standards. In a June 1950 memo by Sierra Berdecía, she stated that this procedure was meant to show the measures taken by the BEM "to assure compliance by airlines with all safety regulations."[53] The governor was kept informed of issues regarding air transportation for migrants and of negotiations with air carriers. For example, in a June 15, 1950, meeting he instructed Sierra Berdecía to get a better offer on airfares from Eastern or Pan Am and to try to procure additional air transportation with other nonscheduled carriers.[54]

In 1951, under intense pressure from the Puerto Rican government, the CAB allowed Eastern to expand its services to the island and compete with Pan Am. Eastern immediately offered a $64 airfare to Puerto Rico, forcing Pan Am to lower theirs. Even at these "lower" rates, the two airlines made huge profits in the Puerto Rican market. As economist Walton Hamilton argued, "the tourist services thus forced upon Pan American and Eastern by the Government of Puerto Rico have served the reluctant carriers well." The "tourist" airfare was nothing more than a euphemism for cheap airfares benefitting migrants. Hamilton concluded that the $64 airfare "is far more than the masses of the people can afford to pay, leaves huge layers of potential traffic untapped, and imposes a barrier against the migration of workers to the mainland and the creation of new jobs at home."[55]

The government of Puerto Rico, through the actions of the Department of Labor, was engaged in airfare negotiations with airlines, agricultural contractors, and federal agencies. Pagán de Colón devoted a long section in her review of the Farm Placement Program to the issue of air transportation of migrant workers. She described how already by 1949 the responsibility for the issue of air transportation had been assumed by the BEM as part of the implementation of Puerto Rico's migration law. By that date, the air transportation of workers to the United States was included in the labor contract that was required by the Puerto Rican government—that is, it was regulated by the BEM. The government also compelled all airlines flying Puerto Rican workers to the United States to be certified by Puerto Rico's TA and required that their airfares were the cheapest available if these were to be paid up front by the worker. By 1949, the Department of Labor was encouraging farmers interested in hiring Puerto Rican workers to group into associations that could enter into contract negotiations directly. The most controversial issue was air transportation, since these associations usually wanted to hire their own unscheduled airline, while Puerto Rican functionaries insisted on hiring one of the scheduled carriers.

In 1950, the Department of Labor signed a contract with the Michigan Field Corporation allowing the transportation of workers on an unscheduled airline, Westair. The first flight to Miami ended in a tragic accident with over fifty dead. After this incident, the Puerto Rican government allowed the transportation of workers only in flights by Pan Am and Eastern.[56] In June 1956, it reached an agreement with the major airlines, the CAB, and the Garden State

Service Cooperative Association to reduce airfare from $59.50 to $52.50 in travel from San Juan to the East Coast.[57] Two years later, in June 1958, Puerto Rico was involved in intense negotiations with the major airlines for airfare reduction. The airlines had reduced their regular airfare from $52.50 to $45 along the San Juan–New York route, and the government wanted the same rate for their charter flights with these airlines. When the airlines refused, the government stopped sending workers on charter flights, which reduced the number of workers moving to the United States.[58]

The Puerto Rican government also mediated with federal air transportation regulatory agencies in favor of the nonscheduled, or irregular, carriers. These carriers, which provided charter flights on their own or by contract with agricultural employers on the mainland, provided cheaper airfares to migrants. In December 1948, Governor Piñero asked the CAB to grant permission to World Airways to fly to Puerto Rico, arguing,

> More than 50,000 people moved into and out of Puerto Rico by nonscheduled carriers last year. This movement was in a very large measure a matter of economic life and death to job-seekers. This large movement could not have taken place at rates charged by scheduled airlines who have, until this month, ignored the island's glaring need for low-priced air service to the mainland.

He asserted also that the elimination of these carriers from Puerto Rican routes would lead to higher airfares from the major airlines. The CAB responded positively to the governor's request.[59]

In 1952, the government of Puerto Rico filed a motion to the CAB in support of a petition by Flying Tigers, a nonscheduled carrier, for authorization to fly farmworkers from Puerto Rico to the United States; both Pan Am and Eastern opposed this petition. The government's motion argued that there were eighteen thousand farmworkers ready to move to the United States, but that Pan Am and Eastern's refusal to lower their airfares made this uncertain; Flying Tigers proposed an airfare of $40 to $45, almost $20 below what the two major airlines had offered. The government argued that the CAB had previously established that a cheap air service was an "imperative" need for the Puerto Rican economy and that migrant workers could not afford the high airfares charged by Pan Am and Eastern.[60] In 1953, the CAB approved Eastern's request for lowering its Miami–San Juan airfare from $64 to $43, a petition supported by the Puerto Rican government.[61]

Puerto Rico's extensive dependence on irregular carriers to transport migrants to the United States became a policy issue. Some favored a ban on these carriers, while others supported their continued use. O'Connor had endorsed the latter position as early as 1948, when he was working on matters related to airfares and the air transportation of migrants.[62] O'Connor argued that cheap transportation was necessary for Puerto Ricans to remain competitive on the mainland, and this meant resorting to the use of irregular carriers. He claimed that air safety "is a relative matter" and that no matter what precautionary measures are taken, "risks to life are inherent in speedy transportation," whether performed by the major airlines or the irregulars. O'Connor concluded that irregular carriers "should still have a place in our scheme of things."[63]

THE INTERNATIONAL AIRPORT

The rising exodus of people—which contributed to the increase in the number of flights to and from the U.S. mainland—justified the construction of a modern airport capable of sustaining the large volume of air passengers and the growing number of flights. The international airport, in turn, made it possible for more flights and more modern airplanes to fly to Puerto Rico and thus to facilitate the ever-increasing outflow of people. The Puerto Rican government played a central role in the construction of the international airport, a role that needs to be understood within the context of its migration program.

In May 1946, while celebrating the approval of Pan Am's direct route between San Juan and New York, *El Mundo* reported that the "rise of large proportions" in the island's air transportation system was due to the "unprecedented exodus" of Puerto Ricans going to New York City. The greatest limitation to the expansion of air transportation in Puerto Rico then was the very limited airport infrastructure on the island. The main facility, the Isla Grande Airport next to the San Juan Bay, was shared by civilian and military flights. The report concluded that "it was essential to construct a civilian airport" in San Juan that could be characterized as an "international airport." Later that year, *El Mundo* regretted the slow progress in the planning of the new airport that was to be constructed in the area of Isla Verde, in the municipality of Carolina, next to San Juan. This situation was due mostly to the opposition of the U.S. Navy to transferring the lands to Puerto Rico. The editorial also noted that Pan Am was threatening to reduce its flights from the United States because the existing airport at Isla Grande could not accommodate its newer and bigger airplanes.[64]

By 1948, the government of Puerto Rico and the CAA had agreed on a plan to build the new airport in Isla Verde. This plan was opposed by the navy on the basis that it would interfere with a naval radar station near the projected construction area. Instead, the navy proposed that the new airport be built in Palo Seco, in the municipality of Cataño, also next to San Juan. The CAA refused to provide any funding for the construction until the opposition by the navy was resolved.[65] After failed negotiations with the navy, Governor Piñero requested that President Truman intervene. Truman sent Admiral William Leahy, the former governor of Puerto Rico, to assess the situation. Leahy sided with the Puerto Rican government and said that he saw no reason for the navy's position. On July 7, 1948, Truman ordered the secretaries of the interior and the navy to begin negotiations between the navy and the Puerto Rican government to transfer the navy's land in Isla Verde to Puerto Rico and land in Sabana Seca to the navy. Earlier that year, on June 1, the CAA had approved the construction of an international airport in Isla Verde. According to government officials, the construction of the airport at Isla Verde would cost $12,612,000, with federal funds amounting to just $5 million.[66] The Puerto Rican government was the main force behind the construction of the international airport.

Construction of the new airport began on August 17, 1949. Puerto Rico's TA was in charge of its construction and management. The cost for the first phase of construction was $3.5 million, coming mostly from local funds; by this time, the total cost of the project was estimated at $15 million.[67] Later that year, the journal *Aviation Operations* estimated that nine hundred thousand persons would fly to and from Puerto Rico in 1949. Among the causes for this rise in air traffic was "the strong migratory flow of Puerto Ricans to New York since the end of the war."[68] A 1949 study of Puerto Rico's future international airport indicated that passenger traffic to the United States would increase from 314,346 in 1949, to 665,000 in 1960, to 968,000 by 1970. It estimated that the biggest share of passenger traffic would be due to family visits to and from Puerto Rico, followed by permanent and temporary worker migration to the mainland.[69]

By mid-1951, the construction of the airport was already behind the initial plans. The Puerto Rican government complained that one reason for this situation was that the federal government was retracting from its original financial commitment. In August of that year, the CAA and the Puerto Rican government were able to convince Congress to advance the promised funding by emphasizing the military uses of the new airport. Federal appropriations increased for 1951 and 1952, but not to the levels promised initially by the federal government. In March 1952, TA director Salvador Caro announced the beginning of the second phase in the construction of the airport; up to that date, the Puerto Rican government had invested $3.83 million, while federal funds amounted to $2.2 million. Caro restated the urgency of the new airport based on the unprecedented number of air travelers, claiming that 434,631 passengers used the Isla Grande Airport in 1951—104,292 more than in the previous year. He displayed the model for the new airport, showing its six-floor terminal with offices for federal and local government agencies, airlines, stores, and waiting areas.[70] When the airport was inaugurated in May 1955, the government reported that its original estimates for the airport's passenger traffic—508,000 travelers in 1955 and 665,000 in 1960—were already outdated. In 1953, 605,000 passengers used air transportation to and from Puerto Rico.[71]

In August 1952, Caro stated that of the estimated $15,062,848 final cost for the airport construction, the Puerto Rican government would provide $10.312 million, while the federal government would give only $4.75 million.[72] In early October 1952, Fernós-Isern requested from Congress the approval of the remaining $2.46 million of the funds promised to Puerto Rico in order to accelerate construction. He emphasized the increasing number of industries opened in Puerto Rico by U.S. investors in recent years, the increase in cargo trade with the United States, and the rising number of tourists coming from the U.S. mainland. Missing from the resident commissioner's account, as with other public pronouncements on the need for the new airport during this period, was migration.[73] Why?

Migration was presented as the main reason for new and modern air transportation facilities, including the airport, immediately after the end of the war. The shift in emphasis away from migration might be explained by the attitudes toward Puerto Rican migrants in the United States and the Puerto Rican government's migration policy. The "Puerto Rican problem" in New York City never went away; it surfaced repeatedly in the coming decades, and it also extended to other communities like Chicago, Hartford, and Philadelphia, where Puerto Ricans began to arrive in increasing numbers after 1948. The Puerto Rican government did not want to appear to be "encouraging" migration, the cornerstone of its public relations on this matter.

"VISITORS," TOURISM, AND AIR TRANSPORTATION

When the Isla Verde International Airport began its operations in May 1955, it was heralded as one of the biggest and most modern facilities in Latin America and the Caribbean, a symbol of Puerto Rico's modernization and economic development.[74] Already by this time, the idea that the modernization and expansion of the air transportation system and infrastructure was linked to tourism and the economic development program in Puerto Rico was widely accepted and reproduced in the media.⁷⁵ This idea, actively promoted by the Puerto Rican government at the time, is still prevalent today, even in academic circles.⁷⁶ I argue here that the major force behind the expansion and modernization of the air transportation infrastructure actually was migration: the number of airlines and flights, airline regulations, airfares, the international airport—all of these elements were linked to the dramatic increase in the number of Puerto Ricans leaving the island for the United States to live or work and those returning to see relatives during the holidays.

I will examine briefly the role of tourism and tourist travel in Puerto Rico at that time so the ahistorical and misguided notion that tourism promoted the increase in air transportation on the island can finally be dispelled. In doing so, I will address only two issues regarding tourism in Puerto Rico during the late 1940s and 1950s that are relevant to this book. First, the impact of tourism on the expansion and modernization of the air transportation infrastructure in the early 1950s was not very significant. Second, the increase in tourism in Puerto Rico came *after* the expansion of the air transportation infrastructure (number of flights, airport, etc.) from 1948 to 1955 and, very importantly, after the 1959 revolution closed the U.S.-financed American tourism industry in Cuba. That is, tourism was not the cause in the expansion of the air transportation system in Puerto Rico but vice versa: it was only after this infrastructure was modernized and expanded that tourism in Puerto Rico began to expand significantly. Furthermore, by the late 1950s and early 1960s, an important segment of the "visitors" (the official designation of tourists) traveling to Puerto Rico were Puerto Ricans living in the United States who went back to see relatives and enjoy their holidays on the island.

Tourism in Puerto Rico was minimal before the Puerto Rican government began in 1947, as part of its economic development program, to promote the construction of new hotels through direct investments by Fomento or by giving incentives to U.S. investors.⁷⁷ Still, by the end of the 1940s, the number of tourists coming to Puerto Rico was insubstantial, so it does not explain the increasing number of air passengers leaving the island at that time. Furthermore, and very importantly, a considerable number of tourists coming to Puerto Rico were doing so by sea and not by air. When the resident commissioner gave a deposition to Congress in 1949 on the "transportation needs of Puerto Rico," he argued for more support not only for air transportation but also for sea transportation; the most important reason to expand sea transportation was its direct impact on the island's tourism.⁷⁸ A survey by Puerto Rico's Tourism Office in 1949 supported the resident commissioner's claim for tourists' preference for traveling by sea.⁷⁹

TABLE 1
ARRIVALS TO AND DEPARTURES FROM PUERTO RICO, 1950-60

	1950-51	1955-56	1960-61
Total Arrivals	146,979	319,303	667,081
From the U.S.	92,956	230,585	500,641
Percentage	63.24%	72.22%	75%
Total Departures	188,898	380,950	680,843
To the U.S.	136,101	287,325	517,409
Percentage	72%	75.42%	76%

Source: Albors and López Mangual, *Selected Statistics*, selected data from pp. 2-5.

TABLE 2
NUMBER OF VISITORS TO PUERTO RICO, 1946-65

YEAR	1946-47	1950-51	1955-56	1960-61	1965-66
Number of Visitors	40,380	78,367	162,522	354,963	723,543
From the U.S.	32,405	65,636	147,219	232,343	613,641
Percentage	80.25%	83.75%	90.58%	65.46%	84.81%

Source: Albors and López Mangual, *Selected Statistics*, selected data from pp. 8-9.

As shown in table 1, the movement of people to and from Puerto Rico increased dramatically during the 1950s, increasing fourfold between 1950 and 1960. The overwhelming majority of travel to and from Puerto Rico was to the United States (by 1960 two-thirds of all departures and arrivals). Almost 98 percent of these passengers traveled by air. That is, between 1955—the year the international airport was inaugurated—and 1960, the air movement of passengers almost doubled. The government's yearly figures for passenger movement in Puerto Rico show that between 1950-51 and 1960-61, some 4,101,684 passengers arrived on the island, while 4,568,892 departed. Of this number, 2,982,750 arrived from the United States, while 3,442,772 departed to the United States. Based on this data, the net migration to the United States was 460,022 passengers.

Estimating the number of tourists is trickier since the government at this time used the category of "visitors." As shown in table 2, although the number of visitors to Puerto Rico increased from 1946-47 to 1955-56, the numbers more than doubled by 1960-61, and again by 1965-66. These figures indicate two important things: first, although the number of visitors rose steadily during the 1950s, this figure increased dramatically after 1960, and second, the

TABLE 3
HOTEL REGISTRATIONS IN SAN JUAN BY ORIGIN, 1950-65

YEAR	1950	1955	1960	1964-65
Total	54,832	99,478	217,035	387,287
Puerto Rico Residents	26,858	31,843	34,617	49,638
Percentage of Total	49%	32%	16%	13%
Nonresidents	27,994	67,635	182,418	337,649
Percentage of Total	51%	68%	84%	87%

Source: Albors and López Mangual, *Selected Statistics*, selected data from pp. 20-25.

overwhelming number of visitors came from the United States. From 1950–51 to 1960–61, there were 2,102,812 visitors in Puerto Rico, the vast majority (1,545,838) coming between 1955–56 and 1960–61. But from 1961–62 to 1965–66 alone, there were 2,714,809 visitors to the island.

Table 3 shows how the same pattern of growth is reflected in the number of hotel registrations in San Juan during the period, if this category can be used as a reflection of tourism. In 1950 there existed almost no difference between local and foreign tourism. By 1955, however, the numbers were different: hotel registrations in San Juan by "nonresidents" more than doubled those of "residents of Puerto Rico." The gap between local and foreign hotel registrations widened after that year, more than doubling in numbers between 1955 and 1960; the numbers almost doubled again between 1960 and 1965. An important reason for this, no doubt, was the dramatic jump in the total number of rooms available to visitors in tourist hotels, commercial hotels, and guest houses in Puerto Rico from the mid-1950s to the mid-1960s: from a total of 1,730 in 1955, to 3,323 in 1960, to 6,777 in 1965.[80] But other factors need to be considered to explain more comprehensively the rise of "visitors" in this period.

The traditional discourse on the rise of the tourist industry in Puerto Rico focuses on the growth of the U.S. tourist market based on the expansion of hotels owned or managed by the United States following the collapse of the U.S.-financed tourist industry in Cuba after the revolution in 1959.[81] This perspective of the development of the Puerto Rican tourist industry is not wrong, but it is too limited. It fails to take into consideration how migration promoted the expansion and modernization of the air transportation infrastructure that made possible the growth of the traditional tourist industry in the 1960s ori-

TABLE 4
TOP EIGHT HOTEL REGISTRATIONS IN SAN JUAN, BY U.S. STATES ORIGIN, 1955-65

YEAR	1954-55	1960-61	1965-66
New York	16,474	75,395	149,857
Florida	4,547	12,611	16,375
Illinois	3,439	5,604	—
New Jersey	3,335	13,311	32,343
Pennsylvania	2,653	8,716	17,956
California	2,526	3,941	11,913
Ohio	2,173	3,454	7,298
Massachusetts	1,872	—	14,871
Connecticut	—	4,581	11,343

Source: Albors and López Mangual, *Selected Statistics*, selected data from pp. 27-28.

ented to U.S. tourism in U.S.-owned or U.S.-managed hotels. It also fails to acknowledge that, beginning in the 1950s, a very significant number of the "visitors" going to the island were Puerto Ricans living in the United States.

The pattern of tourism in Puerto Rico for decades to come was already established by 1955: the majority of tourists came from the United States. In 1954-55, 52,399 of a total of 94,316 hotel registrations were from the "U.S. mainland." The numbers for other years were 165,890 out of 219,058 in 1960-61 and 341,227 out of 433,341 in 1965-66. By 1955, another pattern of tourism in Puerto Rico was emerging: most hotel registrations in San Juan hotels were from states with a growing Puerto Rican population. Table 4 shows the top eight states with hotel registrations in San Juan from 1954-55 to 1965-66. By 1963, the three major U.S. airlines flying to Puerto Rico had established three main routes in flights to the island, all of them in cities with heavily populated Puerto Rican communities (or a major transfer airport, in the case of Miami): the Northeastern United States (New York, Newark, Philadelphia, etc.), with Pan Am having 1,815 flights, Eastern 1,256, and Trans-Caribbean Airways (TCA) 213; Chicago, with 200 Eastern flights; and Miami, with 463 flights by Pan Am and 498 by Eastern.[82] This pattern connecting Puerto Rico to major Puerto Rican communities in the United States remains the same to this day.

These numbers reflect another important factor of tourism in Puerto Rico that the literature on the subject usually neglects: a significant number of "visitors" coming to the island were Puerto Ricans living in the United States.[83] A study of the tourism and travel industry in the 1960s concluded:

> The number of visitors arrivals is very large in Puerto Rico; in 1963 it was over half of the total population of the island. Perhaps an unexpectedly small proportion of these visitors comprise the most noticeable group, those who stay in the hotels and guests houses, about 18 percent. . . . Other visitors, staying in apartments with friends or relatives, or elsewhere, comprise a very important group (36 percent . . .).[84]

According to this study, the impact on the economy of these nontraditional tourists who did not stay in hotels and guest houses was greater than that of the more traditional tourists attracted by government publicity.[85] By the 1960s, the largest number of "visitors" traveling to the island were Puerto Ricans living and working in the United States who came to stay with friends or relatives. A significant number of those considered in official statistics as traditional "tourists" came from states with a large number of Puerto Rican residents, probably islanders vacationing in Puerto Rico.

During the fiscal year 1956–57, the Department of Labor began to publish more detailed information coming from its Bureau of Labor Statistics on migration and the number of air passengers moving to and from the United States. This data provides a more accurate perspective on the character of the movement of people and the kinds of passengers involved in Puerto Rico's air traffic. The department's annual report for this fiscal year indicated that 332,400 persons left the island and that 69 percent (97,800) of the nonresidents departing had stayed in private residences during their visit to the island, while only 26.1 percent stayed in hotels. The department's 1958–59 annual report begins to offer more detailed information on the travel of residents and nonresidents. As table 5 clearly shows, already by this time the pattern of air travel was clearly defined: two-thirds of all departures and three-fourths of all arrivals were from nonresidents. But contrary to the official discourse, most air travelers going to or leaving the island were Puerto Ricans living in the U.S. mainland, not foreign tourists. The most important reasons for residents of Puerto Rico to fly to the U.S. mainland were to look for jobs, to move there permanently, and to see or accompany friends and relatives there. The most important reasons for nonresidents to fly to the island were to see or accompany friends and relatives and tourism.

TABLE 5
AIR TRAFFIC MOVEMENT IN PUERTO RICO, 1956-61, BY CATEGORY

YEAR	1956-57	1958-59	1960-61
Departures	332,400	281,300	368,200
RESIDENTS OF PUERTO RICO	N/A	38%	34.3%
Reason for Departing			
To work or search for jobs	33.8%	29%	21.8%
To see relatives and friends	34.1%	15.9%	20.9%
To accompany friends or relatives	N/A	12.8%	13.9%
Moving to the U.S. permanently	N/A	25%	27.3%
NONRESIDENTS	N/A	62%	65.7%
Reason for Visit			
To work or search for jobs		—	—
To see relatives and friends		43%	38.4%
To accompany friends or relatives		7.4%	8.4%
Tourism		25.5%	28.4%
Business		8.5%	7.1%
Arrivals	281,700	285,500	382,500
RESIDENTS OF PUERTO RICO	N/A	24.9%	22%
Reason for Travel to U.S.			
To visit relatives and friends	45.7%	35%	40.6%
To work or search for work	16%	34.8%	27.5%
To accompany relatives	—	8.6%	—
Tourism	12.4%	7.9%	8.8%
Business	—	5.8%	9.4%
NONRESIDENTS	N/A	75%	77.6%
Reason for Visit			
To visit relatives and friends		34%	32.3%
Tourism		19%	25%
To accompany relatives		11%	11%
Business		—	6.4%

Sources: GPR, Comm. Labor, *Twenty-Third Annual Report 1956-57*, 74-75; *Twenty-Fifth Annual Report 1958-59*, 87-88; and *Twenty-Seventh Annual Report 1960-61*, 90-91. The Commissioner of Labor's annual reports for the years 1956-57, 1957-58, and 1958-59 were incorrectly numbered in the original documents. The numbers 23, 24, and 25 were repeated. To avoid further confusion, hereafter we will use both the number and the year of the report as reference for these documents.[86]

TRAVEL AID AND SAFETY

Providing aid to the migrants who left for the United States on their own was an issue that occupied the government for many years. By the mid fifties, those who migrated to the United States through the auspices of the Labor Department reached some fourteen thousand a year, while those who left on their own reached between forty to fifty thousand.[87] In January 1950, the BEM opened an office at the international airport to orient migrants in problems they could face in the United States.[88] Furthermore, in January 1954, Sierra Berdecía announced the opening of an office to provide travel aid to Puerto Ricans at Idlewild International Airport in New York City. He said the idea came from Muñoz Marín after hearing of the economic exploitation and problems faced by Puerto Ricans when they arrived in New York. Following its policy of not "duplicating services" offered by established agencies in the United States, the government decided to provide these services through the Travel Aid Society of New York. The airport office was staffed by two Spanish-speaking social workers reporting to the Migration Office. The staff provided information, among other things, to help migrants move to other areas of the mainland apart from New York City. The existence and function of the airport office was publicized in Puerto Rico by the BEM and by the Migration Office in New York.[89]

Perhaps the most troubling issue for the government regarding individual migrants was the "smuggling of workers." The Department of Labor, together with the Justice Department and the Public Service Commission (PSC), began a campaign in May 1952 against the illegal hiring of workers. Thousands of migrants went to the mainland through the mediation of travel agencies on the island working with contractors in the United States; many workers were scammed in the process. Other workers were hired on the island by contractors not regulated by the Department of Labor, a practice that violated Puerto Rico's migration law.[90] The legislature passed a law that required travel agencies to register with the PSC after May 1948; their licenses could be revoked if they were found guilty of illegal trafficking of workers. Nevertheless, many travel agencies still worked as intermediaries in recruiting workers for U.S. labor contractors and agricultural employers, placing ads in newspapers and redirecting workers to U.S. contractors and employers. This practice became common in the early 1950s in areas of the American South, particularly in Florida, after the government had prohibited the legal hiring of farmworkers in the region. Many working there would later ask the government for protection. According to Pagán de Colón, "the situation that had occurred in the north in 1947 was reproduced in the southern states," referring to the

"Puerto Rican problem" in New York years earlier. Sierra Berdecía requested *El Mundo* and *El Imparcial* not to publish ads used for illegal recruiting, a petition accepted by the two major dailies.[91] In March 1953, Sierra Berdecía denounced the "contraband of agricultural workers" by New Jersey's Garden State Cooperative Association, one of the biggest employers of island migrants; the association refused to accept the contract's medical insurance clause. Eastern Airlines was providing air transportation for these workers.[92]

CHAPTER 5

"Every Puerto Rican a Potential Migrant"

Migrant Education and the English Language Issue

ONE OF THE areas of Puerto Rican life that was significantly impacted by the growing level of migration from Puerto Rico to the United States was public education. The government's goal of easing the incorporation of its migrants into American society influenced the policy of intensifying English teaching in the public school system. After 1953, the expansion of the English program in the public school curriculum was closely associated with the government's migration policy. The Puerto Rican government used the educational system in Puerto Rico to further the adaptation of Puerto Ricans to the "ethnologically different environment" that awaited them in the United States. The Department of Education's program to teach English for adults gradually transformed into one designed to teaching English to prospective migrants.

Furthermore, the Puerto Rican government used the public educational system to encourage the migration of its people to the United States. The government used public schools to promote and encourage migration among thousands of school students and adults through the expansion of programs created to provide "orientation" and "advice" to prospective migrants. The relationship of the educational system to migration is also important for other reasons. Puerto Rico's migration policy was not only implemented by the Department of Labor; it also engaged the government's largest and most important bureaucratic institution, the Department of Education. One of the reasons for the rejection of island migrants in many communities throughout the United States was their foreign culture and language. As part of its migration policy, the Puerto Rican government implemented several programs to educate prospective migrants; these programs sought not only to teach the fundamentals of the English language but also to provide migrants with a basic background of American culture and society.

This policy is linked to two of the most contentious issues on the island since its U.S. occupation: the teaching of English in the public school system and its relationship to the United States' Americanization policy.

ENGLISH EDUCATION, AMERICANIZATION, AND MIGRATION

The use of English as the language of instruction in the educational system became a political issue as soon as the colonial government was established in Puerto Rico under the Foraker Act of 1900. This policy was usually perceived, by supporters and detractors alike, as a means of Americanization in a predominantly Spanish-speaking society. According to Ismael Rodríguez Bou, in order to understand the "development of education in Puerto Rico since 1898," one needs to realize "that the central theme has been the language problem . . . , the result of an ill-advised and short-sighted policy of Americanization."[1] Alicia Pousada argues that "to study the history of English on the island is to study the history of Puerto Rico's uneasy relationship with the U.S. and its political, economic, and cultural implications."[2] Roamé Torres González contends that the history of the English language in Puerto Rico's educational system is related to the island's colonial status and U.S. colonial policies, calling this relationship "highly troubled and not very harmonious."[3]

The 1900 Foraker Act established a Department of Education; its presidentially appointed commissioners saw in the educational system a tool to further U.S. rule on the island. The policy of Americanization was to turn these backward, uncivilized Spanish-speaking people into colonial subjects imbued with the values and ideals of the great American nation. The imposition of English as the language of instruction in the public school system was understood by U.S. colonial functionaries as the best means of implementing the policy of Americanization.[4] The importance given to education by the new colonial authorities was reflected in its size and budget: for the first thirty years of U.S. rule in Puerto Rico, the Department of Education had the largest government bureaucracy and represented one-third of the government's budget.[5] The number of students enrolled in the school system increased from 95,342 in 1910 to 286,098 in 1940; the number of teachers rose from 1,623 to

6,294 during the same period.⁶ Still, by 1920, 61 percent of Puerto Ricans over the age of ten years and 74 percent of the adult rural population were illiterate, according to a government report.⁷ In 1903, the University of Puerto Rico was created to provide teachers for the Education Department; it would also provide the managerial and professional class essential for an expanding capitalist economy. The university followed the goal of Americanization in its curriculum; classes were taught in English, and graduating teachers were required to master the language.⁸

The granting of citizenship to Puerto Ricans by the Jones Act of 1917 had a clear impact on language policy. Although the act did not include any requirement of English knowledge among the population to extend citizenship to Puerto Ricans, colonial functionaries on the island understood that Americanization of the population was more necessary than ever before.⁹ The turn to a stronger use of English in public schools was made by the first Puerto Rican ever appointed as commissioner of education, Juan B. Huyke, a prominent Republican who saw the public school system as "an agency of Americanization." Huyke's policy was revised by José Padín, appointed commissioner in 1930. A strong believer in the role of Spanish in early education as the native and dominant language of Puerto Ricans, Padín made Spanish the language of instruction through grade 8, with English as a special subject; in high school, English was the language of instruction, while Spanish became a special subject.¹⁰

By the 1930s, Puerto Rican and American functionaries began to promote the idea that knowledge of both languages could be beneficial to Puerto Ricans and to the United States. The idea of "Panamericanism" and of Puerto Rico as a "bridge" between the United States and Latin America became popular among government and educational functionaries. Spanish-speaking Puerto Ricans could be of benefit to United States interests in Latin America, after all. During this period, U.S. functionaries began to emphasize the "functionality" of the English language in Puerto Rico rather than Americanization.¹¹ One area in which English could be beneficial to Puerto Ricans was in the area of migration to the United States. Victor S. Clark, a former commissioner of education and a strong believer in Americanization policy, argued in *Puerto Rico and Its Problems* that one of the island's major "problems," as was to be expected, was overpopulation. For Clark, knowledge of English would allow Puerto Ricans to migrate to the United States in search of jobs. Thus, he supported the idea of strengthening the teaching of English at all levels of the school system, contrary to Padín's policy.¹² Commissioner Padín's reply was to indicate that "it was not convenient to complicate and delay the education of all the Puerto Rican public to benefit the few who could immigrate to New York."[13]

In 1937 President Roosevelt appointed Manuel Gallardo as commissioner of education and, in his letter of appointment, stressed the importance of teaching English in the public school curriculum. He considered it "regrettable" that after twenty years of U.S. citizenship, "hundreds of thousands of Puerto Ricans have little and often virtually no knowledge of the English language." According to Roosevelt, mastery of the English language was central to the meaning of American citizenship in Puerto Rico since it would allow "Puerto Rican Americans [to] secure a better understanding of American ideals and principles." He emphasized that Spanish would remain the language of Puerto Ricans and that there was "no desire or purpose" to diminish the Spanish culture in Puerto Rico. Roosevelt accentuated the "functionality" of the English language for Puerto Ricans by emphasizing "that the American citizens of Puerto Rico should profit from their unique geographical situation and the unique historical circumstance which has brought to them the blessings of American citizenship by becoming bilingual." Furthermore, he was emphatic in pointing out another important function of English in Puerto Rico: allowing Puerto Ricans to migrate to the United States. It is only by mastering English, he said,

> that the Puerto Ricans will be able to take full advantage of the economic opportunities which became available to them when they were made American citizens. . . . Puerto Rico is a densely populated Island. Many of its sons and daughters will desire to seek economic opportunity on the mainland. . . . They will be greatly handicapped if they have not mastered English.[14]

The 1930s were characterized by an intensification of nationalism in Puerto Rico, both politically and culturally. In the midst of this movement was the language debate: Spanish represented the most important symbol of the Puerto Rican nation and culture. The movement to have Spanish declared the language of instruction at all levels of the educational system intensified in this period. The PPD's 1940 platform included the demand to make Spanish the official language of education in Puerto Rican public schools. This was one of the first laws approved by Puerto Rico's first elected governor, Luis Muñoz Marín, in 1949. However, right after this historically important law was passed, the PPD government began to intensify the instruction of English in public schools. This shift in policy was due to the new political direction of the PPD toward a more "permanent union" with the United States and the creation of the Commonwealth in 1952, as well as an increased awareness by government officials of the "functional" benefits of English in Puerto Rico. Perhaps the most important benefit was migration.

During the 1948 campaign for Puerto Rico's first elected governor, Muñoz Marín promised that he would make Spanish the language of instruction through all grades of the school system his government's official policy. One of his first appointments as elected governor in 1949 was Mariano Villaronga as commissioner of education. On August 10, 1949, by an executive order, Villaronga established Spanish as the official language of education in all grades of the public school system, with English as a preferred subject in all grades.[15] According to Torres González, there was no contradiction between the PPD government's language policy in the public school system and its new political standing in favor of Commonwealth. The Spanish language policy presented the party and the government as supporters of cultural nationalism at a time when it was abandoning political nationalism, that is, independence. Furthermore, at the same time that Villaronga was making Spanish the language of instruction in public schools, he also announced the intensification in the teaching of the English language in Puerto Rico's schools. The policy of intensifying English teaching was related to the need for more educated and trained workers and the government's economic policy of Operation Bootstrap, as well as the island's growing integration with the American economy. But Torres González provides another element to explain the intensification of English teaching in Puerto Rican public schools after 1949: migration.[16]

Even if the 1949 language policy in public schools was defined by other factors besides migration, by 1953 the situation would be different. That year, the government of Puerto Rico, through public statements by Governor Muñoz Marín himself, again announced its intention to intensify the teaching of English in public schools. But this time, the reason given for this policy was the need to prepare migrants going to the United States. Already by this date, migration was an integral part of one of the most contentious debates in Puerto Rican society since the United States imposed its colonial regime: the language of instruction in public schools.

POSTWAR MIGRATION AND THE TEACHING OF ENGLISH IN PUERTO RICO

Culture and language were significant factors in the emergence of the "Puerto Rican problem" in New York City after 1946. Puerto Rican migrants were seen as foreigners, as alien in language and culture to the United States. Their lack of knowledge of the English language was an important element in this characterization. The several public and private institutions in the city that took an interest in the incorporation of these migrants pointed to language as an important obstacle in this process: their need to learn English as a path toward assimilation into American society. When the New York City Welfare Committee created its committee in 1947 to study the flow of Puerto Ricans to the city, its first recommendation was to provide them with English classes. One year later, its report made the same recommendation.[17] A few weeks later, Dr. Clare Baldwin, assistant superintendent for schools in Harlem, pointed out the large number of Puerto Rican children registered in the city schools and how they had "created an unusual problem in specialized education." Baldwin stated that the problems faced by those children were similar to those confronting immigrants from countries with a different language and customs than those of the United States. Knowledge of English was essential for these children to function in American society and assimilate.[18] When the *World Telegram* began its inflammatory series on the "Puerto Rican problem" in New York City, one of the first articles was on the problems that Puerto Rican children were creating for the city's school system, which was unprepared to deal with so many children lacking a basic knowledge of English.[19]

The English issue became a major concern for the government functionaries in charge of implementing Puerto Rico's migration policy. When Sierra Berdecía traveled to the United States in December 1947—to, among other things, organize the new migration office in New York, as required by the Migration Law approved weeks earlier—joining him was Assistant Commissioner of Education Francisco Collazo. The main goal of the trip was to discuss migration issues with U.S. functionaries, particularly in New York City. Collazo was there to talk about education matters, particularly how to ease the adjustment of Puerto Rican children to their new environment.[20] In his review of Puerto Rico's migration policy, Sierra Berdecía devoted more than a few pages to the issue of English and migration, underscoring the importance he and his department gave to the matter:

> It is a reality that the greatest problem faced by Puerto Ricans when they move themselves to the United States is their ignorance of the English language. . . . So as to be able to work and advance like all his other fellow citizens in the United States, the Puerto Rican migrant must know English, he must learn it, and the quicker he learns it the more marked the development of his own welfare shall be.[21]

Although the Migration Office in New York began to promote English classes for migrants immediately after it opened its doors in 1948, the program to provide English classes for migrants in Puerto Rico evolved rather slowly. In November 1950, *El Mundo* welcomed a program created by the University of Puerto Rico with Georgetown University to provide English classes to Puerto Rican workers of all kinds, including prospective migrants.[22] In January 1951, the municipal government of Barceloneta began to provide English classes specifically aimed at prospective migrants. This program was created after failed attempts to have the Department of Education offer these courses.[23] Later that year, the Department of Labor hired Harry Kessler to train teachers in Puerto Rico in the method he had used in the Hudson Guild in New York to teach English to Puerto Rican workers in the city.[24]

In January 1952, the Department of Education announced its program for English classes specifically aimed at prospective migrants going to the United States. Like in previous programs, the eight-week tuition-free course would provide basic conversational English classes to those planning to migrate to the United States only. Classes would be at night for persons not currently enrolled in schools—that is, it was aimed at adults in the labor force. Classes were offered in fourteen of the island's largest municipalities. When the program started in February, there were 1,320 persons enrolled in thirty-four groups of forty students each; initially only fourteen groups were anticipated. Department officials stated that no more groups were created due to a lack of facilities.[25] In April the department's Vocational Training Division and the Puerto Rico Employment Service announced a joint program to promote the employment of vocational students in Puerto Rico. As part of the agreement, vocational students had to register with the Employment Service office and vocational schools had to advise students on employment opportunities in the United States.[26]

The role that migration played in the intensification of English teaching in Puerto Rico's public schools became more pronounced and publicly acknowledged in the early part of 1953. In March, the Puerto Rican government sponsored the first Migration Conference between functionaries of the New York City and Puerto Rican governments. The conference was supposed to show the common interests that New York City and Puerto Rican policy makers shared regarding island migrants in New York: how to facilitate the incorporation of island migrants in the United States, for example. Since its creation, the NYC Mayor's Committee on Puerto Rican Affairs in New York (MCPRA) had indicated that the lack of English fluency among island migrants was a major impediment in the migrants' incorporation into the labor market and the broader community in New York.[27] Days before the San Juan conference, Mary Finocchiaro, school supervisor in New York City and advisor to the Puerto Rican government on education matters, announced that the number of Puerto Rican children in city schools was seventy-two thousand, a much higher number than the forty thousand previously announced. Finocchiaro agreed with what many others had indicated before, that the major obstacle to the educational development of Puerto Rican children going to the city was their lack of English knowledge.[28] One day before the start of the conference, MCPRA made its report on Puerto Ricans in New York City public. Among the twelve recommendations presented by the committee on how to improve relations between the migrants and the city was the need for them to learn and have a basic understanding of English.[29] Days after the conference, Superintendent Baldwin—also present in the San Juan conclave—declared that almost a fourth of all children in Manhattan public schools were Puerto Ricans.[30]

On the eve of the first Migration Conference, Muñoz Marín announced that his government would intensify the teaching of English in all public schools and expand the number of English classes for adults in order to facilitate the incorporation of Puerto Rican migrants going to the United States. The governor acknowledged that this was an important issue for New York City functionaries and a common recommendation of many reports on the status of Puerto Ricans in the city. He proposed that the program to teach English to prospective migrants be administered by the Departments of Education and Labor. A main goal of the new program was to "orient" prospective migrants on the "customs and methods of life" they would encounter once they moved the United States, and to advise them on other places apart from New York City that offered better job opportunities.[31] As was to be expected, among the recommendations agreed to by participants in the first Migration Conference was the need to "orient and advise" prospective migrants on the conditions they would encounter in New York City. One widely supported recommendation was to encourage Puerto Rican migrants to move to other places besides the city. Also urged was the need for island migrants to have a basic knowledge of English so they could find jobs more easily and enhance their opportunities for a fruitful incorporation into the United States. As Muñoz Marín had announced earlier, the Puerto Rican government made a commitment to strengthening the teaching of English in public schools.[32]

The idea behind the intensification in the teaching of English in public schools and the offer of English classes to prospective migrants was to support both individual migration (people going on their own) and organized migration (such as through the FPP). Furthermore, and probably more important, by intensifying the teaching of English in public schools and providing orientation and background on migration to mostly poor and rural Puerto Rican children in public schools, the Puerto Rican government was in fact socializing these children in the experience of migration. Migration would not be seen as a distant experience, perhaps mentioned in the community or by relatives already in the United States, but as an idea taught in schools and promoted by the government that was supposed to represent the will of the people.

The obvious contradictions and dilemmas of the English language educational policy and the political stance of the PPD became a major and conflictive issue for the party, the government, and, particularly, the governor in the following decades. A number of PPD ideas became very difficult to incorporate into a coherent doctrine: How could the PPD reconcile its abandonment of independence with its claims to cultural nationalism? How could it reconcile the contradictory notion at the basis of the Commonwealth status— that Puerto Rico was a nation that gave its consent to a relationship with the United States under a so-called pact of free association that in fact reinforced colonialism? Most important for the subject of education and migration, how could the PPD promote a Puerto Rican national identity while also supporting Americanization and migration to the mainland? The new language policy furthered this contradictory discourse; essentially, migration was in the midst of the new cultural debate.

Muñoz Marín tried to reconcile these conflicting principles on the political and cultural basis of Commonwealth in his famous "Agapito's Bar" speech in December 1953, when he spoke to the annual assembly of the Teachers Association, which had been a strong supporter of both the use of Spanish in education and the PPD.[33] The governor emphatically called for the preservation of Spanish as the vernacular language and the axis of identity of Puerto Ricans, while at the same time reiterating his government's policy of accentuating the teaching of English in public schools. For the first time, Muñoz Marín declared that it was his government's goal to make Puerto Ricans bilingual citizens within a generation. He stressed the essential need to maintain the cultural and linguistic identity of Puerto Ricans, which constituted their essence as a people. But, he argued, Puerto Ricans should not confuse this cultural claim with their political reality. Puerto Ricans had agreed to enter into a "political association" with the United States in order to achieve a better material future and to sustain the ties of common citizenship, but in a context that did not require their cultural assimilation. Cultures change through time and are not static, Muñoz Marín reasoned, and they should absorb elements from other cultures. But he warned against assimilating bad elements from American culture, like gross consumerism and the incorrect adoption of English words that diminished the Spanish language. Muñoz Marín questioned the indiscriminate use of English names to identify the titles of persons and places instead of using the correct words in Spanish, pointing out that English was used as a sign of power and distinction. Why did schoolchildren call their teachers "Mister" or "Missis" instead of *"maestro"* or *"maestra,"* *"señor"* or *"señora,"* he asked? The governor wondered why someone in the rural center of the island would call his business Agapito's Bar instead of *Bar de Agapito*:

> Why did you do that, Agapito? If not even once a year you will meet a client walking down the street of your little town whose vernacular is English! Is it that you feel better saying it in a language that is not yours? And if you despise your tongue, are you not somehow despising yourself?

Muñoz Marín warned against making these two great languages of the world—Spanish and English—into a *"burundangoso y emprobecido papiamento"* (a messy and impoverished Papiamento). For him, language was a reflection of the spirit, so Puerto Ricans should not lose their language in order to protect their identity as a people. Learning English would enrich the lives of Puerto Ricans, but they should not lose their spirit. He called on Puerto Ricans to become bilingual but not "semilingual" in two languages. Puerto Ricans could contribute to the Western world, to the Americas in general, and to the United States in particular by preserving their Puerto Rican national identity and culture.

In his speech, Muñoz Marín made an exception regarding a group of Puerto Ricans that did not need to preserve their identity and language— those migrating to the United States:

> Nothing I say here certainly applies to Puerto Ricans migrating and becoming residents anywhere in the United States. From people like this was the United States made. People that individually became adapted to the culture they found there and contributed to it and enriched it. All Puerto Ricans that establish their residence in the United States must adapt to their community, the same way that the Irish, Poles, Italians and Scandinavians did before them. I'm talking about the culture of Puerto Rico in Puerto Rico.

Muñoz Marín made a clear distinction between the preservation of national identity and language in Puerto Rico and the prospect of cultural assimilation that awaited migrants going to the United States. Thus, at the same time that the Puerto Rican government began to boost the teaching of English in public schools in order to facilitate the incorporation of prospective migrants in the United States, the governor was also urging Puerto Ricans to preserve their language as an essential means of maintaining their national identity and culture. At the very moment that the government encouraged migrants to assimilate to American culture and society, the governor warned Puerto Ricans against the nefarious consequences of assimilation through the misuse of English on the island.[34]

José Padín, the former commissioner of education, questioned the new language policy in public schools. He acknowledged that migration was and would continue to be a major element in Puerto Rico's society and that, as citizens, Puerto Ricans had a right to migrate to the United States. In addition, he applauded the government's measures to manage migration and to aid and advise migrants going to the U.S. mainland. But Padín argued that Puerto Rico's society must not be structured in such a way that it existed only to provide cheap labor to the metropolis. Puerto Rico should strive to provide the best economic, social, and educational development to its members, whether they stayed on the island or went elsewhere. Those who migrated would be better prepared to find good jobs and standards of living because of this educational background. Still, Padín questioned the government's policy that linked the teaching of English to migration; it was not fair, he argued, "to revolutionize the school system and attach it to the wave of migration as the tail is attached to a kite. It is not fair to sacrifice two and a quarter million human beings for the benefit of 60,000 people leaving the island every year." He warned against going back to the old policy of using English in schools as a means of Americanization, which he considered a failed and tragic policy. According to Padín, "Agapito's Bar" was but a "collateral effect" of the heightened use of English in Puerto Rico.[35]

EDUCATION FOR MIGRATION

In June 1953, the newly restructured and renamed Department of Public Instruction announced its new plan to "alleviate" the situation of those migrating to the United States by "intensifying" the teaching of English in schools and expanding the program of English education for adults who were prospective migrants. The new plan included vocational training for those planning to migrate to the United States and the provision of advice to school dropouts on job opportunities in the U.S. mainland. Trying to discourage migration to New York City, pamphlets and films were to be used to inform prospective migrants of the job market throughout the United States. These programs were coordinated with the Department of Labor's BEM. Among the proposed goals was to increase the exchange programs between Puerto Rico and New York teachers and education functionaries, to expand the program aimed at the orientation of adults, and to provide orientation to migrant adults and schoolchildren once they moved to New York City.[36]

It is evident that by this time, the Department of Education was an integral part of the government's migration program. Migration was seen by government officials as a means of improving not only the economic and living standards of the population in Puerto Rico but its educational system as well, as is stated in the 1954–55 annual report of the Department of Labor:

> Puerto Rican migration is not only related to living standards in Puerto Rico but also to the program of public education. For example: there are 110,000 Puerto Rican children enrolled at the elementary schools in New York City. We cannot oversee the serious problem which Puerto Rico would face if besides providing schools for the children actually enrolled it should have to provide schools for the 110,000 Puerto Rican children who attend New York schools and for the thousands of children who attend other schools in the rest of the United States. We could also imagine the impact which migration would deal on all aspects of our life if the 650,000 Puerto Ricans living in the United States should decide to return to the island.[37]

As the teaching of English expanded in the island's public schools, it also became more intense when targeted to prospective migrants after the governor's speech. The secretary of education stated that the 1953 fall courses on conversational English for adults would be oriented toward those interested in migrating to the United States. Villaronga noted that the courses were taught in forty-two municipalities, an increase from the previous year, and that the teachers for these courses would be selected based on their professional preparation and their spoken English, giving preference to those who mastered English as their first language or those whose spoken English approximated that of the United States.[38] Dr. Pauline Rojas, director of the department's English program, later pointed out that 2,197 persons took the fall courses organized in sixty-four groups. She noted that the number of courses in rural areas had increased and that the decision of where to hold the courses was made by the Department of Labor's BEM.[39]

In July 1954, Villaronga announced that the literacy program for adults was fused with the program for teaching English to prospective migrants. That is, adult education was now integrated with teaching those with plans to move to the United States. Villaronga summarized the program's goal in the department's 1956–57 annual report:

The Adult English Program is organized for the primary purpose of providing people who go to work in the United States the opportunity to learn the English necessary for their most effective advancement in the Continent. The real situations which migrants go through in their journeys, in their work, and in their adaptation to new communities is usually taken into account in the outlook and content of the courses. The program also tries to educate migrants about those habits, customs, and traditions of the American people that they need to know. . . . The majority of migrants will be doing agricultural work; therefore, the Program has given priority to those needs.[40]

The new program was directed by Dr. Ismael Rodríguez Bou, then secretary of the Council of Higher Education, the institution in charge of overseeing all higher education on the island. The appointment of Rodríguez Bou, a well-known scholar in the field of education, signaled the importance of this new program for the government.[41] By the end of that year, 3,122 students were enrolled in the program in eighty groups in fifty-one island municipalities, almost half of them in rural areas. Villaronga announced that more emphasis was being given to expanding the vocabulary taught to reflect the real-life situations faced by the migrants in the United States, following the recommendations of the migration functionaries at the Department of Labor. Labor Department representatives also gave talks to the students on the job market and the ways of living in the United States.[42]

In December 1954, the *Journal of Educational Sociology* published a special issue on Puerto Rican migration. Prominent among the articles was Villaronga's "Program of Education for Puerto Rican Migrants." He described the goals and the elements of this program as follows:

> We are deeply conscious of the importance of an adequate education to those who seek their fortune in what to many is a completely strange environment. We have, therefore, drawn a definite plan of action with regard to the emigration of our countrymen to the continent. Briefly, our program is designed (a) to extend educational opportunities to an ever greater proportion of our citizens, (b) to intensify our teaching and to promote the formation of habits and attitudes that will contribute to an adequate adjustment of the individual to the new environment, (c) to familiarize our personnel with instructional practices and general environmental factors affecting the adjustment of Puerto Rican children in the continental communities, (d) to assist school authorities in the State [*sic*] in understanding our school system and the cultural and social background of their new Puerto Rican pupils,

and finally (e) to cooperate with other agencies of our Commonwealth in orienting adults and children who plan to emigrate.

Villaronga added that in addition to the better preparation and recruitment of English teachers, the department had prepared a series of English textbooks adapted to children in Puerto Rico, with an emphasis on conversational English. He also mentioned the program of English classes for adults, including the transmission of these classes on radio with the lesson published a day earlier in *El Imparcial*. The social studies program was also designed to provide students with "information about living conditions in the continental United States." At the elementary level, particular attention was given to "the study of life in the United States as one aspect of education related with situations in the daily life of students." At the secondary level, the topics included

(a) the living conditions of the American people, (b) the migration of Puerto Ricans to the continental United States and the problems the migrants must face, (c) the agencies responsible for orienting Puerto Rican migrants and the work they are doing, (d) employment opportunities in the different parts of the United States, and (e) the advantages and disadvantages of migration.

In a word, the social studies program was designed to orient and prepare the students in all aspects of migration to the United States. Villaronga also mentioned the expansion of the vocational schools program, which although not designed specifically to address migration, would "have the effect of bettering the employment opportunities of those who choose to migrate to the continental United States in the future."

Villaronga declared that the department had developed a "Pupil Transfer Card" that included all the information required for Puerto Rican students to register in New York City and other U.S. school systems. He also mentioned the exchange programs with the New York City school system, which the department was extending to other cities and areas of the United States. For example, New York City teachers participated in a summer workshop at the University of Puerto Rico (UPR) sponsored by the UPR and New York University. In collaboration with the Migration Division, UPR offered a summer workshop for New York social workers to get them acquainted with the culture and problems of island students. Villaronga stressed the role of Assistant Secretary Francisco Collazo in maintaining a working relationship between the department and the New York Board of Education, particularly in their plan to promote the incorporation and better adaptation of Puerto Rican students in the city's school system, including hiring island teachers in New York.

Collazo, along with functionaries of the Migration Division, worked closely with the Ford Foundation to organize and fund *The Puerto Rican Study*, an extensive research study on the educational status of Puerto Rican children in New York. Similar actions were taken in other areas outside of New York, particularly in Chicago, where a significant migrant population was already established.[43]

By this time, the Department of Education was playing an active role in the implementation of the Puerto Rican government's migration policy. An undated memo for U.S. agencies—one that certainly corresponds to Villaronga's course of action—stated that the department "has assumed the leadership in all educational activities for the benefit of Puerto Rican migrants. The Secretary of Education of Puerto Rico has appointed a coordinating committee composed of central office staff members, with the Assistant Secretary of Education as chairman." The committee was to "coordinate" all activities between the Puerto Rican and New York school agencies and would "act as a liaison body in coordinating the educational activities of other Puerto Rican agencies in behalf of the migrants." The memo added that special literature was available regarding the ways of life, language, customs, and school practices in New York to be given to "parents, teachers, and prospective migrants." The document also stated: "We are making every effort to locate in advance children who are planning to move to New York in order to give them special orientation and training in vocational skills and conversational English."[44] The fine line between providing "orientation" and "advice," on the one hand, and encouraging migration among individuals coming into contact with the department's educational programs, on the other hand, became thinner and thinner for the Department of Education, as it did for the Department of Labor. Through the public school system, the government was reaching "prospective migrants," be they adults or children, in a way that the Department of Labor could not do. By using the Department of Education, the government was able to expand the pool of "prospective migrants" it could reach. By the mid-1950s, two agencies of the Puerto Rican government—the Departments of Labor and Education—were instrumental in the promotion and organization of migration for the colonial state.

In the spring of 1955, Rodríguez Bou announced a shift in the program to teach English to prospective migrants: it would now focus more strongly on rural areas. This new emphasis coincided perfectly with the Department of Labor's migration policy then. By this time, the department's Farm Placement Program was in full force. The program's aim was to move the surplus labor force from the decaying sugar industry in the rural areas of Puerto Rico to the United States. In this case, as on other occasions, the Department of Education supported the Department of Labor's migration policy. As Rodríguez Bou stated while announcing the new shift, "the rural area is the main source of Puerto Rican migrants to the North, so the need for instruction is greater there." According to him, while in the previous year only forty-six of the 101 groups in the program were in the rural areas, that year ninety-six groups were in the rural areas, while only forty-six were organized in the urban areas. Rodríguez Bou indicated that the dates when the courses were offered coincided with the period of migrants returning home after the harvest season in the United States, as reported by the Department of Labor. He also asserted that priority would be given to those with immediate plans of migrating to the United States. The topics and the vocabulary for these courses were decided in collaboration with the Department of Labor's migration functionaries, who also provided the material to be used by teachers in their preparation for the courses.[45] The following year, Villaronga appointed five hundred teachers for these courses and requested that school superintendents promote and support the program in their respective districts.[46] That is, the teaching of English for prospective migrants had to be regarded as a regular program in the department's agenda.

The Department of Education's regular English program also became more intense in rural areas. In her study of the school system under the Commonwealth, Sylvia Eliza Colón emphasizes how, by 1955, the teaching of English dominated the Department of Education's general curriculum. She points out how students at the high school level devoted twice the amount of time to English classes compared to any other subject per day or week. This practice was even more intense in rural areas: ninety minutes of the students' daily schedule was devoted to English, with ninety minutes for agriculture. All other subjects received only forty-five minutes each. English classes were taught daily, but all other subjects were taught once every other day. Eliza Colón questioned this practice:

> This expenditure of time, energy, and resources for teaching English to rural children is especially striking as it was a language they almost never heard or used in their daily life. At the official level, no one raised the question as to whether there was a connection between their low performance level in the basic skills and the huge amount of time they had to spend in ineffectual study of this foreign language.[47]

This policy did not make any pedagogical sense, but it was not an irrational one: it was part of Puerto Rico's migration policy. By intensifying the instruction of English in public schools in rural areas, the Department of Education was fulfilling its task of supporting the Department of Labor's migration program, which at the time focused its organized migration plans in the rural areas.

In June 1956, through Circular Letter 91, the secretary of education announced another major revision to the department's English program: the effort to "departmentalize" the teaching of English from fourth to sixth grades. According to this new policy,

> the teaching of English is carried out only by the most qualified teachers, based on their mastery of the English language, their specialization in the subject, their demonstrated proficiency in practice and other factors. This change was implemented in conformity with the Department's goal to intensify and continually improve the teaching of English.[48]

From then on, the teaching of English in the higher grades of the public school system was guided by the department's central bureaucracy. Furthermore, aware of the failures and shortcomings of previous English programs in Puerto Rico, including the use of texts developed for American students, the department developed its own texts for island students; this project was heralded as "a contribution from Puerto Rico to education in the field of language teaching."[49]

The secretary's report for 1957–58 underscored the department's continued efforts to strengthen the English program. English teachers received priority in recruitment, training, and compensation. That year, 138 teachers received fellowships to study English in U.S. universities, and several program supervisors were sent to receive master's degrees on the subject. In addition to studying the English language in all its facets, the teachers were also required to take courses on U.S. history and culture and to live with American students and in close contact with their host communities in order to learn the American way of living.[50]

Villaronga praised the effectiveness of the program for teaching English to prospective migrants in his late 1956 review. A total of 27,520 adults had enrolled in the program in the previous three years, with a retention rate of 80 percent. A total of 772 groups were organized in sixty-six municipalities, with 450 groups in rural areas and 272 in urban areas; the initial number of 147 teachers now surpassed 500. The secretary stated that the program's target audience had expanded from just prospective migrants for farm labor to include all of those who might think of moving to the United States at some point. That year, the department began to present the program's graduates with a certificate in English that they could use when looking for work in the

United States.[51] Rodríguez Bou reported that by early 1958, forty-four thousand adults had taken the courses since 1954, and that nearly fifteen thousand persons were enrolled in the previous academic year. He announced that the Council of Higher Education began publishing the weekly supplement *Semana* (*Week*) to help students practice at home what they learned in their English classes. He also announced that the number of contact hours were increased from 72 to 120 to "provide prospective migrants a more solid basis" in their command of English.[52]

The publication and distribution of *Semana* illustrates the integration of the English education for adults program with that of English for prospective migrants. *Semana* is an excellent example of the department's efforts to "educate" the masses on the advantages of migration and on how to "adapt" to the new and culturally foreign environment in the United States. In 1955, the Department of Education took the responsibility of publishing *Semana*—the first number came out on September 10—with a circulation of two hundred fifty thousand distributed in public schools. On the recommendation of Muñoz Marín and Sierra Berdecía, an additional fifteen thousand copies were distributed among Puerto Rican farmworkers in the United States. The weekly was designed as a vehicle to provide information to common people on the current events in Puerto Rico, the United States, and the rest of the world. It was also supposed to enhance the cultural knowledge of the masses, with articles and texts by Puerto Rico's most celebrated authors. The newspaper was given to students to take to their homes. *Semana* was aimed at educating not only public school students but their relatives and acquaintances as well. From its first edition, *Semana* also included a supplement on *Lecciones de Inglés* (English lessons).[53] Each issue of *Semana* included a series of vocabulary and grammar exercises that could be mailed to the department's English for Adults program for grading. When the public television station WIPR was inaugurated in 1958, one of its first regular programs was English courses for adults; the registration for these courses and the exercises were published in *Semana*.[54] This weekly publication and its English supplement were used as a teaching text throughout the department's regular adult education program.[55]

A cursory look at *Semana*'s English lessons shows their emphasis on familiarizing the reader with life in the United States: U.S. history, American patriots, the flag and the Pledge of Allegiance, and American culture and traditions like Thanksgiving and Christmas. Most of the lessons on grammar and vocabulary were based on aspects of day-to-day life in the United States: how to order a meal; how to travel by train, bus, or plane; services like mail and garbage collection; different ways of life in urban and rural America; differences regarding the American way of life on matters related to diet, work, vacationing, travel, education, and family structure; laws of etiquette; seasonal changes and its respective clothing (coats in winter are a must); the workings of the public school system in the United States; getting professional services like doctors and lawyers; laws on taxes and voting; and services available to the migrant from the Migration Division or local governments on matters regarding health, welfare, and employment, among others. The lessons on the American way of life were aimed at sustaining traditional American gender and class roles, like the one on "The family":

> The American family is small. The father is the head of the family. He works in a factory, an office, a school, a store or some other business place. Some men work as policemen, drivers or some other outdoor job. Some work on farms. The mother works in the house. She takes care of the children, she cooks and irons. She keeps the house clean. Some mothers work out. The children help their parents with housework. Each child has certain responsibilities. They learn that everybody must work.[56]

Other information considered Puerto Rican life in the United States. For example, only the cities and states with the largest Puerto Rican population were reviewed (New York, Chicago, and New Jersey). After surveying some of the states' main attributes, the lesson on New Jersey, for example, pointed out the jobs available and the settlement areas for Puerto Ricans.[57] Some of the lessons were designed to orient those interested in doing farmwork in the United States:

> This is José. He lives in Guayama. He goes to the United States every year. He is an agricultural worker. He is seeking information for his trip. José wants to know what state he can go this year. He went to New Jersey last year. He receives orientation from the Department of Labor office. Go under contract for work in the States. You and your family will be protected.[58]

Much of the "regular news" referred to Puerto Ricans moving to the United States: one read, for example, "Many Puerto Rican farm workers arrived in the United States this month. They are going to work on farms."[59] Other lessons emphasized the benefits of learning English in Puerto Rico or in the United States: "Ana and Alberto are learning English. They go to night school. They work during the day. Knowing more English is good for them. They plan to live in the States. If you know English you make more money."[60] In general, the lessons underscored the benefits of living in the United States: "Look at

Pedro. Look at Ana. Pedro and Ana are from Puerto Rico. They live in Chicago now. They lived in Puerto Rico before. Pedro and Ana are very happy."[61]

A brief outline of the Department of Education's programs to aid migrants was presented in the spring 1957 newsletter *Educación*, in an article titled "The Public School Orients Migrants." The editor of this monthly newsletter, whose goal was to provide "information and orientation to teachers," was Assistant Secretary Collazo, the department's point man on issues of migration. The article summarized all the programs provided by the department to orient and advise those willing to migrate to the United States and described how the overall education of Puerto Rican children better prepared them for migrating to the U.S. mainland. Among the programs mentioned was the production of teaching materials showing the "practical situations that migrant families face" in the United States.[62] For example, the department's English program produced the text *La familia Vázquez en los Estados Unidos* (*The Vázquez Family in the United States*), which included "forty practical lessons for persons that think about moving to the United States." The lessons in the book were similar to those presented in *Semana* but were oriented mostly to guiding the migrant family moving to an urban area from the moment they boarded the plane in Puerto Rico to the moment they were settled in the United States.[63]

Another text to orient public school children and adults was *Emigración* (*Emigration*), one of the *libros para el pueblo* (books for the people) produced by the department's División para la Educación de la Comunidad (Community Education Division). The division, created in 1949, aimed at providing the poor rural masses with education and the basic tools for developing their communities, mostly using artistic means like pamphlets, films, theater, and radio programs.[64] It recruited some of Puerto Rico's most renowned artists at the time. The migration booklet was written by René Marqués, one of Puerto Rico's best-known writers, and had illustrations by celebrated painters like Luis Cajigas and Carlos Raquel Rivera. It answered common questions and subjects: "Why do people today emigrate?" "Why is migration so easy for Puerto Ricans?" "Do Puerto Ricans know the country they emigrate to?" "New York is not the only city." "Housing in the big U.S. cities." "Why sick workers should not migrate." "Work in the American farms." "Do I stay or do I go?" It also discussed topics like culture in the United States, the nature of prejudice, the differences between Puerto Ricans in Puerto Rico and those living in the United States, moving to places other than New York, farm labor, and the offices of the Puerto Rican government in New York and Chicago.[65] *Emigración* was used as a text in the regular adult education program, including at the elementary level.[66]

In February 1958, Governor Muñoz Marín publicized the steps his government was taking to implement the recommendations from the third Migration Conference, held in San Juan the previous month. Once again, he promised to implement measures to intensify the teaching of English in public schools and the English program for prospective migrants. Among the recommendations mentioned by the governor to expand and improve the teaching of English on the island was to use the new public TV station—WIPR, inaugurated in 1958—for this purpose. The recommendations included the following:

> To explore new techniques for the orientation of a greater number of *migrants and potential migrants* in the United States and Puerto Rico. The inauguration of a new educational television channel in Puerto Rico provides an excellent opportunity to show movies and establish other programs *to familiarize potential migrants with the conditions in the United States.*[67]

The recently created WIPR became the new mechanism to orient and advise prospective migrants. Its English programs were managed by the department's English for Adults program; the exercises were made available through *Semana* and other publications.[68] After 1959, English classes were also offered by this program through the government's public radio station.[69] In the fiscal year 1958–59, the department's English for Adults program included four areas: the regular curriculum in schools, teaching farmworkers in their places of work, English courses via public television, and English courses by public radio.[70]

By this time, all the means of socialization available to the government—public schools, community organization, print, radio, and TV—were employed in the organization and promotion of migration to the United States. Every Puerto Rican became a "prospective" or "potential" migrant. What may be significant is how the numerous texts used throughout the public school curriculum in English classes and the readings and English lessons in publications like *Semana* recall the previous U.S.-implemented policy of Americanization of the early decades of the twentieth century, with its texts emphasizing U.S. history, American patriots, and the American way of life. However, mastery of English and even literacy rates were not what colonial functionaries expected given the expenditure on education by the colonial state. There are many reasons why this policy failed. The texts used in schools, imported from the U.S. educational system, were foreign to Puerto Rican children: after all, it never snows on the island, Puerto Ricans do not sing Christmas carols, and the people in those pictures do not resemble them. But in the English programs of the 1950s, the people in the pictures looked Puerto Rican, and by moving to the

United States, Puerto Ricans became part of that country's history. The English lessons learned then had an impact in the daily life of Puerto Ricans. The previous Americanization policy was an effort to Americanize Puerto Ricans in Puerto Rico in order to sustain the colonial regime. The PPD's policy was aimed at infusing migrants and prospective migrants with the language and way of life in the United States to facilitate their adaptation there; it was now aimed at Americanizing those Puerto Ricans going to the United States.

By promoting the intensification and expansion of the teaching of English throughout the public school system and by expanding the education programs—with their heavy content of teaching the American culture and way of life—for prospective migrants as a means of easing their incorporation in the United States, the colonial government under the PPD was able to do what decades of U.S. colonial functionaries were not able to achieve. By treating every Puerto Rican as a potential migrant and by trying to prepare them for migration accordingly, the PPD government—headed by former *independentistas* and defenders of Spanish as the vernacular language of the island and of a Puerto Rican national identity—implemented policies that furthered the influence of English and American ideals and values on the island like never before.

ENGLISH AND MIGRANT INCORPORATION IN THE UNITED STATES

The issue of English was also prominent in the news reports that came from Muñoz Marín's tour of the United States in commemoration of the tenth anniversary of the Migration Division creation in 1958. Muñoz Marín made important stops in Chicago and New York, the two cities with the largest Puerto Rican communities and the two most important Migration Division offices. In Chicago, where issues of poverty and youth gangs in the Puerto Rican community were important topics of discussion with government and community representatives, the governor reiterated the measures taken by his administration to ease the incorporation of migrants into the mainland communities, including the intensification of English education on the island. While in Chicago, Muñoz Marín asserted that Puerto Rican migration would cease by 1975, when Puerto Rico would have achieved the level of economic development prevalent in the United States. *El Mundo* questioned both statements by the governor, declaring that English teachers in Puerto Rico were not well prepared or well paid, which explained the continuing problems of English education in Puerto Rico. It further argued that Puerto Rico would never achieve the level of economic development of the United States, thus making migration a continuing escape valve for the island's unemployed.[71]

In New York, Puerto Rican government officials also had to face issues of migrant incorporation. San Juan Mayor Felisa Rincón de Gautier complained that Puerto Ricans were still regarded as "foreigners" and blamed "those who have not cooperated to accelerate our integration" for the migrants' lack of progress. Muñoz Marín touched a more familiar note, stating that ignorance of English was "the main problem that delays the integration of Puerto Ricans to metropolitan life."[72] The governor mentioned all the measures that his government was taking to ease the incorporation of migrants, particularly the intensification in the teaching of English through schools and other institutions, including the new public TV station. He announced the production of short films to be shown on WIPR and in cinemas in Puerto Rico and the United States to orient and advise migrants moving to the U.S. mainland. Muñoz Marín also announced that he had asked island mayors to make a census of prospective migrants so the government could be better prepared to help them in their journey to the United States, including through the teaching of English.[73]

By the time that Muñoz Marín toured those cities in the United States with the most important Puerto Rican communities (Detroit, Chicago, New York, and Lorrain, Ohio) in 1958, the Puerto Rican government was promoting its plan to encourage island migrants to integrate into their communities in the U.S. mainland. Leading the program was Rincón de Gautier, who made frequent tours to the United States, particularly to New York. According to her, Puerto Ricans had to "integrate" to their communities in the United States— socially, politically, and culturally—in order to become better citizens. They could help themselves and Puerto Rico, for example, by engaging in electoral politics, a right they could enjoy immediately as U.S. citizens. Integration also required assimilation, learning the culture and language of their new society. The Puerto Rican government was doing everything possible to achieve these goals with programs in Puerto Rico and the United States. Through integration and assimilation, there would be no more "Puerto Rican problem" in the United States, she argued.[74] In a previous visit to New York in 1957, Muñoz Marín had already declared that with assimilation, "the current problems would disappear quickly." Eliminating the "language barrier" was a step in that direction. For the Puerto Rican government and for institutions like *El Mundo*, providing more access to English education in Puerto Rico and the United States was an important means of eradicating the language barrier for Puerto Rican migrants.[75]

At the Migration Division's tenth anniversary ceremony in New York, Muñoz Marín characterized Puerto Rican migration as one more "internal migration" in the United States, similar to that of hundreds of thousands of U.S. citizens who move from one state to another. He recognized, nevertheless, that due to the economic stagnation in the United States, some "return migration" had been noticeable in the previous year and argued that this was part of the process of migration. The governor acknowledged the "adaptation" that Puerto Ricans had experienced in the United States and how this had improved their lives there. He praised the role played by the Migration Division in the advancement of Puerto Rican incorporation in the United States, characterizing the division as "probably unique in the history of the United States, as it is the first time that the place of origin of a migrant has established offices in the United States for the purpose of helping its people to get adjusted to their new home fast and successfully."[76]

The inconsistencies of the official discourse on migration by the Puerto Rican government were apparent by that time. At the same time that it insisted that Puerto Ricans were another "internal migration" group in the United States, it had acknowledged the similarities with other immigrant groups that had to "adapt" to an "ethnologically different environment" there. While the governor emphasized the commonalities that Puerto Ricans shared with other U.S. citizens, he praised the work of the Migration Division in advancing the adaptation of island migrants to the United States; it was an office that no previous immigrant group had established before.

During the New York tour, Department of Labor functionaries announced a new program to provide English classes to migrants working in farms in the United States. The program, with an initial funding of $60,000, would start in farms in New York and New Jersey. Classes would be taught early in the morning before work or late in the evening after work, with the authorization of the employers; the program would be administered by the Departments of Education and Labor. The bill was signed into law by Muñoz Marín in July 1958.[77] The original bill was submitted in May 1958 by the Speaker of the House, Ernesto Ramos Antonini. It was based on the conclusions of a report by the House Labor Committee on their investigation of working conditions faced by Puerto Rican farmworkers in the United States. The report concluded that one major problem faced by farmworkers was their lack of English knowledge; this situation created problems not only in terms of labor relations but also in terms of their relationship with the local communities in general. The bill's preamble stated that the political, economic, and cultural relations with the United States required intensifying the teaching of English in public schools. But foremost, the increasing levels of migration to the United States made knowledge of English indispensable. It should be an "imperative" goal of the Puerto Rican government to adequately train and prepare Puerto Ricans migrating to the United States. To achieve these goals, it was "a primary factor that they should possess the ability to communicate in English." The bill concluded: "Common citizenship and the increase in mass transportation and communication between Puerto Rico and the United States make *every Puerto Rican a potential migrant.*"[78]

After Congressman Marcantonio was defeated in 1950, the Puerto Rican government identified the language barrier as the main issue in the continued "Puerto Rican problem" in the United States. By the end of the 1950s, mainland communities and employers still rejected Puerto Rican migrants; island functionaries explained this by the fact that these migrants were still identified as foreigners from a strange land and not as U.S. citizens. They argued that the main reason for this identification was their cultural difference, mostly in terms of language. By eradicating this difference, the government could ease the incorporation of these migrants into American society and thus assure the continuation of the migration program. By the mid-1950s, the intensification in the teaching of English for Puerto Rican children in schools and for prospective migrants became a main goal of the government's migration policy. That this language policy was never truly effective is a reminder of the difficulties of imposing a new language of communication (English) on a society that had been using another language (Spanish) as a central part of its identity and culture for centuries.[79]

But perhaps a more important lesson to be learned regarding the relationship of language and migration may be the fact that the language barrier might have not been the most significant obstacle in the incorporation of these island migrants in the United States, as the Puerto Rican government and many U.S. public and private officials argued for many decades. The U.S. Civil Rights Commission's 1976 report on the status of Puerto Ricans in the United States, entitled "An Uncertain Future," determined that "mainland Puerto Ricans generally continue mired in the poverty facing first generations of all immigrant or migrant groups." Contrary to the expectation that the second generation would fare better in social and economic terms, it argued: "One generation later, the essential fact of poverty remains little changed. Indeed, the economic situation of the mainland Puerto Ricans has worsened over the last decade." The report concluded:

> The United States has never before had a large migration of citizens from offshore, distinct in culture and language and also facing the problem of color prejudice. After 30 years of significant migration, contrary to conventional

wisdom that once Puerto Ricans learned the language the second generation would move into the mainstream of American society, the future of this distinct community in the United States is still to be determined.[80]

As the commission concluded, other factors besides the language barrier are required to explain the difficult incorporation of Puerto Ricans in the United States, like racism and prejudice, their exclusion from high-paying jobs, their concentration in cheap labor areas like agriculture and the service sectors, a lack of educational opportunities, school and residential segregation, and concentration in cities and regions that were experiencing deindustrialization. The Puerto Rican government might have achieved some success in turning "every Puerto Rican into a potential migrant," but that in itself did not improve the chances of its people achieving a successful incorporation in the United States.

1. Cover, DIVEDCO booklet *Emigración*.

2. Farmworkers in front of BEM office ready to depart, circa 1953. AGPR, Photographic Archives, *Colección Departamento de Instrucción Pública* (Department of Education Collection). Photo by Miguel A. Landrón.

3. Ad in Arecibo bar announcing airfares to New York, September 1946. AGPR, Photographic Archives, *Colección Departamento de Instrucción Pública* (Department of Education Collection). Photo attributed to Charles Rotkin.

4. Ad in Arecibo bar announcing airfares to New York, September 1946 (close-up). AGPR, Photographic Archives, *Colección Departamento de Instrucción Pública* (Department of Education Collection). Photo attributed to Jack Delano.

5. Aerial view of Isla Grande Airport, March 1948. AGPR, Photographic Archives, *Colección Departamento de Instrucción Pública* (Department of Education Collection). Photo by Charles Rotkin.

6. Aerial view of the International Airport at Isla Verde, Carolina, Puerto Rico, after inauguration. AGPR, Photographic Archives, Puerto Rico Industrial Development Company Collection.

7. Pan Am building at Isla Grande Airport in San Juan, August 1946. AGPR, Photographic Archives, *Colección Departamento de Instrucción Pública* (Department of Education Collection). Photo by Charles Rotkin.

8. Main lobby at the International Airport after inauguration. AGPR, Photographic Archives, Puerto Rico Industrial Development Company Collection.

9. Passengers and mother and child boarding unscheduled flight by Waterman Airlines at Isla Grande Airport in San Juan, July 1946. AGPR, Photographic Archives, *Colección Departamento de Instrucción Pública* (Department of Education Collection). Photo by Charles Rotkin.

10. Farmworkers at Isla Grande Airport ready to depart, circa 1953. AGPR, Photographic Archives, *Colección Departamento de Instrucción Pública* (Department of Education Collection). Photo by Miguel A. Landrón.

11. Farmworkers on their way to the United States in unscheduled airline, Salinas, Puerto Rico, July 1946. AGPR, Photographic Archives, *Colección Departamento de Instrucción Pública* (Department of Education Collection). Photo by Louise Rosskam.

12. Governors Averel Harriman of New York and Luis Muñoz Marín of Puerto Rico at the tenth anniversary of the Migration Division in New York City, 1958. Photo from the Migration Division Records, Archives of the Puerto Rican Diaspora, Centro de Estudios Puertorriqueños, Hunter College, CUNY.

13. Farmworkers arriving at farm housing, circa 1953. AGPR, Photographic Archives, *Colección Departamento de Instrucción Pública* (Department of Education Collection). Photo by Miguel A. Landrón.

14. Puerto Rican functionaries visiting farmworkers at camp, no date. Standing from left to right, Commissioner of Labor Fernando Sierra Berdecía, Governor Luis Muñoz Marín, and Migration Division Director José Moserrat. Photo from the Migration Division Records, Archives of the Puerto Rican Diaspora, Centro de Estudios Puertorriqueños, Hunter College, CUNY.

Vol. IV No. 41   **SEMANA**   Nov. 14, 1960
ENGLISH SUPPLEMENT

Readings in Elementary English
Adult Education Program
A Publication of the Department of Education of Puerto Rico

Thanksgiving Day is November 24. It will be a holiday.

Look at Pedro.
Look at Ana.
Pedro and Ana are from Puerto Rico.
They live in Chicago now.
They lived in Puerto Rico before.
Pedro and Ana are very happy.

Vocabulary

now — ahora
before — antes

15. English lesson from *Semana*, November 14, 1960.

16. "Our Holocaust: United States—Puerto Rico, 204 Deaths." Editorial cartoon by Filardi. *El Mundo,* April 15, 1952.

CHAPTER 6

The Beets of Wrath

Migration Policy and Migrant Discontent in Michigan, 1950

AS PART OF its migration policy, the Puerto Rican government was engaged in the authorization of worker recruitment in Puerto Rico. No U.S. employer could hire a Puerto Rican worker without a contract approved by the Puerto Rican government. Furthermore, by the early 1950s, the Puerto Rican government itself organized the movement of labor from Puerto Rico to the United States. Thus, many workers saw the government as part of the contract labor process when doing farmwork in the United States. As a consequence, on several occasions worker discontent emerged in these farm labor expeditions to the United States; disappointed with their working and living conditions and engaged in labor disputes with farmers, workers directed their dissatisfaction against the Puerto Rican government, which usually intervened to mediate between the workers and the employers. Concern for the workers' plight must be related to the government's interest in keeping the migration program running and preventing major political harm on the island.

In 1950, serious worker dissatisfaction with working and living conditions and a dispute with employers among Puerto Rican farmworkers in the sugar beet fields of Michigan forced the government to intervene directly in the situation to prevent major damage to the migration program and to the government's image on the island, as well as to promote stability in the labor relations between migrant workers and employers. The Michigan incident is one of the earliest and most important episodes of Puerto Rican migrant discontent in the United States.[1] This experience in Michigan would have a lasting impact on Puerto Rico's migration policy thereafter. The aftermath of this experience made clear that Puerto Rican farmworkers under the government's Farm Placement Program (FPP) had become part of that group of agricultural laborers in the United States known as migratory labor and that the Puerto Rican government had become for all purposes a labor contractor to American agricultural interests.

The events in Michigan are of further interest for several additional reasons, all of them related to other aspects of the Puerto Rican migration experience. The Michigan affair illuminates what can be called the migration politics of the time. The workers' expedition to this sugar beet state once again linked migration to the island's political status debate. This time, it involved the relationship of Puerto Rico's government with Fred L. Crawford, representative of Michigan's sugar beet interests and a leading congressman on issues pertaining to Puerto Rico's political status in Congress at a moment when the Puerto Rican government was seeking reforms to the island's political status.

Furthermore, an examination of the Michigan experience allows this book to return to its beginnings—colonialism, citizenship—and, in addition, to consider U.S. sugar politics. The same factors that explain the beginnings of U.S. rule on the island after 1898 can be seen at work with regard to migration in the 1950s. The Michigan experience highlights the workings of the U.S. sugar industry and its intricate relationship with American colonial territories in the twentieth century. When the Bracero Program came under heavy attack after World War II, Michigan sugar beet interests tried to replace Mexican labor with Puerto Rican farmworkers. The labor surplus created by the decline of the sugar industry in Puerto Rico—largely due to restrictions supported and promoted in Congress by sugar beet producers—made it possible that the colonial labor from the "racially inferior" sugar-producing proletariat in Puerto Rico could satisfy the labor needs of the Michigan sugar beet producers. Thus, the 1950 Michigan experience is but a reflection of U.S. colonial policies echoed in the interests, debates, and conflicts regarding the U.S. sugar industry and its ties with colonial populations.

The Michigan experience is also related to the issue of air transportation and safety for migrant workers discussed previously in this book. The very first flight taking island farmworkers to Michigan crashed en route to the United States, one of the worst airplane tragedies involving Puerto Ricans up to that moment. More than in previous air disasters, this particular crash produced strong public reactions to the government's farmworkers' program, reactions that directly and seriously questioned its migration policy for the first time. The Michigan experience prompted the Puerto Rican government to implement new policies and guidelines for the movement of Puerto Rican labor to the United States.

Sending Puerto Rican farm laborers to Michigan in 1950 was important for the Puerto Rican government for several reasons. The Michigan contract was the second major contract approved by the Department of Labor since the approval of the migration law in 1947. According to Commissioner of Labor Fernando Sierra Berdecía, the significance of this contract lay in its status as "the first contract beyond the Northeast area and it was believed to be the opening wedge to the great Middle West for our program of employment for the workers of Puerto Rico since it is located in the great industrial area around the Great Lakes."[2] There might be an additional reason why the Puerto Rican government was interested in sending migrant workers to Michigan in an attempt to replace Mexican *braceros* here: this expedition must be understood as part of that campaign by the Puerto Rican government to promote the use of Puerto Rican farmworkers as domestic labor in place of foreign workers, the most important source of competition for Puerto Rican labor in U.S. agriculture. Negotiations to send Puerto Rican workers to the sugar beet fields of Michigan between the government of Puerto Rico and the Michigan Field Corporation (MFC)—the representative of the Michigan sugar beet growers—began in March 1950. By May 9, a final agreement was reached on a contract to regulate working conditions between workers and employers. Like all other government-sponsored contracts, it had to be signed by the workers and the employer. The MFC initially placed an order of 1,500 workers with the Department of Labor after certification by the U.S. Employment Service (USES); it later ordered an additional 5,314 men for the program.[3]

But before discussing the events in Michigan during the summer of 1950, it is necessary to provide a brief background on the many ways that Puerto Ricans—particularly those working in the island's sugar cane fields—were linked to the production of beet sugar in Michigan.

SIX DEGREES OF (COLONIAL) SEPARATION: SUGAR BEET PRODUCTION IN MICHIGAN AND PUERTO RICAN POLITICS

The paths of Puerto Rican farmworkers and sugar beet growers intertwined in a complex way in the fields of Michigan in 1950. It would be the culmination of decades of U.S. sugar politics and colonial policies. These two had been related since the United States began its overseas imperial venture in 1898.[4] U.S. sugar politics, determined by conflicting sugar interests, was at the center of the debate regarding the overseas empire in 1898: domestic sugar producers—particularly sugar beet producers—were strong supporters of protectionism and thus maintained postures in favor of anti-imperialism, while colonial/foreign sugar producers supported free trade and imperialism. Domestic sugar producers were strongly opposed to the "incorporation" of Puerto Rico and the Philippines; they were particularly adamant against granting citizenship to Puerto Ricans in the 1900 Foraker Act. Similarly, domestic sugar producers—specifically sugar beet producers—were strongly opposed to the Supreme Court declaring Puerto Rico a domestic territory in the early Insular Cases, particularly in *Downes v. Bidwell*.[5]

Sugar beet farmers and beet sugar producers feared the competition of cheaper cane sugar from foreign/colonial markets and the powerful Sugar Trust, particularly from Cuba and the Philippines. They not only presented their interests behind a veil of protectionism but also used a racist and white supremacist discourse so common among anti-imperialists. Protecting the production of beet sugar was protecting not only the American farm but also American "civilization": "Would the United States rely on sugar grown on large aristocratic plantations by 'coolie' labor or would it consume sugar from small family farms tended to by white farmers and white workers? Simply put, did the United States want 'barbaric' or 'civilized' sugar?"[6] The economic crisis at the end of the 1920s pushed the price of sugar to new lows and threatened the position of domestic sugar producers in the American market. What came as a result of the actions of the U.S. sugar beet lobby was one of their most important political victories: they were able to protect the domestic market from "colonial" sugar and force the independence of the Philippines. In 1934, Congress passed the Jones-Costigan Act, which imposed a quota on the entry of sugar from Cuba, the Philippines, and Puerto Rico, ending the existing free trade with the latter two colonies.[7] The political consequences of the Jones-Costigan Act in Puerto Rico were dramatic.[8] The quota on sugar produced in Puerto Rico marked the beginning of the sugar industry's decline on the island, and with it, its political power and influence. The quota led to the breakdown of the alliance between central owners (led by four U.S. corporations) and *colonos,* or independent sugar farmers.[9] This event was linked to the rise of the reformist PPD and the collapse of the conservative and pro-statehood Republican forces. The Jones-Costigan Act also affected the Puerto Rican labor movement and its political affiliations. It led to the 1934 sugar strike—the biggest in Puerto Rico to that point—and altered the political spectrum for workers' politics; many workers abandoned the Socialist Party and its related Free Federation of Labor, joining a more radical workers' organization and later the PPD.[10]

The economic and political weakening of the dominant sugar interests on the island, closely related to the economic crisis and the Jones-Costigan quota on sugar production, accelerated the push for economic and social reform from both local and U.S. government forces. With its "Puerto Rican New Deal" sabotaged by the conservative Republican-Socialist Coalition that controlled the local government, the Roosevelt administration allied with local reformers in the Liberal Party led by Luis Muñoz Marín in presenting a program of economic and social reform that dramatically impacted the sugar industry.[11] The promises of agricultural and land reform made by the PPD in 1940 never fully materialized, and by 1947 the PPD-led government placed all its bets for modernization on the industrialization of the economy. Ironically, many of the sugar workers who became labor surplus after being expelled from the sugar industry would be the migrant workers that the PPD government's FPP would send to farms in the United States after 1947.[12] Many of them would be among the five thousand–plus who went to the sugar beet fields in Michigan in 1950.

The other major victory for sugar beet producers was the push for the independence of the Philippines. In 1934, Congress passed the Tydings-McDuffie Act, allowing for the independence of the Philippines (it also restricted the number of Filipinos to be admitted to the United States and created a system for the repatriation of Filipinos living then in U.S. territory). Senator Millard Tydings, the new chair of the Insular Affairs Committee, was instrumental in approving this law.[13] In 1936 Tydings submitted—with the support of the Roosevelt administration—what would be the first of three bills he authored in the next ten years granting Puerto Rico its independence. According to Gattel, for Tydings Puerto Rican independence "would be in harmony with the United States policy of imperial disengagement and help improve Latin American relations."[14] Tydings's 1936 independence bill was extremely punitive for Puerto Ricans, even more restrictive in economic terms than the one he proposed for the Philippines.[15] This bill exacerbated rifts in the Liberal Party, which led to the creation of the PPD in 1938 and later to its victory in the 1940 elections. Tydings's two other bills for independence, in 1943 and 1945, created rifts within the governing PPD by encouraging its pro-independence sectors. In 1946, after Tydings's third bill, Muñoz Marín was forced to expel *independentistas* from the party. They immediately created the Puerto Rican Independence Party (PIP) and became the strongest opposition to the rising PPD and its political and economic programs.

Why did Puerto Rican farmworkers go to the sugar beet fields of Michigan in 1950? After World War I, when the entry of European labor was drastically reduced by the conflict and by restrictionist forces pushing for limited immigration, sugar beet farmers in Michigan found a new source of labor: Mexican migrants. Their dependence on this labor was so pronounced that the sugar beet lobby was able to prevent the 1924 Johnson-Reed Act from curtailing Mexican labor from entry to the United States. Sugar beet interests were able to promote what Mapes calls a "racialized and nationalized" system of labor. The federal government would create the structure to provide the sugar beet farms with Mexican labor, while at the same time, sugar beet producers would satisfy the concerns of restrictionists and nativists by arguing that these laborers were not immigrants but temporary migrant workers. They were to be considered laborers, but not future citizens to be assimilated.[16]

Sugar beet farming, along with cotton farming, was among the areas of American agriculture to experience mechanization the latest, and some of its production, like early harvesting, required large amounts of manual, or "stoop," labor. This made this industry highly dependent on migratory labor. According to the report by the president's Commission on Migratory Labor, in 1945 less than 1 percent of the acreage devoted to sugar beet in Michigan was mechanized. Although the rate of mechanization increased thereafter, there was still a large need for manual labor: by 1950, the industry required fifteen thousand seasonal workers for spring work and another five thousand for harvesting work.[17] Sugar beet interests were supportive of the Bracero Program created by the U.S. government during World War II to satisfy U.S. agricultural labor needs. They were also instrumental in the approval of Law 78, which reinstated the program in 1951, after a brief interlude when critics were able to stop the program. It was precisely during this interval that Puerto Ricans would migrate to the sugar beet fields in Michigan as migrant labor.[18]

The Bracero Program came under attack by nativists and by labor unions in the late 1940s and by the Mexican government's refusal to allow Mexican migrant laborers to work in the sugar beet industry due to its brutal working conditions. By 1948, the National Farm Labor Union pressured the federal government to end the Bracero Program under the assumption that there was no shortage of domestic labor to fulfill U.S. agricultural needs.[19] The Michigan sugar beet interests found an answer to their labor problem by looking again south of the border, this time to the Caribbean. As Dennis Valdés argues: "The ever resourceful Michigan sugar beet industry turned to Puerto Rico, hoping to find workers as poor and easily controlled as the *braceros*. Because they were U.S. citizens, hiring Puerto Ricans would protect the industry from criticism for hiring foreign workers."[20] According to an MFC representative, they were forced to recruit Puerto Ricans after their "plans in Chicago went awry . . . when the Immigration Service deported some 1,800 illegal Mexican entries and the balance of the Latin American population remained in the city hoping to obtain the industrial jobs vacated by these illegal aliens."[21] The Michigan project would not only have made it possible for Puerto Rican farmworkers to make an inroad in the Midwest, as Sierra Berdecía stated, but it also might have been the ideal opportunity to show agricultural employers that they could replace and displace Mexican *braceros* and undocumented workers and thus open a new space for island workers.

Puerto Rican workers and sugar beet producers in Michigan were linked in multiple ways by U.S. sugar and colonial politics. But there was another link between them that would lead Puerto Rican migrant workers to the sugar beet fields of Michigan in 1950. His name was Congressman Fred L. Crawford.

PUERTO RICO'S NEW "BEST FRIEND IN CONGRESS": FRED L. CRAWFORD AND PUERTO RICAN POLITICS

Crawford, elected to Congress as a Republican by Michigan's 8th District in 1934, was secretary of the Michigan Sugar Company in 1925, and by 1932 he operated several sugar factories in Michigan; he was also director of the Michigan National Bank and of the Refiners Transport and Petroleum Corp. of Detroit. He belonged to the group of Republicans sent to Congress after Franklin Roosevelt's election in 1932 and led the Republican opposition to New Deal policies in agriculture. Crawford was a founding member of the Farmers Independence Council, a very conservative organization created to oppose New Deal reforms and federal legislation in agriculture.[22]

As representative of sugar beet interests in Michigan for decades, Crawford had to deal with the issue of the industry's labor needs. In 1929, Congress held hearings on the tariff to foreign sugar coming to the United States, and sugar beet interests were clearly present during these hearings. One of the most contentious issues they faced was related to their opposition to the entry of foreign sugar produced by nonwhite cheap labor in the colonial/neocolonial territories while, at the same time, they used Mexican labor at home. Testifying on behalf of the Michigan Sugar Company, Crawford addressed the question of where sugar beet producers would find labor to substitute for Mexican workers by arguing, "If we cannot get the Mexican, we are going to pull the colored people out of the South and take them out of the cotton fields."[23]

By the early 1940s, Crawford was already an influential member of the House Committee on Insular Affairs, which oversaw the administration of U.S. colonial territories. Like many Republicans in Congress, he was extremely critical of the reforms that were implemented in Puerto Rico then by Governor Tugwell and by the newly elected PPD government. Crawford and the other Republicans accused the Puerto Rican government of turning the island into a Communist paradise. Crawford's first inroad into Puerto Rican politics was not well received by the PPD/Tugwell government, particularly by PPD leader and Senate president Muñoz Marín. In January 1943, Crawford submitted a resolution in the House that would have allowed Congress to annul any law approved by the Puerto Rican government. This act aimed to stop the social and economic reforms that were being implemented by the PPD and Tugwell, such as the creation of public corporations, land reform, and the economic program based on state-owned industries.[24] Muñoz Marín reacted furiously to this resolution, calling it

> the most outrageous assault on democracy attempted in any part of the world, whether under democratic or axis domination. . . . If Congress were to annul this legislation, the obvious meaning . . . would be that democracy can be made a hoax by the highest parliamentary body of democracy.[25]

The PPD-controlled Puerto Rican legislature condemned Crawford's resolution. He replied that his proposed action was allowed by the Puerto Rican Organic Acts approved by Congress.[26] Although his resolution was not passed in the House, it nevertheless played an important role in moving the House Committee on Insular Affairs to take a closer look at the political events and government reforms in Puerto Rico.[27] The House committee's investigation occurred near the same time as a similar one by the Senate's Committee on Territories and Insular Affairs.

Crawford actively participated in the House Committee on Insular Affairs, chaired by Representative C. Jasper Bell, which held hearings in Puerto Rico in 1943 during its investigation of PPD-Tugwell policies. Its final report, briefly mentioned in chapter 1 (one if its main recommendations was the need to promote Puerto Rican migration to the United States) was highly critical of the Puerto Rican government.[28] It is evident throughout the thousand-plus pages of the report that Crawford was a leading voice in these hearings. He expressed concerns with issues like the government's land reform; the creation of public corporations in communications, the water system, and electricity; public planning; the creation of state-owned manufacturing enterprises; the influence of *independentistas* in the Puerto Rican government; and particularly the situation of the Puerto Rican sugar industry. What is most interesting is that Crawford's views in 1943 were no different from those that he would hold in the late 1940s and early 1950s. Crawford maintained his economic and political ideas regarding Puerto Rico throughout this period, while the PPD government and Muñoz Marín changed theirs. It comes out clearly in his statements in 1943 that, for Crawford, Puerto Rico ought to remain under U.S. jurisdiction for strategic considerations. By extension, he believed that Puerto Ricans needed to be economically self-sustaining, which meant advocating for a reduction of federal expenditures on the island.

One of the most discussed issues during the 1943 congressional hearings was that of Puerto Rico's political status. By this time, President Roosevelt had requested that Congress reform the Jones Act, including allowing Puerto Ricans to elect their own governor.[29] Senator Tydings had submitted his second bill for Puerto Rico's independence in reaction to this measure, which roused pro-independence supporters who were already a significant voice inside the PPD. Muñoz Marín faced particularly pointed questions on the status issue during the hearings, which led to heated debates between him and members of the committee. In an exchange during the 1943 hearings, Crawford pressed Muñoz Marín on the issue of the elective governor—a reform not requested at the time by the PPD—asking if that reform would "take Puerto Rico out of the so-called colonial status." He replied, "Probably it would be to a large extent interpreted by many Puerto Ricans as not removing it basically, as long as the right to take away that right remains outside the sovereignty of Puerto Rico."[30] Although Crawford openly opposed the right of Puerto Ricans to elect their own governor in 1943, the 1947 law that allowed Puerto Ricans to do this for the first time in their history carried Crawford's name and was hailed by Muñoz Marín as a great step in reforming Puerto Rico's colonial status. Furthermore, Muñoz Marín recognized Crawford's significant role in approving this reform.[31]

During the 1943 congressional hearings, Crawford made it evident that he opposed statehood for fiscal reasons—the "inability" of Puerto Ricans to sustain the economic burdens of statehood—and independence for strategic reasons. In 1944, Crawford told *El Mundo* that there would be no status change of any kind—neither statehood nor independence—for Puerto Rico in twenty-five years. At that time, he was willing to consider the elective governor reform but not the right of Puerto Ricans to write their own constitution for fear that they could adopt "any kind of constitution that they wished, fascist, communist, or of other nature."[32] Crawford believed that Puerto Ricans would be easy prey for international communism.[33] Nevertheless, by 1950 Crawford supported Law 600, allowing Puerto Ricans to write their own constitution, probably because this law clearly limited the type of constitution Puerto Ricans could enact: it had to be compatible with and subordinate to the U.S. Constitution.

Another issue on which Crawford presented his opinion during the hearings in 1943—views that he maintained in later years—was Puerto Rican migration to the United States. He questioned why foreign workers like Jamaicans were given jobs in the sugar beet industry while Puerto Ricans—U.S. citizens—remained unemployed.[34] For Crawford, the reforms to the status of Puerto Rico and the promotion of migration to the United States were related. Political and economic stability in Puerto Rico would decrease the need to send federal funds to the island, while the United States would maintain a less conflictive presence there; at the same time, all the surplus labor in Puerto Rico could be employed as cheap labor on the mainland.

During the hearings on Law 600 by the House Interior and Insular Affairs Committee, Crawford made it perfectly clear that he supported Muñoz Marín.[35] The conservative Crawford was the perfect answer to those in Congress who still harbored concerns about Muñoz Marín and his government's supposed radicalism. It is important to emphasize the relationship that emerged between Crawford and Muñoz Marín in the late 1940s. If at the beginning of the decade Muñoz Marín and the PPD relied on Marcantonio—Puerto Rico's "best friend in Congress" then—to protect and promote Puerto Rico's interests in Washington, by the end of the decade they relied on a newfound "best friend" in Washington, Congressman Crawford.[36] After 1945, Muñoz Marín and the PPD began to have conflictive differences with Marcantonio with regard to Puerto Rico's political status, social and economic reforms, and migration policy to the United States.[37] At the same time that they distanced themselves from the radical Marcantonio, Muñoz Marín got closer to the conservative Crawford. R. Brian Ferguson noticed the changing relationship between Crawford and Muñoz Marín and its importance for Puerto Rican affairs by the late 1940s. He contends that Muñoz Marín and Crawford cut a deal in 1945 where the PPD would let go of its social and economic reforms in exchange for Crawford supporting the PPD's political reforms to the island's status. By 1947, Crawford had become a strong supporter of reforms to the political status of Puerto Rico. Ferguson argues that Crawford was crucial for those reforms to become reality: "It was the newfound support of conservative Republicans that paved the way for the status plebiscite and the invited-industrial-development program of Fomento. . . . After Muñoz Marín and Tugwell, no individual is more important for understanding mid-twentieth century colonial policy than the beet man from Michigan, Fred Crawford."[38]

Muñoz Marín and Crawford maintained their relationship even after Crawford left Congress in 1953 following his first electoral defeat since being elected to Congress in 1934. Crawford opened a lobbying office offering his services to the governments of the U.S. territories, including Puerto Rico. In January 1953, Muñoz Marín appointed Crawford as "Special Assistant to the Governor" in charge of studying the possibility of increasing Puerto Rico's trade with its Caribbean neighbors.[39] This contract might have been in gratitude to Crawford's defense of the Puerto Rican government's policies during his last years in Congress—particularly in relation to the island's sugar industry—but also in recognition of his political stance in the 1950 Michigan sugar beet strike by Puerto Rican workers. Both issues were considered by many in Puerto Rico and Michigan as causes leading to Crawford's electoral defeat in 1952.[40] In May 1951, Crawford submitted a report on Operation Bootstrap to the House Committee on Insular Affairs, where he praised the PPD's economic reforms and argued that organized migration to different parts of the United States would provide the greatest relief to Puerto Rico's population level.[41] Crawford's contract with the government of Puerto Rico was canceled by Muñoz Marín in April 1953 in order to avoid—according to the governor—any "embarrassment, both ways, to the public interest."[42] In 1951, Crawford had gained further notoriety in Puerto Rico after it was disclosed, during the trial of Nationalist leader Pedro Albizu Campos for his role in the 1950 Nationalist uprising, that Nationalists planned an unsuccessful plot to assassinate the congressman during a visit to the island.[43]

The relationship between Crawford and Muñoz Marín became strained in the summer of 1950, when discontented Puerto Rican farm laborers launched a strike against the sugar beet farmers in Michigan. Representing the sugar beet interests was Crawford, also running a close race for reelection. The Puerto Rican government came to represent the Puerto Rican workers by default, and it presented a complicated political dilemma for Muñoz Marín's government. On one hand, they could not abandon the workers for fears of both political repercussions on the island and the potential consequences to the FPP and their migration project. On the other hand, going against the interests of farm owners could raise questions about the reliability of Puerto Rican workers and the government's farm labor program in the United States. Furthermore, Public Law 600, which allowed Puerto Ricans to write their own constitution and thus provided a basis for the PPD's political power in Puerto Rico, was under debate in Washington, and Muñoz Marín had no better friend there than Crawford. To complicate things even further for the Puerto Rican government, the October 30, 1950, Nationalist uprising in Puerto Rico was accompanied by an attempt on President Truman's life by two Nationalists, an event that further clouded the image of Puerto Ricans in the United States and the prospects for continued migration there. Once again, status politics and migration politics proved to be closely intertwined and difficult to separate.

THE "BIGGEST LABOR AIRLIFT IN HISTORY" BEGINS IN DISASTER

Sierra Berdecía provided the official account of how the Michigan expedition came to be in his 1949–50 annual report to the governor. He stated that in August 1949, 181 contract workers in the Northeast were transferred to MFC for work in Saginaw, Michigan, with the approval of the department. After information given by the workers themselves and from payrolls, the department concluded

> that the working conditions and earnings in that area were satisfactory. When the Michigan Field Corp., Inc., contacted this Department for the purpose of negotiating a contract to take a large group of workers to the Midwestern area, the Department judging from the results of the first group who worked for this company, approved a contract which is admittedly the best ever negotiated for best workers in the Mainland.[44]

There is no mention here of Congressman Crawford's direct intervention with Governor Muñoz Marín on behalf of MFC. In April 1950, MFC placed an order of 1,500 workers, followed by an additional order in May that increased the number Puerto Rican farmworkers going to Michigan to 5,314.

The Michigan farmworkers' expedition began in disaster. On June 5, a plane owned by Westair Lines—the nonscheduled carrier contracted by MFC to transport sixty-one Puerto Rican workers—crashed near the Florida coast; twenty-eight workers died in the crash. The C-46 plane left the Isla Grande Airport at 6:26 p.m. on its way to Wilmington, North Carolina, and then on to Saginaw, Michigan. Another Westair plane, en route to San Juan to pick up additional workers, notified the authorities of the disaster. Not all of the survivors were able to board the life rafts; some had to spend the night floating with life jackets and were attacked by sharks, to the horror of the others. Thirty-seven were rescued by the coast guard—thirty-four workers and three crew members, including the pilot—and were later taken to Charleston, North Carolina. There, the Westair representative offered the men the choice of a flight to San Juan or to Saginaw.[45] Muñoz Marín ordered the immediate suspension of all Westair flights carrying workers to the United States and commissioned Sierra Berdecía to investigate the situation. BEM's Pagán de Colón announced that the plane had been inspected as required by law and that it fulfilled all the requirements of federal and local laws. The Westair crash was the fifth air disaster since 1947 and came just one year after the tragic plane crash of Punta Salinas that shook public opinion in Puerto Rico.[46]

The Westair crash caught Washington's attention immediately. Several members of Congress, including Marcantonio, called for an immediate investigation of the accident. Jacob Javits demanded that Puerto Rican migrants should be fully protected from any exploitation and that all measures should be taken to prevent another horrible accident for the U.S. citizens from Puerto Rico. Senator Owen Brewater, pointing out previous air crashes in Puerto Rico, stated: "Here we have one more crash carrying Puerto Rican workers to their death."⁴⁷ More important yet, and with greater repercussions on the island, the very same day that the *New York Times* first covered the crash, it also reported that the Civil Aeronautics Administration (CAA) had recommended to the Civil Aeronautics Board (CAB) in the previous fall that the operating certificate to the Aviation Corporation of Seattle, which did business as Westair Transport, be suspended. The CAA stated that this company was "guilty over a long period of time of careless and reckless operation of aircraft." It charged that Westair's three planes were operated in such a manner "as to endanger the life and property of others." The CAB charged Westair of operating in the Caribbean without the required authorization and violating numerous regulations.⁴⁸

The statement by the CAA fell like a bomb in Puerto Rico. Muñoz Marín immediately prohibited Westair from flying farmworkers to Michigan. The director of Puerto Rico's Transportation Administration (TA), which had authorized Westair's flight, denied any knowledge of the CAA accusations. Muñoz Marín stated that Westair "should have never been used to transport laborers whose contracts are supervised by the insular Government."⁴⁹ That very same day, *El Imparcial* published the first of several editorials on the air crash. Pointing to the tragic repetition of these airplane accidents, it called for a more secure form of transporting farmworkers to the U.S. mainland, be it by regularly scheduled airlines or by sea.⁵⁰

Sources close to the government said that the prohibition on Westair flights was "an open disavowal of the Commissioner of Labor." Some blamed him for demanding a lower airfare for the workers from MFC.⁵¹ Muñoz Marín announced that he would be in charge of the crash investigation and that thirty-two of the thirty-five survivors had opted to continue to Michigan. The governor also announced that the government was in negotiations with Pan Am and Eastern for the air transportation of the remaining workers already under contract for the Michigan expedition.⁵² *El Imparcial* reported that Sierra Berdecía had approved the use of Westair only after the TA had certified the use of the airline based on previous reports by the CAA, which had not informed the TA about its recommendation to the CAB to decertify Westair. A TA functionary acknowledged that the person in charge of inspecting the

Westair plane never did so.[53] Upon his return to Puerto Rico, Sierra Berdecía declared that he would take responsibility for any failure of the Department of Labor but claimed that the department was not responsible for the inspection and certification of these flights.[54]

On June 9, *El Imparcial* published its strongest-worded editorial in many years, accusing the PPD government of being "the real masterminds of this latest massacre." After describing the lack of regulations and oversight over these flights taking Puerto Rican workers to the United States, the editorial blamed the government and its migration policy for these deaths: "The government of Puerto Rico . . . which has established, drawn, guided, and encouraged this absurd policy of mass migrations—to escape their responsibilities to create sources of welfare and work here—is the real culprit for these deaths."[55] *El Imparcial*'s statement was a direct questioning of the policy itself, not of its implementation. Days later, the PPD mayor of a sugar municipality also questioned the government's policy of migration, asking why former workers in the island's sugar industry had to emigrate to work in the sugar beet fields in the United States.[56]

After a period of negotiations that included the government of Puerto Rico and MFC, the transportation of workers resumed after an agreement was reached with Pan American and Eastern Airlines. By June 18, all 5,314 workers were in Michigan.[57] The negotiations to achieve this conclusion involved Muñoz Marín. On June 10, while Muñoz Marín was in direct negotiations with Pam Am and Eastern, Crawford reminded him of the urgency of getting Puerto Rican workers to Michigan. Days later, Pan Am agreed to move 3,500 Puerto Ricans to Michigan in "one of the biggest airlifts in its history." This agreement was reached between Pan Am president Juan T. Trippe and Muñoz Marín.[58] Sierra Berdecía claimed that "the largest civilian airlift in history . . . comparable only to the Berlin airlift . . . was carried on much faster than if the original transportation scheduled had been adhered to by Westair."[59] For the Puerto Rican government, the "beet airlift" served as evidence that it could be counted on by U.S. agricultural employers to deliver massive amounts of workers in a short time.

In June 1951, after Lloyds of London finally agreed to pay for the deaths of those killed in the Westair air crash in June 1950, there was still no final report on the accident by the federal or Puerto Rican government agencies in charge of the investigation.[60] After it left the Puerto Rican market, Westair continued to do business from its Washington State base, expanding its routes to Alaska and Hawaii well into the 1960s. After the Charleston tragedy, the CAA had requested the CAB to revoke Westair's certificate of operation, an action that was never implemented.[61]

The Westair tragedy had important repercussions for Puerto Rico's migration policy, specifically on the air transport of farmworkers to the United States. According to Pagán de Colón in her review of the FPP, new regulations were implemented by the Department of Labor after the accident. Now the employer had to notify the department forty-five days in advance with the specific date and airline on which the workers were to be transported. Puerto Rico's TA had to certify that the agreement between the employer and the airline satisfied all the security provisions mandated by the Puerto Rican government and that the airline fulfilled all federal regulations and certifications to operate. Nevertheless, the policy established by Muñoz Marín to use only scheduled airlines had to be ignored in 1951 when U.S. employers could not reach an agreement with Pan Am and Eastern to move the nearly twelve thousand workers required for that year's harvest. The Department of Labor instructed the TA to allow the use of nonscheduled chartered airlines that were certified by the CAA and the CAB. Furthermore, the selected airline had to provide a $10,000 life insurance policy per worker at a fee of $0.50 per person. The department assumed responsibility for ensuring that the airlines would follow the specific date and time scheduled for the flight as agreed with the employers, seeking to make sure that workers would be to their final destinations in less than ten hours; it also regulated life insurance companies and the life insurance fee paid by the workers.[62]

The farmworkers' expedition to Michigan in 1950 began with the tragedy of the Westair plane crash on June 5. For those who survived the crash and went on to work in the sugar beet fields of Michigan, and for the thousands more who joined them later, the tragedy continued with the entire experience. Those workers who rose in discontent with the working and living conditions they encountered in Michigan, the many who left the sugar beet farms and moved elsewhere or went on strike, presented the first real challenge to the Puerto Rican government's migration policy.

MIGRANT DISCONTENT IN MICHIGAN

Ironically, the first news report from farmworkers in Michigan on June 21 declared that they were satisfied with the working and living conditions they encountered there.[63] But complaints from other workers in Michigan and their families in Puerto Rico began to be heard on the island shortly thereafter. *El Imparcial* began to publish news stories on the workers' situation in Michigan on June 27.[64] In letters addressed to Sierra Berdecía, workers told about the "horror" stories they were experiencing there, expressing unhappiness about overcrowded living quarters, no beds, no drinking water, inadequate food, no pay, and no bathrooms.⁶⁵ Other workers complained that they "have been deceived like children by the American companies in Puerto Rico," that the $5 they were paid a week for food was insufficient, and that since they had not received any wages, they could "send no money to our children, which means they will have to eat wind." This letter ended: "Tell us, Mr. Sierra, would you agree with these conditions if you were working here with us?"⁶⁶ The situation of farmworkers in Michigan was so dire that they requested and received help from the American Red Cross.⁶⁷

On July 9, *El Imparcial* published a report titled "Horrors Described in the Fields of Michigan," in which farmworkers there depicted their situation as "slavery in the twentieth century and under the American flag." They protested that under their labor contract—approved by the Puerto Rican government—they were supposed to earn $10 per acre, but that after working "from six in the morning to six in the afternoon," they were told that they "had not earned enough even to pay for the food." Workers reported that they were told by the employers that, contrary to their contract, they would be paid by piecework rates and that "only Americans were paid by the hour." They added: "We were first deceived in our own country and then we are deceived in Michigan." Deploring that they had received no pay after working for five weeks, the workers—alluding to the Puerto Rican government—added, "They offered us to end unemployment on the island and what they have done is to let our children go hungry and needy."⁶⁸ Other workers made similar complaints in a letter addressed to the commissioner of labor: "We do not have money to send to our families, not even for our own expenses. Do you think, Mr. Sierra, that this is just? Would you like to be one of us?"⁶⁹ Another letter signed by dozens of workers claimed that they were protesting directly to Muñoz Marín but wanted to have their situation made public so their wives knew the reason why they were not sending home any money.⁷⁰ Other workers from Michigan requested Muñoz Marín's "cooperation for an early solution to our problem," indicating that because they were sending what little money they had earned to their families back home, they had been going hungry for days.⁷¹

In a letter signed by more than two dozen workers, they lamented that after working more than 187 hours in nineteen days, instead of receiving $112—based on sixty cents an hour, as stipulated in their contract—they were paid only $42: "We get paid at the rate of two dollars a day, with which we have to pay the debt of the airfare, pay for our meals and send money to our families. It seems that this contract was not made by a worker but by someone that wants to live off the workers."⁷² Many of the letters by Michigan workers published by *El Imparcial* deplored the lack of supervision of their working and living conditions and of support by the Department of Labor, many blaming Sierra Berdecía directly: "Mr. Berdecía has not taken care of us after we left the airport in Isla Grande. Tell me Mr. Governor, if you were one of us, what would you do?"[73]

Workers held the government responsible for their situation, including the governor himself, and asked him to intervene in the situation: "You are the one called to solve this critical situation of ours, since we are the ones that have taken you to the position in which you are now."[74] Other workers lamented that the Puerto Rican government "has left us at the mercy of the whims of our employers. . . . Either we get paid or we run away."[75] Addressing "the government of Puerto Rico," workers in Owosso, Michigan, declared that "the abuse and exploitation by farmers has been so oppressive that many of our comrades have gone on strike." The workers charged that after hearing their complaints, the representative of the Department of Labor urged them to keep working. "Is this what our government representative has to say to us?" they asked. "If so, we will have no alternative but to escape or kill ourselves."[76]

On July 18, *El Imparcial* requested a government investigation into the situation of workers in Michigan, stating that the vast number of letters describing the same situation showed that it was not merely the complaints of a few lazy workers or of those feeling nostalgia for their country. The newspaper charged that "there is enough proof that there exists a state of oppression and exploitation against Puerto Rican workers in Michigan" and urged for a government investigation "to see what the true state of affairs is and to protect Puerto Ricans, if the situation requires it." The editorial, referring to John Steinbeck's classic novel recounting the hardships experienced by a migrant family during the Dust Bowl era, *The Grapes of Wrath*, argued for "a protective hand to be extended to our brothers, so they do not have to pick the 'grapes of wrath.'" The newspaper also requested that the government should have a permanent representative in Michigan to deal with the problems facing the migrant workers there.[77] Earlier, *El Imparcial* had reported on the contradiction implied by the expedition of Puerto Rican workers to save the sugar beet crop in Michigan. Some asserted that the government's migration policy was leaving the island's agriculture (particularly sugar) without enough of a labor force. Others raised the issue that since Congress had reduced Puerto Rico's sugar quota to 86,718 tons while keeping that of domestic sugar beet at 1.8 million tons, by sending workers to Michigan, the island's sugar industry was hurt: Puerto Rico's sugar could replace Michigan's quota if its sugar beet crop was lost.[78]

Some of the letters regarding the Michigan situation questioned the rationale for a migration policy. After demanding the "repatriation" of workers from Michigan, farmworker Serafín Ramos urged that "this sad affair should serve as a warning so that in the future the government does not sponsor migrations of this kind, which always end in failure."[79] Pedro Cruz and twelve other workers in Michigan decried their terrible working and living conditions, claiming to be without work and pay, suffering physical abuse by their employer, and living in conditions "worse than in a jail." The letter continued, "This is the second time I've been on these expeditions and I think this is the last one for me."[80] Joan Menéndez, from the Michigan fields, also questioned the validity of migratory labor: "I'm sure that no Puerto Rican will return here to give away his labor to these Yankee millionaires. We will not be fooled again."[81]

People in Puerto Rico began to share the pains suffered by farmworkers in Michigan, blaming the government for their awful situation there:

> What is the government of Puerto Rico doing, since it was the insular Department of Labor which sponsored emigration of Puerto Rican workers to foreign lands? Will it allow our compatriots to be worked like slaves and their families perish of hunger? What do Sierra Berdecía and Muñoz Marín have to say about this?[82]

During this period, *El Imparcial* began to publish letters from people in Puerto Rico affected by the situation of farmworkers in Michigan. Angela Vargas Pagán showed *El Imparcial* her husband's letters from Michigan, which described his situation there as a "concentration camp" and "worse than hell." His only remittance was one dollar, given to him by an American woman to buy milk; he decided to send the money home to feed his six children.[83] The newspaper also reported on the situation of Dora Torres de Rivera Oquendo, pregnant with two children, who had received no word or money from her husband working in Michigan and had been evicted from her public housing apartment.[84] By the end of July, many farmworkers were returning from Michigan—with no money, sick, and undernourished—telling their "horror" stories regarding their experience in sugar beet fields there.[85]

Perhaps as disconcerting for Muñoz Marín and the government's migration policy makers as the Michigan situation was what it meant for their migration policy; the political implications of migrant discontent in Michigan were evident in the workers' letters. In a letter addressed to Muñoz Marín by "Five thousand workers from Alma, Michigan," titled "We are no longer

Populares" (PPD supporters), the workers threatened the governor with political reprisals in the next election, stating that

> the five thousand workers that are here now are no longer '*Populares.*' Do not count on us for the next elections . . . we will snatch from you the [electoral] victory. With the votes of suffering people you will not be elected again since you have to know how we are suffering and you have sent no one.[86]

Another letter from workers in Michigan, this time addressed to Santiago Mari Ramos, president of the Puerto Rican Independence Party chapter in Mayagüez, clearly stated, "You can count on our votes, we will make you win in '52, because after what Governor Muñoz Marín has done to us none of the 5,400 workers who are working here want to have anything to do with him ever again."[87] Incidentally, in the 1952 election, the PIP received 19 percent of the vote, its highest ever.

The Puerto Rican government had to contend not only with the negative press coverage that the Michigan experiment was receiving in Puerto Rico but also with the attention paid by the Michigan press to the plight of Puerto Rican farmworkers in the sugar beet fields there. Reports in the Michigan press described the "deplorable plight" of Puerto Rican workers in the sugar beet fields and accused the employers of a "policy of short-sightedness combined with a cold, impersonal attitude toward the workers." It noted that island workers vowed not to return to Michigan and that many were already leaving.[88] Many island workers discontented with their conditions ran away from the farms and moved to nearby communities, particularly to Detroit. The accusations and complaints raised by the farmworkers in the Puerto Rican press were confirmed by the press coverage and several state investigations that were carried out in Michigan. Puerto Ricans found in Detroit a comforting hand in the Mexican neighborhood, particularly in the Catholic parish, whose priest was deeply involved in the plight of the previous wave of Mexican migratory workers in the Michigan sugar beet fields. According to him, some 10 percent of Puerto Ricans working in the sugar beet fields in 1950 came to his parish seeking some kind of aid after leaving the farms before the end of their contract. He and others helped many Puerto Rican farmworkers to find jobs in the area, particularly in steel and auto plants. As Valdés noted, "a significant consequence of Operation Farmlift was that it resulted in the formation of a permanent Puerto Rican community in Detroit. Almost five hundred men who walked out of the beet fields in 1950 ultimately settled in the city."[89]

NEGOTIATING DISCONTENT

Many of the complaints expressed by the workers were known to the Puerto Rican government from the beginning of the Michigan expedition. From May 30 to June 19, two employees of Puerto Rico's Migration Office in the United States, Eulalio Torres and Antonio Vega, went to Michigan to investigate the working conditions faced by Puerto Rican workers in the sugar beet fields. Their report voiced many of the complaints expressed by workers in the Puerto Rican press. The workers complained that the growers were breaking the contract in terms of payment, paying by piecework instead of by the hour; that they were given only $5 a week as advance for food, which was not enough to cover their expenses; that their living quarters were overcrowded and unhealthy, with no running water or electricity; and that after weeks of work, they had received no payment at all. The report recommended more interpreters to facilitate relations between the workers and the employer and more orientation to the workers so they could finish their work contracts.[90]

After workers' complaints kept surfacing on the press, Sierra Berdecía sent another team to investigate the situation in Michigan. This one was headed by Alan Perl, labor adviser to the Puerto Rican government. His July 17 report confirmed most of the complaints workers expressed in the press, which were also presented in the Torres report. Perl concluded that the biggest source of worker dissatisfaction was wage payment since workers had no idea of how they were paid or when. He criticized the employers for using different forms of payment not stipulated in the contract. But he stated that further discrimination must be employed in recruitment to avoid those workers not capable of doing the field work. Perl also suggested that additional analysis of the situation was warranted and recommended that the commissioner of labor should investigate the situation in person.[91]

After the recurring allegations of mistreatment and hardships in the local press by Puerto Rican workers in Michigan, Sierra Berdecía met with Muñoz Marín on July 19 to discuss the situation there. The governor requested the commissioner of labor to head a delegation that would investigate the farmworkers' program in Michigan. Along with Sierra Berdecía, the delegation included Francisco Collazo, of the Bureau of Conciliation and Arbitration; Howard Davidson, of the BEM; and Perl, Torres, and Vega. Each would look into a different area of Michigan where Puerto Ricans were working.[92] *El Mundo*, closer to the government's position on migration and relatively silent on the Michigan situation during this period, welcomed Sierra Berdecía's investigation, stating that he should guarantee that the Michigan project would not fail since it would make possible future expeditions to other parts of the United States and assure the continuance of Puerto Rico's migration program.[93] *El Imparcial*, more critical of the PPD government and its migration policy, added to this assessment of the situation that the success or failure of the Michigan expedition would have consequences for the legitimacy of the Puerto Rican government.[94]

Crawford welcomed Sierra Berdecía's investigation. He had a big stake in the Michigan situation since he represented the sugar beet interests in Michigan and as such had lobbied the Puerto Rican government to send workers to that area. He was also one of the strongest supporters of granting Puerto Rico its own constitution, a bill for which was under discussion precisely at that time.[95] It was widely acknowledged in Michigan that Puerto Rican workers had saved that year's sugar beet crop. William Dorvillier, an *El Mundo* correspondent in Washington, stated that "Crawford's devotion to Puerto Rican interests has been paid in a practical way locally in his district." He added that Crawford's friendship with Muñoz Marín not only saved the sugar beet crop but probably also furthered Crawford's reelection campaign in the coming November elections. Dorvillier claimed that Puerto Rican officials were deeply concerned that the government's biggest supporter in Congress might not be reelected.[96] Meanwhile, discontent among Puerto Rican workers was still running high. Some complained that they had no knowledge of Sierra Berdecía's investigation, nor had they seen the commissioner visit the Michigan fields. Others said they had sent their complaints to Congressman Marcantonio in search for remedy to their plight.[97]

Sierra Berdecía submitted his report to Muñoz Marín on his investigation of the situation of workers in Michigan on August 16, 1950. He confirmed the seriousness of the situation facing Puerto Rican workers in Michigan, characterized by inadequate housing and food services, as well as breach of contract in terms of the amount of wages paid and the method of payment. Michigan growers had repeatedly violated a contract signed with the workers and approved by his department. Puerto Rican workers were paid less than half of the average wage paid in the beet industry; further, their low earnings were not paid every two weeks, as stipulated in the contract. Workers' complaints that they had no money to satisfy their basic needs and to send back home to sustain their families were more than justified. In addition, workers had been paid by a fixed scale determined by the growers and not by the amount specified in the contract.[98] *El Mundo* welcomed the results of Sierra Berdecía's "impartial" investigation, requesting that the government do everything in its power to uphold the contract signed by workers and remedy their situation; if not, the government should not allow any more workers to go to Michigan.[99] *El Imparcial* also applauded Sierra Berdecía's report and its conclusions, acknowledging that the government finally realized "the importance of this issue, since it was related to the success or failure of the export of workers on a large scale." After questioning the political motives of the Michigan project (to support Crawford), it agreed that future emigration plans could be implemented only if the government assured the workers that the farmers would comply with the contracts.[100]

Prior to the publication of the report, Sierra Berdecía had written to MFC's director, Max Henderson, that he would not support the continuance of Puerto Rican workers in Michigan unless growers "completely rectify the situation," including additional payment for work already done and full compliance with all the terms of the contract. Two days after Sierra Berdecía's report, Crawford wrote to Muñoz Marín requesting a rapid solution to the situation, "in view of the fact of the unsettled attitude of the Puerto Rican workers."[101] Crawford accused Sierra Berdecía of playing politics with his report and denied any abuse of Puerto Rican workers in Michigan, adding that any complaints about wages and working conditions in the sugar beet fields should be sent to the U.S. secretary of agriculture, who was in charge of setting the standards in those areas. Henderson also accused Sierra Berdecía of playing politics and accused him of being responsible on equal terms for the situation of Puerto Rican workers in Michigan.[102] In response to Crawford, the commissioner of labor defended his report and blamed MFC for the situation of Puerto Rican workers in Michigan. Furthermore, Sierra Berdecía publicly rebuffed Henderson's proposal to employ fifteen thousand Puerto Ricans in the future, stating that what MFC's farmers should do is to abide by the contract already signed with the workers.[103] Even *El Imparcial,* not given to praising Sierra Berdecía, defended him from the accusations raised by Crawford and Henderson and supported the measures approved by the government to benefit the workers in Michigan.[104]

On August 20, the Puerto Rican legislature approved a bill providing $117,400 to aid workers in Michigan. The bill, sponsored by Muñoz Marín, declared a state of emergency regarding the living conditions faced by Puerto Ricans in Michigan. The law was signed by the governor on August 24 and allowed the commissioner of labor to provide financial aid to any worker who was under contract in Michigan and had started working between May 31 and June 18, whether he was still in Michigan or had moved to any other state. The worker had to be in economic need and in the process of moving to a job in any part of the United States or returning to Puerto Rico.[105] The *New York Times* claimed that the appropriations allowed by the bill were not only to "meet the workers' needs but to prevent them from becoming social burdens on the community in which they were situated."[106] This was probably one of the major concerns for the Puerto Rican government in the Michigan situation and in agreement with its migration policy.

On August 25, Governor Muñoz Marín sent a letter to Puerto Rican workers in the sugar beet fields in Michigan. He stated that he had requested the Division of Public Welfare to provide financial aid to the neediest of those worker's families that had not received remittances due to the lack of payment by employers. The governor also announced new working conditions agreed with the MFC, including a salary of not less than sixty-five cents per hour to be paid weekly, an effort to improve housing conditions, and additional pay of one dollar per acre worked in the sugar beet harvest. He affirmed: "Under these conditions and in view of the Company's agreement with me, my advice is that you stay on the job. . . . In order to keep a relationship of good faith with the people of Michigan . . . you should make every effort to finish the harvest." He added that the government was willing to provide aid to those interested in finding jobs in other parts of the United States after the harvest in Michigan was finished. The governor asked the workers to write to him directly if there was a breach of contract so that "it could be resolved with the company, which I am sure will be eager to correct any inadvertent breach of their commitment to me."[107] On August 21, Muñoz Marín informed both Crawford and Henderson that he would ask Puerto Rican workers to remain in Michigan and finish the harvest. In this communication, Muñoz Marín implied that he was playing a delicate balancing act between the workers and the Michigan sugar beet interests. On August 22, Henderson thanked Muñoz Marín, since "your timely intervention has saved this program both for present and future."[108] Later that year, Crawford won his reelection, news reported on *El Mundo*'s front page, along with the other headline that Senator Tydings and Congressman Marcantonio—both "champions of independence"—had lost their bids for reelection.[109]

By the end of August, the situation appeared to have changed little, as indicated by two official accounts. In a letter to Muñoz Marín, Luis Rivera Santos, administrator of social programs of the International House in Chicago, recounted his recent visit to the Michigan fields to interview Puerto Rican workers. He declared that workers were still disappointed that they had not been paid for the first half of the harvest and that they could not send money back home. He criticized MFC and indicated that many workers had looked for employment in industries near the area.[110] A report from the Migration Office's Torres reaffirmed the situation. He indicated that only about two thousand workers remained in Michigan, most of them working in the pickle fields until the end of the sugar beet harvest began. He stated that "the workers have developed an anxiety state of mind to leave the sugar beets territory, that it will take super salesmanship to retain them for the harvesting of the sugar beets." He denounced the MFC for not improving the working conditions and not paying workers the hours agreed on in the contract. He reaffirmed that many workers were leaving the Michigan fields and getting jobs elsewhere, making the coming sugar beet harvest uncertain in terms of required manpower.[111]

A memo from the Migration Division's director, Manuel Cabranes, to Sierra Berdecía dated August 23, 1950, is even more specific on the Michigan situation. Cabranes stated that only $53,925 was used from the amount approved by the Puerto Rican government. Of the 5,300 workers in Michigan sugar beet fields at the beginning of the season, only 1,709 received any government help; the remaining 3,591 went back to Puerto Rico or moved to other parts of the U.S. mainland. Cabranes claimed that the discontent that Sierra Berdecía witnessed during his July visit to the camps was "complicated with the confusion created in workers' minds with the approval of the law." To this he added: "This confusion was encouraged and exploited in New York by followers of former congressman Marcantonio and other elements disaffected with the Puerto Rican government."[112]

Problems with the application of the law appeared immediately. Workers who had been employed in Michigan but were working in other places appeared in New York's Migration Office demanding funds to return to Puerto Rico. Sierra Berdecía argued that those holding jobs could not benefit from the law and that doing so could set a bad precedent, since many workers in the East Coast would make the same demand. He asserted that the money approved by the law could provide for transportation to only 1,565 workers.[113] Puerto Rican workers picketed the Migration Office, demanding to be flown back to the island. Cabranes declared that only the sick or incapacitated could be repatriated to Puerto Rico; otherwise, money would be given only to those seeking new jobs on the mainland.[114]

The *New York Times* reported that of the 5,500 Puerto Rican farmworkers in Michigan, only 900 were flown back to the island; around 3,000 stayed in the United States, with nearly 1,300 moving to farms in New Jersey and others staying in Detroit or going to New York.[115] *El Imparcial* reported that Torres and two other migration functionaries remained in Michigan to ensure that the beet farmers abided by the labor contract. It also noted that of the 5,500 initial workers in Michigan, only 916 renewed their contracts with MFC.[116] According to Sierra Berdecía, of the 5,514 workers in Michigan that summer, 1,721 received a total of $80,961.48 in compensation. He also declared that as of June 1951, the Migration Division had collected $87,661.62 from MFC on behalf of workers due to claims of unpaid labor.[117] In December 1950, Cabranes informed BEM director Pagán de Colón that Torres had returned to the New York office since the sugar beet season had ended, and any worker remaining in Michigan would be on his own.[118] The 1950 Michigan expedition for Puerto Rican farmworkers had officially ended.

But the 1950 fiasco experienced by Puerto Rican migrant workers in Michigan did not end the relationship of island laborers with that state's sugar beet industry. In mid-March 1952, Crawford sent a letter to Muñoz Marín requesting another expedition of Puerto Rican migrant workers to the sugar beet fields of Michigan. The plea included a new contract by MFC that guaranteed a specific number of working hours to laborers and a set wage standard. They requested a thousand workers from Puerto Rico. Crawford asked the governor for a prompt consideration of the proposal, since the sugar beet crop was to begin soon.[119] It seems to be no coincidence that Crawford's new petition happened to arrive during the congressional debate for the approval of the Commonwealth constitution in 1952—much like his first petition to Muñoz Marín for workers in 1950 was delivered in the midst of the debate in Congress for the approval of Public Law 600, allowing Puerto Ricans to write their own constitution.

An ad hoc committee was created to discuss Crawford and MFC's proposal. It was chaired by the University of Puerto Rico's chancellor, Jaime Benítez, and included Sierra Berdecía, BEM's Pagan de Colón, Pedro Muñoz Amato from the Planning Board, and economic adviser Millard Hansen. Sierra Berdecía elaborated on the 1950 experience of Puerto Rican workers in Michigan and "expressed his interest in trying to help Mr. Crawford in a way that could be satisfactory to the workers." Although there was some questioning about sending workers to Michigan again, the committee concluded:

> However, in view of the necessity that the Michigan Field Corps has for Puerto Rican workers to take in the crop, and *in view of the friendship which Congressman Crawford has shown for the Island* it was thought that every effort should be made to arrange for workers to go to Michigan.

The committee then agreed that workers should not be sent unless sufficient working hours were guaranteed, standards of employment were satisfied, and the Department of Labor was assured that the contract terms were going to be complied with. Muñoz Marín later informed Crawford of the committee's discussion, stating that some workers could be sent to Michigan.[120] Eventually some 190 workers were sent there to work on the 1952 harvest. Still, some government officials expressed doubts about allowing Puerto Ricans to return to Michigan and questioned the working arrangements.[121] *El Diario de Nueva*

York, the most important Hispanic daily in the city, criticized the Puerto Rican government for allowing Puerto Rican farmworkers to return to Michigan, arguing that this action was a measure to placate Crawford in a period when the Puerto Rican constitution was under debate in Congress.[122] Even after the 1950 fiasco, employers in Michigan showed their interest in recruiting Puerto Rican workers, without any success.[123] The Puerto Rican government never again organized another farmworkers' expedition to the state.

IN THE AFTERMATH OF MICHIGAN

The incidents related to the Michigan expedition in 1950 had important consequences for Puerto Rico's migration policy. The Michigan incident makes visible the active role played by Muñoz Marín not only in the formulation but also in the implementation of Puerto Rican migration policy and illustrates the importance of migration for the governor and the PPD government. Migration policy was not an afterthought for Muñoz Marín and other top government policy makers, a policy to be formulated and implemented by second-level functionaries. Michigan demonstrates how Muñoz Marín was directly involved in approving farmworkers' expeditions to the North and in the approval of labor contracts. When discontent emerged in Michigan, the governor intervened directly to mediate between workers and employers. Furthermore, when workers' discontent threatened to wreck the Michigan expedition and thus endanger future migration expeditions to the United States, Muñoz Marín used his legitimacy to keep workers in Michigan, appealing to them directly as the charismatic leader of the island. Muñoz Marín and Sierra Berdecía intervened personally to make sure labor contracts were complied with by employers, that air transportation was safe and reliable, and that labor discontent in U.S. farms was minimal and taken care of by government officials. Finally, the Michigan incident shows the workings of the Puerto Rican government as a labor contractor, a subject I will examine more carefully in the next chapter.

Valdés points out another lesson of the Michigan expedition for the Puerto Rican government and U.S. employers: not to underestimate the unwillingness of Puerto Rican farmworkers to accept abuses by the government or employers:

> Industry calculations erred first by underestimating the Puerto Rican workers, who had many years of experience in agriculture on the island, were much more aggressive in defending their rights than were Mexican Ameri-

cans, and who expected employers to abide by contract terms. They preferred not to work rather than endure abuses.[124]

Indeed, Puerto Rican farmworkers going to the United States came mostly from the sugar industry and were highly radicalized, politicized, and well organized in Puerto Rico. They were very supportive first of the *Federación Libre de Trabajadores* (FLT) and then of the Socialist Party, the main working class organization and political party, respectively, of Puerto Rican workers in the first three decades of the twentieth century. After the 1934 strike, sugar workers abandoned both the FLT and the Socialist Party and supported the radical General Confederation of Workers and the PPD.[125] After Michigan, the Puerto Rican government would be more conscious of screening workers going to do farmwork in the U.S. mainland, but it also became more attentive to workers' demands and complaints in the United States.

The Michigan incident brings to mind the 1947 "Puerto Rican problem" in New York City, and in a sense, they might be comparable. In both cases there was a sustained public debate in the press and calls for the Puerto Rican government to assume a more active role in the situation. But there are important differences to keep in mind. The "Puerto Rican problem" in New York was caused by individual, or "spontaneous," migration to that city; it was a reaction by the host society to the entry of these migrants. This incident is significant in Puerto Rican migration history because it was a central factor in the formulation of the government's migration policy. The incidents in Michigan, in contrast, reflected the travails and dilemmas of organized migration under the Puerto Rican government's Farm Placement Program. Migrant discontent in Michigan called into question the government's organized migration program for the first time.

CHAPTER 7

Puerto Ricans as Migratory Labor, the State as a Labor Contractor

U.S. COLONIALISM in Puerto Rico created an economic space in the territory that allowed U.S. corporations to exploit Puerto Ricans as cheap labor beginning in 1898. The economic, social, and political changes that emerged after the 1940s did not change this situation. Under Operation Bootstrap, the Puerto Rican government gave subsidies to U.S. corporations that included local tax exemption and a vast source of cheap labor that was not fully protected by U.S. labor laws. One of the areas of autonomy of the reconstituted colonial state under the Commonwealth status was its continued exclusion from specific federal laws approved by Congress, like minimum wage and environmental protection.

Puerto Ricans also became a significant source of cheap labor in the United States after 1945. They were regarded as such from the time they began to move to the United States. What was qualitatively and quantitatively new was the massive number of Puerto Ricans leaving the island after World War II. For over a decade, tens of thousands of Puerto Ricans moved to the United States, most of them on their own, to areas of the American Northeast. They worked mostly in low-paying jobs in labor-intensive manufacturing industries, in the service industry, and in agriculture. Thousands more left the island every year as farmworkers under contract, in expeditions organized and managed by the Puerto Rican government. They were considered migrant workers, as part of that army of exploited farmworkers moving from one place to another in search of agricultural work in the U.S. mainland.

One consequence of the Michigan expedition was the insertion of Puerto Rican farmworkers into the debate regarding the status of migratory labor in the United States at the end of the 1940s. As migratory labor, they joined large numbers of domestic workers, largely African Americans and Chicanos, and of alien laborers who worked in U.S. agriculture, mostly Mexicans—both legal *braceros* and undocumented immigrants—and West Indians. Reflecting the status of their homeland, Puerto Rican farmworkers occupied a liminal position within the structure of U.S. migratory labor: they were not deemed domestic labor by the U.S. government and employers but neither were they completely alien, given their citizenship. They enjoyed the protection of a government-sponsored contract, like Mexican and West Indian alien labor, but they could not be deported, like domestic labor.

In the first section of this final chapter, I use the report by President Truman's Commission on Migratory Labor to examine the status of Puerto Rican farmworkers as migrant labor in the United States and the working of the Puerto Rican government as a labor contractor: an intermediary between Puerto Rican farmworkers and U.S. agricultural interests. The Puerto Rican government became a provider of reliable cheap labor to American agricultural employers. This is an important reason why Puerto Rican farmworkers were hired in American agriculture for decades.

The last two sections discuss the specific workings of the Farm Placement Program (FPP) and the Migration Division in the United States. The FPP is the clearest example of an organized migration program by the Puerto Rican government and reflects its role as a labor provider to American agricultural interests. Once Puerto Rican migrants moved to the United States, the Migration Division would provide information on jobs and social services to facilitate their incorporation in American society. Furthermore, through its employment program, the Migration Division also functioned as a labor provider of unskilled labor to low-paying manufacturing industries in the United States.

THE PRESIDENT'S COMMISSION ON MIGRANT LABOR: PUERTO RICANS AS MIGRATORY WORKERS

The director of the Bureau of Employment and Migration (BEM), Petroamérica Pagán de Colón, stated in a report to Governor Muñoz Marín in December 1949, "Our workers have joined the group of migratory workers in the United States and they move from region to region where there are job opportunities."[1] By 1950, particularly after the incidents in the sugar beet fields of Michigan, Puerto Rican farmworkers became part of the United States' debate on migrant labor. In June 1950, President Truman appointed a presidential commission to study the situation of migratory workers in the United States. The plight of Puerto Rican migrant workers figured prominently in the hearings held by the presidential commission.

According to Kirsten, the commission "represented a noble but futile effort on the part of the Truman administration to bridge the difference between organized labor and agribusiness over immigration policy and to rationalize the use of alien labor."[2] A major concern that led to the creation of this commission was the issue of Mexican labor, both legal *braceros* and undocumented immigrants. Representatives of labor argued that Mexican workers, both *bracero* and undocumented, were displacing American workers; they stressed that agricultural interests preferred undocumented workers, who were more easily exploited and subject to deportation after their work contract ended. Agricultural interests contended that the continued need for alien labor resulted from a lack of interest by American workers in performing agricultural work. Representatives of American labor reasoned that domestic labor would carry out farmwork if wages and working conditions improved. After the NAACP and other African American and Hispanic organizations complained that the conditions of domestic labor were not included in the commission's proposed agenda, Truman ordered the commission to study the labor conditions of this group as well. Nevertheless, Truman did not appoint any African American or Hispanic representatives to the commission.[3]

Hearings by the president's Commission on Migratory Labor were held in Trenton, New Jersey, and the situation of Puerto Rican migrants workers there figured prominently in those proceedings. Asked if all Puerto Ricans went back to the island after finishing their contract, John G. Sholl, from the New Jersey migrant labor bureau, answered that some went to New York in the first year, and added: "New Jersey has not had a single case of relief for Puerto Ricans, however. Most of them go back to their home island with a good roll of bills in their pockets." He stated that farmers were satisfied with their work. New Jersey's secretary of agriculture also praised Puerto Rican workers, saying that farmers generally preferred them because they were "good workers, came from rural areas, were well behaved and single."[4]

The last round of hearings by the commission was held in Saginaw, Michigan, in the heart of Congressman Crawford's district. There, too, the plight of Puerto Rican workers in that state would play an important part in the hearings. Crawford argued that the hearings, scheduled to start a day before primary elections, were aimed at hurting him politically—that unions trying to organize agricultural workers were behind the commission's hearings in an attempt to harm agricultural interests and him in particular. He criticized Sierra Berdecía for playing into the hands of union interests by criticizing sugar beet farmers in his report on Puerto Rican workers in Michigan. Crawford maintained that even if it hurt him politically in Michigan, he would still defend the right of Puerto Ricans to work in the Michigan fields. Muñoz Marín had to intervene to indicate that the Puerto Rican government still considered Crawford a friend of the island and had no political agenda against the Michigan congressman.[5] The Puerto Rican government was trying hard to maintain Crawford's crucial support for its agenda of political reforms in Congress. Crawford won the primary and the right to represent his Michigan district once again.[6]

The first person to testify in the Saginaw hearings was precisely Crawford. He stated that Puerto Rico's "fantastic overpopulation" required an extensive plan of migration of at least twenty-five thousand per year. According to Crawford, the American government had two options: "Either we let them work or we send them financial aid. If we cannot provide them with opportunities for work they will disintegrate at the expense of the American taxpayer."[7] Also testifying that day was MFC's Henderson, who declared that enforcing federal regulations would have ruinous consequences on Michigan's sugar beet industry. In his statement, Henderson elaborated on the disastrous situation experienced by Michigan sugar beet farmers with Puerto Rican farmworkers in the 1950 season, claiming that difficulties with these workers arose from several misunderstandings regarding working conditions and pay. He basically blamed the Puerto Rican government, arguing that "a very poor job of briefing the men in Puerto Rico was done with the result that the men did not understand the terms and conditions of work properly and many of them came under the impression they were working on an hour basis" instead of being paid by piecework. He found fault with their living conditions in the fact the "these men being without the women" were not able to do their cooking and cleaning and "soon found themselves living in filth." Henderson stated that MFC would still hire a small number of Puerto Ricans in the future, but under a "special system of supervision, housing, feeding, and payment." The MFC representative argued that until sugar beet production was fully mechanized, a foreign labor program would still be required in the industry.[8]

The panorama presented by several Puerto Ricans who had worked in the Michigan sugar beet farms in the 1950 season was vastly different from that portrayed by Crawford and Henderson. Santos Cintrón, who left a wife and seven children in Puerto Rico to go to work there in June, testified that after eight weeks of work, the Michigan Sugar Company contended that he owed them $9.69 for deductions of food, housing, and transportation. Cintrón left the Michigan farms and moved to Detroit, where he made $75 a week working in a steel plant and was able to send $45 a week to his family back home. A similar story was told by Martín González, who had survived the June Westair crash and, like Cintrón, had abandoned the sugar beet field for a steel plant in Detroit. Father Clement Kern, of the Holy Trinity Church in Detroit, gave testimony of similar stories from the more than one hundred Puerto Ricans who had gone to this parish seeking aid and shelter. He testified about pay statements of $10, $13, and $16 for a period of four weeks' work. A spokesman for the Michigan sugar beet industry told the commission that the workers' working and living conditions could not be improved "until we prove that the sugar beet industry is profitable." The deputy commissioner of Michigan's Department of Labor testified that the farmers had the resources to pay the workers fair salaries and provide them with decent living conditions.[9]

After several days of hearings before the presidential commission, it was evident that Puerto Rican workers in Michigan were mistreated and deceived. Representatives of social service agencies in Saginaw explained how the workers were misled and not properly advised in terms of the working and living conditions and wages to be expected in Michigan. A representative of Michigan's Labor Department argued for stricter federal regulations on migratory farm labor, particularly on the sugar beet industry. There were no complaints against Puerto Rican workers from the community or agricultural representatives.[10]

The commission's report to the president was made public on April 7, 1951. It presented a strong condemnation of the appalling working and living conditions of migratory workers in the United States.[11] The report remains the best document on the working and living conditions of this group of workers in American agriculture at this time of history. Nevertheless, none of the main recommendations presented by the commission—like giving domestic labor priority over foreign labor in agricultural jobs—were implemented. In fact, a year after the report was made public, Congress approved Public Law 78, extending the *Bracero* Program, in blatant contradiction to a major recommendation by the commission.

The report established that what made a person a migratory worker was not the kind of work he did but "whether he maintains a stable home the year round." Other areas of the economy depended on seasonal work, but "it is only in agriculture that migratory labor has become a problem of such proportions and complexity" as to require government intervention and study.

The single most important reason for workers to become migrant laborers "is that many people find it impossible to make a living in a single location and hence have had to become migratory" (5).[12] By 1950, migratory labor represented almost one-fourth of the agricultural labor in the United States. Of the close to one million migratory workers, half were domestic workers and the other half were foreign workers, most of them Mexicans, with a smaller number of West Indians and Puerto Ricans (3, 6).[13]

The report characterized migrant workers as "children of misfortune," be it in the United States or in foreign lands: "They are the rejects of those sectors of agriculture and of other industries undergoing change." Domestic and foreign migratory workers shared many experiences of work and exploitation; they moved through the nation in search of work, "but they neither belong to the land nor does the land belong to them." Both were marginal and excluded in the nation and in the communities they worked for. The differences between domestic and foreign migratory workers in the terms of economic and social status and job security were none: "Under the law, the domestic migrants are citizens of the United States but they are scarcely more a part of the land of their birth than the alien migrants working beside them." They worked everywhere but belonged nowhere. Communities wanted their labor, yet declined "to accept them as full members of the community." Although migratory workers worked in the same places, doing similar jobs, they did not join forces in defending their common interests (3). Not only citizenship status divided them, but race and ethnicity, too.

One characteristic element faced by all migratory workers was that their work was seasonal, and they worked for specific periods of time, sometimes very short, at the whims of the employers. Farm employers

> want a labor supply . . . ready and willing to meet the short-term work requirements and which, on the other hand, will not impose social and economic problems on them or on their communities when the work is finished. . . . The demand for migratory workers is thus essentially twofold: To be ready to go to work when needed; to be gone when not needed.

To avoid the problems related to family migrants, "many farm employers prefer alien labor" (16). Wages for migratory workers were very low, particularly compared to manufacturing jobs; in 1949 the average earning for farmwork was $5 per day, with a yearly income of $514. Migratory workers worked an average of 101 days per year (70 days of farmwork and 31 days of nonfarmwork) (125, 128). Harsh treatment, low wages, and no job security explained why very few farmworkers returned the next year to their previous employer.

Migratory workers enjoyed almost none of the social protections extended to industrial workers, like unemployment benefits, social security, disability insurance, sickness pay, or minimum wage protection (17–19).

Migratory laborers worked mostly in cotton, fruits, vegetables, and sugar beets. Although they provided only 3 to 4 percent of the American agricultural output, their labor was significant at the critical periods of crop production. Migratory farmworkers were employed in a small number of large and highly specialized farms that employed a great quantity of labor. The approximately 125,000 such farms represented 2 percent of all American farms, and their crop production constituted 7 percent of all farm products. These laborers proliferated in those crops less amenable to mechanization. After the end of the war, increased agricultural production did not imply more jobs, as mechanization extended throughout. By 1949, only 40 percent of all farmworkers could get eight or more months of work per year (7–10). The commission's report questioned the contradictory nature of U.S. policy on alien labor. Most alien labor was used in large-scale farms that represented only 2 percent of all of the nation's farm units. The use of cheap alien labor gave these large farms, owned by big agricultural companies or corporations, a competitive advantage over smaller, family-owned farms (22).

Although North American migratory workers and alien labor in agriculture faced similar working and living conditions, they experienced different situations that were defined by their citizenship status. Ironically, alien labor enjoyed more government-provided protections than did American farmworkers:

> Domestic migratory farm workers not only have no protection through collective bargaining but employers as a rule refuse to give them the guarantees they extend to alien contract workers whom they import. These include guarantees of employment, workmen's compensation, medical care, standards of sanitation, and payment of the cost of transportation.

Like the Mexican *bracero* and the West Indian laborer, the Puerto Rican farmworker enjoyed a contract and the protection and representation of his government. Domestic farmworkers, nevertheless, "have one security which alien contract labor does not have: Whether they quit or are discharged, they cannot be deported" (5). Although considered in most ways as alien labor, Puerto Ricans enjoyed one right in common with other domestic workers: as U.S. citizens, they could not be deported. Puerto Rican farmworkers were, in a sense, in a more advantageous position than alien and domestic migratory workers.

THE PRESIDENT'S COMMISSION ON MIGRANT LABOR: THE PUERTO RICAN GOVERNMENT AS A LABOR CONTRACTOR

Puerto Ricans occupied a peculiar position within the structure of the U.S. migratory labor system: like the status of their island or their citizenship, they moved within the borders of the domestic and the foreign in the American polity. Even though they were U.S. citizens, their status had many similarities with that of foreign labor; however, even though they were considered by many as alien labor, they enjoyed rights of citizenship. Unlike the domestic migrant labor force, Puerto Ricans were protected by their government, like Mexicans and West Indians—that is, like foreign labor. But like domestic workers, they could move within the borders of the nation without fear of deportation. Although they were not usually considered part of the domestic supply of labor, they were not seen as alien labor, either. When the president's Commission on Migratory Labor reported in its main conclusion that the United States should decrease its dependence on alien labor for agriculture and create more jobs opportunities for its workers, it also recommended: "To meet any supplemental needs for agricultural labor that may develop, preference [should] be given to citizens of the offshore possessions of the United States, such as Hawaii and Puerto Rico" (36). That is, when the need arises, these particular U.S. citizens should receive preference over alien workers.

One important conclusion that comes from reading the report by the president's Commission on Migratory Labor is the extensive and significant role that governments played in providing alien labor to American agriculture. As the report concluded, during and after World War II, "government was the labor contractor." The report is referring here to the U.S. government, but the same could have been said of the foreign governments that were supplying labor to American agriculture, like Mexico, the Bahamas, and Jamaica. The same can also have been said of Puerto Rico, which, although technically not a foreign government, is treated as such throughout the report. In all of these cases, these governments were functioning as a labor contractor, that is, as intermediary agents regulating and organizing the movement of labor from their territories to the United States in order to provide labor to agricultural employers. There is a difference, though, in the procedure to implement this movement of labor between the Mexican experience and the West Indian and Puerto Rican ones. In the case of the *Bracero* Program, the governments of Mexico and the United States entered into an agreement that was later accepted by the workers and the employer. In this agreement, employers paid transportation costs, and there was no penalty for the workers if they abandoned work. In the West Indian and Puerto Rican cases, agricultural employers came to an agreement directly with these governments, which provided a contract stipulating the working conditions and responsibilities for both the employers and employees. Recruitment was mostly carried out by the government, and transportation was organized by the employer but paid for by the worker. The agreement allowed the employer to make deductions from the worker's pay to cover transportation costs, meals, and housing, as well as any other expenses included in the agreement. There was no mechanism established to settle disputes related to working and living conditions, as existed in the Mexican agreement. Work desertion in the West Indian case—as it would be in the Puerto Rican experience—was lesser than in the Mexican program due to the "vulnerability of the British West Indian workers to financial discipline, as provided in their agreements" (48). The report made clear the difference between the Mexican agreement and the West Indian and Puerto Rican ones:

> Mexico is the only country which requires an intergovernmental agreement; by coincidence, Mexico is the country which is ostensibly least interested in having its nationals do farm work in the United States. The greater concern of the British West Indies and of Puerto Rico to allow their people to enter into farm employment is reflected in the terms of their agreements, all of which are somewhat less costly to employers in one respect or another than is the Mexican agreement. (51)

Puerto Rican policy makers—from Muñoz Marín down—asserted throughout many decades that it was the government-approved contract and thus their government's protection that differentiated island farmworkers from other domestic workers in the United States. They claimed that the Puerto Rican government had to fight farm employers to get them to accept the contract and thus provide some basic protections and benefits for island migrant workers. But contrary to what these government functionaries argued, it was precisely because these workers had a contract that they were employed in the United States.

This discussion leads us to important questions: Why were Puerto Ricans hired to do farmwork in the United States? What was their comparative advantage over other alien workers or other domestic workers? The contract might be a reason: although it offered some important protections for Puerto Rican workers that other domestic workers did not enjoy, it also provided certain benefits to employers that made these workers attractive for hiring. To agricultural employers, dealing directly with the Puerto Rican government as a provider of labor guaranteed a reliable and safe source of labor when needed. And unlike agreements with contract alien labor, dealing with the Puerto Rican government, an authority from a U.S. territory, avoided all the bureaucratic entanglements of diplomatic understandings with foreign nations like Mexico, the Bahamas, or Jamaica. The Puerto Rican government provided a reliable labor force since it did all the screening and selection before signing the workers into a contract and did its best to ensure that the workers would return to the island. Through its migration agencies in Puerto Rico and the United States, the Puerto Rican government encouraged its workers to comply with their contract and return home and never to disturb the communities where they worked. Even when these workers did not return home, which was often, they would move to cities far away from the communities where they had been working, and once they were there, the Puerto Rican government would do its best through its Migration Division offices to find them work and help in their incorporation into American society. One stipulation that benefitted employers in the labor contract provided by the Puerto Rican government was the so-called prevailing wage agreement. Puerto Rican functionaries boasted that their contract guaranteed Puerto Rican workers the same wages earned by other domestic workers and that island labor did not lower wages in the areas where they worked. Nonetheless, the prevailing wage was not set by the federal government nor by collective negotiations, but by the farmers themselves before the beginning of each season. The presidential commission's report characterized the prevailing wage as "worse than meaningless." It argued that a wage that was set by the employer with "no regard to whether it is a sufficient wage to attract workers" has no value in determining the price of labor in this area. It continued: "This is especially true when contract foreign workers are brought in at the arbitrary wage rate which then inevitably tends to set the pattern of wages in the locality." That is, the prevailing wage was used by employers to keep wages below their true value in the labor market. As a consequence, the prevailing wage standard set in the contracts with foreign labor, including Puerto Rico, was used to depress wages for domestic farmworkers. Contrary to the prevailing wage standard in industrial employment, there was no collective bargaining in agriculture setting the price of labor. As a consequence of this mechanism, domestic labor was not attracted to agricultural work, and thus an artificial scarcity of labor would require the importation of foreign labor (59–61).

The hiring of Puerto Rican workers was possible only after USES had established a shortage of domestic workers for the industry and allowed the importation of foreign workers to satisfy that demand. But the presumed labor shortage existed because the prevailing wage rate was insufficient to attract domestic workers. Domestic workers also faced another disadvantage with regard to alien and Puerto Rican workers since they had no contract that provided certain benefits and protections. Thus, the Puerto Rican government reproduced and benefitted from a system that kept wages depressed for domestic workers and allowed the employment of Puerto Rican farmworkers in the United States for wages that were lower that what the market would establish. That is, Puerto Ricans were employed in agriculture because their labor was cheaper than the available domestic labor supply.

But would not the other workers' benefits of the Puerto Rican labor contract increase the price of their labor with respect to domestic workers? Indeed, but the contract also offered another element that was beneficial to employers: the Puerto Rican government as a labor contractor. By accepting the contract, the Puerto Rican government guaranteed employers an organized and reliable source of labor, something that domestic migratory labor could not offer. Although USES determined labor shortages and the areas in need of labor, it did not organize the movement of labor from one region to the other; in fact, the commission's report was highly critical of the agency in this regard.[14] Migrant workers had to move on their own, often with families, or get work through the use of private labor contractors. The latter served as intermediaries between the workers and the employers. As the report stated: "The labor contractor system is essentially a means by which the employer of migratory farm workers avoids the responsibilities of obtaining and managing his labor" (91). But the use of private labor contractors was often problematic for employers. Although employers would have little contact with the workers, the workers would often have conflicting relationships with contractors. Many contractors would steal from the workers' pay, charge exorbitant fees for finding employment, and mislead them regarding their working and living conditions; more often than not, they would leave the farm after delivering the workers. The first expeditions of Puerto Rican farmworkers after the end of the war were organized by private contractors; the host of problems these created for workers and local communities was one of the given reasons for the government's intervention in the migration of farmworkers.

According to the commission's report, worker desertion in farms using labor contractors was high, and workers would not return the next year to work in the same place, forcing employers to devote time and resources every year to the process of contracting of workers. The use of labor contractors was not the most efficient means of getting labor. On the other hand, "when the employment occurs under the contractual relationship which legal aliens and Puerto Ricans have, there is no occasion for the labor contractor or the crew leader to introduce himself as an employment intermediary." Although "foreign and Puerto Rican work contracts" provided workers with guaranteed wages and terms of employment that could increase labor costs for the employer, they also provided "stability in the employer-employee relationship" (105). The contract and the intervention of governments provided alien and Puerto Rican contract labor with a means to deal with grievances, contrary to what "the typical domestic migrant has, which is to move on to something else, if he feels he has been treated unjustly" (106).

Another major advantage of alien and Puerto Rican contract labor was that their governments could guarantee large numbers of workers to associations of agricultural employers, something that individual migrant workers or even private labor contractors could not do. By the early 1950s, the Puerto Rican government was dealing almost exclusively with farmers' associations like the Michigan Fields Corp., the Garden State Service Cooperative Association, the Glassboro Service Association in New Jersey, and the Minnesota Canners Association. These were four of the best examples of agricultural associations mentioned in the commission's report, and all four hired labor from Puerto Rico. Encouraged by the U.S. government, these associations proliferated during World War II as a mechanism to provide labor to American agriculture. They allowed farmers and companies to pool their resources to hire large numbers of workers and guaranteed that they could fulfill the requirements of the labor contracts.[15] The Puerto Rican government would provide many workers, but only to these associations. These associations allowed individual farmers to have access to a secure source of Puerto Rican workers through the pooling of labor, that is, sharing workers throughout a season in order to guarantee the minimum number of working hours required by the Puerto Rican contract (160 hours for a four-week period). Organizing the pooling of labor on such a scale with domestic migrant workers was much more time-consuming and costly for farm employers. Furthermore, the Puerto Rican government implemented a very exhaustive process of screening and selecting workers in Puerto Rico in order to provide U.S. agricultural employers with a reliable labor force for the duration of the contract.

As the report by the Presidential Commission on Migratory Labor concluded, the labor contract given to alien labor, the relationship with foreign governments, and the creation and expansion of farmers' associations provided American agriculture with some "orderly" relations. In fact, the commission concluded that it was having an impact in improving working conditions for domestic migrant labor (174). By the early 1950s, Puerto Rican farmworkers, through the government's FPP, had become part of American agriculture's migratory labor system. The Puerto Rican government played a fundamental role in this process.

ORGANIZING PUERTO RICAN LABOR FOR U.S. AGRICULTURE

After the United States took over the island in 1898, Puerto Rico became a source of cheap labor for U.S. corporations largely based on certain constitutional and legal exclusions from the American polity sustained by the notion of the unincorporated territory justified by the Supreme Court in 1901. But these exclusions remained even after Puerto Ricans became U.S. citizens under the Jones Act of 1917. For example, Puerto Ricans were excluded for decades from the federal minimum wage approved by Congress under the New Deal, something that Congress could do under the legal and constitutional exceptions approved by the Supreme Court for the territory. And even though the PPD had emerged in 1938 as a party of reform and of "social justice" for workers and peasants, by 1947 its Operation Bootstrap model for economic development was designed to market Puerto Ricans as cheap labor to U.S. corporations as one major incentive for these to settle on the island. The Commonwealth status approved in 1952 allowed Puerto Rico to enjoy fiscal autonomy over local matters so that the island government could keep offering local tax exemptions and cheap labor to U.S. corporations going to Puerto Rico. And although the Commonwealth status was supposed to represent a new era in U.S.–Puerto Rico relations, the island remained an unincorporated territory of the United States. Thus, the island's marginal standing in the American polity allowed Puerto Rico's government to use the territory's exclusion from certain federal laws—like minimum wage and environmental protection—as incentives to attract American capital to the island.

Months after the government approved the Industrial Incentives Act in 1947 that launched Operation Bootstrap, another act with far-reaching consequences for the island was approved: the Migration Law. Although less remembered than its economic counterpart, this law is of equal significance for the island's postwar social and economic development. It acknowledged that the organization and encouragement of migration would be government policy from then on. Migration functionaries liked to say that the government's migration policy was the other face of Operation Bootstrap. And, indeed, it was. While Operation Bootstrap sought to provide cheap labor to U.S. corporations going to Puerto Rico, its migration policy allowed Puerto Ricans to work in U.S. agriculture and other areas of the American economy as cheap labor as well.

The Puerto Rican government became a labor contractor that, by moving farm labor from Puerto Rico to the U.S. mainland, provided a source of cheap labor to U.S. agriculture. According to Sierra Berdecía, the BEM, "facing the surplus of unemployed workers in agriculture during the dead season . . . has acted as an intermediary between workers and mainland employers who need workers precisely during the same season."[16] The BEM became part of USES after the approval of the Wagner-Peyser act of 1950. Under this system, U.S. agricultural employers justified their demand for labor and requested Puerto Rican workers to satisfy these needs. Through its employment offices in Puerto Rico, the BEM evaluated and selected the workers able to go to the United States. These workers would go there with a contact approved by the Puerto Rican government. Once in the United States, these contract workers were serviced by the Migration Division. It made sure that employers abided by the contract and provided services for the "integration and adaptation" of the workers to their new environment. BEM opened regional offices in Puerto Rico's major municipalities: San Juan, Ponce, Mayagüez, Arecibo, Aguadilla, Caguas, Humacao, and Guayama. Another branch office was opened in 1950 at the airport.[17]

The BEM's Farm Placement Program was designed to move the surplus labor from the decaying sugar industry to U.S. farms. Unlike other sugar-producing areas, the sugar industry in Puerto Rico did not experience mechanization because of the excess supply of cheap labor on the island; "as a consequence, the agricultural phase of the sugar industry in Puerto Rico finds itself in a primitive state of technological development which hinders it from paying wages adequate to the living necessities of our workers."[18] Total employment in agriculture decreased from 203,000 workers in 1950–51 to 164,000 in 1954–55, and the total number of unemployed workers in agriculture increased from 21,000 in 1946–47 to 37,000 in 1950–51. The overwhelming majority of the unemployed in agriculture came from the sugar industry: from 15,000 in 1946–47 to 27,000 in 1950–51.[19] The number of unemployment benefit claims in the sugar industry increased from 98,628 in 1949–50 to 125,099 in 1952–53, with almost all claims coming from workers in the agricultural field. Nevertheless, the number of unemployment claims in the sugar industry decreased to 85,690 in 1956–57, in large measure as a consequence of migration and the government's FPP.

Even with the impact of migration in providing employment for the workers in the sugar industry, the unemployment rate in agriculture increased from 14.9 percent in 1953–53 to 17.8 percent in 1954–55. By 1960, agricultural workers represented only 24 percent of the island's labor force, and sugar workers represented only 36 percent of all those working in agriculture.[20] Not only was agriculture decaying in Puerto Rico, particularly the sugar industry, but the wages on the island were far lower than those in American agriculture. In 1959–60, for example, the prevailing wage set by the Puerto Rican government's contract for farmworkers going to the U.S. mainland was 80 cents per hour, with higher rates in tobacco harvesting, at 95 cents per hour, and $1 per hour in flower farms and greenhouses. In Puerto Rico that same year, the highest hourly wage in agriculture was paid in the industrial phase of sugar manufacturing, at 68 cents, while working in the cane fields paid 44 cents. Hourly wages in other agricultural areas were even lower: 45 cents at poultry farms, 43 cents in pineapple farms, 40 cents processing tobacco leaves, 37 cents at flower farms, and 28 cents at minor crop farms.[21]

One of the consequences of the Michigan experience in 1950 was that the Puerto Rican government placed more attention on the screening and selection process of farmworkers going to the United States under the FPP. In order to avert the extensive discontent among farmworkers due to the living and working conditions in farm camps and to reduce the number of workers abandoning work before the end of their contract, labor functionaries made clear to prospective migrants the duties and conditions they would face on the U.S. mainland. The Department of Labor described the orientation process by 1952 as follows:

> Local offices receive copies of the clearance orders from the central office and the quota of workers allocated to each of them. The local farm labor representative makes a preliminary selection of the best qualified workers to fill the order and called-in them. Complete orientation is given to the workers before selection by the employer or his representative as to the following points: 1) place of employment 2) name of employer 3) transportation to the mainland 4) wages 5) duration of the work agreement 6) kind of work to be performed 7) working conditions in labor camp 8) insurance policies 9) duties and rights of workers 10) compliance with the contract 11) importance of identification cards 12) any other matter of interest to the workers.[22]

By this time, the local offices of the Farm Placement Program had to provide the BEM with a register of not only those interested in migration but those ready to move at little notice.[23]

By 1952 the Department of Labor had intensified the screening and selection process for prospective farmworkers going to U.S. farms. For example, it required a set of documents necessary for the worker to apply to go to U.S. farms under the government's contract, including a birth certificate, a health certificate from a government health clinic (no more than six months old), a police certificate of good behavior to attest that the applicant had no criminal record (not older than six months), a reference letter from a farmer confirming that the applicant was a "bona-fide" farmworker, $30 for air transportation, and an identification photo. The signed reference letter from the farmer had to include information regarding the applicant's agricultural jobs and whether the worker was "efficient and responsible in carrying out agricultural tasks." The purpose of this requirement was to exclude all those unable to do the arduous and demanding farmwork in the United States and thus prevent worker desertion. The application form for the FPP also required that workers detail their working experience and the specific agricultural tasks performed. The police certificate would exclude not only those with a criminal record but also those linked to political or labor union activism. After workers were selected, labor officials provided them with a photo ID to be presented at the time of departure in Puerto Rico and arrival at a United States airport and at the farm contracted for work. The ID was used for identification purposes for the placement program, as proof of citizenship in the U.S. mainland, and to prevent unauthorized persons from going to the United States under the placement program. Recruitment was held at the local offices of the Department of Labor or at specific town halls throughout the island.[24]

A flyer for the BEM's Farm Placement Program is quite indicative of the department's marketing toward prospective migrants. It featured a big drawing of a *jíbaro con pava* (the traditional peasant with a straw hat—also the symbol of the PPD) with the words "TRABAJADOR AGRICOLA" (farmworker). "If you are planning to work in the United States" described the advantages of going to do farmwork with a government contract, which guaranteed a $10,000 air flight insurance paid by the employer; an employer's bond to provide payment, health insurance, compensation insurance for work-related accidents, wages and work for 160 hours per four weeks, and adequate housing; and no labor contractor fee.[25]

As shown in table 6, the number of Puerto Ricans leaving the island to settle in the United States increased dramatically after 1947–48, according to Department of Labor statistics. Net migration (departures minus arrivals) in the 1950s reached a peak of close to 75,000 in 1952–53 and a low of nearly 14,000 in 1960–61. Total migration from 1947–48 to 1960–61 was 558,388, for an average of nearly 40,000 migrants per year during this period. The Department of Labor argued that the ebb and flow in the number of people leaving the island was due to pull factors (job availability) in the United States. During this period, the department characterized these migration statistics as "individual migrants" leaving the island on their own; this conclusion was based on the idea that workers going to the U.S. mainland under the FPP returned to the island after ending their work contract.[26] On the other hand, as shown in table 7, the flow of agricultural workers going to the United States under the FPP kept a steady pace throughout the decade. From 1951–52 to 1960–61,

TABLE 6
NET YEARLY MIGRATION, 1947–48 TO 1960–61, BY FISCAL YEAR

1947–48	28,031
1948–49	33,053
1949–50	34,155
1950–51	41,919
1951–52	60,642
1952–53	74,603
1953–54	44,209
1954–55	31,182
1955–56	61,647
1956–57	48,284
1957–58	25,956
1958–59	37,203
1959–60	23,742
1960–61	13,762

Sources: GPR, Comm. Labor: *Eighteenth Annual Report 1948–49*, table 5; *Nineteenth Annual Report 1949–50*, 63; *Twenty-Seventh Annual Report 1960–61*, 60.

some 129,372 farmworkers were placed in U.S. farms (a total of 152,253 since 1947–48) for an average of close to 13,000 per year; this movement of workers reached its peak during this decade in 1956–57, with nearly 16,000 placements. The number of farm placements by the government program stayed the same throughout the decade, while the number of migrants going on their own varied from year to year, influenced by the vagaries of the labor market forces. In fact, while net migration decreased during the 1960s, in part due to better economic conditions on the island, the number of workers placed in the United States by the FPP increased steadily during this period. That is, while individual migration fluctuated and even decreased in the 1960s, the migration flow organized by the government kept a steady pace and even increased in this period. In addition, the Department of Labor estimated that between 10,000 and 15,000 farmworkers went on their own to the United States every year to work in agriculture.[27]

The first group of Puerto Rican farmworkers going to the United States under the government's placement program went to New Jersey; later, other farm employers began to hire Puerto Ricans in Pennsylvania, Connecticut, Massachusetts, Indiana, New York, Minnesota, Washington, Delaware, Michigan, and Wisconsin.[28] As shown in table 8, by the mid-1950s the overwhelming majority of Puerto Rican workers in the FPP went to four states: New

TABLE 7
BEM JOB PLACEMENTS IN THE UNITED STATES, BY FISCAL YEAR

YEAR	FARM PLACEMENTS BEM-PR*	MIGRATION DIVISION	TOTAL
1947–48	2,533	—	2,533
1948–49	5,796	—	5,796
1949–50	8,846	3,966	12,812
1950–51	5,706	—	—
1951–52	12,491	8,108	20,599
1952–53	14,417	13,167	27,584
1953–54	14,088	10,751	24,839
1954–55	11,628	10,683	22,311
1955–56	11,750	13,885	25,635
1956–57	15,776	11,720	27,496
1957–58	12,180	11,147	23,327
1958–59	11,728	10,482	22,210
1959–60	11,733	12,767	24,500
1960–61	13,581	10,954	24,535

*Placements of farmworkers by the Bureau of Employment and Migration in Puerto Rico.
Sources: GPR, Comm. Labor: *Nineteenth Annual Report 1949–50*, 60; *Twenty-First Annual Report 1951–52*, 39; *Twenty-Third Annual Report 1953–54*, 47–48; *Twenty-Fourth Annual Report 1954–55*, 55; *Twenty-Third Annual Report 1956–57*, 51; *Vigésimo Cuarto Informe Anual 1957–58*, 66–67; *Twenty-Fifth Annual Report 1958–59*, 42, 57; and *Twenty-Seventh Annual Report 1960–61*, 53, 61.

Jersey, Pennsylvania, New York, and Connecticut, with the largest contingent by far going to New Jersey. During this decade, New Jersey agricultural interests hired around half of all Puerto Rican contract laborers.

The number of agricultural cooperatives and individual employers hiring Puerto Ricans under contract increased after the creation of the FPP in Puerto Rico. In 1948, four employers hired island farmworkers, eight did so in 1949, fourteen in 1950, and thirty-six in 1951. But by the end of the decade, the vast majority of farm placements by the Puerto Rican government were concentrated in just a few agricultural associations. In 1957–58, for example, 9,948 of the 12,180 farm placements were hired by the Garden State Service Association, a mega-union of agricultural cooperatives and associations in the Northeast, mostly in New Jersey, New York, Pennsylvania, and Connecticut. But even here, the distribution was highly skewed: the Glassboro Service Association from New Jersey alone hired 5,772 Puerto Ricans, close to half of all placements that year.[29] By the end of the 1950s, the Puerto Rican govern-

TABLE 8
PUERTO RICO FARM PLACEMENTS IN THE UNITED STATES, BY STATE AND SELECTED FISCAL YEARS

	1955–56	1957–58	1958–59	1959–60	1960–61
Connecticut	1,200	829	1,992	1,477	2,070
Delaware	210	591	863	1,127	1,284
Illinois	—	—	—	—	20
Indiana	—	—	62	95	25
Maine	9	33	30	28	41
Maryland	106	161	175	164	252
Massachusetts	875	512	457	453	563
Michigan	—	56	23	22	—
New Hampshire	46	101	84	78	100
New Jersey	6,704	6,503	6,619	6,476	6,882
New York	2,536	1,788	1,108	962	1,446
Ohio	—	—	4	7	6
Pennsylvania	1,903	1,600	1,443	818	875
Rhode Island	21	6	25	—	5
Wisconsin	—	—	6	26	12
Total	12,180	13,610	11,728	11,733	13,581

Sources: GPR, Comm. Labor: *Twenty-Fifth Annual Report 1955–56*, 47; *Vigésimo Cuarto Informe Anual, 1957–58*, 79; *Twenty-Fifth Annual Report 1958–59*, 42; *Twenty-Seventh Annual Report 1960–61*, 69.

ment was indeed a labor contractor for American agriculture, but just for a few major farm conglomerates.

The Puerto Rican government functioned not only as a provider of farm labor from Puerto Rico to U.S. agricultural interests but also as an intermediary between Puerto Rican labor and other employers in the U.S. mainland. The Migration Division was created to facilitate the integration and adaptation of Puerto Ricans in the United States. Among its many functions was to find employment for Puerto Ricans already settled in the U.S. mainland. From 1951–51 to 1960–61, the division's employment program placed 113,664 persons in the United States (see table 7). Like the FPP in Puerto Rico, the division's job placement program kept a constant pace throughout the decade of close to 12,000 placements per year. The majority of job placements by the Migration Division in the United States were in low-paying manufacturing jobs. The total number of job placements in the United States by the Puerto Rican government during this period—be it through the Farm Placement Program in Puerto Rico or the Migration Division in the United States—reached 243,036.

THE MIGRATION DIVISION: GUIDING THE INCORPORATION OF INDIVIDUAL MIGRATION

While the FPP provided farm labor to U.S. agricultural interests, the Migration Division's functions were more complicated. It also functioned as an intermediary between Puerto Rican labor and U.S. employers, and in addition it had to fulfill the task of promoting the incorporation of Puerto Ricans in the United States. While the government in Puerto Rico could mobilize the administrative structures of the colonial state to organize and encourage migration, the workings of the Migration Division in the United States were somewhat more complex and delicate. This extension of the Puerto Rican government in the United States functioned as a labor provider to U.S. employers, but it had additional functions as an intermediary between Puerto Ricans and the American polity: between Puerto Ricans and the different state structures in the United States (federal, state, local) and between islanders and the American community in general. For several decades, the Puerto Rican government through the Migration Division became the "representative" of Puerto Ricans in the United States for employers and government institutions at multiple levels.[30]

The primary function of the Migration Division was to "orient and advise" those Puerto Ricans living in the United States in their "adaptation" and incorporation to American society. For the most part, the division focused on those going to the U.S. mainland on their own; that is, it was created to oversee the flow of individual migration settling in the United States. Since the formulation of its migration policy, the Department of Labor tried to influence the movement of those who migrated to the United States on their own, always a greater number than those going to work on government contract. As stated in the department's 1948–49 annual report:

> The Bureau tries to reach these people through the radio with talks on climate, food, living and working conditions and information on requirements for entrance into the public schools. They are constantly warned of the danger of unscrupulous persons who might attempt to swindle them out of their money in their ticket fares, in cost of transportation upon arrival from the airport to their residence. They are advised as to the duties and responsibilities of citizenship and information required by individual cases is gladly furnished. Conferences before groups are given in addition to printed and mimeographed material and personal interviews. The material is distributed through mayors, public welfare offices, vocational schools and other agencies of the Government.[31]

In 1956, the department opened its Traveler Orientation Section, with offices throughout the island; its main function was to "orient and inform" prospective migrants regarding job and housing opportunities in the United States outside of New York City.

This program underlined for those planning to migrate the need to know English, to have a job or skill, to be in good health, and to be prepared to adapt to the culture and customs of the new country. That year, orientation committees for the island's mayors were organized in a majority of municipalities, using these government structures to orient prospective migrants. Initially, the orientation program focused on agricultural workers going under contract to the United States, but after 1951 a greater emphasis was placed on those going on their own, which represented the bulk of Puerto Rican migration. In 1959–60, for example, migration functionaries made visits to 123 towns and 70 rural districts to provide orientation to prospective migrants, using both films and printed material. The department estimated that 170,000 persons were oriented though this program that year.[32] The department's orientation office at the San Juan International Airport provided information and advice to those going on their own to the United States on issues regarding jobs, education, and housing; it also offered counseling on other areas of settlement outside of New York City and tried to discourage those interested in moving to Florida and other Southern states.[33]

The Migration Division was in charge of providing orientation and services to Puerto Ricans once they moved to the U.S. mainland, including those who came under the FPP. By 1956, the Migration Division had twelve offices in the United States, mostly in the Northeast, where Puerto Ricans were working or settling by then. In addition to the central office in New York and the two main offices in New York and Chicago, there were local offices in Hartford, Connecticut; Boston; Keyport and Camden in New Jersey; Rochester, Middletown, and Riverhead in New York, and Hamburg, Pennsylvania.[34] *La oficina de Puerto Rico* (or the Commonwealth office) became a kind of consular office for many Puerto Ricans in the United States. Even in New York City, the oldest U.S. community, the division replaced Congressman Marcantonio as a provider of services and protection for the tens of thousands of newcomers from the island. As table 9 shows, as the Puerto Rican community increased in size during the 1950s, so did the number of visitors to division offices throughout the United States. Even though the operations of the Chicago office increased during this decade—reflecting the growing community there—the New York office remained the biggest in terms of functionaries and services provided, a reflection of the status of the city as the major Puerto Rican settlement in the United States.

TABLE 9
TOTAL SERVICE REQUESTS IN MIGRATION DIVISION, BY FISCAL YEAR

YEAR	TOTAL SERVICES RENDERED*	NEW YORK OFFICE	CHICAGO OFFICE	EMPLOYMENT PROGRAM
1948–49	19,320	19,320	—	10,815*
1949–50	18,450	18,450	7,451	14,361**
1950–51	16,332	16,332	—	9,874**
1951–52	26,833	26,833	—	20,022**
1952–53	45,321	33,783	11,538	23,141**
1953–54	54,835	37,348	17,487	27,578**
1954–55	57,673	41,118	16,555	30,112**
1955–56	61,973	41,961	20,012	32,462**
1956–57	70,027	45,374	24,553	54,980***
1957–58	84,671	53,792	19,533	53,996***
1958–59	82,487	54,128	17,977	59,202****
1959–60	80,884	52,672	21,378	66,326****
1960–61	77,523	52,987	19,815	67,483****

*Total number of persons seeking services in all of the U.S. offices of the Migration Division.
**New York Office only.
***New York and Chicago offices only.
****All Migration Division offices.
Sources: Data from GPR, Comm. Labor: *Nineteenth Annual Report 1949–1950*, 62; *Twenty-Fifth Annual Report 1955–56*, 53, 63; *Twenty-Third Annual Report 1956–57*, 56, 58; *Vigésimo Cuarto Informe Anual 1957–1958*; *Twenty-Fifth Annual Report 1958–59*, 57; *Twenty-Sixth Annual Report 1959–60*, 56–57; *Twenty-Seventh Annual Report 1960–61*, 53, 61.

As indicated by table 9, the most numerous of the services provided by the Migration Division was giving employment information to migrants; the majority of visits to its offices were people in search of jobs. When the Department of Labor began to produce data in 1956–57 on the movement of people to and from the island, 33.8 percent of those who departed by air that year went to the United States in search of jobs; 70 percent were between the working ages of fifteen and forty-four years old.[35]

In 1955–56, the Employment Section of the New York office of the Migration Division referred a total of 11,835 persons for employment, out of which 6,999 were hired. The overwhelming majority (74 percent) of old and new applicants that year were unskilled, and another 11 percent were semiskilled; the majority was male. Most of these placements (66 percent) were in manufacturing, followed by agriculture (15 percent), service (13 percent), and office and professional (6 percent). According to the Department of Labor, the major reason for these people not finding jobs was their lack of skills and English fluency. In that same year, the Chicago office referred 8,710 persons for employment, out of which 7,009 were hired, mostly in manufacturing, followed by services and lastly in agriculture.[36] While a majority of placements by the BEM in Puerto Rico itself were in manufacturing, supplying labor to *Fomento*-subsidized plants, most of their placements in the United States were in agriculture, under the FPP. On the other hand, the majority of placements by the Migration Division were in nonagricultural jobs. For example, in 1954–55, 5,768 of the 6,999 placements by the New York office and 2,480 of the 3,684 placements by the Chicago office were in nonagricultural work.[37] As with its counterpart in Puerto Rico, the BEM, the Migration Division placed Puerto Ricans in the United States in low-paying jobs in labor-intensive manufacturing industries.

Besides its employment placement program, the Migration Division was structured to provide information and services to Puerto Ricans in other areas of their incorporation to American society. The Service Section was in charge of providing aid and support to Puerto Rican farm and manufacturing workers in the United States placed by the government's placement programs on the island and the U.S. mainland. The services provided included direct negotiation for employment, inspection of agricultural camps and living quarters, visits to camps and factories to investigate working and living conditions and accidents in and outside the job, and intervention in wage claims and medical assistance. The section serviced 16,834 migrant workers in the United States in 1951–52, up to 22,088 in 1953–54, and 24,127 in 1954–55. In 1960–61, there were 20,145 island farmworkers spread over eleven states in the Northeast and Midwest. That year, division field workers made 1,113 visits to camps and farms where the Puerto Ricans worked: 516 visits were related to complaints filed by workers and employers, and 597 visits were to instruct both workers and employers about the labor contract and its related rights, duties, and responsibilities. Some 5,948 workers were contacted personally that year.[38]

The major purpose of the division's Identification Section was to give proof of citizenship to Puerto Ricans for employment, education, health, and welfare services. The section also worked with state and city agencies regarding the correct verification and interpretation of documents from Puerto Rico. In addition, along with federal and state agencies, it implemented a campaign against the fraudulent use of Puerto Rican birth certificates by undocumented immigrants. In 1957–58, some 7,325 persons requested services from this section.[39]

The aim of the division's Social Service Section was to aid Puerto Rican families in confronting the major issues of adaptation to U.S. society, like insufficient economic resources, domestic relations, health and welfare, juvenile delinquency, and other matters in the field of social work. The majority of problems presented by clients were related to economic matters, followed by housing concerns and complaints and compensations. In 1957–58, a year characterized by an economic downturn, the New York and Chicago offices received 7,346 visits to the Social Service Section, mostly related to unemployment, housing, and welfare issues.[40] In 1957–58, some 9,679 Puerto Ricans received assistance by the Travel Aid Society at the Idlewild International Airport; two Puerto Rican social workers employed by the Migration Division worked in this office to take care of island migrants.[41]

The Education Section functioned mostly to provide access to English learning materials and classes for Puerto Rican adults and children living in the United States. Its "Learn English" campaign distributed fifty thousand copies of the pamphlet *"La llave del exito"* ("The Key to Success") in 1953–54; it distributed two hundred and forty thousand pamphlets in 1957–58. In that year, the English campaign extended to twenty additional cities in the United States, and the New York City public school system expanded its English classes for Puerto Rican children and adults throughout the city.[42] The Department of Labor claimed that ten thousand Puerto Ricans were enrolled in English classes for adults in the autumn of 1954 as a result of the Migration Division campaigns. This section also coordinated a teacher exchange program between Puerto Rico and schools in the United States.[43]

Throughout the 1950s, the division's Education Section and Community Organization Section organized the *"Inscríbase y vote"* ("Register and Vote") campaign, distributing tens of thousands of *"Use su derecho a votar"* ("Exercise Your Right to Vote") pamphlets. In its 1960–61 annual report, the Department of Labor claimed that one of the "outstanding achievements" of the division's work that year was "the tangible demonstration of the awakening interest in politics" by U.S. Puerto Ricans as a consequence of "the registering and voting campaign during the elections" in the United States that year.[44] From 1957 to 1959, the Information and Public Relations Section produced 1,422,200 prints of the division's many publications. These included ones aimed at the Puerto Rican public, providing information on English programs, electoral registration, housing, employment, health services, and welfare services. There were also publications directed at the American public in general: these provided information on Puerto Ricans as American citizens, their culture, and their contributions to the local community.[45]

PUERTO RICO'S GOVERNMENT AND PUERTO RICANS' UNCERTAIN FUTURE IN THE UNITED STATES

In the most extensive study of the Migration Division so far, Lapp argues that this institution failed to become an "ethnic representative" of the Puerto Rican community in the United States. He called it "an ethnic bureaucracy manque," an extension of the Puerto Rican government in the United States that had no constituency of its own and responded to the goals of the PPD government on the island.[46] In the 1960s, the U.S. Puerto Rican communities developed their own leadership and agendas, pushing the division to the margins and developing their own representation in the American polity. The election of a pro-statehood government under the New Progressive Party in 1968 further delegitimized the division's goals and internal functioning. Although the FPP lasted well into the 1970s, a lawsuit by apple growers questioning the need to hire Puerto Ricans under a labor contract finally put an end to the program.[47]

The limited success of the Puerto Rican government's placement programs in Puerto Rico and the United States in finding not only good jobs, but jobs in general in the U.S. mainland, shows the limits of the colonial state as a labor contractor. Be it in agriculture, through the FPP, or in manufacturing, mostly through the Migration Division's employment program, the Puerto Rican government for the most part channeled migrants to low-paying jobs with no long-term employment security and benefits. And although the government's labor contract offered protections and benefits to island farmworkers that domestic farmworkers largely did not enjoy, the actions of the Puerto Rican government in protecting these workers were not always the best. In general terms, the FPP benefitted U.S. agricultural interests. The fact that it sustained and reproduced the prevailing wage reflects how the labor contract was beneficial to American farm interests, in addition to providing them with a reliable and continued source of cheap labor.

Furthermore, the literature on Puerto Rican migration and the government's own records attest to the extensive and continued instances where farm employers broke the labor contracts with no major penalties and consequences. Hundreds of boxes in Puerto Rico's national archives belonging to the Department of Labor's FPP are filled with farmworkers' claims of contract violations.[48] Furthermore, the fact that more Puerto Ricans decided to work in U.S. agriculture on their own with no government contract, as the department continuously complained, reflects on how little farmworkers thought of the celebrated contract or the government's protection. In general, the Puerto Rican government failed to confront farm interests with contract violations, be it in terms of contract duration, wages, or working and living conditions. The government's own track record in enforcing the contract and its ideology of cooperation with farming companies undermined the validity of the labor contract itself.[49] At the end, the Puerto Rican government's FPP maintained and sustained the migratory labor system that benefitted U.S. agricultural interests in the postwar period at the expense of the laborers it was supposedly designed to protect.[50]

Despite the programs and services provided to Puerto Rican migrants in the United States by Puerto Rico's government through the Migration Division, significant sectors of the mainland community faced persistent rates of poverty and economic and social marginalization for decades. Although many Puerto Ricans experienced economic, social, and educational improvements after the 1950s, particularly second-generation cohorts, the economic and social indicators of the Puerto Rican community by the 1970s were rather dismal, according to the U.S. Commission on Civil Rights: in 1974, 32.6 percent of Puerto Rican families living in the United States remained in poverty, and 85 percent of New York City's one million Puerto Ricans lived in low-income neighborhoods. Puerto Rican family earnings were only 59 percent of the national average, 24.5 percent of Puerto Rican families received income from public welfare, and in 1972, 8.8 percent of Puerto Rican men and 17.6 percent of women were unemployed—rates higher than the national average. In addition, 60 percent of all Puerto Rican families living in poverty were headed by a female single parent.[51] Not only were Puerto Ricans employed in low-paying jobs in agriculture, manufacturing, and services, but they settled primarily in areas of the Northeast facing deindustrialization in the postwar period—New York City is the best example—factors that were not conducive to their economic and social mobility. Characterized by lower job skills, limited English fluency, and less education, large sectors of the immigrant generation continuously faced lower indicators of economic and social achievements than the second generation.[52] In addition to these factors, the commission stated that "the evidence is compelling that racial, ethnic, and sex discrimination are barriers to job opportunities for Puerto Ricans."[53]

While the Puerto Rican government cannot be blamed for the poverty that existed in Puerto Rico by 1945, its postwar economic model largely benefited U.S. capital and sustained an economic and colonial order that marketed Puerto Ricans as a source of cheap labor. Similarly, while the Puerto Rican government was not the cause of postwar migration, its postwar migration policies encouraged, promoted, and even organized the mass movement of people from Puerto Rico that forever transformed the lives of Puerto Ricans in the years to come. As Acosta-Belén and Santiago indicate, while traditional human capital models of migration argue that it is the highly skilled in the homeland society that are most likely to move, in the case of Puerto Rico, it was those considered surplus labor that the government encouraged to migrate to the United States in the postwar period.[54] Despite its efforts to facilitate their incorporation into and adaptation to the metropolitan society, the Puerto Rican government's policies could not overcome the economic and social obstacles these migrants faced in the U.S. mainland. In concluding his widely influential study of the Migration Division, Lapp contends that the Puerto Rican government became an "apologist for an economic order that marginalized Puerto Ricans."[55]

The Puerto Rican government's Operation Bootstrap and migration programs were designed to provide economic, social, and political stability to Puerto Rico in the postwar period. While Operation Bootstrap presented an economic development plan to provide economic growth and industrialization as a means of turning the island into a modern and politically stable society, migration was supposed to ease the pressures created by the island's overpopulation and allow the realization of the PPD's economic and political goals. In the minds of Puerto Rican and American policy makers, the 1950s became the golden era of economic and political development in Puerto Rico. During the Cold War period, in an attempt to win the "hearts and minds" of peoples in the so-called Third World, the U.S. government presented Puerto Rico as a showcase of capitalist development and political democracy imbued with American ideals and institutions.[56] Nowhere in the local, national, and global campaigns showcasing Puerto Rico was the mass migration of Puerto Ricans to the metropolitan territory mentioned as one major reason for the apparent economic success of this era.

The limits of Operation Bootstrap in providing continued economic growth became obvious by the late 1960s, as the labor-intensive, low-paying manufacturing enterprises that the program attracted to the island began to leave for other areas of the global economy with lower wages and restrictions. The situation became so critical that by the early 1970s, the federal government had to intervene to prevent a furthering of the economic crisis and a possible social and political crisis as well. The increase in federal transfers to Puerto Rico sustained a weakened economy and a growing poor and marginal sector, as well as the colonial government. In addition, the metropolitan state once again used the island's marginal position within the American polity as an unincorporated territory to create a special and protected space for U.S. capital with the Internal Revenue Service's Section 936, which allowed American transnational corporations to produce huge amounts of profits on the island as the new bootstrap for economic growth and development. Although this metropolitan strategy benefitted American corporations, it created few jobs since mostly capital-intensive manufacturing plants came under this corporate welfare scheme. The end of Section 936, along with massive corruption and incompetence by successive PPD and *Partido Nuevo Progresista* (PNP [New Progressive Party]) administrations, plunged the island in a spiral of economic and social disarray that has persisted into the twenty-first century. The result has been a massive flow of people from the island, comparable to the great migration of the 1950s. By 2005, more Puerto Ricans lived in the U.S. mainland than in Puerto Rico. The 2010 census, for the first time in Puerto Rico's history, marked an absolute decrease in population from the previous census. For many Puerto Ricans today, migration is seen as their best exit strategy in a crumbling economic, social, and political system. If in 1947 Operation Bootstrap and migration were seen as two sides of the same strategy, by the beginning of the new century, when Operation Bootstrap is no more than a evanescent memory of a seemingly golden past, migration remains for hundreds of thousands of Puerto Ricans the only plausible alternative facing a collapsing colonial order that was created more than a century earlier. The postwar migration history of past generations of Puerto Ricans should not be lost to those following their paths today.

NOTES

NOTES TO THE INTRODUCTION

1. In September 2013, *El Nuevo Día* published a series of articles examining migration to the United States, discussing topics like the young face of migrants; the "airbus" to Florida; the island's dramatic loss of population and the growing number of Puerto Ricans now living on the U.S. mainland. See ElNuevoDia.com, accessed on September 29, 2013. On a more scholarly approach to Puerto Rico's economic crisis and the related increase in migration to the United States, see Meléndez and Vargas-Ramos, *Puerto Ricans*.
2. See, e.g., "Puerto Ricans Seeking New Lives Put Stamp on Central Florida," August 25, 2015, A1, and "Anxiety Builds as Puerto Ricans Face Debt Crisis," July 4, 2015, A1, in the *New York Times*.
3. Puerto Rican migration falls between the cracks in the study of U.S. migrations. Even a standard text on "multicultural" America like Takaki's *A Different Mirror* does not devote any attention to Puerto Ricans. Another text on "immigrant" America by two scholars knowledgeable of U.S. Hispanic history also fails to mention Puerto Rican migration; see Portes and Rumbaut, *Immigrant America*. Puerto Rican migration is also absent from studies of internal migration; it is not even mentioned in one of the standard texts on this subject: Greenwood, "Research on Internal Migration."
4. Senior, "Migration and Puerto Rico's Population Problem," 135; also Senior, *The Puerto Ricans*.
5. Senior, *The Puerto Ricans*; see also Senior, *Our Citizens*. This view is contrary to the assertion presented in *The Puerto Rican Journey*, which Senior coauthored with C. Wright Mills, where it is argued that for racial and other historical factors, Puerto Rican migration was different from previous migrations. See Mills, Senior, and Goldsen, *The Puerto Rican Journey*.
6. Centro de Estudios Puertorriqueños, *Labor Migration*.
7. See, e.g., Bonilla and Campos, "A Wealth of Poor."

8. Lapp, "Managing Migration."
9. Ibid., *passim,* particularly ch. 2.
10. See, e.g., Basch, Schiller, and Szanton Blanc, *Nations Unbound*; Portes, Guarnizo, and Landolt, "The Study of Transnationalism"; Smith and Guarnizo, *Transnationalism*; Castles, "Migration and Community Formation"; Portes and DeWind, "A Cross-Atlantic Dialogue"; and Levitt, De Wind, and Vertovec, "International Perspectives."
11. Ostergaard-Nielsen, *International Migration*; Baubock, "Towards a Political Theory"; Itzigsohn, "Immigration"; and Levitt and de la Dehesa, "Transnational Migration."
12. Ostergaard-Nielsen, *International Migration,* 11.
13. For elaboration of this argument, see Meléndez, "Puerto Rican Migration."
14. Duany, "The Orlando Ricans"; Duany, *Blurred Borders.* Also Duany, *Puerto Rican Nation on the Move.*
15. Grosfoguel, *Colonial Subjects*; Pérez, *The Near Northwest Side Story*; and Aranda, *Emotional Bridges.*
16. DeSipio and Pantoja, "Puerto Rican Exceptionalism?"
17. Duany, *Nation on the Move,* ch. 7; Duany, "The Orlando Ricans"; and Duany, "A Transnational Colonial Migration," 247–48. On Puerto Rico's migration policy from the perspective of migration to Chicago, Philadelphia, and Michigan, respectively, see Pérez, *The Near Northwest Side Story,* ch. 3; Whalen, *From Puerto Rico to Philadelphia*; and Findlay, *We Are Left without a Father Here.*
18. Duany, *Nation on the Move,* 169–71, and most recently, Duany, *Blurred Borders,* 84–85.
19. Duany, "A Transnational Colonial Migration," 247–49. Duany examines these arguments further in *Blurred Borders.*
20. Grosfoguel has compared Puerto Ricans to other Caribbean "colonial migrants" who also enjoy metropolitan citizenship and have unrestricted access to the colonial metropolis, and whose migration there has been espoused by government agencies (metropolitan or colonial). For Grosfoguel and other scholars, colonial migrants engage in transnational relations similar to those coming from nation-states. See Grosfoguel, *Colonial Subjects,* ch. 6; and also Grosfoguel, Cervantes-Rodríguez, and Mielants, "Introduction."
21. Fernando Sierra Berdecía, commissioner of labor and framer of the government's migration policy, acknowledged the particular role played by the Puerto Rican government in this arena in his crucial text on this matter: *Puerto Rican Emigration.*
22. Meléndez, "Puerto Rican Migration."
23. See Meléndez, "Citizenship."
24. The idea that Puerto Ricans are seen as "foreign" to the United States is used by scholars like Duany to argue that Puerto Rican migration is a transnational—although colonial—migration; Duany, "A Transnational Colonial Migration," 247–49. For the notion that French citizens from the Caribbean—like Puerto Ricans—are also seen as "foreign" in France, see Milia-Marie-Luce, "Puerto Ricans in the United States," 98.
25. Puerto Rico is by far the largest of the U.S. overseas territories in terms of population and size. On the U.S. territories, see Leibowitz, *Defining Status,* and Sparrow, *The Insular Cases.*
26. See, e.g., Glazer and Moyniham, *Beyond the Melting Pot,* chapter "The Puerto Ricans," and Mills, Senior, and Goldsen, *The Puerto Rican Journey.*
27. Williams, *The Tragedy*; LaFeber, *The New Empire.*
28. For a review of this literature, see McCoy, Scarano, and Johnson, "On the Tropic of Cancer," particularly 1–12.
29. Kaplan and Pease, *Cultures.*
30. Kaplan, "Left Alone with America."
31. Kaplan discusses Puerto Rico's status within the American empire when she examines *Downes v. Bidwell* in order to explore the interrelationships between the "domestic" and the "foreign" in U.S. affairs; see her introduction to *The Anarchy of Empire.*
32. McCoy, Scarano, and Johnson, "On the Tropic of Cancer."

33. Cabán, *Constructing a Colonial People*.
34. Go, *American Empire*.
35. Thompson, *Imperial Archipelago*.
36. Briggs, *Reproducing Empire*.
37. del Moral, *Negotiating Empire*.
38. See the chapters by Santiago-Valles, del Moral, Barreto, Navarro-Rivera, Scarano, Schmidt-Nowara, Duffy Burnett, Rodríguez Beruff, and García Muñiz and Campo, in McCoy and Scarano, *Colonial Crucible*.
39. Duffy Burnett and Marshall, *Foreign in a Domestic Sense*; Duffy Burnett, "Untied States"; Rivera Ramos, *The Legal Construction of Identity*; and Sparrow, *The Insular Cases*.
40. Cabranes, "Citizenship and the American Empire"; Venator-Santiago, "Extending Citizenship to Puerto Rico"; Erman, "Puerto Rico"; Duffy Burnett, "They say I am not an American . . ."; and Baldoz and Ayala, "The Bordering of America."
41. On the need for more research linking U.S. empire to colonial migrations to the United States, see Green, "Labor of Empire."
42. For an excellent study of Filipino migration to the United States within the context of U.S. empire, see Baldoz, *The Third Asiatic Invasion*, particularly chs. 1 and 2. Also see Fujita-Rony, *American Workers*. For an account on the relationship between Filipino migration to the United States and the independence of the Philippines, see Kramer, *The Blood of Government*.
43. A similar perspective on Puerto Rican migration is presented by McGreevy, "Borderline Citizens." A comparative study of Filipino and Puerto Rican workers in Hawaii at the beginning of the twentieth century is provided by Poblete, *Islanders in the Empire*.
44. Magoon, *Report*, 72.
45. Cabranes, "Citizenship and the American Empire," 433.
46. The major issues in *Downes v. Bidwell*, as well as the decision itself and its several opinions, are examined in Rivera Ramos, *The Legal Construction of Identity*, chs. 4 and 5; Sparrow, *The Insular Cases*, chs. 4 and 5; Torruella, *The Supreme Court and Puerto Rico*, ch. 3.
47. *Downes v. Bidwell* (182 U.S. 244, 1901), quotes from 279–80, 282, and 287, respectively.
48. *Downes v. Bidwell* quotes from 299, 306, 312–13, and 341–42, respectively; my emphasis. Similar concerns regarding the incorporation of the "uncivilized tribes" incapable of "self-government" were raised in the dissenting opinion written by Justice McKenna and joined by Shiras and White in *De Lima v. Bidwell* (182, U.S. 1), 219.
49. See Meléndez, "Citizenship."
50. *Gonzales v. Williams* (192 U.S. 1, 1904).
51. A comprehensive examination of the Jones Act and the grant of U.S. citizenship to Puerto Ricans requires a discussion that is not possible here. The Jones Act also introduced reforms to the Puerto Rican government (i.e., an elected senate) and granted Puerto Ricans their own bill of rights, in itself a topic that should require an appropriate discussion. That is, even as citizens, the Bill of Rights would not be fully applied to these new citizens. For many years previous to the act, some in Congress and among the colonial functionaries debated whether to grant citizenship to Puerto Ricans through a collective naturalization—as it happened—or by individual ("voluntary") naturalization. The context where citizenship was granted—World War I—also raises a number of questions regarding this event, including the strategic and political concerns involved in this decision. For an excellent discussion of the reasons for granting citizenship to Puerto Ricans, see Rivera Ramos, *The Legal Construction of Identity*, ch. 7. The standard text regarding congressional debates on citizenship for Puerto Ricans remains Cabranes, "Citizenship and the American Empire," 391–492. On the debates around the Jones Act, see also Fors, "The Jones Act."
52. *Balzac v. People of Porto Rico* (258 U.S. 298, 1922), quotes from 309, 306, and 311, respectively; my emphasis.
53. *Balzac v. the People of Porto Rico*, 308, statement reiterated in 311.

54. See Kramer, *The Blood of Government*, ch. 6, quote on 426. As Kramer stated in another writing, "Decolonization would be racial exclusion by other means." Kramer, "Race, Empire," 209. See also Ngai, *Impossible Subjects*, ch. 3.
55. See McGovney, "Our Non-Citizen Nationals ...," 621-22. Erman has argued that citizenship "ensured their freedom of movement within the U.S. borders": in "Puerto Rico," 288. Congress imposed a very limited quota for Filipino immigration after it promised the Philippines independence in the 1934 Tydings-McDuffie Act. Numerous policies encouraging Filipino repatriation, particularly in the American West, increased during this period. See Ngai, *Impossible Subjects*, ch. 3; Baldoz, *The Third Asiatic Invasion*, ch. 5.
56. Cabranes, "Citizenship and the American Empire." See also Cabán, *Constructing a Colonial People*, and Estades Font, *La presencia militar*, ch. 6.
57. Rivera Ramos, *The Legal Construction of Identity*, ch. 7.
58. On U.S. formal and informal empire, see McCormick, "From Old Empire to New," and Sparrow, *The Insular Cases*, ch. 8. On Root, see Johnson, "Understanding the American Empire."
59. Vega, *Memoirs, passim*; Thomas, *Puerto Rican Citizen*, chs. 1 and 2; McGreevy, "Borderline Citizens" and "Empire and Migration"; and Meléndez, "Citizenship."
60. On the Puerto Rican migrant experience, see, for example, Duany, *Nation on the Move*; Whalen, *From Puerto Rico to Philadelphia*; Sánchez Korrol, *From Colonia to Community*; Vega, *Memoirs*; Thomas, *Puerto Rican Citizen*; Pérez, *The Near Northwest Side Story*; Aranda, *Emotional Bridges to Puerto Rico*; Whalen and Vázquez-Hernández, *The Puerto Rican Diaspora*; Findlay, *We Are Left without a Father Here*; Fernández, *Brown in the Windy City*; and Gerena Valentín, *Gilberto Gerena Valentín*.

NOTES TO CHAPTER 1

1. See, e.g., Maldonado Denis, *The Emigration Dialectic*, ch. 2.
2. McCoy, Scarano, and Johnson, "On the Tropic of Cancer," particularly 24-26.
3. McCoy and Scarano, *Colonial Crucible*, passim; Go and Foster, *The American Colonial State*; Go, *American Empire*; Cabán, *Constructing a Colonial People*; and Kramer, *The Blood of Government*, ch. 3.
4. Go, *American Empire*.
5. Kramer, "Race, Empire," 206.
6. Go, "Introduction," 5.
7. Ibid., 10.
8. For a review of the literature on this issue, see Meléndez Vélez, *Partidos*, ch. 1.
9. Cabán, *Constructing a Colonial People*, 8.
10. See Baldrich, "Class and the State," and González Díaz, "El Estado."
11. Dietz, *Economic History*, 219.
12. See Pantojas-García, *Development Strategies*, particularly 24-25.
13. See, e.g., Ames, "Labor Conditions."
14. Centro, *Sources*, 15.
15. Ibid., 97, 100.
16. Ibid., 45. Also McGreevy, "Borderline Citizens," ch. 2. A recent study of the Hawaii experience appears in Poblete, *Islanders in the Empire*.
17. Centro, *Sources*, 54-64, also 16-53 for other documents on the Hawaiian experience.
18. Ibid., 65-94.
19. Ibid., 96.
20. Ibid., 140.
21. Ibid., 187-93.

22. Ibid., 68–70.
23. McGreevy, "Borderline Citizens," ch. 5; Centro, *Sources*, 104.
24. Centro, *Sources*, 5, 127, and 112–26 for this topic.
25. Ibid., 194–95.
26. Ibid., 202–3.
27. Ibid., 206–10.
28. Senior, "Toward a Balance Sheet," 701.
29. Sánchez Korrol, *From Colonia to Community*.
30. Atherton Lee to William Leahy, April 8, 1940; in Archivo General de Puerto Rico (AGPR), Fondo Oficina del Gobernador (FOG), tarea 96-20, box 269.
31. Leahy to Harold Ickes, April 9, 1940; in ibid.
32. Ridley to Leahy, May 21, 1940; in ibid.
33. Atherton to Carlos Gallardo, June 6, 1940; in ibid.
34. Rivera Martínez to Colóm, June 14 and 15, and July 2, 1940; in ibid.
35. Daley to Leahy, October 2, 1940; in ibid.
36. Stimson to the U.S. secretary of interior, October 25, 1940; in ibid.
37. López to Guy J. Swope, governor of Puerto Rico, February 25, 1941; in ibid.
38. Glen E. Edgerton to Swope, March 27, 1941; in ibid.
39. Swope to Edgerton, April 8, 1941; in ibid.
40. "La emigración sería de 500,00 portorriqueños," *El Mundo*, April 14, 1942, 1; "Risky Undertaking," *Detroit News*, April 15, 1942. See also "Transfer of Puerto Ricans," *Shreveport, LA., Journal*, April 10, 1942. The latter two are found in AFLMM, section IV, series 16, subseries "Migración América Latina," folder 57, docs. 1 and 2.
41. "La propuesta emigración portorriqueña," editorial, *El Mundo*, May 30, 1942, 10.
42. "Se estudia la compra de terrenos en Santo Domingo," *El Mundo*, December 8, 1942, 1.
43. Carlos Chardón, "Brief Report to the Governor of Puerto Rico on Emigration of Puerto Ricans to Venezuela," February 21, 1945, and letter from Chardón to Tugwell, March 2, 1945. Both in AGPR, FOG 96-20, 269.
44. Frank Corrigan, "Proposal to Settle Puerto Rican Families in Venezuela," confidential report to the secretary of state, September 1, 1945; in AFLMM, Section IV, Series 15, subseries 195a, doc. 1.
45. "Informal Committee on Migration: Called together by Field Office II, National Resources Planning Board, Room 211, Federal Building," dated December 26, 1942; in AGPR, FOG, tarea 96-20, box 269.
46. "La propuesta emigración a Estados Unidos," editorial, *El Mundo*, October 3, 1942, 6.
47. "Washington estudia emigración de P. R.," *El Mundo*, October 10, 1942, 1.
48. "Logran favor proyecto emigración portorriqueña," *El Mundo*, October 18, 1942, 1.
49. Iglesias Jr. to Tugwell, October 21, 1942; in AGPR, FOG 96-20, 2256.
50. "Aprobada en principio emigración boricua a EE.UU.," *El Mundo*, December 16, 1942, 5.
51. Senior, *Puerto Rican Emigration*, 24.
52. "Vasto plan para llevar obreros de la isla a los Estados Unidos," *El Mundo*, March 10, 1943, 5.
53. Edwin Maldonado, "Contract Labor," 108–10.
54. Whalen, *From Puerto Rico*, 49–50.
55. As quoted in Whalen, *From Puerto Rico*, 51.
56. Senior, *Puerto Rican Emigration*, 25.
57. Maldonado, "Contract Labor," 111.
58. Quoted in Whalen, *From Puerto Rico*, 52; also Maldonado, "Contract Labor," 107–8.
59. "Emigration of Puerto Ricans to work in the copper industry in the United States," memo from Pérez to Tugwell, February 20, 1945; in AGPR, FOG 96-20, 269. Reports from September 1944 indicated that four hundred out of one thousand Puerto Ricans working for

the Baltimore and Ohio Railroad Co. had abandoned their jobs; in "Dos mil obreros del país desean trabajar en E. U.," *El Mundo,* September 3, 1944, 2.
60. See Rosario Natal, *Luis Muñoz Marín,* and Anderson, *Gobierno y partidos,* 73–83.
61. See Anderson, *Gobierno y partidos,* 78–79; Rosario Natal, *Luis Muñoz Marín,* 198; Senior, *Puerto Rican Emigration,* 123.
62. U.S. Congress, Senate Committee on Territories, *Economic and Social Conditions,* 302–3.
63. U.S. Congress, House of Representatives, House Committee on Insular Affairs, *Investigation* 41–42.
64. U.S. Tariff Commission, *The Economy of Puerto Rico.*
65. Rosario Natal, *Luis Muñoz Marín,* 198–200.
66. *New York Times,* March 29, 1946, 13.
67. U.S. Tariff Commission, *The Economy of Puerto Rico,* 31; *El Mundo,* April 30, 1945, 1.
68. U.S. Tariff Commission, *The Economy of Puerto Rico,* 31 and 19, respectively.

NOTES TO CHAPTER 2

1. "Muchedumbre puertorriqueña aclamó ayer a Piñero en el homenaje de Nueva York," August 16, 1946, 1. *El Mundo* criticized the island government for not fulfilling "its obligations with those Puerto Ricans that migrate to New York." "El homenaje a Piñero," editorial, August 17, 1946, 6; both in *El Mundo.*
2. The significance of the "Puerto Rican problem" was noted by the Puerto Rican community's premier chronicler, Bernardo Vega, in Vega, *Memoirs,* 275–80. More recently, it is examined in Briggs, *Reproducing Empire,* 167–69, and Thomas, *Puerto Rican Citizen,* ch. 4. An example of previous media denigration of Puerto Ricans is Hewitt, "Welcome: Paupers and Crime."
3. Baldoz, *The Third Asiatic Invasion,* particularly chs. 4 and 5.
4. Briggs, *Reproducing Empire,* ch. 3.
5. Ramírez de Arellano and Seipp, *Colonialism,* 97.
6. Ibid., 97, 98.
7. Asociación de Salud Pública, *El problema poblacional,* 22.
8. Ibid., 3–4.
9. On the notion of how migration lowered population growth, see Sierra Berdecía's statements in his 1954–55 annual report to the governor; in GPR, Comm. Labor, *Twenty-Fourth Annual Report* 9.
10. "Foro Público sobre el Problema Poblacional de P. R.," Resumen de las Soluciones Ofrecidas por los Ponentes en la Sesión de Julio 19, 1946; in AFLMM, Section IV, series 2, folder 16, doc. 9, 1–3. Tió was an ardent advocate of migration to Latin America and opposed migration to the United States on cultural, racial, and climatic grounds. See Salvador Tió, "El desastre de Arizona," *El Mundo,* September 28, 1947, 1; also his paper "Sobre la necesidad de encauzar parte de nuestra emigración hacia Hispano-América," n.p., n.d.; in AGPR, FOG 96-20, 2274.
11. "Foro Público," 5; location in note 10, above.
12. Senior, "Migration and Puerto Rico's Population Problem," 130.
13. Davis, "Puerto Rico," 116–17.
14. "Informe preliminar sobre los trabajadores puertorriqueños," n.d.; in AFLMM, Section IV, Series 2, Subseries 9—Department of Labor, Folder 277, doc. 23.
15. Munita Muñoz Lee to Muñoz Marín, December 9, 1946; in ibid., doc. 22.
16. Pérez to Muñoz Marín, December 18, 1946; in AFLMM, IV:2, Sub. 9, Folder 251, doc. 11.
17. Pérez to Muñoz Lee, December 17, 1946; in ibid, doc. 12.
18. Pérez to the Director of *El Imparcial,* December 17, 1946; in ibid., doc. 13.

19. Whalen, *From Puerto Rico*, 52.
20. Isales to Muñoz Marín, April 3, 1947; in AFLMM, IV:2, Sub. 9, Folder 277, doc. 14.
21. "Report on Cases of Puerto Rican Laborers Brought to Chicago to Work as Domestics and Foundry Workers under Contract with Castle, Barton, and Associates, Inc.," confidential report by Carmen Isales, Chicago, Illinois, March 22, 1947; in ibid., doc. 16.
22. Carmen Isales, "Situación de los obreros puertorriqueños contratados por la Agencia de Empleos Castle, Barton and Assoc.," December 1946; in ibid., doc. 25
23. "Géigel partió en una misión especial ayer," January 3, 1947, 1, and "Géigel presentará enmienda a la ley de emigración obrera," January 24, 1947, 8; both in *El Mundo*.
24. "Caucus de la mayoría aprobó medida de emigración obrera," *El Mundo*, April 2, 1947, 1. Text of the law in GPR, Legislatura, *Leyes de la Tercera Legislatura Ordinaria*, 210–15.
25. Meléndez, *"The Puerto Rican Journey* Revisited," 195–97; Vega, *Memoirs*, 275–80.
26. *PM*'s articles were translated and published in "PM relata las vicisitudes de portorriqueños," February 8, 1947, 1; "PM informa se controlará el éxodo boricua," February 11, 1947, 1; "Miseria y abandono esperan a emigrantes boricuas en N. Y.," February 16, 1947, 5; and "Problema de boricuas en Nueva York sin resolver," February 20, 1947, 2; all in *El Mundo*.
27. "Puerto Rico Seeks to Curb Migration," *New York Times*, February 20, 1947, 20.
28. "Fernós pide supervisión para emigración boricua," *El Mundo*, February 15, 1947, 3.
29. The New York *World Telegram* series includes "The Miserables Find Grim Promised Land," October 20, 1947, 1; "City's Disease Rate Raised by Migrant Tide," October 21, 1947, 1; "Tide of Migrants Swell Relief Load," October 22, 1947, 1; "Migration to Go on Island Officials Warn," October 24, 1947, 1. News clips of the series are found in Muñoz Marín's files in AFLMM, IV:15, subseries 196. The series was reproduced in *El Mundo* from October 21 to 31, 1947. The *World Telegram* had published an earlier series on Puerto Ricans, also reproduced in *El Mundo*, May 3, 5, and 6, 1947.
30. "Officials Worried by Influx of Migrant Puerto Ricans," August 2, 1947, 1; "Puerto Rican Drift to Mainland Gains," July 31, 1947, 18; "Crime Increasing in 'Little Spain,'" August 3, 1947, 12; and "Solution is Sought to Migrant Influx," August 4, 1947, 19; all in *New York Times*. Among the few American politicians who raised a voice in defense of Puerto Ricans during the "Puerto Rican problem" was Marcantonio; see, e.g., "Defends Puerto Ricans: Marcantonio Sees Them Forced into Second-Class Citizenship," *New York Times*, September 23, 1947, 18.
31. "'Newsweek' comenta la emigración de boricuas," and "Uno de cada 22 neoyorquinos es boricua," *El Mundo*, March 21 and 23, 1947, 2 and 1, respectively; "Sugar-Bowl Migrants," *Time*, August 11, 1947.
32. A. Fernós-Isern, "Economy of Puerto Rico," *New York Times*, August 7, 1947, 20.
33. Mills, Senior, and Goldsen, *The Puerto Rican Journey*, and Meléndez, *"The Puerto Rican Journey* Revisited."
34. "Suggestions for a New Approach to Migration," confidential report from Monserrat to Muñoz Marín, February 9, 1961; in AFLMM, V:1, folder 137, doc. 1, p. iii.
35. Machuca to D. E. López Ramírez, secretary to the governor, February 3, 1947, and the attached memo from Machuca to Muñoz Marín, "Sugestiones [sic] en torno al momento actual" n.d.; in AGPR, FOG 96–20, 468.
36. D. J. O'Connor, "No Panaceas for Puerto Rico," n.d. The accompanying letter to Governor Piñero from O'Connor is dated March 4, 1947; in AGPR, FOG 96–20, 236.
37. D. J. O'Connor, "Addendum on an Internal Migration of Puerto Ricans," n.d.; the document is stamp-marked as April 2, 1947; in AGPR, FOG 96–20, 236.
38. D. J. O'Connor, "Notes for the Hon. Andrew L. Sommers on a Project to Locate Puerto Ricans in the Dominican Republic," n.d. This document was attached to a memo from O'Connor to Resident Commissioner Fernós-Isern, March 14, 1947, along with a draft letter to the U.S. president on the Dominican Republic plan, dated March 1947. In AGPR,

FOG 96-20, 236. The latter two also are found in AFLMM, IV:2, folder 22, docs. 20 and 23, respectively.

39. O'Connor, "A Basis for Preliminary Conversation on a Resettlement Project for Puerto Ricans in Venezuela," June 11, 1947; in AFLMM, IV:1, series 1, folder 13, doc. 4; and "Estado se opone a plan emigración de boricuas a República Dominicana," *El Imparcial,* July 3, 1947, 17.

40. Senior, *Puerto Rican Emigration,* 122; emphasis in the original.

41. Ibid., quote from 119, and also 119–22.

42. On this notion see Lapp, "Managing Migration," 67–74; Duany, *Nation on the Move,* 170–71; Whalen, *From Puerto Rico,* 35–36.

43. Senior, *Puerto Rican Emigration,* quotes from 101 and 103, respectively.

44. Pons to Rafael Picó, July 14, 1947. Pons told Sierra Berdecía that he was "specially qualified to successfully solve the problem that this committee will face" in his letter to the commissioner, July 14, 1947. Both letters in AGPR, FOG 96-20, 422.

45. Russell C. Derrickson, acting chief of the Caribbean Branch of the Division of Territories and Island Possessions, U.S. Department of the Interior, to Reck, July 29, 1947; in ibid.

46. Minutes of the third meeting of the Emigration Advisory Committee, August 18, 1947, and attached memo to members from Reck, August 28, 1947; in ibid.

47. Minutes of the fourth meeting of the Emigration Advisory Committee, August 23, 1947, emphasis added; in ibid.

48. Minutes of the Emigration Advisory Committee, September 11, 1947; in ibid.

49. "Fernós llevará al Congreso el caso de boricuas en Nueva York," *El Mundo,* August 3, 1947, 1.

50. Sierra Berdecía lived in the United States from 1925 to 1927, and upon his return to the island he began to work in journalism, including as director of the newspaper *La Correspondencia,* chief editor of *El Imparcial,* and correspondent for *El Mundo.* He became director of the Minimum Wage Board in 1942 and in 1945 was appointed director of the Labor Relations Board. Sierra Berdecía was also a novelist and a distinguished playwright. Among his best known plays is *Esta noche juega el Joker* (*The Joker Is Playing Tonight*), based on his experience in New York City. Sierra Berdecía acknowledged many times how his days living in the United States made him particularly sensitive to the conditions that Puerto Rican migrants faced in a society with a different culture and social practices like racism. See, e.g., Sierra Berdecía, *Puerto Rican Emigration,* 11. On the evolution of his political thinking, see "Sierra Berdecía se solidariza con unión permanente a E. U.," *El Mundo,* December 16, 1950, 1.

51. "Sierra Berdecía designado para dirigir Departamento Trabajo," June 30, 1947, 1; "Bien acogido nombramiento Sierra Berdecía," July 1, 1947, 1. Pagán de Colón was associate director of the Vocational Rehabilitation Division. Manuel Cabranes was appointed director of the Migration Office in New York; at the time, he was executive director of Melrose House in New York. See "Seleccionado ya el personal de Migración," December 31, 1947, 1. All in *El Mundo.*

52. Sierra Berdecía resigned as commissioner of labor in December 1960 due to health reasons. He died of a thrombosis at age fifty-nine on January 21, 1961. He was given the highest honors a public servant could receive at the time in Puerto Rico. See "Muñoz accede, acepta renuncia a Sierra Berdecía," December 29, 1960, 1; "Sierra Berdecía muere de trombosis a los 59," "Muñoz apenado por fallecimiento del 'amigo Sierra,'" January 22, 1962, 1; all in *El Mundo.* Also "Fernando Sierra Dies; Former Secretary of Labor in Puerto Rico was 59," *New York Times,* January 22, 1962. *El Mundo* described his funeral services as "one of the greatest expressions of public mourning seen in recent years in Puerto Rico"; January 23, 1962, 1. Sierra Berdecía was also remembered by Puerto Ricans in the United States. See "Lamentan en urbe deceso Fernando Sierra Berdecía," January 24, 1962, 17; and

"Boricuas en Chicago; mas de 1,000 van a misa en memoria de Sierra," February 16, 1962, 9, both in *El Mundo*.
In an editorial titled "Mission Accomplished," *El Mundo* praised the devotion of the commissioner to public service, concluding that after "a mission fully accomplished, Puerto Rico owes the highest recognition" to Sierra Berdecía; January 3, 1961, 6. Although he played an important role in postwar Puerto Rican government and politics, as of now there is no single article or book on Sierra Berdecía's life or work

53. "Bien acogido nombramiento Sierra Berdecía," *El Mundo*, July 1, 1947, 1.
54. "Sierra define actitud de Trabajo ante los obreros y los patronos," *El Mundo*, September 7, 1947, 1. This presentation was published as Sierra Berdecía, *Protecting Puerto Rico's Labor*.
55. GPR, Comm. Labor, *Twenty-First Annual Report 1951–1952*, 7; emphasis added.
56. "Sierra fija las normas para las migraciones," *El Mundo*, September 19, 1947, 1.
57. Sierra Berdecía, "Migración de Trabajadores Puertorriqueños a Estados Unidos."
58. "Caso boricua discutido en Nueva York," *El Mundo*, October 29, 1947, 1.
59. "Sierra dictará cambio radical en emigración," *El Mundo*, October 31, 1947, 5.
60. "Esperan que Sierra Berdecía regrese en la próxima semana," November 1, 1947, 5; "Sierra discute un plan para dar empleo a los puertorriqueños," November 5, 1947, 7; and "Sierra afirma hará cambios en emigración," November 11, 1947, 1; all in *El Mundo*.
61. "Sierra va a iniciar plan vocacional," *El Mundo*, November 9, 1947, 1.
62. "Sierra elogía normas de vida de los boricuas en Nueva York," *El Mundo*, November 13, 1947, 1.
63. "Pronta acción para alivio a los emigrantes," *El Mundo*, November 16, 1947, 1.
64. Sierra Berdecía, "Migración de Trabajadores Puertorriqueños." Page numbers of quoted passages from this source will appear parenthetically in the text.
65. Sierra Berdecía claimed repeatedly that the island's migration policy was the result of consultation with functionaries and institutions in New York City. While visiting New York in December 1947, he asserted that the new migration policy was the result of the "consensus of ideas" discussed in his previous visit to review "the problem of Puerto Ricans" in the city. See "Sierra expone labor oficina de New York," *El Mundo*, December 19, 1947, 1.
66. "Senado aprobó el proyecto que define política sobre migración," *El Mundo*, November 28, 1947, 1. *El Mundo* welcomed the bill's approval and called Sierra Berdecía the right man to fulfill this job. "El proyecto sobre migración," *El Mundo*, November 29, 1947, 6.
67. Gov. PR, Legislatura, *Leyes de la Cuarta y Quinta Legislaturas*, 386–94.
68. Memo from Sierra Berdecía to Muñoz Marín, "'Financing Migration from Puerto Rico' by D. J. O'Connor," March 23, 1949; in AGPR, FOG 96–20, 2275.
69. A. W. Maldonado, *Teodoro Moscoso*, 144–46.

NOTES TO CHAPTER 3

1. President's Commission, *Migratory Labor*, 16–88, 105–8; also Whalen, *From Puerto Rico*, ch. 3. Donald O'Connor, "Contract Migrant Labor," memo to Roberto Sánchez Vilella and Sierra Berdecía, June 26, 1950; in AGPR, FOG 96–20, 2273.
2. See, e.g., Fernández, "Of Immigrants and Migrants."
3. According to Senior, Puerto Ricans' "legal status as citizens . . . conflict in the public mind with their role as Spanish-speaking bearers of another culture, and they are often treated as immigrants." Senior, "Patterns of Puerto Rican Dispersion," 93.
4. President's Commission, *Migratory Labor*, 49; emphasis added.
5. Ibid., 2.

6. Quotes and statistical data are from ibid., 38–39. Already by the 1920s, U.S. farmers stated their preference for Mexican workers over Puerto Ricans, based on the former's deportability versus the latter's U.S. citizenship. See Molina, *How Race is Made*, 34–38.
7. President's Commission, *Migratory Labor*, 16.
8. See letter from H. Rex Lee, acting director of the Division of Territories and Island Possessions, to Juan A. Pons, acting governor, July 21, 1947, and letter from Lee to Governor Piñero, July 24, 1947; both in AGPR, FOG 96-20, 422. A 1950 report by the agency acknowledged the need of Puerto Ricans to migrate and the benefits for U.S. employers in hiring them. See Office of Territories, U.S. Department of Interior, "The Potential Contribution of Puerto Rico's Migrant Workers to the Mainland's Need for Workers" (Washington, DC, October 1, 1950); in AGPR, FOG 96-20, 2272.
9. Barr to Cecil Morales, Department of Labor, December 3, 1947; in AGPR, FOG 96-20, 454.
10. Pagán de Colón, *Programa*, 13–14; Monserrat, "The Development," 11.
11. Agreement signed by Goodwin and Sierra Berdecía on February 10, 1949; press release, February 11, 1949, in OGPRUS, box 2907, folder 22. See also Pagán de Colón, *Programa*, 13–15, and Sierra Berdecía, *Puerto Rican Emigration*, 10–11.
12. Agreement signed by Goodwin and Sierra Berdecía on February 10, 1949; press release, February 11, 1949, in OGPRUS, box 2907, folder 22.
13. Memo from Sierra Berdecía to José Raúl Cancio, governor's executive assistant, August 18, 1949; in AGPR, FOG 96-20, 2275.
14. Confidential Memo from Draper to Sierra Berdecía, October 24, 1949; in ibid.
15. Draper, "Report of Meeting of Special Farm Labor Committee, USES," January 19, 1950; in AGPR, FOG 96-20, 2273.
16. Perl to Sierra Berdecía, January 19, 1950; in ibid. Support from the U.S. labor movement is reflected in a letter from David Sternback, CIO representative in Puerto Rico, urging colleagues in Connecticut to support the hiring of Puerto Ricans over West Indians in that state. Sternback to Ed. McCrone, June 14, 1951; in AGPR, FOG 96-20, 2276.
17. President's Commission, *Migratory Labor*, 62.
18. Kirsten, "Agribusiness," 633.
19. Robinson, "Taking the Fair Deal," 381–402.
20. Memo from Tobin to Goodwin, "Importation of Foreign Labor," January 9, 1950; in AGPR, FOG 96-20, 2273.
21. Hilliard to Tobin, February 15, 1950; in ibid. For similar "pleas . . . made by members of Congress with large numbers of Puerto Rican voters," see "Alien Farm Labor Protested Amid Political, Racial Rifts," *New York Times*, April 4, 1950, 1.
22. "Alien Labor Barred in State," *New York Times*, April 5, 1950, 32.
23. See "Alien Labor's Rise Arouses Concern," *New York Times*, September 7, 1950, 33. On the issue of racism, a *New York Times* report noted: "Leaders in the fight against foreign contract labor deny that any question of race is involved. They point out that many of the Puerto Ricans for whom they are seeking farm jobs are Negroes, and insist that the only issue is protection of United States citizens from unfair competition with imported contract labor." In "Alien Farm Labor Protested," *New York Times*, April 4, 1950, 33.
24. As quoted in "Alien Farm Labor Protested," *New York Times*, April 4, 1950, 33.
25. Sierra Berdecía to Tobin, May 23, 1950; in AGPR, FOG 96-20, 2273.
26. Tobin to Sierra Berdecía, June 14, 1950; in ibid.
27. GPR, Comm. Labor, *Vigésimo Informe Anual 1950–1951*, 39. Puerto Rico's political status almost prevented the law from being extended there. According to Monserrat, the basis for this exclusion was that Puerto Ricans paid no federal taxes. The impasse was resolved when it was determined "that Puerto Rico provided a service to U.S. growers." Monserrat, "The Development," 10
28. Monserrat, "The Development," 11.
29. GPR, Comm. Labor, *Vigésimo Informe Anual 1950–1951*, 40.

30. President's Commission, *Migratory Labor,* 36.
31. Robinson, "Taking the Fair Deal," 389–92.
32. "Estudian envío de trabajadores boricuas a E. U.," *El Mundo,* May 12, 1951, 1.
33. "Hacen planes para emigrar más boricuas," *El Mundo,* July 16, 1952, 1.
34. "Senior pide se favorezca obreros isla," *El Mundo,* March 29, 1952, 1.
35. Holdeman to Mitchell, October 21, 1958; in AGPR, FOG 96-20, 2277.
36. GPR, Comm. Labor, *Vigésimo Informe Anual 1950–1951,* 41.
37. The two-flow migration thesis became a mantra for Puerto Rican migration policy makers: Pagán de Colón, *Programa,* 2; Sierra Berdecía, *Puerto Rican Emigration,* 10–11; Senior, "Migration and Economic Development," 151–52.
38. Scholarly attention to the FPP includes Whalen, *From Puerto Rico,* ch. 3; Duany, "A Transnational Colonial Migration," 225–51; Lapp, "Managing Migration," 173–203.
39. BEM's goals and workings are described in detail in GPR, Comm. Labor, *Nineteenth Annual Report 1949–1950,* 55.
40. See Monserrat, "The Development," 15.
41. According to Monserrat, the migration of agricultural workers "is and has been an intrinsic part and basic factor in the economic growth and development of the island." Monserrat, "The Development," 27. Also Senior in Dept. Labor, Migration Division, *Annual Report 1955–1956,* 117; in OGPRUS, box 2733, folder 2.
42. Sierra Berdecía in GPR, Comm. Labor, *Twenty-First Annual Report 1951–1952,* 7.
43. GPR, Comm. Labor, *Eighteenth Annual Report 1948–1949,* vii–viii.
44. Pagán de Colón, *Programa,* 31–36; Monserrat, "The Development," 26–36; Senior, "Migration and Economic Development"; and Sierra Berdecía in GPR, Comm. Labor, *Twenty-Fourth Annual Report 1954–1955,* 58–59.
45. "Sierra fija norma para emigración," *El Mundo,* September 17, 1947, 1, 5. Also, Pagán de Colón, *Programa,* 39; Monserrat, "The Development," 14. On the positive elements of Puerto Rico's labor contract for farmworkers, see Lyon, "The Legal Status," 24–25. Senator Hubert Humphrey praised the Puerto Rican labor contract in "Alegan dan un mejor trato los boricuas," *El Mundo,* April 22, 1952, 1.
46. See President's Commission, *Migratory Labor,* particularly chs. 1 and 3, and Lyon, "The Legal Status," ch. 1.
47. See President's Commission, *Migratory Labor,* 42–48. Puerto Rican officials boasted that their contract offered more benefits and protections than the Mexican and West Indian ones; in Virginia Maldonado, "El trabajador boricua en los E. U.," part 1, *El Diario de Nueva York* (Suplemento Dominical), January 3, 1960, 1; part 2, January 4, 1960, 12.
48. Pagán de Colón, *Programa,* 16–17. See also Monserrat, "The Development," 16–18. Lyon's study also holds that these workers were mostly unprotected by federal and state legislation. Lyon, "The Legal Status," 202–3.
49. Sierra Berdecía, *Puerto Rican Emigration,* 12–14. Also, Pagán de Colón, "Migration," 137–41.
50. Monserrat, "The Development," 35–40.
51. By the early 1950s, the typical labor contact approved by the Puerto Rican government included over fifteen stipulations that regulated farmworkers' working and living conditions, ranging from the type of food that they could eat to housing, workers' compensation, health insurance, transportation costs, and the right to belong to unions. The contract is described in Monserrat, "The Development," 19–21.
52. One of the most important clauses in the contact prohibited any kind of discrimination, including racial discrimination, against Puerto Rican workers. Sierra Berdecía rejected any contract that would take Puerto Rican workers to the American South, arguing that it was almost impossible to protect Puerto Rican workers from racial prejudice and discrimination there and that their presence could cause conflicts in local communities, something that the government was trying to avoid. "Sierra no aprobara contratos para ir a trabajar al sur E. U.," *El Mundo,* April 7, 1951, 17.

According to Monserrat, officials from USES tried to attach Puerto Rico to the regional office in Atlanta when it became part of this agency. Sierra Berdecía "refused that suggestion on the grounds that racial segregation was practiced" in that region; Puerto Rico eventually became part of the New York City regional office. Monserrat observed that Sierra Berdecía refused to send workers to the South even though he came under constant pressure from farmers in Florida and Georgia to do so. Monserrat, "The Development," 12. On this racial policy, see also Sierra Berdecía, *Puerto Rican Emigration*, 18, and Pagán de Colón, *Programa*, 49. In his memoirs, the only reference that Muñoz Marín made on the issue of Puerto Rican migration to the United States was to acknowledge his refusal to send Puerto Ricans to the South due to the rampant racism there. In Luis Muñoz Marín, *Memorias: autobiografía pública 1940–1952* (San Germán, P. R.: Universidad Interamericana de Puerto Rico, 1992), 315.

53. President's Commission, *Migratory Labor*, 59. The "prevailing wage" will be discussed further in chapter 7.
54. "Sierra deniega petición para emigración debido a jornal bajo," *El Mundo*, January 17, 1948, 1; GPR, Comm. Labor, *Eighteenth Annual Report 1948–1949*, 49–51; Pagán de Colón, *Programa*, 15–16.
55. President's Commission, *Migratory Labor*, 61.
56. GPR, Comm. Labor, *Eighteenth Annual Report 1948–1949*, 50.
57. The process of recruitment and selection of workers is described by Pagán de Colón, *Programa*, 28–30.
58. GPR, Comm. Labor, *Eighteenth Annual Report 1948–1949*, 49–53.
59. The functions and workings of the FPP carried out by the BEM's Farm Placement Division were described in GPR, Comm. Labor, *Twenty-First Annual Report 1951–1952*, 39.
60. "No emigre para trabajar como agricultor el que no le sea," May 29, 1950, 10, and "Devolverían a obreros boricuas que no satisfagan a granjeros," May 7, 1952, 3; both in *El Mundo*.
61. GPR, Comm. Labor, *Nineteenth Annual Report 1949–1950*, 56. An analysis of FPP labor contracts carried out by Whalen for the years 1949 and 1950 clearly shows the overwhelming rural character of these migrants; see Whalen, *From Puerto Rico*, 80–81. See also Pérez, *The Near Northwest Side Story*, ch. 2.
62. GPR, Comm. Labor, *Twenty-First Annual Report 1951–1952*, 38–39, 43–44.
63. Monserrat, "The Development," 25; yearly figures in 32. The number given by Monserrat must be understood as the total number of placements or farmworkers going to the United States under FPP's labor contracts and not as the total number of individuals moved by the program. Many workers returned to Puerto Rico and then came back to the mainland with a new yearly contract.
64. Pagán de Colón, *Programa*, 34. On the government's policy of migrant dispersion, see report from Senior to Sierra Berdecía, "Factors Affecting the Dispersion of Puerto Ricans in the States," August 13, 1956, in AGPR, FOG 96-20, 2277; and Senior, "Dispersion of Puerto Rican Migration," speech prepared for the annual conference of the Welfare and Health Council of New York City, held on May 7, 1953, in AGPR, FOG 96-20, 2280. Also Senior, "Puerto Rico: Migration to the Mainland."
65. Maldonado, "Contract Labor"; Whalen, *From Puerto Rico*, 123–36 and ch. 5; Pérez, *The Near Northwest Side Story*, ch. 3.
66. On the impact of migration on Puerto Rico's rural municipalities, see Myers, "Migration and Modernization"; also Whalen, *From Puerto Rico*, ch. 4.
67. Pagán de Colón, *Programa*, 17–18.
68. Ibid., 31.
69. For example, the 1953 agreement between the New Jersey Garden State Service Cooperative and the Puerto Rican government was negotiated directly by Muñoz Marín; "Hay acuerdo sobre viajes obreros a EU," *El Mundo*, April 22, 1953, 1.
70. "Gobierno proyecta emplear 100,000 boricuas en E. U.," *El Mundo*, February 26, 1952.

71. See the confidential memo from Draper to Sierra Berdecía, October 24, 1949; in AGPR, FOG 96-20, 2275; also memo from Blas Oliveras, assistant commissioner of labor, to Muñoz Marín, October 27, 1949; in ibid.
72. See the series of articles published by Salvador Tió in *El Mundo* during the fall of 1947: "La emigración necesita similitud cultural, afirma Tió," September 7, 1947, 5 and September 14, 1947, 7; September 28, 1947, 4; and October 5, 1947, 14. Tió and other intellectuals contended that Puerto Ricans in the United States also experienced the loss of their cultural and national identity; Tió, "La emigración," and Fernández Méndez, "¿Asimilación o enquistamiento?"
73. Letter from Lee to Governor Piñero, July 24, 1947; in AGPR, FOG 96-20, 422.
74. "Brasil abre sus puertas al éxodo portorriqueño," August 27, 1946, 12, 17, and "El interior de Brasil: Están colonizando su centro para atraer a los inmigrantes," August 18, 1946, 1, 12; both in *El Mundo*.
75. Memo from O'Connor to Piñero, Muñoz Marín, Fernós-Isern, Sierra Berdecía, Moscoso, and others, "Subject: San Francisco River Valley- Brazil," August 4, 1948; in AFLMM, Section IV, Series 2, Folder 18, doc. 10.
76. Hanson to Muñoz Marín, January 5, 1949, 1; in AGPR, FOG 96-20, 2275.
77. Ventura Barnes Jr. to Rafael Picó, January 24, 1949; in ibid.
78. José Raúl Cancio, January 31, 1949, and letter from Cancio to Sierra Berdecía, February 17, 1949; both in ibid.
79. See letter from Sierra Berdecía to Alvaro Adolfo, Senate of Brazil, June 9, 1949; letter from Adolfo to Sierra Berdecía, May 30, 1949; and letter from Sierra Berdecía to Cancio, June 10, 1949; all in ibid.
80. These notes have no author, title, or date; in ibid. Muñoz Marín's handwritten note dates the document February 21.
81. O'Connor to Hanson, October 26, 1949; in ibid.
82. This account is based on Maldonado's *Teodoro Moscoso*, 150-54.
83. "Ultiman planes para emigración boricua a Brasil," December 28, 1954, 1, and "Alentaría la migración si dan tierra Boricuas," December 31, 1954, 22; both in *El Mundo*.
84. "Preparan una emigración a Venezuela," December 26, 1947, 1; "Verán a Muñoz sobre obreros para Venezuela," January 9, 1948, 1; and "Esbozan proyecto de emigración por lapso 20 años a Venezuela," February 8, 1948, 1; all in *El Mundo*. Government officials continued to contemplate the export of laborers to Venezuela as an option; see the letter from Vernon R. Esteves, economic adviser to the governor, to Sierra Berdecía, June 21, 1950, in AGPR, FOG 96-20, 2275.
85. "'Miami Herald' acoge la idea sobre Surinam," March 19, 1947, 4; "Harán estudio de emigración a Sudamérica," November 2, 1947, 1; and "Fomentarán la inmigración a zona Surinam," July 22, 1948, 1; all in *El Mundo*.
86. "Delegación Costa Rica discutirá emigración," March 7, 1955, 1; "Hay oposición a inmigración en Costa Rica," October 6, 1955, 1; "Gobierno no tiene un interés especial se vaya a Costa Rica," October 12, 1955, 1; all in *El Mundo*.

NOTES TO CHAPTER 4

1. Sánchez, *La guagua aérea*; Torre, Rodriguez Vecchini, and Burgos, *The Commuter Nation*; Duany, *Nation on the Move*.
2. Dept. Labor, "Requirements for the Transportation of Workers from Puerto Rico to the United States." In AFLMM, V:1, folder 138, doc. 16.
3. Button and Vega, "The Effects of Air Transportation," 74-76.
4. Fleisher, "Some Aspects," 245-53, quotes from 251 and 252.

5. Hamilton, "The Puerto Rican Economy," 76–84, quotes from 79 and 80.
6. "Piden JAC autorice expansión en servicio aéreo en la Isla," *El Mundo,* July 15, 1948, 1.
7. "Muñoz insiste en un mayor servicio de transportación aérea para la Isla," *El Mundo,* February 1, 1949, 1.
8. "El Gobierno pide amplíen rutas aéreas," *El Mundo,* May 25, 1949, 1.
9. "Isla pide mejoren el servicio aéreo," *El Mundo,* March 20, 1950, 1.
10. Letter from Muñoz Marín to Ryan, August 29, 1950, in AFLMM, V:12 (January–December 1950), doc. 59.
11. Fernós-Isern, *Transportation Needs,* quotes from 28–29.
12. Ibid., 36.
13. Antonio Fernós-Isern, "Air Service for Puerto Rico," *New York Times,* June 30, 1950, 20.
14. "Recomiendan más servicio aéreo a isla," *El Mundo,* September 25, 1950, 1, 18.
15. Dierikx, *Clipping the Clouds,* 33.
16. "Air Currents," September 29, 1940, 131, and "Tropical Airways," November 3, 1957, 382; both in *New York Times.*
17. See Dierikx, *Clipping the Clouds,* ch. 2 *passim*; data from appendix, 145–46.
18. "Tropical Airways"; "Aviation: Puerto Rico; A Model Airport to Open Next Month," *New York Times,* April 10, 1955, Travel, XX21.
19. "Heavy Volume of Winter Travel," January 13, 1952, Travel, XX16, and "Overseas First-Class Rates to Rise 10 Per Cent," November 27, 1955, Travel, X21; in *New York Times.*
20. "Inauguran hoy el vuelo directo S. J.–New York," *El Mundo,* July 1, 1946, 1.
21. "Eastern establece récord al iniciarse ruta directa," *El Mundo,* March 27, 1951, 1.
22. "Best Year for the Airlines," February 19, 1950; "Aviation: A Good Year," July 1, 1951; in *New York Times.*
23. "Puerto Rico Is Aided by Emigration to U.S.," January 4, 1952, 52; also "Island's Summer; Off-season Vacationing," September 2, 1951, 61; in *New York Times.*
24. Dierikx, *Clipping the Clouds,* ch. 2 *passim,* and 41, 58.
25. "JAC suspende 42 líneas de las independientes," *El Mundo,* October, 24, 1947, 1.
26. Quoted in Fleisher, "Some Aspects," 249.
27. Hamilton, "The Puerto Rican Economy," 76.
28. Antonio Fernós-Isern, "Air Service for Puerto Rico," *New York Times,* June 30, 1950, 20.
29. "Se matan 22 Puertorriqueños al caer avión en Florida," 6, and "Patéticas y conmovedoras escenas hicieron familiares de pasajeros," 1, July 14, 1947; "Causa consternación en Nueva York tragedia aérea," July 15, 1947, 7; in *El Imparcial.* "21 Killed, 15 Hurt in Crash of a DC-3 in Florida Swamp," *New York Times,* July 14, 1947, 1.
30. "Senado inicia investigación del desastre," July 16, 1947, 3; "Llegada de cadáveres resultó un severo e imponente espectáculo," July 19, 1947, 3; in *El Imparcial.*
31. "Revelaciones sensacionales," editorial, *El Imparcial,* July 16, 1947, 11. Similar concerns were expressed in New York City by *La Prensa;* "Un desastre aéreo mas," editorial, July 15, 1947, 8.
32. "Puede Senado actúe en caso de Savannah," *El Mundo,* January 10, 1948, 1.
33. "Mueren quince puertorriqueños," and "Ante la desgracia," editorial, January 8, 1948, 6, in *El Mundo.* Many ads published in *La Prensa* during this period announced flights to Puerto Rico by travel agencies (mostly Puerto Rican–owned); all promoted chartered flights by unscheduled airlines (Waterman Airlines, Trans-Tropic Airlines, TLA Airlines, Universal Airlines, etc.). They competed in terms of stops (nonstop versus one-stop in Miami) and price (nonstops from $113 to $130 in 1946 and from $50 to $65 in 1947). See, e.g., *La Prensa,* July 12, 1946, 8, and May 5, 1947, 11.
34. "J. A. C. realizará investigación del accidente," "Llevarán 300 trabajadores a Lorain, Ohio," and "Verán a Muñoz sobre obreros para Venezuela," in *El Mundo,* January 9, 1948, 1.
35. "Puede Senado actúe en caso de Savannah," and "Coastal Airways se encargará de traer los cadáveres y heridos," *El Mundo,* January 10, 1948, 1.

36. "Sigue en el misterio caso de Savannah," *El Mundo*, January 23, 1948, 1.
37. "Boricuas resultan ilesos en un acuatizaje forzoso en Maryland," *El Mundo*, May 29, 1948, 1.
38. "23 Saved in Crash of Charter Plane," *New York Times*, October 5, 1948.
39. Quote from "Desaparece avión en la ruta de Puerto Rico a Nueva York con 27 pasajeros boricuas," December 29, 1948, 1; "Estuvo dos meses en reparación el avión que se desapareció," December 30, 1948, 14; in *El Mundo*.
40. "Ahora es el momento," editorial, *El Mundo*, December 30, 1948, 6.
41. "Cierran el caso del avión DC-3 desaparecido," *El Mundo*, July 19, 1949, 1. This tragic incident became part of the Bermuda Triangle legend.
42. "Mueren 53 en desastre de avión C-46," June 8, 1949, 2, and "Es falso el manifiesto del avión," June 11, 1949, 6; in *El Imparcial*. Also, "Creen desastre habrá afectar líneas aéreas," June 9, 1949, 1, and "Piden supervisión de aviones se realice en forma más severa," June 10, 1949, 1; in *El Mundo*. See also "54 Die in Plane Crash at Sea; Puerto Ricans Bound for U.S.," *New York Times*, June 8, 1949.
43. "Gobernador investigará el desastre," June 9, 1949, 1, and "Marcantonio pide Congreso proceda," June 11, 1949, 1; in *El Mundo*.
44. "Informe secreto de JAC indica deficiencias del avión C-46," and "Muñoz ordena tomen medidas de protección en Isla Grande," June 11, 1949, 1; "Entra en vigor un reglamento para vuelos aéreos irregulares," June 17, 1949, 1, in *El Mundo*.
45. "CAA Grounds Airline in Crash That Killed 53 off Puerto Rico," *New York Times*, July 15, 1949, 1.
46. "Atribuyen a desperfecto en motor accidente aéreo ocurrido en Punta Salinas," *El Imparcial*, February 12, 1950, 4; "C. A. B. Challenged on Crash of Plane," *New York Times*, October 6, 1949; and "Junta de Aeronáutica le recovoca la licencia a la Strato Freight," *El Mundo*, October 29, 1949, 1.
47. "El desastre de Punta Salinas," and "Problemas de la emigración," June 9, 1949, 17; also "Después del desastre," June 10, 1949, 19, in *El Imparcial*.
48. See "Mueren 52 en accidente aéreo," and "La JAC envia 2 inspectores a Puerto Rico," April 12, 1952, 1, in *El Mundo*. Also, "52 Die, 17 Survive in U.S. Plane Crash at San Juan, P. R.," *New York Times*, April 12, 1952, 1.
49. "Accidente en la Isla eleva cifra muertes a 118 durante este año," *El Mundo*, April, 15, 1952, 1.
50. "Record Toll Seen for Air Disaster," *New York Times*, July 1, 1956.
51. Fernós-Isern, "Air Service for Puerto Rico," *New York Times*, June 30, 1950, 20.
52. Letter from Glen Lawrence to Muñoz Marín, February 21, 1949; in AGPR, FOG 96-20, 2275.
53. See memo from Pagán de Colón to Sierra Berdecía, "Information Regarding Airline Contracts," June 12, 1950; in AFLMM, V:1, folder 138, doc. 7. In this regard, see the letters from Pagán de Colón to Eddie Holohan on September 28, 1949, and May 10, 1950, both in ibid., docs. 10 and 14.
54. See memo from Alberto Arrillaga, military assistant to the governor, June 15, 1950; in AGPR, FOG 96-20, 2273.
55. Hamilton, "The Puerto Rican Economy," 80.
56. Pagán de Colón, *Programa*, 19-28.
57. "Rebaja en pasajes: representa economía $35,000 para obreros," *El Mundo*, June 28, 1956, 26.
58. "Petición rebaja en tarifas aéreas reduce migración obreros hacia EU," *El Mundo*, June 11, 1958, 1.
59. Letter from Piñero to O'Connell, November 8, 1948; also letter from O'Connell to Piñero, stamp-dated December 14, 1948; both in AGPR, FOG 96-20, 454.
60. "Creen oposición vuelos baratos perjudica migración de obreros," *El Mundo*, March 27, 1952, 5.

61. "La tarifa a Miami," editorial, *El Mundo*, September 29, 1953, 6.
62. "O'Connor vino a discutir el caso de ampliación de servicio aéreo."
63. "Contract Migrant Labor," memo from O'Connor to Roberto Sánchez Vilella and Sierra Berdecía, June 26, 1950; in AGPR, FOG 96-20, 2273.
64. "Nuestro futuro aéreo," *El Mundo*, November 30, 1947, 6.
65. "La Marina definitivamente en favor aeropuerto en Palo Seco," January 17, 1948, 1; "ACC retiene fondos aeropuerto esperando decisión de la Marina," February 14, 1948, 17; in *El Mundo*.
66. Partsch, *Jesús T. Piñero*, 144-50; "Administración de Aeronáutica aprobó aeropuerto Isla Verde," *El Mundo*, June 2, 1948, 1.
67. "Labor a realizarse representa inversión inicial de $3,550,000," *El Mundo*, August 18, 1949, 1.
68. "Esperan Isla tenga tráfico aéreo mayor," *El Mundo*, October 26, 1949, 1.
69. "Prevén auge en industria de aviación,"May 20, 1955, 1; "Autoridad Puerto NY ve gran auge aviación Isla," June 12, 1958, 14; and "Aceleran la expansión pistas del aeropuerto," October 22, 1959, 1; in *El Mundo*.
70. "Trazan plan para acabar obra nuevo aeropuerto para el 1953," August 1, 1951, 1; "Aeropuerto Isla Verde estará terminado a principios de 1954," March 8, 1952, 5; and "Acelerarán aeropuerto de Isla Verde," July 31, 1952, 1; in *El Mundo*. The new airport's design included spacious departing and receiving areas made specifically to accommodate the Puerto Rican tradition of welcoming and saying farewell to travelers. The TA director claimed that 1,086,577 persons went to the airport to see out or receive relatives, more or less three per passenger.
71. "Puerto Rico's $15,000,000 Airport," *New York Times*, May 22, 1955, Travel, X28.
72. "AT invertirá suma $9,370,500 en el aeropuerto de Isla Verde," *El Mundo*, August 16, 1952, 5.
73. "Se pedirá asignación para el aeropuerto internacional," *El Mundo*, October 3, 1952, 4.
74. "Puerto Rico 'Fair" to Open Airport," May 15, 1955, 45, and "Puerto Rico Airport Hailed at Opening," May 21, 1955, 36; in *New York Times*. The *Times* reported that in 1954, the Isla Grande Airport served more than two million people. It also informed readers that the federal government apportioned only $2.5 million of the airport's estimated $15 million final cost, an amount much lower than that reported elsewhere.
75. "Puerto Rico's $15,000,000 Airport"; also "Aviation: Puerto Rico; A Model Airport to Open Next Month," *New York Times*, April 10, 1955, Travel, XX21.
76. See, e.g., Merrill, *Negotiating Paradise*, 186-87. Partsch links the expansion of air transportation facilities to Puerto Rico's economic development program; see *Jesús T. Piñero*, 144.
77. For Fomento's role in tourism, see Ross, *The Long Uphill Path*, 100-105. Also, Merrill, *Negotiating Paradise*, ch. 5; and Vaughan, "Tourism in Puerto Rico."
78. Fernós-Isern, *The Transportation Needs of Puerto Rico*, 31.
79. "Encuesta revela que turistas prefieren venir a la isla por mar," *El Mundo*, June 15, 1949, 20.
80. Albors and López Mangual, *Selected Statistics*, table 7, 16.
81. Vaughan, "Tourism in Puerto Rico," 276-77; Merrill, *Negotiating Paradise*, 188-92, 216-18.
82. Goldsmith, "The Impact of the Tourism," table 5.2, 93.
83. Mings, "The Role of the Commonwealth Government," 57.
84. Goldsmith, "The Impact of the Tourism," 109.
85. Ibid., 110, 124-25.
86. The Commissioner of Labor's annual reports for the years 1956-57, 1957-58, and 1958-59 were incorrectly numbered in the original documents. The numbers 23, 24, and 25 were repeated. To avoid further confusion, hereafter we will use both the number and the year of the report as reference for these documents.

87. BEM, "Programa de Orientación en Puerto Rico a personas que se proponen salir para los Estados Unidos u otros países," San Juan, January 24, 1956; in AGPR, FOG 96-20, box 2274, 2.
88. "Abren oficina de información en aeropuerto," El Mundo, January 30, 1950, 12.
89. Press release by the Migration Division; in OGPRUS, box 3072, folder 16. Also, "Oficina ayuda a migrantes en Idlewild," June 11, 1954, 1; "Intensifica orientación boricuas que llegan a NY," August 12, 1958, 13; in El Mundo.
90. "Perseguirán envío ilegal obreros E. U.," May 14, 1952, 1, and "Perseguirán envío ilegal de obreros al continente," August 22, 1953, 13; in El Mundo.
91. Pagán de Colón, Programa, 48-49; "Procesan a cinco agentes de pasajes," El Imparcial, June 11, 1949, 3. A large file on these cases appears in "Migraciones clandestinas 1953," AGPR, Box "Correspondencia de la División de Colocaciones en Fincas 1953," Tarea 63-37, series 5.
92. "Sierra Berdecía apela a la Policía para acabar contrabando de obreros," El Mundo, March 31, 1953, 1.

NOTES TO CHAPTER 5

1. Rodríguez Bou, "Significant Factors," 159.
2. Pousada, "The Singularly Strange Story," "33.
3. Torres González, Idioma, 2-3.
4. Negrón de Montilla, La americanización. For a recent perspective of Americanization in educational policy, see del Moral, Negotiating Empire.
5. Cabán, Constructing a Colonial People, 128-29.
6. del Moral, Negotiating Empire, 72.
7. Cabán, Constructing a Colonial People, 130-39.
8. See Picó, "Origins," 175-94.
9. See del Moral, Negotiating Empire, ch. 3.
10. Pousada, "The Singularly Strange Story," 38-41.
11. Torres González, Idioma, ch. 6.
12. Ibid., 102.
13. Algren de Gutiérrez, The Movement against Teaching English, 103.
14. As quoted in Rodríguez Bou, "Significant Factors," 162-63.
15. Torres González, Idioma, 163-69; Rodríguez Bou, "Significant Factors," 163-69. For a review of the language issue in public schools during the 1930s and 1940s, see Algren de Gutiérrez, The Movement against Teaching English, chs. 3 and 4.
16. Torres González, Idioma, 168-75.
17. "Problema de boricuas en Nueva York lo constituye el inglés," El Mundo, February 22, 1947, 1, 12; Welfare Council, Puerto Ricans in New York City.
18. "Boricuas han creado problema en las escuelas," El Mundo, March 20, 1947, 1.
19. This World Telegram article was translated as "Problema de escolares boricuas en Nueva York," El Mundo, May 6, 1947, 12.
20. "Collazo y Sierra Berdecía harán nuevas gestiones en Nueva York," El Mundo, December 18, 1947, 7.
21. Sierra Berdecía, Puerto Rican Emigration, 20-21.
22. "Inglés para trabajadores," editorial, El Mundo, November 12, 1960, 6.
23. "En Barceloneta enseñan inglés a los obreros bajo nuevo plan," El Mundo, January 22, 1951, 4.
24. "Harry Kessler enseñara idioma a obreros que vayan al norte," El Mundo, August 7, 1951, 11.

25. "Instrucción anuncia cursos para aprendizaje del inglés," January 26, 1952, 7, and "1,320 adultos estudian aquí cursos de inglés," February 16, 1952, 21; in *El Mundo*.
26. "Establecen un plan cooperativo para el empleo vocacional," *El Mundo*, April 21, 1952, 3.
27. The Mayor's Committee on Puerto Rican Affairs in New York City, "Interim Report," September 1949 to September 1953; in AGPR, FOG 96–20, 2281.
28. "Ascienden a 72,000 los alumnos boricuas en las escuelas de N. Y.," *El Mundo*, February 26, 1953, 4.
29. "Señalan logros de los boricuas en Nueva York," *El Mundo*, March 2, 1953, 1.
30. "Alumnos boricuas constituyen 24% de matrícula de Manhattan," *El Mundo*, March 31, 1953, 7.
31. "Aumentarán la enseñanza del inglés," *El Mundo*, March 2, 1953, 1, 16.
32. "Conferencia pide gobierno federal siga ayuda a Isla," *El Mundo*, March 9, 1953, 1. *El Mundo* questioned the government's late acknowledgment of this issue in an editorial, "La enseñanza del inglés," March 9, 1953, 6. The second Migration Conference was held in San Juan in July 1954. According to the Labor Department's 1953–54 annual report, the "purpose of this conference was to study the most effective means to aid in the integration and adjustment of the Puerto Ricans in New York." In GPR, Comm. Labor, *Twenty-Third Annual Report 1953–54*, 59.
33. "Muñoz insta preservar español e intensificar la enseñanza del inglés," *El Mundo*, December 30, 1953, 1; quotes are from 16.
34. After the governor's speech, *El Mundo* supported the government's policy of intensifying English language education in public schools in "La enseñanza del inglés," editorial, December 30, 1953, 6.
35. Jose Padín, "Influencia inglés: Relación de isla con EU," *El Mundo*, April 3, 1954, 11.
36. "Instrucción tiene un programa de ayuda a obreros migrantes," *El Mundo*, June 29, 1953, 1. Although the department changed its name to *Departamento de Instrucción Pública* (Department of Public Instruction) in 1953, it kept using the name Department of Education in English texts. To avoid any confusion, and because the word *instrucción* might imply a different meaning in English as well, I will keep referring to this government agency as the Department of Education in the text that follows.
37. GPR, Comm. Labor, *Twenty-Fourth Annual Report 1954–55*, 58–59.
38. "Se repetirán cursos inglés para adultos," *El Mundo*, October 7, 1953, 1.
39. "A migrantes potenciales; 2,197 toman los cursos de inglés conversacional," *El Mundo*, November 18, 1953, 4.
40. GPR, Departamento de Instrucción Pública, *Informe Anual, 1956–57*, 55.
41. "Integraron la enseñanza para adultos," July 3, 1954, 13, and also "Inglés para migrantes," editorial, June 22, 1954, 6; in *El Mundo*.
42. "Toman aquí los cursos inglés para emigrantes," November 23, 1954, 12, and "Clases de inglés," editorial, November 24, 1954, 6; in *El Mundo*.
43. Villaronga, "Program of Education," 146–50.
44. Department of Education, "The Educational Situation of the Puerto Rican Migrant," n.d., n.p.; in OGPRUS, box 2951, file 21, 4.
45. "En la zona rural; intensifican curso inglés a emigrantes," *El Mundo*, April 21, 1955, 15; GPR, Departamento de Instrucción Pública, *Informe Anual, 1955–56*, 77.
46. "Organizan programa de inglés," July 25, 1955, 1, and "Villaronga explica cursos a migrantes," July 20, 1956, 14; in *El Mundo*.
47. Eliza Colón, "Colonialism and Education in Puerto Rico," 129–30, quote from 130.
48. GPR, Departamento de Instrucción Pública, *Informe Anual, 1955–56*, 26–27.
49. Ibid., 26.
50. GPR, Departamento de Instrucción Pública, *Informe Anual, 1957–58*, 26–30.
51. "Enseñanza de inglés; programa ha beneficiado a 27,520 adultos en isla," *El Mundo*, November 19, 1956, 4; GPR, Departamento de Instrucción Pública, *Informe Anual, 1956–57*, 56.

52. "44,000 toman cursos inglés en cuatro años," *El Mundo*, February 8, 1958, 1. The Department of Education's 1958–59 annual report pointed out that 59,304 persons had completed the program's courses since its creation in 1953. GPR, Departamento de Instrucción Pública, *Informe Anual, 1958–59*, 47.
53. GPR, Departamento de Instrucción Pública, *Informe Anual, 1955–56*, 54–56.
54. I was able to examine *Semana* issues only from 1959 to 1961, but the weekly's emphasis then should not be different from that of previous years. In AGPR, Fondo Departamento Instrucción Pública, Section: Programa de Inglés Adultos, Tarea 65–95, Lista 65–21, Serie 8: Publicación Escolar "Semana," box 28.
55. Programa de Alfabetización y Enseñanza Elemental de Adultos, *Informe Anual año fiscal 1960–61* (Hato Rey, PR: Departamento de Instrucción Pública, n.d.), appendix, n.p.; in AGPR, Fondo Departamento Instrucción Pública, Sección Programa de Inglés Adultos, Tarea 65–95, Lista 65–21, Series 1: Correspondencia Administrativa, box 3.
56. *Semana*, January 25, 1960, 4.
57. *Semana*, October 31, 1961, 4.
58. *Semana*, February 13, 1961, 2.
59. *Semana*, April 25, 1960, 1.
60. *Semana*, February 13, 1961, 3.
61. *Semana*, November 14, 1960, 1.
62. "La escuela pública orienta al emigrante," *Educación*, VI:50 (March 1957), 2.
63. Rizzo Costa and Robinett, *La Familia Vázquez*.
64. For a description of this program and its goals, see GPR, Departamento de Instrucción Pública, *Informe Anual, 1957–58*, 63–71. For this fiscal year, thirty-seven community organizers worked in 336 communities throughout the island, making over ten thousand visits and organizing more than five thousand community meetings with an average of forty-five adults per meeting.
65. GPR, Departamento de Instrucción Pública, DIVEDCO, *Emigración*.
66. GPR, Departamento de Instrucción Pública, *Informe Anual, 1955–55*, 76.
67. "Plan ayuda a migrantes; Muñoz urge intensificar la enseñanza del inglés," *El Mundo*, February 12, 1958, 2, emphasis added. The English fluency of Puerto Rican migrants was again a major issue in the fourth Migration Conference held in New York City in 1960. See "Pide aumento de enseñanza inglés en isla," *El Mundo*, June 6, 1960, 1.

The Puerto Rican government had already produced films to advise and orient migrants by 1953. Among the events of the 1953 Migration Conference was a showing of the film *A Friend in New York*, in which migrants were advised on the conditions they would face in the United States and the services provided by the migration offices in the U.S. mainland were advertised. See "Puerto Rico Film Warns Migrants," *New York Times*, March 7, 1953, 17.
68. In AGPR, Fondo Departamento Instrucción Pública, Sección Programa de Inglés para Adultos, Tarea 65–95, Lista 65–21, Series 6: Programa de Televisión, box 24. There are dozens of boxes on WIPR's English programs, including the graded exercises.
69. By the fiscal year 1961–62, 6,025 persons were registered in the television courses and 4,365 were taking the courses offered by radio. Like the English for Adults/English for Prospective Migrants program, most of the participants came from the rural areas. See "Informe Anual de la Sección de Inglés para Adultos Correspondiente al año fiscal 1961–62," Memo from Félix R. Guzmán, director Sección de Inglés para Adultos, to Federico José Modesto, assistant secretary, Programa de Educación de Adultos, July 13, 1962, 5–6; in AGPR, Fondo Departamento Instrucción Pública, Sección Programa de Inglés Adultos, Tarea 65–95, Lista 65–21, Series 1: Correspondencia Administrativa, box 3. The English for Adults program offered in WIPR consisted of eighty half-hour classes three days a week.
70. GPR, Departamento de Instrucción Pública, *Informe Anual, 1958–59*, 46.
71. "La enseñanza del inglés," editorial, September 9, 1958, 6, and "Nivel arriba, nivel abajo," editorial, September 11, 1958, 6; in *El Mundo*.

72. "Exponen causas retardan progreso de boricuas N. Y.," *El Mundo*, September 11, 1958, 16.
73. "Utilizarán aquí TV para enseñar el idioma inglés," September 10, 1958, 1; also "La televisión y el inglés," editorial, September 13, 6; in *El Mundo*.
74. "Boricuas en Nueva York, Alcaldesa impulsará programa de integración," June 21, 1956, 21; "La alcaldesa traza curso integración," June 25, 1956, 23. Also "Hacia asimilación; Alcadesa de SJ exhorta a puertorriqueños en NY," September 23, 1957, 14; "De Oficina de PR; intensificarán NY plan de adaptación de boricuas," March 30, 1959, 16; "Alcaldesa SJ; insta boricuas NY traten integrarse a vida allí," February 17, 1960, 24; in *El Mundo*.
75. "En Nueva York; Muñoz insta puertorriqueños acelerar proceso de asimilación," October 17, 1957, 1; "La barrera del idioma," editorial, October 16, 1957, 6; in *El Mundo*.
76. "Muñoz espera los boricuas en E. U. regresen alguna vez a Puerto Rico," *El Mundo*, September 13, 1958, 18.
77. "En fincas EU; se iniciará la enseñaza inglés a puertorriqueños," *El Mundo*, September 13, 1958, 18.
78. "Bill Cámara: Lleva enseñanza inglés a obreros boricuas EU," *El Mundo*, May 3, 1958, 40, emphasis added. In 1959-60, there were 345 farmworkers taking these courses, organized in twenty groups; in 1960-61, 654 workers participated in the program in twenty-nine groups. In "Informe Anual de la Sección de Inglés para Adultos Correspondiente al año fiscal 1961-62," n.p.
79. On the limited success that English education in public schools has had on making Puerto Ricans fluent in this language, see Torres González, *Idioma*, 288-98; Rodríguez Bou, "Significant Factors," 160-89; and Pousada, "The Singularly Strange Story," 47-55.
80. U.S. Commission on Civil Rights, *Puerto Ricans in the Continental United States*, 145.

NOTES TO CHAPTER 6

1. On migrant discontent among Puerto Rican farmworkers in the United States, see García Colón, "Claiming Equality." For a recent analysis of the Michigan incidents, see Findlay, *We Are Left without a Father Here*; also Asencio Camacho, *Itinerario de muerte*.
2. Sierra Berdecía, "Report for the Governor of Puerto Rico: Living and Working Conditions of Puerto Rican Workers Under Contract in Michigan," August 16, 1950, 1. In AGPR, FOG 96-20, 2273.
3. Ibid.
4. Ayala, *American Sugar Kingdom*; Mapes, *Sweet Tyranny*, ch. 1; and Sparrow, *The Insular Cases*, chs. 1-3.
5. Mapes, *Sweet Tyranny*, 26-28; Sparrow, *The Insular Cases*, ch. 4.
6. Mapes, *Sweet Tyranny*, 24.
7. See ibid., ch. 8.
8. See Mathews, *Puerto Rican Politics*, ch. 5.
9. See Ayala, *American Sugar Kingdom*, ch. 5.
10. Quintero-Rivera, *Conflictos de clase*; García and Quintero-Rivera, *Desafío y solidaridad*; and Meléndez, *Puerto Rico's Statehood Movement*, ch. 4.
11. See Mathews, *Puerto Rican Politics*, passim; Pantojas-García, *Development Strategies*, ch. 2; and Dietz, *Economic History of Puerto Rico*, ch. 3.
12. Ferguson, "Class Transformations in Puerto Rico," 318-44; Ayala, "The Decline of the Plantation Economy."
13. Mapes, *Sweet Tyranny*, 188-205; Kramer, *The Blood of Government*, 424-28.
14. Gatell, "Independence Rejected," 31. Also Mathews, *Puerto Rican Politics*, ch. 4 and 25-44.
15. Mathews, *Puerto Rican Politics*, 254; Gatell, "Independence Rejected," 31-36.

16. Mapes, *Sweet Tyranny*, chs. 4, 5, and 6, quotation is from 129; Valdés, *Al Norte*, chs. 2 and 3.
17. President's Commission, *Migratory Labor*, 13–14.
18. Valdés, *Al Norte*, chs. 5 and 7.
19. Fernández, "Of Immigrants and Migrants," 15; Valdés, *Al Norte*, ch. 5.
20. Valdés, *Al Norte*, 118.
21. President's Commission, *Migratory Labor*, 110.
22. "Who Was Who in the Michigan Sugar Industry," *History of Michigan's Beet Sugar Industry* at http://beetsugarhistory.blogspot.com, and Crawford, Fred Lewis, "Biographical Directory of the United States Congress" at http://bioguide.congress.gov. "F. L. Crawford, 72, Attorney is Dead," April 14, 1957, and "Organize to Protect Farmer's 'Freedom,'" June 9, 1935; in *New York Times*. On New Deal policies in the sugar beet industry, see Mapes, *Sweet Tyranny*, ch. 8.
23. In Mapes, *Sweet Tyranny*, 193.
24. "Resolución para quitarle poderes a Tugwell," February 9, 1943, 1, and "El senador Vanderberg presentará un proyecto para ponerle fin a la gobernación de Tugwell," January 4, 1943, 1; in *El Mundo*. Crawford's resolution wanted to annul the laws creating the Land Authority, the Development Bank, the Economic Development Company (Fomento), the Communications Authority, the Transportation Authority, the Water Resources Authority, and the Sugar Industry Regulatory Board. Although signed by Tugwell, these laws were important pieces of legislation in the PPD's reform program. See Lugo Silva, *The Tugwell Administration*, 142–43.
25. See "Statements by Luis Muñoz Marín, President of the Puerto Rican Senate," January 14, 1943, AFLMM, IV:15, file 12, docs. 16 and 17.
26. "Senado condena enérgicamente resolución del Repte. Crawford," February 9, 1943, 5, and "Representante Crawford le responde a Muñoz," January 18, 1943, 1; in *El Mundo*.
27. Barreto Velázquez, *Redford G. Tugwell*, 133.
28. "El Comité Bell condena en su informe la socialización de economía de Pto. Rico," May 1, 1944, 1, and "El Comité Bell desilucionado con Compañía de Fomento," July 19, 1944, 1; in *El Mundo*.
29. Lugo Silva, *The Tugwell Administration*, 53–54.
30. U.S. Congress, House of Representatives Committee on Insular Affairs, "Investigation," part 3, 280–81.
31. See the letter from Muñoz Marín to Crawford, June 11, 1947; in AFLMM, IV:1, file 137, doc. 27.
32. "El status de la Isla no se decidirá en 25 años," May 26, 1944, 2; "Crawford afirma que P. R. no tendrá ni independencia ni estadidad en 25 años," July 19, 1944, 1; in *El Mundo*.
33. U.S. Congress, House of Representatives Committee on Public Lands, "Election of Governor," 53–55.
34. U.S. Congress, House of Representatives Committee on Insular Affairs, "Investigation," part 4, 313.
35. U.S. Congress, House of Representatives Committee of Interior and Insular Affairs, "Puerto Rico Constitution," 17.
36. Muñoz Marín urged Crawford to reply to Marcantonio's plea during the congressional hearings to approve Public Law 600 to counteract his influence in the House debates; cablegram from Muñoz Marín to Crawford, June 26, 1950; in AFLMM, V:12 (January–December 1950), doc. 41. Muñoz Marín acknowledged Crawford's role in pushing the constitution bill through Congress in a letter to Crawford, March 5, 1952; in AFLMM, V:2 (January–June 1952), doc. 79. *El Mundo*'s William Dorvillier acknowledged that Crawford's initial conflictive relationship with Muñoz Marín changed after Tugwell left the governorship; in "Informe Crawford es obra de estudio," May 4, 1951, 6.
37. Meléndez, "Vito Marcantonio," 199–233.

38. Ferguson, "Restudying *Cañamelar,*" 238–39. Also Ferguson, "Class Transformations," 323–26.
39. Letter from Muñoz Marín to Crawford, January 14, 1953; in AFLMM, V:12 (January–June 1953), doc. 64.
40. Crawford lost the 1952 Republican primaries to Alvin Morell Bentley. *El Mundo* acknowledged Crawford's role in getting reforms through Congress and the negative role that his work on behalf of Puerto Rico played in this contest in "Agradecidos, Señor Crawford," editorial, October 29, 1952, 6. Even *El Imparcial,* not particularly fond of Crawford, agreed with this argument; "Justicia a Crawford," editorial, September 7, 1950, 19.
41. "Instan alza en la quota azúcar aquí," *El Mundo,* May 4, 1951, 1, 25.
42. Muñoz Marín to Crawford, April, 23, 1953; in AFLMM, V:12 (January–June 1953), doc. 171. Also, "Muñoz anuncia Fred Crawford ya no trabaja para el gobierno," *El Mundo,* June 13, 1953, 1.
43. "Dos Nacionalistas planeaban el asesinato del Congresista Crawford," *El Mundo,* August 1, 1951, 1. Ironically, Congressman Bentley, who replaced Crawford in Congress in 1952, was one of five House members shot by Puerto Rican Nationalists after they opened fire in the House chambers on March 1, 1954.
44. GPR, Comm. Labor, *Nineteenth Annual Report 1949–50,* 57.
45. A first-person account of the crash and its aftermath by one of its survivors is presented in Asencio Camacho, *Itinerario de muerte.* A review of the Michigan incident appears in Findlay, *We Are Left without a Father Here,* ch. 4.
46. "Rescatan 37 de avión caído con 62 boricuas," *El Imparcial,* June 7, 1950, 3. Also "Plane with 65 Down in Atlantic; C-46 on Flight from Puerto Rico," June 6, 1950, 1, and "C-46 Survivors Reach Charleston; 37 Tell of Night among Sharks," June 8, 1950, 1; in *New York Times.*
47. "Fernós aboga mayor seguridad en transportación obreros," *El Mundo,* June 7, 1950, 7.
48. Quotes from "37 of 65 on Plane Saved in Atlantic," June, 7, 1950, *New York Times,* 1; also "Congreso investiga el desastre aéreo," *El Mundo,* June 8, 1950.
49. Quote from "Plane Crash Study Set," *New York Times,* June 9, 1950; also "Viaje del avión no ofrecía seguridad," *El Imparcial,* June 8, 1950, 3.
50. "El último desastre," *El Imparcial,* June 8, 1950, 23.
51. "Eluden responsabilidad por desastre de avión," *El Imparcial,* June 9, 1950, 45.
52. "Muñoz busca culpable de la tragedia aérea," *El Imparcial,* June 9, 1950, 3.
53. "Contrataron Westair a base aprobación ACC," June 10, 1950, 2; also, "Otro testigo corrobora no inspeccionaron avión," June 11, 1950, 3; from *El Imparcial.* This testimony and statements were reiterated during the CAB investigation weeks later; "Revelan Trabajo pidió informe sobre la Westair desde 1949," *El Mundo,* June 29, 1950, 23.
54. "Sierra Berdecía dice no rehuirá responsabilidad," *El Imparcial,* June 13, 1950, 5.
55. "La causa del desastre," *El Imparcial,* June 9, 1950, 19. While *El Imparcial* linked these tragic air crashes to the government's migration policy, *El Mundo,* whose editorials strongly supported it, blamed the lack of implementation of rules and regulations already in paper; see "El caso de la Westair," editorial, *El Mundo,* July 7, 1950, 6.
56. "Alcalde censura sistema de emigración obreros," *El Imparcial,* June 14, 1950, 2.
57. Sierra Berdecía, "Report for the Governor of Puerto Rico," 1–2; also, "Grupo de 29 se encuentra en Míchigan, *El Mundo,* June 12, 1950, 1.
58. "'Beet Airlift' Runs from Puerto Rico," and "Air Lift of Puerto Ricans Averts Wide Beet Crop Loss in Michigan," June 18, 1950; in *New York Times.*
59. GPR, Comm. Labor, *Nineteenth Annual Report 1949–50,* 57–58.
60. "Transigen caso de la Westair con la Lloyds," *El Mundo,* June 24, 1951. The CAB declared the unspecified failure of the two engines as probable cause for the accident. See "Vistas públicas sobre tragedia aérea Westair," *El Imparcial,* June 17, 1950, 4; and Asencio Camacho, *Itinerario de muerte,* 104–5.

61. Asencio Camacho, *Itinerario de muerte*, 64–65. Also, "Piden de la JAC revocación del certificado de la Westair," *El Mundo*, July 6, 1950, 1.
62. Pagán de Colón, *Programa*, 24–28.
63. "Boricuas en Míchigan dicen están muy bien," June 21, 1950, 6; also "Obreros se sienten satisfechos," July 13, 1950, 19; in *El Imparcial*.
64. "Boricuas se quejan de maltrato en Míchigan," *El Imparcial*, June 27, 1950, 5. There are hundreds of letters from farmworkers in Michigan complaining to Muñoz Marín about their situation there in Box 2273 of the Governor's Office fund at Puerto Rico's General Archives. I decided to use those letters from farmworkers that were published in newspapers since these became part of the public debate on the Michigan issue.
65. "Maltrato en Míchigan," July 5, 1950, 17, and "Mal trato," July 6, 1950, 17; in *El Imparcial*.
66. "Quejas de Míchigan," *El Imparcial*, July 7, 1950, 19.
67. "Cruz Roja se hace cargo de boricuas en Míchigan," *El Imparcial*, August 10, 1950, 4.
68. "Describen horrores en campos de Míchigan," *El Imparcial*, July 9, 1950, 5. Also "Grupo obreros Míchigan alega que se les engañó con contrato," *El Mundo*, July 26, 1950, 22.
69. "Le agradaría a usted," *El Imparcial*, July 10, 1950, 19; signed by Pedro Rodríguez and others.
70. "Sigue el maltrato," *El Imparcial*, July 16, 1950, 17.
71. "Nueva quejas," *El Imparcial*, August 5, 1920, 19; signed by Emilio Guzmán and many others.
72. "Quieren vivir de nosotros," *El Imparcial*, July 12, 1950, 19.
73. "Desesperación en Míchigan," July 22, 1950, 17. Also "Están hastiados," July 1, 1950, 21; in *El Imparcial*.
74. "Obreros Míchigan piden Muñoz Marín intervenga," July 14, 1950, 7. Also "Más atropellos," July 27, 1950, 17; in *El Imparcial*.
75. "Quieren fugarse," *El Imparcial*, July 15, 1950, 17.
76. "Obreros desesperados," *El Imparcial*, July 18, 1950, 17.
77. "Urge se investigue," *El Imparcial*, July 18, 1950, 17.
78. "Ayuda boricua a Míchigan perjudica a Puerto Rico," *El Imparcial*, July 2, 1950, 5.
79. "El caso de Míchigan," *El Imparcial*, July 23, 1950, 17.
80. "Pegan a los obreros"; also "$15 por 40 días," in *El Imparcial*, July 27, 1950, 17.
81. "No es cierto," *El Imparcial*, July 27, 1950, 17.
82. "Siguen las quejas," July 9, 1950, 17; also "Los obreros de Míchigan," July 16, 1950, 17; in *El Imparcial*.
83. "Relata miseria familia de obrero en Míchigan," July 26, 1950, 5; also "Lo engañaron," July 3, 1950, 21; in *El Imparcial*.
84. "Desalojan esposa de obrero," *El Imparcial*, July 21, 1950, 5.
85. See, e.g., "Obreros alegan maltrato al regreso de Míchigan," July 22, 1950, 5; "Obrero enfermo relata horrores de Míchigan," August 5, 1950, 22; "Obrero enfermo denuncia atropellos en Míchigan," September 9, 1950, 10; all from *El Imparcial*.
86. "No somos mas Populares," *El Imparcial*, July 19, 950, 15; like many others from the Michigan situation, this news clipping was found in the governor's papers in AGPR, FOG 96-20, 2273.
87. "Situación en Míchigan," *El Imparcial*, August 15, 1950, 15.
88. "Puerto Rican Farm Workers Embittered by Deplorable Plight," August, 6, 1950; also "Puerto Ricans Vow Not to Return," August 8, 1950, both in *Bay City (Michigan) Times*; in AGPR, FOG 96-20, 2276.
89. Valdés, *Al Norte*, ch. 6, quote from 132.
90. Memo from Torres to Estella Draper, "Visita a Míchigan," June 26, 1950; in AGPR, FOG 96-20, 2273.
91. Memo from Perl to Sierra Berdecía, "Field Trip-Michigan," July 17, 1950; in AGPR, FOG 96-20, 2273.

92. "F. Sierra Berdecía partió ayer junto con Howard Davidson," July 25, 1950, 2. Sierra Berdecía repeatedly stated that the goal of his trip to Michigan was "to help both our boys and employers as well." In "Sierra empieza investigación en Míchigan," July 27, 1950, 12; from *El Mundo*.
93. "El viaje de Sierra Berdecía," editorial, *El Mundo*, July 24, 1950, 6. Also "Migrant Labor Inquiry; Puerto Rican Commissioner in Michigan on Inspection," the *New York Times*, July 25, 1950.
94. "Protestas en Míchigan," editorial, *El Imparcial*, July 24, 1950, 17.
95. "Crawford afirma visita Sierra es bien recibida en Míchigan," July 26, 1950, 3, and "Crawford analiza intervención en la contratación de obreros," August 10, 1950, 18; in *El Mundo*. Muñoz Marín informed Crawford of Sierra Berdecía's trip to Michigan in a July 26, 1950, letter; in AGPR, FOG 96-20, 2273.
96. Dorvillier, "Obreros boricuas ayudan salvar carrera Crawford," *El Mundo*, July 10 1950, 6.
97. "Varios obreros envían quejas desde Míchigan," *El Mundo*, August 8, 1950, 7; "Sierra ignora a los obreros en Míchigan," *El Imparcial*, August 16, 1950, 8.
98. Sierra Berdecía, "Report for the Governor of Puerto Rico." Also "Indigna a Sierra la situación de los boricuas en Míchigan," *El Mundo*, August 19, 1950.
99. "Frente al maltrato," editorial, *El Mundo*, August 19, 1950, 6.
100. "Situación en Míchigan," editorial, *El Imparcial*, August 20, 1950, 17.
101. Letter from Sierra Berdecía to Henderson, and letter from Crawford to Muñoz Marín, both August 8, 1950; in AGPR, FOG 96-20, 2273. Crawford's letter was sent on a "Farmers and Manufacturers Beet Sugar Association" letterhead.
102. "Acusa a Sierra hacer política en caso obreros," August 21, 1950, 1; "Alegan Sierra no coopera en caso Míchigan," August 23, 1950, 2; and "Crawford alega investigación le perjudica," September 1, 1950, 1; in *El Mundo*. Also "Puerto Rico Seeks Workers' Return," *New York Times*, August 20, 1950, 32.
103. "Míchigan no puede acoger 15,000 obreros: Sierra," August 18, 1950, 6, and "Sierra Berdecía refuta acusación de Crawford," August, 23, 1950, 7; in *El Imparcial*. Also "Commissioner Pledges Aid," the *New York Times*, August 22, 1950.
104. "Los obreros en Míchigan," editorial, *El Imparcial*, August 25, 1950, 19.
105. "Muñoz plantea emergencia en Míchigan," August 21, 1950, 1, and "Firman ley para ayudar trabajadores," August 25, 1950, 1; in *El Mundo*.
106. "Puerto Rico to Pay for Migrant's Aid," *New York Times*, August 21, 1950.
107. "Dear friend and fellow-citizen," letter from Muñoz Marín, August 25, 1950; in AGPR, FOG 96-20, box 2273. The letter was made public in "Muñoz aconseja obreros que sigan en Míchigan," August 29, 1950, 5; also, "Ordenan ayudar familias de obreros en Míchigan," August 23, 1950, 3; in *El Imparcial*.
108. See telegrams from Muñoz Marín to Crawford and Henderson, August 21, 1950; and Henderson to Muñoz Marín, August 22, 1950. On August 24, Muñoz Marín's assistant, Roberto Sánchez Vilella, informed Henderson that the governor would send him three thousand copies of his letter to the Michigan workers so these could be distributed in the farms. All documents in AGPR, FOG 96-20, 2273. See also "Michigan Beet Labor to Get Hourly Rate," *New York Times*, August 23, 1950. In his telegrams to Crawford and Henderson, Muñoz Marín made it clear that he was trying to mediate between the workers and the sugar beet producers. During his deposition before Truman's Commission on Migratory Labor, Crawford stated that in visits to Michigan farms, he saw Puerto Rican workers with copies of Muñoz Marín's letter. "Crawford declarará en la vista hoy sobre migración obreros," *El Mundo*, September 11, 1950, 10.
109. Crawford es vencedor en su distrito; se van Tydings y Marcantonio," *El Mundo*, November 9, 1950, 1. The newspaper reported that Crawford was reelected with the vote of areas where sugar beet production was dominant, where many believed that the last harvest had been saved by Puerto Ricans "brought" there by him.

110. Letter to Muñoz Marín, August 27, 1950; in AGPR, FOG 96-20, 2273.
111. Memo from Torres to Manuel Cabranes, "Progress Report about the Michigan Situation," August 30, 1950; in AGPR, FOG 96-20, 2273.
112. Memo from Cabranes to Sierra Berdecía, "Ayuda prestada a trabajadores mediante la ley no. 1," August 23, 1950; in OGPRUS, box 3056, Folder 6 (Reports and Aid for Agricultural Workers, 1950-51).
113. Memo from Sierra Berdecía to Muñoz Marín, September 27, 1950; in AGPR, FOG 96-20, 2276.
114. "Hay situación difícil en obreros boricuas; piden la repatriación," *El Mundo*, October 1, 1950, 1.
115. "Migrants to Stay in U. S.," *New York Times*, October 30, 1950.
116. "Obreros se niegan a renovar contrato en fincas de Míchigan," October 22, 1950, 2, and "Gobierno anuncia personal para ayuda en Míchigan," September 13, 1950, 2; in *El Imparcial*.
117. GPR, Comm. Labor, *Vigésimo Informe Anual, 1950-51,* 44.
118. Cabranes to Pagán de Colón, December 7, 1950; in OGPRUS, box, 2991, folder 5.
119. Crawford to Muñoz Marín, March 14, 1952; in AGPR, FOG 96-20, 2276. Also "Crawford insta Muñoz acelerar envío trabajadores a Míchigan," *El Mundo*, March 22, 1952, 5.
120. Memo "Possibilities of Sending Puerto Rican Farm Workers to Michigan," meeting at the University of Puerto Rico on March 19, 1952; also letters from Sierra Berdecía to Muñoz Marín, March 24, 1952, and Muñoz Marín to Crawford, March 27, 1952; all in AGPR, FOG 96-20, 2276. Emphasis added in the quote.
121. See memo from Senior to O'Connor, "Migrant Farm Labor, Michigan," March 20, 1953; in AGPR, FOG 96-20, 2278. Also "Aceptan salida de 184 obreros para Míchigan," *El Mundo*, May 7, 1952, 3.
122. "Siervos a Míchigan," editorial, March 25, 1952, and "El desastre de Míchigan," editorial, March 28, 1952; both in *El Diario de Nueva York*; in AGPR, FOG 96-20, 2272.
123. "Se informa que obreros nativos pueden trabajar en Míchigan," *El Mundo*, March 31, 1953, 4. On March 11, 1953, O'Connor sent a memo on Michigan to Sierra Berdecía, Pagán de Colón, Senior, and several of the governor's advisors arguing that sugar beet producers there were again interested in seeking Puerto Rican labor. He claimed that this could present "an opportunity to lay the groundwork for the Middlewest 'colonies,' [sic] which should serve to deflect some of the migratory stream into metropolitan New York." In AGPR, tarea 63-37, Series 5, "Correspondencia de la División de Colocaciones en Fincas 1953," File "Migraciones Clandestinas 1953."
124. Valdés, *Al Norte*, 133.
125. Quintero-Rivera, *Conflictos de clase y política*; García and Quintero-Rivera, *Desafío y solidaridad*.

NOTES TO CHAPTER 7

1. Report from Pagán de Colón to Muñoz Marín, "Resumen de las actividades llevadas a cabo en mi visita a la ciudad de Miami durante los días 19 al 27 de noviembre de 1949," December 2, 1949, 1; in AGPR, FOG 96-20, 2275.
2. Kirsten, "Agribusiness," 650.
3. Kirsten, "Agribusiness," 650-58.
4. "Jersey Welcomes Migrant Workers," *New York Times*, September 6, 1950, 29.
5. "Crawford alega investigación le perjudica," September 1, 1950, 1; "Crawford defiende el derecho de boricuas a ganarse la vida," September 5, 1950, 1; "Muñoz juzga Fred Crawford amigo de la isla," September 7, 1950, 1; in *El Mundo*.

6. See "Fernós Isern considera idea ir a Míchigan," September 8, 1950, 1, where the resident commissioner declared his support for "our friends in Congress." In the editorial "Las primarias en Míchigan," September 15, 1950, 6, *El Mundo* celebrated Crawford's primary victory.
7. "Inician vistas del trabajo migratorio," *El Mundo*, September 12, 1950, 1.
8. "No U. S. Curbs Urged on Migrant Labor," *New York Times*, September 12, 1950, 28.
9. "His Wages 'Minus,' Migrant Relates," *New York Times*, September 13, 1950, 30.
10. "Dama de Míchigan hace relato de necesidades de los boricuas," September 13, 1950, 17; "Impresiona el relato de obreros a Comité Trabajo Migratorio," September 14, 1950, 1; in *El Mundo*.
11. "Top Federal Agency Urged for Migrant Farm Workers," *New York Times*, April 8, 1951, 1. On the commission's report and its aftermath, see Lyon, "Legal Status," 425–37; Kirsten, "Agribusiness"; and Robinson, "Taking the Fair Deal."
12. President's Commission, *Migratory Labor*. Page numbers of quoted passages from this source will appear parenthetically in the text.
13. Using a different method and sources, Lyon argues that in 1952 there were close to 2.162 million migratory workers, *excluding* foreign labor. See Lyon, "Legal Status," 30.
14. President's Commission, *Migratory Labor*, 98; also Lyon, "Legal Status," 76–77, 455–61. USES managed the Farm Placement Service, whose main function was to provide labor to U.S. agriculture.
15. Lyon, "Legal Status," 81–82. According to Lyon, there were some four hundred agricultural associations in 1949.
16. Government of Puerto Rico (GPR), Department of Labor, Commissioner of Labor (Comm. Labor), *Vigésimo Segundo Informe Anual, 1952–53*, 37. From here on this source will be cited as GPR, Comm. Labor.
17. The selection process and the contracting of farmworkers going to the United States is discussed in GPR, Comm. Labor, *Vigésimo Informe Anual, 1950–51*, 38–39.
18. GPR, Comm. Labor, *Twenty-Third Annual Report 1953–54*, 14.
19. GPR, Comm. Labor, *Twenty-Fourth Annual Report 1954–55*, 67; and GPR, Comm. Labor, *Vigésimo Informe Anual, 1950–51*, 80.
20. The data comes from GPR, Comm. Labor, *Twenty-Third Annual Report 1953–54*, 107; *Twenty-Fourth Annual Report 1954–55*, 70; *Twenty-Third Annual Report 1956–57*, 106; and *Twenty-Sixth Annual Report 1959–60*, 73, 75.
21. GPR, Comm. Labor, *Twenty-Sixth Annual Report 1959–60*, 86–87.
22. GPR, Comm. Labor, *Twenty-First Annual Report 1951–52*, 40.
23. See memo from Pagán de Colón, "Registro de Personas Interesadas en Migrar," April 4, 1952; in Correspondencia de la División de Colocaciones en Fincas 1953, Departamento del Trabajo, in AGPR, Tarea 63-37, Serie 5, File: Memorandum a las Oficinas Locales 1952. In 1957 there were 14,435 workers registered for migration, 4,399 ready to migrate and 7,659 newly registered. In GPR, Comm. Labor, *Vigésimo Cuarto Informe Anual, 1957–58*, 58.
24. Notices to farmworkers, application forms, and office memos are found in Correspondencia de la División de Colocaciones en Fincas, Departamento del Trabajo, in AGPR, Tarea 63-37, Serie 5, File: Material Impreso de Migración, 1952; the quote is from "La carta del agricultor," by the Employment Section, Department of Labor, n.d. On the importance of all farmworkers having their photo ID when going to the United States, see the memo on this subject by Pagán de Colón to all local office managers on May 19, 1952; in Correspondencia de la División de Colocaciones en Fincas 1953, Departamento del Trabajo, in AGPR, Tarea 63-37, Serie 5, File: Memorandum a las Oficinas Locales 1952.
25. In Correspondencia de la División de Colocaciones en Fincas, Departamento del Trabajo, in AGPR, Tarea 63-37, Serie 5, File: Material Impreso de Migración, 1952.

26. I have found no data from the Department of Labor or any other source indicating the percentages of worker desertion under the FPP. Data on the number of migrant farmworkers under contract that returned were not reported by the department.
27. GPR, Comm. Labor, *Vigésimo Cuarto Informe Anual, 1957–58,* 66.
28. GPR, Comm. Labor, *Vigésimo Informe Anual, 1950–1951,* 43.
29. GPR, Comm. Labor, *Vigésimo Cuarto Informe Anual, 1957–1958,* 79.
30. Lapp, "Managing Migration," 144–47.
31. GPR, Comm. Labor, *Eighteenth Annual Report 1948–49,* 52–53.
32. GPR, Comm. Labor, *Vigésimo Cuarto Informe Anual, 1957–1958,* 64; *Twenty-Fifth Annual Report 1958–59,* 62; *Twenty-Sixth Annual Report 1959–60,* 64.
33. See GPR, Comm. Labor, *Vigésimo Cuarto Informe Anual 1957–1958,* 60–61. That year, 1,995 prospective migrants received orientation at the airport's office.
34. GPR, Comm. Labor, *Twenty-Fifth Annual Report 1955–56,* 51.
35. GPR, Comm. Labor, *Twenty-Third Annual Report 1956–57,* 84.
36. GPR, Comm. Labor, *Twenty-Fifth Annual Report 1955–56,* 64, 66, 82.
37. GPR, Comm. Labor, *Twenty-Fourth Annual Report 1954–55,* 55. Also Lapp, "Managing Migration," 151–56.
38. Description of services in GPR, Comm. Labor: *Twenty-Third Annual Report 1953–54,* 55; *Twenty-First Annual Report 1951–52,* 43; *Twenty-Fourth Annual Report 1954–55,* 59; *Twenty-Seventh Annual Report 1960–61,* 63–64.
39. GPR, Comm. Labor, *Vigésimo Cuarto Informe Anual 1957–1958,* 71–72.
40. GPR, Comm. Labor, *Vigésimo Cuarto Informe Anual 1957–1958,* 69.
41. Ibid., 70.
42. Data from GPR, Comm. Labor: *Twenty-Third Annual Report 1953–54,* 53; *Twenty-Fifth Annual Report 1955–56,* 76; *Twenty-Third Annual Report 1956–57,* 59; *Vigésimo Cuarto Informe Anual, 1957–1958,* 70.
43. GPR, Comm. Labor, *Twenty-Fourth Annual Report 1954–55,* 60, and *Vigésimo Cuarto Informe Anual, 1957–58,* 70.
44. GPR, Comm. Labor, *Twenty-Seventh Annual Report 1960–61,* 59.
45. GPR, Comm. Labor, *Vigésimo Cuarto Informe Anual 1957–58,* 72–73.
46. Lapp, "Managing Migration," 145–46.
47. Ibid., chs. 4 and 5.
48. According to the Department of Labor's 1960–61 annual report, division functionaries handled 3,304 claims that year, out of which 2,630 came from agricultural workers. That year some $157,299 were recovered from workers' claims, out of which $139,211 went to agricultural workers. GPR, Comm. Labor, *Twenty-Seventh Annual Report 1960–61,* 61–62. On contract violations by farmers and the employment of farmworkers without a government contract, see Whalen, *From Puerto Rico to Philadelphia,* 154ff.
49. Lapp, "Managing Migration," 187–97; on contract violations and working and housing conditions, see Whalen, *From Puerto Rico to Philadelphia,* 154–56.
50. Lapp, "Managing Migration," 196–99.
51. U.S. Commission on Civil Rights, *Puerto Ricans in the Continental United States,* 44, 47–48, 52, 56.
52. Acosta-Belén and Santiago, *Puerto Ricans in the United States,* 126–44.
53. U.S. Commission on Civil Rights, *Puerto Ricans in the Continental United States,* 61.
54. Acosta-Belén and Santiago, *Puerto Ricans in the United States,* 129.
55. Lapp, "Managing Migration," 203.
56. See, e.g., "Puerto Rico: A Study in Democratic Development," the special issue of the *Annals of the American Academy of Political and Social Science* 285 (January 1953) devoted entirely to Puerto Rico's postwar transformations.

BIBLIOGRAPHY

Acosta-Belén, Edna, and Carlos E. Santiago. *Puerto Ricans in the United States: A Contemporary Portrait.* Boulder, CO: Lynne Rienner Publishers, 2006.

Albors, Juan A., and Juan López Mangual. *Selected Statistics on the Visitors and Hotel Industry in Puerto Rico.* San Juan: Economic Development Administration, January 1967.

Algren de Gutiérrez, Edith. *The Movement against Teaching English in Schools in Puerto Rico.* Langham, MD: University Press of America, 1987.

Ames, Azel. "Labor Conditions in Porto Rico." *Bulletin of the Department of Labor* 34 (May 1901): 377–439.

Anderson, Robert. *Gobierno y partidos políticos en Puerto Rico.* Madrid: Editorial Tecnos, 1970.

Aranda, Elizabeth M. *Emotional Bridges to Puerto Rico: Migration, Return Migration, and the Struggles of Incorporation.* Lanham, MD: Rowman and Littlefield, 2007.

Asencio Camacho, Luis. *Itinerario de muerte.* Yauco, PR: Editorial Coquí, 2012.

Asociación de Salud Pública de Puerto Rico. *El problema poblacional de Puerto Rico.* San Juan: Administración General de Suministros, 1946.

Ayala, César J. *American Sugar Kingdom: The Plantation Economy of the Spanish Caribbean, 1898–1934.* Chapel Hill: University of North Carolina Press, 1999.

———. "The Decline of the Plantation Economy and the Puerto Rican Migration of the 1950s." *Latino Studies Journal* 7, no. 1 (Winter 1996): 62–90.

Baldoz, Rick. *The Third Asiatic Invasion: Empire and Migration in Filipino America, 1898–1946.* New York: New York University Press, 2011.

Baldoz, Rick, and César Ayala. "The Bordering of America: Colonialism and Citizenship in the Philippines and Puerto Rico." *Centro: Journal of the Center for Puerto Rican Studies* 25, no. 1 (Spring 2013): 76–105.

Baldrich, José Juan. "Class and the State: The Origins of Populism in Puerto Rico, 1934–1952." PhD diss., Yale University, 1981.

Barreto Velázquez, Norberto. *Redford G. Tugwell: el último de los tutores.* Río Piedras, PR: Ediciones Huracán, 2004.

Basch, Linda, Nina Glick Schiller, and Cristina Szanton Blanc. *Nations Unbound: Transnational Projects, Postcolonial Predicaments, and Deterritorialized Nation States.* Langhorne, PA: Gordon and Breach, 1994.

Baubock, Rainer. "Towards a Political Theory of Migrant Transnationalism." *International Migration Review* 37, no. 3 (Fall 2003): 700–723.

Bonilla, Frank, and Ricardo Campos. "A Wealth of Poor: Puerto Ricans in the New Economic Order." *Daedalus* 110 (1981): 134–35.

Briggs, Laura. *Reproducing Empire: Race, Sex, Science, and U.S. Imperialism in Puerto Rico.* Berkeley: University of California Press, 2002.

Button, Kenneth John, and Henry Vega. "The Effects of Air Transportation on the Movement of Labor." *GeoJournal* 71, no. 1 (2008): 67–81.

Cabán, Pedro A. *Constructing a Colonial People: Puerto Rico and the United States, 1898–1932.* Boulder, CO: Westview Press, 1999.

Cabranes, José A. "Citizenship and the American Empire: Notes on the Legislative History of the United States Citizenship of Puerto Ricans." *University of Pennsylvania Law Review* 127, no. 2 (December 1978): 391–489.

Castles, Stephen. "Migration and Community Formation under Conditions of Globalization." *International Migration Review* 36, no. 4 (Winter 2002): 1143–68.

Centro de Estudios Puertorriqueños, History Task Force. *Labor Migration under Capitalism: The Puerto Rican Experience.* New York: Monthly Review Press, 1979.

———. *Sources for the Study of Puerto Rican Migration, 1879–1930.* New York: Centro de Estudios Puertorriqueños, 1982.

Cervantes-Rodríguez, Margarita, Ramón Grosfoguel, and Eric Mielants, eds. *Caribbean Migration to Western Europe and the United States: Essays on Incorporation, Identity, and Citizenship.* Philadelphia: Temple University Press, 2009.

Davis, Kingsley. "Puerto Rico: A Crowded Island." *Annals of the American Academy of Political and Social Science* vol. 285 (January 1953): 116–22.

del Moral, Solsiree. *Negotiating Empire: The Cultural Politics of Schools in Puerto Rico, 1898–1952.* Madison: University of Wisconsin Press, 2013.

DeSipio, Louis, and Adrian D. Pantoja. "Puerto Rican Exceptionalism?: A Comparative Analysis of Puerto Rican, Mexican, Salvadoran, and Dominican Transnational Civic and Political Ties." In *Latino Politics: Identity, Mobilization, and Representation*, edited by Rodolfo Espino, David L. Leal, and Kenneth Meier, 104–20. Charlottesville: University of Virginia Press, 2007.

Dierikx, Marc. *Clipping the Clouds: How Air Travel Changed the World.* Westport, CT: Praeger, 2008.

Dietz, James. *Economic History of Puerto Rico: Institutional Change and Capitalist Development.* Princeton: Princeton University Press, 1986.

Duany, Jorge. *Blurred Borders: Transnational Migration between the Hispanic Caribbean and the United States.* Chapel Hill: University of North Carolina Press, 2011.

———. "The Orlando Ricans: Overlapping Identity Discourses among Middle-class Puerto Rican Immigrants." *Centro Journal* 22, no. 1 (Spring 2010): 84–115.

———. *The Puerto Rican Nation on the Move: Identities on the Island and in the United States*. Chapel Hill: University of North Carolina Press, 2002.

———. "A Transnational Colonial Migration: Puerto Rico's Farm Labor Program." *New West Indian Guide* 84, nos. 3–4 (2010): 225–51.

Duffy Burnett, Christina. "'They say I am not an American . . .': The Noncitizen National and the Law of American Empire." *Virginia Journal of International Law* 48, no. 4 (2008): 559–718.

———. "*Untied* States: American Expansion and Territorial Deannexation." *University of Chicago Law Review* 72, no. 3 (Summer 2005): 797–879.

Duffy Burnett, Christina, and Burke Marshall, eds. *Foreign in a Domestic Sense: Puerto Rico, American Expansion and the Constitution*. Durham, NC: Duke University Press, 2001.

Eliza Colón, Sylvia M. "Colonialism and Education in Puerto Rico: Appraisal of the Public Schools during the Commonwealth Period, 1952 to 1958." PhD diss., Washington University, 1989.

Erman, Sam. "Puerto Rico and the Promise of United States Citizenship; Struggles around Status in a New Empire, 1898–1917." PhD diss., University of Michigan, 2010.

Estades Font, María Eugenia. *La presencia militar de Estados Unidos en Puerto Rico 1898–1918: Intereses estratégicos y dominación colonial*. Río Piedras, PR: Ediciones Huracán, 1988.

Fujita-Rony, Dorothy B. *American Workers, Colonial Power: Philippine Seattle and the Transpacific West, 1919–1941*. Berkeley: University of California Press, 2003.

Ferguson, R. Brian. "Class Transformations in Puerto Rico." PhD diss., Columbia University, 1988.

———. "Restudying *Cañamelar* of *The People of Puerto Rico*." *Identities: Global Studies in Culture and Power* 18 (2011): 234–43.

Fernández, Lilia. *Brown in the Windy City: Mexicans and Puerto Ricans in Postwar Chicago*. Chicago: University of Chicago Press, 2012.

———. "Of Immigrants and Migrants: Mexican and Puerto Rican Labor Migration in Comparative Perspective, 1942–1964." *Journal of American Ethnic History* 29, no. 3 (Spring 2010): 6–39.

Fernández Méndez, Eugenio. "¿Asimilación o enquistamiento?: Dos polos del problema de la emigración transcultural puertorriqueña." *La Torre* 1, no. 3 (January–May 1956): 137–46.

Fernós-Isern, Antonio. *The Transportation Needs of Puerto Rico*. Washington, DC: Office of Puerto Rico, 1949.

Findlay, Eileen. *We Are Left without a Father Here: Masculinity, Domesticity, and Migration in Postwar Puerto Rico*. Durham, NC: Duke University Press, 2014.

Fleisher, Belton M. "Some Aspects of Puerto Rican Migration to the United States." *The Review of Economics and Statistics* 45, no. 3 (August 1963): 245–53.

Fors, Bonnie D. "The Jones Act for Puerto Rico." PhD diss., Loyola University of Chicago, 1976.

García, Gervasio, and A. G. Quintero-Rivera. *Desafío y solidaridad: Breve historia del movimiento obrero puertorriqueño*. Río Piedras, PR: Ediciones Huracán, 1991.

García Colón, Ismael. "Claiming Equality: Puerto Rican Farmworkers in Western New York." *Latino Studies* 6 (2008): 269–89.

Gatell, Frank Otto. "Independence Rejected: Puerto Rico and the Tydings Bill of 1936." *Hispanic American Historical Review* 38, no. 1 (February 1958): 25–44.

Gerena Valentín, Gilberto. *Soy Gilberto Gerena Valentín: Memorias de un puertorriqueño en Nueva York*. New York: Centro de Estudios Puertorriqueños, Hunter College, City University of New York, 2013.

Go, Julian. *American Empire and the Politics of Meaning: Elite Political Cultures in the Philippines and Puerto Rico During U.S. Colonialism*. Durham, NC: Duke University Press, 2008.

———. "Introduction: Global Perspectives on the U.S. Colonial State in the Philippines." In Go and Foster, *The American Colonial State in the Philippines*, 1–42.

Go, Julian, and Anne L. Foster, eds. *The American Colonial State in the Philippines: Global Perspectives*. Durham, NC: Duke University Press, 2003.

Goldsmith, William W. "The Impact of the Tourism and Travel Industry on a Developing Regional Economy: The Puerto Rican Case." PhD diss., Cornell University, 1968.

González Díaz, Emilio. "El Estado y la clases dominantes en la situación colonial." *Revista Mexicana de Sociología* 40, no. 3 (July–September 1978): 1141–52.

Government of Puerto Rico, Departamento de Instrucción Pública. *Informe Anual del Departamento de Instrucción Pública 1955–56*. San Juan: Departamento de Instrucción Pública, 1956.

———. *Informe Anual del Departamento de Instrucción Pública 1956–57*. San Juan: Departamento de Instrucción Pública, 1957.

———. *Informe Anual del Departamento de Instrucción Pública 1957–58*. San Juan: Departamento de Instrucción Pública, 1958.

———. *Informe Anual del Departamento de Instrucción Pública 1958–59*. San Juan: Departamento de Instrucción Pública, 1959.

———. División de Educación de la Comunidad (DIVEDCO). *Emigración*. 2nd ed. San Juan: Departamento de Instrucción Pública, 1966.

Government of Puerto Rico, Department of Labor, Commissioner of Labor. *Eighteenth Annual Report of the Commissioner of Labor Submitted to the Governor of Puerto Rico, Fiscal Year 1948–1949*. San Juan: Department of Labor, 1949.

———. *Nineteenth Annual Report of the Commissioner of Labor Submitted to the Governor of Puerto Rico, Fiscal Year 1949–1950*. San Juan: Government Service Office, Printing Division, 1951.

———. *Vigésimo Informe Anual del Comisionado del Trabajo al Gobernador de Puerto Rico, año fiscal 1950–1951*. San Juan: Departamento de Hacienda, 1951.

———. *Twenty-First Annual Report of the Commissioner of Labor, Fiscal Year 1951–1952*. San Juan: Government Service Office, Printing Division, 1954.

———. *Vigésimo Segundo Informe Anual al Gobernador de Puerto Rico año fiscal 1952–1953*. San Juan: Departamento de Hacienda, 1953.

———. *Twenty-Third Annual Report of the Secretary of Labor Submitted to the Governor of Puerto Rico for the Fiscal Year 1953–54*. San Juan: Printing Division, Treasury Department, 1955.

———. *Twenty-Fourth Annual Report of the Secretary of Labor, Fiscal Year 1954–1955*. San Juan: Government Service Office, 1956.

———. *Twenty-Fifth Annual Report of the Secretary of Labor Submitted to the Governor of Puerto Rico for the Fiscal Year 1955–56*. San Juan: Printing Division, Treasury Department, 1957.

———. *Twenty-Third Annual Report of the Secretary of Labor Submitted to the Governor of Puerto Rico for the Fiscal Year 1956–57*. San Juan: Printing Division, Treasury Department, 1957.

———. *Vigésimo Cuarto Informe Anual del Secretario del Trabajo al Gobernador de Puerto Rico, año fiscal 1957–1958*. San Juan: Departamento de Hacienda, 1959.

———. *Twenty-Fifth Annual Report of the Secretary of Labor Submitted to the Governor of Puerto Rico for the Fiscal Year 1958–59*. San Juan: Printing Division, Treasury Department, 1960.

———. *Twenty-Sixth Annual Report of the Secretary of Labor Submitted to the Governor of Puerto Rico for the Fiscal Year 1959-60*. San Juan: Printing Division, Treasury Department, 1961.

———. *Twenty-Seventh Annual Report of the Secretary of Labor Submitted to the Governor of Puerto Rico for the Fiscal Year 1960-61*. San Juan: Printing Division, Treasury Department, 1962.

Government of Puerto Rico, Department of Labor, Migration Division. *Informe Anual*, año fiscal 1958-59, Office of the Government of Puerto Rico in the United States (OGPRUS), Center for Puerto Rican Studies Library and Archives, box 2733, Administration Program, Agency Reports series, 1939-1992, folder 6.

———. *Annual Report 1955-1956*. New York: Migration Division, 1956, OGPRUS, box 2733, folder 2.

Government of Puerto Rico, Legislatura. *Leyes de la Tercera Legislatura Ordinaria de la Decimosexta Asamblea Legislativa de Puerto Rico*. San Juan: Administración de Suministros, División de Imprenta, 1947.

———. *Leyes de la Cuarta y Quinta Legislaturas Extraordinarias de la Decimosexta Asamblea Legislativa de Puerto Rico*. San Juan: Administración de Suministros, División de Imprenta, 1947.

Green, Julie. "Labor of Empire: Recent Scholarship on U.S. History and Imperialism." *Labor: Studies in Working-Class History of the Americas* 1, no. 2 (2004): 113-29.

Greenwood, Michael J. "Research on Internal Migration in the United States: A Survey." *Journal of Economic Literature* 13, no. 2 (June 1975): 397-433.

Grosfoguel, Ramón. *Colonial Subjects: Puerto Ricans in a Global Perspective*. Berkeley: University of California Press, 2003.

Grosfoguel, Ramón, Margarita Cervantes-Rodríguez, and Eric Mielants. Introduction. In Cervantes-Rodríguez, Grosfoguel, and Mielants, *Caribbean Migration to Western Europe and the United States*, 1-17.

Hamilton, Walton. "The Puerto Rican Economy Linked with the Mainland." *Annals of the American Academy of Political and Social Science* 285 (January 1953): 76-84.

Hewitt, Charles E., Jr. "Welcome: Paupers and Crime: Porto Rico's Shocking Gift to the United States." *Scribner's Commentator* 7, no. 5 (March 1940): 11-17.

Itzigsohn, José. "Immigration and the Boundaries of Citizenship: The Institutions of Immigrants' Political Transnationalism." *International Migration Review* 34, no. 4 (Winter 2000): 1126-54.

Johnson, Courtney. "Understanding the American Empire: Colonialism, Latin Americanism, and Professional Social Science, 1898-1920." In McCoy and Scarano, *Colonial Crucible*, 175-90.

Kaplan, Amy. *The Anarchy of Empire in the Making of U.S. Culture*. Cambridge, MA: Harvard University Press, 2002.

———. "Left Alone with America: The Absence of Empire in the Study of American Culture." In Kaplan and Pease, *Cultures of United States Imperialism*, 3-21.

Kaplan, Amy, and Donald Pease, eds. *Cultures of United States Imperialism*. Durham, NC: Duke University Press, 1993.

Kirsten, Peter N. "Agribusiness, Labor, and the Wetbacks: Truman's Commission on Migratory Labor." *The Historian* 40, no. 4 (August 1978): 650-67.

Kramer, Paul. *The Blood of Government: Race, Empire, the United States and the Philippines*. Chapel Hill: University of North Carolina Press, 2006.

———. "Race, Empire, and Transnational History." In McCoy and Scarano, *Colonial Crucible*, 199-209.

LaFeber, Walter. *The New Empire: An Interpretation of American Expansion, 1860–1898*. Ithaca, NY: Cornell University Press, 1963.

Lapp, Michael. "Managing Migration: The Migration Division of Puerto Rico and Puerto Ricans in New York City, 1948–1968." PhD diss., John Hopkins University, 1991.

Leibowitz, Arnold H. *Defining Status: A Comprehensive Analysis of United States Territorial Relations*. Leiden, Boston: Martinus Nijhoff, 1989.

Levitt, Peggy, and Rafael de la Dehesa. "Transnational Migration and the Redefinition of the State: Variations and Explanations." *Ethnic and Racial Studies* 26, no. 4 (July 2003): 587–611.

Levitt, Peggy, Josh De Wind, and Steven Vertovec. "International Perspectives on Transnational Migration: An Introduction." *International Migration Review* 37, no. 3 (Fall 2003): 565–75.

Lugo Silva, Enrique. *The Tugwell Administration in Puerto Rico, 1941–1946*. Río Piedras, PR: Enrique Lugo Silva, 1955.

Lyon, Richard Martin. "The Legal Status of American and Mexican Migratory Farm Labor: An Analysis of U.S. Farm-Labor Legislation, Policy and Administration." PhD diss., Cornell University, 1954.

Magoon, Charles E. *Report of the Legal Status of the Territory and Inhabitants of the Islands Acquired by the United States During the War with Spain, Considered with Reference to the Territorial Boundaries, the Constitution and Laws of the United States*. Washington, DC: U.S. Government Printing Office, 1900.

Maldonado, A. W. *Teodoro Moscoso and Puerto Rico's Operation Bootstrap*. Gainesville, FL: University Press of Florida, 1997.

Maldonado, Edwin. "Contract Labor and the Origins of Puerto Rican Communities in the United States." *International Migration Review* 13, no. 1 (Spring 1979): 103–21.

Maldonado-Denis, Manuel. *The Emigration Dialectic: Puerto Rico and the USA*. New York: International Publishers, 1980.

Mapes, Kathleen. *Sweet Tyranny: Migrant Labor, Industrial Agriculture, and Imperial Politics*. Urbana: University of Illinois Press, 2009.

Mathews, Thomas. *Puerto Rican Politics and the New Deal*. Gainesville: University of Florida Press, 1960.

Mayor's Committee on Puerto Rican Affairs in New York City. "Interim Report, September 1949 to September 1953." New York: MCPRA, 1953.

McCormick, Thomas. "From Old Empire to New: The Changing Dynamics and Tactics of American Empire." In McCoy and Scarano, *Colonial Crucible*, 63–79.

McCoy, Alfred W., and Francisco Scarano, eds. *Colonial Crucible: Empire in the Making of the Modern American State*. Madison: University of Wisconsin Press, 2009.

McCoy, Alfred W., Francisco Scarano, and Courtney Johnson. "On the Tropic of Cancer: Transitions and Transformations in the U.S. Imperial State." In McCoy and Scarano, *Colonial Crucible*, 1–12.

McGovney, Dudley O. "Our Non-Citizen Nationals, Who are They?," *California Law Review* 22, no. 6 (September 1934): 593–635.

McGreevy, Robert C. "Borderline Citizens: Puerto Ricans and the Politics of Migration, Race, and Empire, 1898–1948." PhD diss., Brandeis University, 2008.

———. "Empire and Migration: Coastwise Shipping, National Status, and the Colonial Legal Origins of Puerto Rican Migration to the United States." *The Journal of the Gilded Age and Progressive Era* 11, no. 4 (October 2012): 553–73.

Meléndez, Edgardo. "Citizenship and the Alien Exclusion in the Insular Cases: Puerto Ricans in the Periphery of American Empire." *Centro: Journal of the Center for Puerto Rican Studies* 25, no. 1 (Spring 2013): 106–45.

———. "The Puerto Rican Journey Revisited: Politics and the Study of Puerto Rican Migration." *Centro Journal* 22, no. 2 (Fall 2005): 192–221.

———. "Puerto Rican Migration, the Colonial State, and Transnationalism." *Centro: Journal of the Center for Puerto Rican Studies* 27, no. 2 (Fall 2015): 50–95.

———. *Puerto Rico's Statehood Movement*. Westport, CT: Greenwood Press, 1988.

———. "Vito Marcantonio, Puerto Rican Migration, and the 1949 Mayoral Election in New York City." *Centro Journal* 22, no. 2 (Fall 2010): 199–233.

Meléndez Vélez, Edgardo. *Partidos, política pública y status en Puerto Rico*. San Juan: Ediciones Nueva Aurora, 1998.

Meléndez, Edwin, and Carlos Vargas-Ramos, eds. *Puerto Ricans at the Dawn of the New Millennium*. New York: Center for Puerto Rican Studies, 2014.

———. *The State of Puerto Ricans 2013*. New York: Center for Puerto Rican Studies, 2013.

Merrill, Dennis. *Negotiating Paradise: U.S. Tourism and Empire in Twentieth-Century Latin America*. Chapel Hill: University of North Carolina Press, 2009.

Milia-Marie-Luce, Monique. "Puerto Ricans in the United States and French West Indian Immigrants in France." In Cervantes-Rodríguez, Grosfoguel, and Mielants, *Caribbean Migration to Western Europe and the United States*, 94–110.

Mills, C. Wright, Clarence O. Senior, and Rose K. Goldsen, *The Puerto Rican Journey: New York's Newest Migrants*. New York: Russell and Russell, 1950, reprint ed., 1967.

Mings, Robert C. "The Role of the Commonwealth Government in the Growth and Development of the Puerto Rico Tourist Industry." PhD diss., Ohio State University, 1966.

Molina, Natalia. *How Race Is Made in America: Immigration, Citizenship, and the Historical Power of Racial Scripts*. Berkeley: University of California Press, 2014.

Monserrat, Joseph. "The Development, Growth and Decline of the Puerto Rican Farm Workers Contract Program." Unfinished manuscript, no date. In Joseph Monserrat Papers, Centro de Estudios Puertorriqueños, box 17 (Subject Files, 1968–1992).

Muñoz Marín, Luis. *Memorias: autobiografía pública 1940–1952*. San Germán, PR: Universidad Interamericana de Puerto Rico, 1992.

Myers, George C. "Migration and Modernization: The Case of Puerto Rico, 1960–1960." *Social and Economic Studies* 16, no. 4 (December 1967): 425–31.

Negrón de Montilla, Aida. *La americanización de Puerto Rico y el sistema de instrucción pública, 1900–1930*. San Juan: Editorial de la Universidad de Puerto Rico, 1976.

Ngai, Mae. *Impossible Subjects: Illegal Aliens and the Making of Modern America*. Princeton, NJ: Princeton University Press, 2004.

Ostergaard-Nielsen, Eva, ed. *International Migration and Sending Countries: Perceptions, Policies and Transnational Relations*. New York: Palgrave Macmillan, 2003.

Pagán de Colón, Petroamérica. "Migration: Its Problems." *Extramuros* 1, no. 3 (June 1968): 137–41.

———. *Programa de Colocaciones de Trabajadores Agrícolas Puertorriqueños*. San Juan: Department of Labor, [195–?].

Pantojas-García, Emilio. *Development Strategies as Ideology: Puerto Rico's Export-led Industrialization Experience.* Boulder, CO: Lynne Rienners Publishers; Río Piedras, PR: Editorial de la Universidad de Puerto Rico, 1990.

Partsch, Jaime. *Jesús T. Piñero: el exilado en su patria.* San Juan: Ediciones Huracán, 2006.

Pérez, Gina M. *The Near Northwest Side Story: Migration, Displacement, and Puerto Rican Families.* Berkeley: University of California Press, 2004.

Picó, Isabel. "Origins of the Puerto Rican University Student Movement under U.S. Domination." In *Puerto Rico and Puerto Ricans: Studies in History and Society,* edited by Adalberto López and James Petras, 175–94. Cambridge, MA: Schenkman, 1974.

Poblete, JoAnna. *Islanders in the Empire: Filipino and Puerto Rican Laborers in Hawai'i.* Urbana: University of Illinois Press, 2014.

Portes, Alejandro, and Josh DeWind. "A Cross-Atlantic Dialogue: The Progress of Research and Theory in the Study of International Migration." *International Migration Review* 38, no. 3 (Fall 2004): 828–51.

Portes, Alejandro, Luis E. Guarnizo, and Patricia Landolt. "The Study of Transnationalism: Pitfalls and Promise of an Emergent Research Field." *Ethnic and Racial Studies* 22, no. 2 (1999): 217–37.

Portes, Alejandro, and Ruben G. Rumbaut. *Immigrant America: A Portrait.* 3rd ed. Berkeley: University of California Press, 2006.

Pousada, Alicia. "The Singularly Strange Story of the English Language in Puerto Rico." *Milenio* 3 (1999): 33–60.

President's Commission on Migratory Labor. *Migratory Labor in American Agriculture.* Washington, DC: Report by the President's Commission on Migratory Labor, 1951.

Puerto Rico Policy Commission. *Report of the Puerto Rico Policy Commission.* San Juan: Puerto Rico Policy Comission, June 14, 1934.

Quintero-Rivera, A. G. *Conflictos de clase y política en Puerto Rico.* Río Piedras, PR: Ediciones Huracán, 1986.

Ramírez de Arellano, Annette B., and Conrad Seipp. *Colonialism, Catholicism, and Contraception: A History of Birth Control in Puerto Rico.* Chapel Hill: University of North Carolina Press, 1983.

Rivera Ramos, Efrén. *The Legal Construction of Identity: The Judicial and Social Legacy of American Colonialism in Puerto Rico.* Washington, DC: American Psychological Association, 2001.

Rizzo Costa, Clara, and Betty Wallace Robinett. *La Familia Vázquez en los Estados Unidos.* Hato Rey, PR: Departament of Education, 1954.

Robinson, Robert S. "Taking the Fair Deal to the Fields: Truman's Commission on Migratory Labor, Public Law 78, and the Bracero Program, 1950–1952." *Agricultural History* 84, no. 3 (2010): 381–402.

Rodríguez, Clara. *Puerto Ricans: Born in the USA.* Boston: Hyman, 1989.

Rodríguez Bou, Ismael. "Significant Factors in the Development of Education in Puerto Rico." In United States-Puerto Rico Commission on the Status of Puerto Rico. *Selected Background Studies,* Washington, DC: Government Printing Office, 1966.

Rosario Natal, Carmelo. *Luis Muñoz Marín y la independencia de Puerto Rico (1907–1946).* San Juan: Producciones Históricas, 1994.

Ross, David. *The Long Uphill Path: A Historical Study of Puerto Rico's Program of Economic Development.* San Juan: Editorial Edil, 1976.

Sánchez, Luis Rafael. *La guagua aérea*. Río Piedras, PR: Editorial Cultural, 1994.

Sánchez-Korrol, Virginia. *From Colonia to Community: The History of Puerto Ricans in New York City*. Berkeley: University of California Press, 1994.

Senior, Clarence O. "Migration and Economic Development in Puerto Rico." *Journal of Educational Sociology* 28, no. 4 (December 1954): 151–56.

———. "Migration and Puerto Rico's Population Problem." *Annals of the American Academy of Political and Social Science* 285 (January 1953): 130–36.

———. *Our Citizens from the Caribbean*. New York: McGraw Hill, 1965.

———. "Patterns of Puerto Rican Dispersion in the Continental United States." *Social Problems* 2, no. 2 (October 1954): 93–99.

———. *Puerto Rican Emigration*. Río Piedras, PR: Social Science Research Center, University of Puerto Rico at Río Piedras, 1947.

———. *The Puerto Ricans: Strangers—Then Neighbors*. Chicago: Quadrangle Books, 1965.

———. "Puerto Rico: Migration to the Mainland." *Monthly Labor Review* 78, no. 12 (December 1955): 1354–58.

———. "Toward a Balance Sheet of Puerto Rican Migration." In United States-Puerto Rico Commission on the Status of Puerto Rico. *Selected Background Studies*, Washington, DC: U.S. Government Printing Office, 1966.

Sierra Berdecía, Fernando. *Frente del Trabajo: Hombres y mujeres que laboran*. San Juan: Departamento del Trabajo, 1951.

———. "Migración de Trabajadores Puertorriqueños a Estados Unidos." Report to Governor Jesús T. Piñero, November 17, 1947. In AGPR, FOG, Tarea 96–20, box 454.

———. *Protecting Puerto Rico's Labor*. San Juan: Department of Labor, 1948.

———. *Puerto Rican Emigration: Reality and Public Policy*. San Juan: Department of Labor, 1957.

Smith, Michael Peter, and Luis E. Guarnizo, eds. *Transnationalism from Below*. New Brunswick, NJ: Transaction Publishers, 1998.

Sparrow, Bartholomew H. *The Insular Cases and the Emergence of American Empire*. Kansas City: University Press of Kansas, 2006.

Takaki, Ronald. *A Different Mirror: A History of Multicultural America*. Boston: Little, Brown, and Co., 1993.

Thomas, Lorrin. *Puerto Rican Citizen: History and Political Identity in Twentieth-Century New York City*. Chicago: University of Chicago Press, 2010.

Thompson, Lanny. *Imperial Archipelago: Representation and Rule in the Insular Territories under U.S. Dominion after 1898*. Honolulu: University of Hawai'i Press, 2010.

Tió, Salvador. "La emigración: Cambios en la política pública." *La Torre* 1, no. 3 (January–May 1956): 113–36.

Torre, Carlos A., Hugo Rodríguez Vecchini, and William Burgos, eds. *The Commuter Nation: Perspectives on Puerto Rican Migration*. Río Piedras, PR: Editorial de la Universidad de Puerto Rico, 1994.

Torres González, Roamé. *Idioma, bilingüismo y nacionalidad: la presencia del inglés en Puerto Rico*. San Juan: Editorial de la Universidad de Puerto Rico, 2002.

Torruella, Juan R. *The Supreme Court and Puerto Rico: The Doctrine of Separate and Unequal*. Río Piedras, PR: Editorial de la Universidad de Puerto Rico, 1985.

U.S. Commission on Civil Rights. *Puerto Ricans in the Continental United States: An Uncertain Future*. Washington, DC: U.S. Commission on Civil Rights, 1976.

U.S. Congress, House of Representatives, Committee on Insular Affairs. "Condition of Puerto Rican Sugar Industry." Hearings before the Committee, 79th Congress, First Session, Washington, DC, March 1, 2, 3, 5, 6, 7, 8, and 9. Washington, DC: U.S. Government Printing Office, 1945.

———. "Investigation of Political, Economic, and Social Conditions in Puerto Rico." Hearings before Subcommittee, 78th Congress, First Session, Pursuant to H. Res. 159. Part 3, San Juan, P. R., June 1 and 2, 1943; part 4, San Juan, P. R., June 3, 4 and 7, 1943; part 12, San Juan, P. R., June 17, 1943. Washington, DC: U.S. Government Printing Office, 1943.

———. *Investigation of Political, Economic, and Social Conditions in Puerto Rico*. Report of the Committee on Insular Affairs, House of Representatives, 79th Congress, First Session, pursuant to H. Res. 159 (78th Cong.) and H. Res. 99 (79th Cong.). Washington, DC: Government Printing Office, 1945.

U.S. Congress, House of Representatives, Committee of Interior and Insular Affairs. "Puerto Rico Constitution." Hearings before the Committee on H. J. Res. 430, "A Joint Resolution Approving the Constitution of the Commonwealth of Puerto Rico, which was Adopted by the People of Puerto Rico on March 3, 1952." 82nd Congress, Second Session, April 25, 1952. Washington, DC: U.S. Government Printing Office, 1952.

U.S. Congress, House of Representatives, Committee on Public Lands. "Election of Governor." Hearings before the Subcommittee on Territorial and Insular Possessions, 80th Congress, First session, on H. R. 3309, "A bill to Amend the Organic Act of Puerto Rico," May 19, 1947. Washington, DC: U.S. Government Printing Office, 1947.

U.S. Congress, Senate Committee on Territories and Insular Affairs. *Economic and Social Conditions in Puerto Rico*. Hearings before a Subcommittee of the Committee on Territories and Insular Affairs, 78th Congress, February 10–19, 1943. Washington, DC: Government Printing Office, 1943.

U.S. Tariff Commission. *The Economy of Puerto Rico: With Special Reference to the Economic Implications of Independence and Other Proposals to Change Its Political Status*. Washington, DC: U.S. Tariff Commission, 1946.

Valdés, Dennis Nodín. *Al Norte: Agricultural Workers in the Great Lakes Region, 1917–1970*. Austin: University of Texas Press, 1991.

Vaughan, Mary K. "Tourism in Puerto Rico." In *Puerto Rico and Puerto Ricans: Studies in History and Society*, edited by Adalberto López and James Petras, 271–95. Cambridge, MA: Schenkman Publishing, 1974.

Vega, Bernardo. *Memoirs of Bernardo Vega*. Edited by César Andreu Iglesias. New York: Monthly Review Press, 1984.

Venator-Santiago, Charles R. "Extending Citizenship to Puerto Rico: Three Traditions of Inclusive Exclusion." *Centro: Journal of the Center for Puerto Rican Studies* 25, no. 1 (Spring 2013): 50–75.

Villaronga, Mariano. "Program of Education for Puerto Rican Migrants." *Journal of Educational Sociology* 28, no. 4 (December 1954): 146–50.

Welfare Council of New York City. *Puerto Ricans in New York City*. New York: Welfare Council of New York City, 1948.

Whalen, Carmen T. *From Puerto Rico to Philadelphia: Puerto Rican Workers and Postwar Economies*. Philadelphia: Temple University Press, 2001.

Whalen, Carmen Teresa, and Víctor Vázquez-Hernández. *The Puerto Rican Diaspora: Historical Perspectives*. Philadelphia: Temple University Press, 2005.

Williams, William Appleman. *The Tragedy of American Diplomacy*. New York: Dell, 1962.

INDEX

Albizu Campos, Pedro, 169
Allen, Charles, 35
air crashes (Puerto Rico), 103–8; Airborne Transport, 105; Holy Friday, 107–8; Melbourne (Florida), 103; and migration, 107; and migration policy, 107; Punta Salinas, 105–6, 170; Savannah (Georgia), 103–4; West Air, 107, 109, 170–73, 190
air transportation in Puerto Rico, 23, 98–99, 100–101; and air crashes/accidents, 94, 98, 102, 103–8, 160; airfares, 96, 97, 98–99, 102, 108–11; and air safety, 93, 102, 111, 120–21; categories of air passengers, 118–19; infrastructure, 93, 114; and major U.S. airlines, 96, 100, 101–2, 107, 110, 173; and migration, 93–94, 95, 96–97, 98, 99–100, 111, 112, 113, 114, 173; and nonscheduled/irregular airlines, 98, 99, 101–2, 103, 107, 110–11, 173; number of flights, 102, 111, 117; number of passengers, 101, 111, 112–13, 115; and tourism, 23, 24, 101, 113–19; "visitors," 114, 115 table 1, 115–16, 117–18. See also Puerto Rico government, migration policy

Baldwin, Clare, 127, 128
Balzac v. the People of Porto Rico, 9, 13, 15–16, 19
Barnes, Ventura, 90
Bonilla, Frank, 4–5
bracero(s), 43, 81, 161, 164–65, 187, 188, 192
Bracero Program, 84, 85, 160, 164, 190, 193
Bureau of Employment and Migration (BEM), 3, 5, 20, 31–32, 33, 34, 68, 70, 80, 82–88, 132, 133, 199; field offices in Puerto Rico, 85, 199; field offices in the U.S., 85, 206; and illegal hiring of workers, 120–21; and job placements in Puerto Rico, 86–87, 208; and job placements in the United States, 83, 86–87, 208. *See also* Department of Labor
Bureau of Employment and Security (BES), 80
Bureau of Insular Affairs (U.S. Department of War), 36

Cabán, Pedro, 28–29
Cabranes, Manuel, 77, 182
Campos, Ricardo, 4–5
Caro, Salvador, 112–13
Castle, Barton and Associates Employment Agency, 53, 55
Centro de Estudios Puertorriqueños (Center for Puerto Rican Studies), 4, 95
Chardón, Carlos, 40–41
Chicago: and migration policy, 52; Puerto Rican migration to, 23, 50, 53, 66; Puerto Ricans in, 53–56, 67, 143
Civil Aeronautics Administration (CAA), 103, 104, 106, 107, 171
Civil Aeronautics Board (CAB), 95, 97, 98–99, 100, 102, 103, 104, 106, 107, 109, 110, 111–12, 171
Clark, Victor, 124
Collazo, Francisco, 62, 127, 135–36, 141, 178
Colón, Sylvia Eliza, 137

255

colonial state in Puerto Rico, 8, 20, 26–29; and migration, 5, 8, 20, 26–27, 29, 30–33; relative autonomy of, 20, 26, 29, 30–33, 90, 94

Commonwealth status (Puerto Rico), 19, 20, 28, 44, 125, 129, 186, 198; Constitution, 19, 44, 79, 167, 168

Contract labor (Puerto Rican), 35; abuses against, 35, 36. *See also* Puerto Rico Government, migration policy

Crawford, Fred L., 24, 160, 165–69, 179–80, 181, 183, 188–89; and Puerto Rican migration to the United States, 168, 189

Crist, Raymond, 62

Davis, Kingsley, 52

Departamento de Instrucción Pública (Department of Public Instruction), 132. *See also* Department of Education

Department of Education (Puerto Rico), 123–24, 136, 137, 145; English for adults program, 132, 133–35, 139, 142; English for prospective migrants program, 122, 123, 128, 129, 132–33, 136–37, 141; and migration, 32, 34, 122, 133, 134–36, 141

Department of Labor (Puerto Rico), 55, 134, 136–37, 145, 161; and migration/migration policy, 34, 122, 137–38, 173; reports, 118, 133

Dietz, James, 30

División para la Educación de la Comunidad (Community Education Division), 141

Domestic labor, Puerto Ricans as, 23. *See also* Puerto Rican migrants in the U.S.

Dorfman Report, 46–47

Downes v. Bidwell, 13–14, 18, 85, 162. *See also* Insular Cases

Draper, Estella, 77

Duany, Jorge, 7, 9

Eastern Airlines, 97, 98, 101, 102, 107, 109, 110, 117, 121, 171, 172, 173

Economic Development Administration (EDA; Fomento), 31, 86. *See also* Operation Bootstrap

education policy in Puerto Rico: and Americanization, 23, 123–25, 129, 132, 142–43; and migration, 23, 131, 132; and Spanish as language of education, 125–26, 130

El Barrio (New York City), 57

El Imparcial, 54, 103, 106–7, 135, 171, 172, 173–76, 179, 180, 182

El Mundo, 40, 41, 104, 111, 143, 144, 178, 179, 181

Emigración, 141

Emigration law 1919 (Puerto Rico), 35–36

Emigration Office, 60–61, 63. *See also* Migration Division

English language education in Puerto Rico, 23, 123–26, 130, 138; for adults, 132, 139, 142; intensification of, 125–26, 129, 132, 137, 143–44, 145; and migration, 122, 124, 125, 126, 127–28, 142–43, 144; to prospective migrants, 128, 134–35, 136–37, 138–39, 142. *See also* Department of Education; education policy in Puerto Rico

farmer's associations (U.S.), 88, 109, 197, 203–4; and Puerto Rican farmworkers, 88; and Puerto Rican labor contract, 88. *See also* Garden State Service Cooperative Association; Glassboro Service Association; Michigan Field Corporation

Farm Placement Program (FPP), 3, 23, 64, 72, 83, 85, 86–88, 109, 136, 160, 185, 187, 197, 199, 200–204, 210; job placements in the U.S., 201–4 tables 7 and 8. *See also* Bureau of Employment and Migration

Ferguson, R. Brian, 168

Fernández García, Rafael, 91

Fernós-Isern, Antonio, 57, 58, 62, 67, 77, 99–100, 103, 108, 114

Filipino migration to the U.S., 16–17, 50

Fleisher, Belton, 96

Fomento, 114, 168. *See also* Operation Bootstrap

Foraker Act, 2, 13, 28, 123, 162

Free Federation of Labor, 162, 185

Gallardo, Carlos, 39

Gallardo, Manuel, 125

Garden State Service Cooperative Association, 109–10, 121, 197, 203

Géigel Polanco, Vicente, 55, 62, 63

Glassboro Service Association, 197, 203

Go, Julian, 27–28,

Gonzales v. Williams, 15, 16

Goodwin, Robert, 76, 77–78, 81

Hamilton, Walton, 96–97, 109
Hanson, Earl Parker, 90
Henderson, Max, 180, 181, 189
Hilliard, Raymond M., 78

Ickes, Harold, 38, 42
Iglesias, Santiago, Jr., 41, 42
Impelliteri, Vincent, 101
Independence (Puerto Rico), 44, 46, 47
individual (or voluntary) migration, 4, 37, 41, 82–83, 86. *See also* Puerto Rican migration to the U.S.
Industrial Incentives Act. *See* Operation Bootstrap
Insular Cases, 9, 162
international airport (Puerto Rico), 93, 111–13, 114; and migration policy, 111; opposition by U.S. Navy, 111–12; and Puerto Rico government, 94, 111
Isales, Carmen, 54–55
Isla Grande airport, 111

Jones Act(s), 16, 17, 28, 124, 198, 217n51
Jones-Costigan Act, 162–63

Kaplan, Amy and Donald Pease, 11
Kramer, Paul, 16, 27

Labor Bureau (Puerto Rico), 35, 37
labor contracts (Puerto Ricans), 36, 54, 55, 84–85, 193–95; and Puerto Rican government, 33, 39, 55–56. *See also* Puerto Rico government, migration policy
Lapp, Michael, 5, 7, 83, 209–10, 212
Leahy, William, 38, 39, 112
Lee, Atherton, 38, 39
Lee, H. Rex, 89
López, William D., 39–40

Machuca, Julio, 59
Maldonado, A. W., 70
Maldonado, Edwin, 43
Marcantonio, Vito, 33, 56, 57, 106, 146, 168, 171, 181, 182, 206
Mayor's Committee on Puerto Rican Affairs in New York (MCPRA), 128
McCoy, Alfred and Francisco Scarano, 11, 12, 27

Michigan Field Corporation (MFC), 107, 109, 161, 170, 172, 180, 181, 182, 183, 197
Michigan: Puerto Rican farmworkers' strike in, 169, 175; and Puerto Rican migrant discontent in, 21, 24, 159–60, 173–77, 189; Puerto Rican migrants in, 33, 161, 164, 170, 174–75, 177, 180, 182, 184, 188–90
Migration Advisory Committee, 58, 61–64, 65, 89
Migration Conference(s), 128, 129, 142
Migration Division, 3, 5, 20, 21, 31, 33, 34, 61, 64, 80, 83, 135, 140, 143, 145, 182, 187, 195, 199, 205–9; English classes for migrants, 209; job placements in the U.S., 203–4, 207–8, 210; and migrant incorporation and adaptation, 204, 205, 208; migrant orientation and services, 206–7 table 9
migration law (Puerto Rico), 32, 64, 65, 67, 69–71, 72, 82, 83, 84, 198
Migration Office, 34, 69, 70, 83, 127, 182. *See also* Migration Division
migration policy (Puerto Rico), 2, 4, 20, 68, 82, 137, 146, 172, 175, 212; critique of, 172, 174–76, 185; formulation of, 22, 51, 65–69, 223n65; and racism in the U.S., 86; study of, 3, 5, 6, 21. *See also* Puerto Rico government, migration policy
migratory labor/workers in the U.S., 84–85, 187, 190–92
Monserrat, José (Joseph), 58, 80, 85, 86
Moscoso, Teodoro, 52, 61, 62, 91
Muñoz Lee, Muna (Munita), 53
Muñoz Marín, Luis, 44, 46, 61, 62, 63, 67, 83, 91, 92, 97–98, 99, 106, 107, 120, 125–26, 129, 139, 142, 143–45, 163, 170, 171, 172, 173, 174, 176, 187, 189; and Congressman Crawford, 166–69, 183; and language policy, 130–32; and migration/migration policy, 6, 90, 108–9, 168, 184; and negotiations in Michigan farmworkers unrest, 178–81; and overpopulation/population control, 51–52

New Progressive Party, 85, 210, 212
New York City, Puerto Ricans in, 56–57, 66, 67, 144; Puerto Rican migration to, 3, 37, 49, 56–57, 78, 82, 101; and welfare, 57
New York Times, 46, 56, 57, 101, 171, 180, 182
New York World Telegram, 57

O'Connor, Don, 59–60, 62, 70, 90, 91, 111

O'Dwyer, William, 66, 67–68
Operation Bootstrap, 31, 64, 65, 79, 126, 169, 186, 198, 212–13
Organized (mass) migration, 38, 82–83
Ostergaard-Nielsen, Eva, 6
overpopulation in Puerto Rico, 35, 38, 45, 51, 189; and migration/migration policy, 2, 35, 4, 22, 25–26, 37, 41, 51–52, 59, 72, 124

Padín, José, 124–25, 132
Pagán, Bolívar, 42
Pagán de Colón, Petroamérica, 64, 83, 85, 86, 88, 108–9, 120, 170, 173, 183, 187
Panama Canal Zone, 38, 39–40
Pan American Airlines, 97, 98, 99, 100–101, 102, 107, 108, 109, 110, 111, 117, 171, 172, 173
Pérez, Manuel A., 43, 53–54
Perl, Alan, 77, 178
Philippines, 162–63
Picó, Rafael, 61, 62, 90
Piñero, Jesús T., 44, 49, 62, 63, 64, 67, 92, 97, 110, 112
PM (New York), 56
political status (Puerto Rico): and migration, 44–46
Pons, Juan A., 61
Popular Democratic Party (Partido Popular Democrático—PPD), 18–19, 44, 79, 129, 162–63; and government reforms, 30, 198, 212; and migration, 6; and political status of Puerto Rico, 44
population control in Puerto Rico, 47, 51, 96; and migration, 23, 50, 51–52, 70
Pousada, Alicia, 123
President's (Truman) Commission on Migratory Labor, 73, 74, 75, 81, 86, 164; hearings, 188–90; report, 74, 187, 190–92, 193–94, 195, 196–97
Public Health Association of Puerto Rico, 51
public school system in Puerto Rico: and migration, 23, 122
Puerto Rican Emigration (Senior), 52, 60
Puerto Rican farmworkers in the U.S.: competition with Mexican and West Indian labor, 74, 77, 79, 80; as migratory workers in the U.S., 75, 160, 164, 187, 188, 192; and Puerto Rican communities in the U.S., 87; work desertion, 194, 219–20n59

Puerto Rican Independence Party (PIP), 163, 177
Puerto Rican migrants in the U.S.: as alien/foreign to the U.S., 8, 9, 10, 15, 16, 18, 19, 74–75, 85, 126, 144, 146, 192, 197, 216n24, 223n3; and assimilation, 144; discontent, 91, 159–60, 173–77, 184–85; as domestic workers/labor in the U.S., 33, 72, 74, 76–77, 85, 161, 187, 192, 193–94; and English education, 66, 67, 127, 144, 145; preference as U.S. citizens, 85, 86, 193; remittances, 84, 174, 176; U.S. employer's reluctance to hire, 75, 77, 87. *See also* Puerto Rico government, migration policy
Puerto Rican migration: to Brazil, 41, 42, 62, 90–91; to Costa Rica, 92; to Cuba, 35; to Detroit, 177, 190; to Dominican Republic, 35, 40, 59, 62, 89; to Hawaii, 34–35; to Latin America, 23, 32, 34, 40, 45, 47–48, 52, 59, 60, 63, 88–92; to Mexico, 35; to Panama, 34, 38–40; as planned, 40–41, 43, 47, 59, 60; and race/racism, 63, 89; to Suriname, 92; to Venezuela, 38, 42, 59–60, 62, 63, 89, 92; of women, 59
Puerto Rican migration to the United States, 2, 42, 47–48, 60, 63, 64, 86; and air transportation, 21, 23, 33, 49; as colonial migration, 2, 8, 9, 10, 22; during World War I, 34, 36; during World War II, 22, 37, 42–43; early twentieth century, 2; early twenty-first century, 2, 212, 215n1; as "ethnologically different," 7, 67, 69, 82, 145; from rural areas in Puerto Rico, 87, 226n61; as individual migration, 4, 70–71, 129, 185, 201, 205; as labor migration, 95; and migrant incorporation, 4, 21, 146–47; and migration/immigration studies in the U.S., 3; net migration, 201–2 table 6; as organized migration, 73, 129, 185, 186; postwar, 186–87; and race/racism, 41, 79, 224n23, 225–26n52; and structural economic forces, 4; study of, 10, 215n3; as transnational migration, 6–7, 9, 216n20; two migration flows, 82–83; in U.S. agriculture, 67, 83, 201–4; and U.S. colonialism and citizenship, 2, 9, 10, 12, 22; as U.S. internal migration, 8, 145. *See also* Puerto Rico government, migration policy
"Puerto Rican problem," 25, 34, 45, 63, 65, 66, 67, 88–89, 113, 121, 127, 144, 146, 185; in New York City, 21, 22, 26, 49–50, 56–58, 61, 71, 82; and Puerto Rico's migration policy, 49–50, 58, 73

INDEX • 259

Puerto Ricans as cheap labor, 36, 37, 186, 196, 198, 211
Puerto Rico: as periphery of American empire, 8, 12–13
Puerto Rico government: and federal government, 5, 18; and U.S. citizenship, 5, 18, 20, 23, 79, 85
Puerto Rico government, migration policy: and air transportation, 5, 21, 23, 93–94, 95, 97–100, 109; and airfares, 108–11, 109; as labor contractor, 5, 73, 86, 88, 160, 187, 193–97, 198, 210; and migrant adjustment, 69, 71, 89; and migrant incorporation, 2–3, 7, 8, 20, 32–33, 50, 126–27, 129, 131, 135, 139–40, 143–44, 145, 187, 195, 212, 232n32; and migrant labor contracts, 75, 77, 81, 83, 84–85, 86, 88, 109, 159–60, 174, 178, 184, 196–97, 210, 225n51, 225–26n52; and migrant orientation/advice, 68, 120–21, 122, 129, 136, 144, 200, 205–6, 233n67; and migration away from New York City, 59, 84, 129; and prevailing wages, 76, 86, 195, 199–200, 210; and prospective migrants, 68, 142–43, 144, 206; role in migration, 2–3, 5, 8, 20, 29, 32, 50, 211–12; and screening and selection of migrant workers, 43, 60, 68, 83, 87, 178, 185, 195, 197, 200–201. *See also* air crashes; air transportation; Department of Education; English education; international airport; Migration Division; migration policy
Puerto Rico politics: and migration, 22; political status, 20, 160, 167
Puerto Rico Transportation Authority (TA), 95, 106, 112, 171

Ramos Antonini, Ernesto, 145
Reck, Daisy, 61, 62
Rincón de Gautier, Felisa, 144
Rivera Martínez, Prudencio, 39
Rivera-Ramos, Efrén, 17
Rodríguez Bou, Ismael, 123, 134, 136–37, 139
Rojas, Pauline, 133
Roosevelt, Franklin D., 38, 125, 165
Root, Elihu, 13, 17
Rosario Natal, Carmelo, 46

Sánchez-Korrol, Virginia, 37
Semana, 139–40, 141, 142
Senior, Clarence, 4, 5, 7, 43, 52, 60–61, 62, 63, 81, 83

Sierra Berdecía, Fernando, 6, 22, 54, 61, 62, 63, 64–65, 76–77, 79–81, 82, 83, 86, 90, 120, 121, 127, 139, 165, 170, 171–72, 183, 184, 189, 198, 222n50, 223n52; and industrial peace, 64–65, 84; and Michigan farmworkers unrest, 173–75, 178–80, 182; and migrant adaptation/adjustment, 66, 67, 68; and migration policy, 51, 65–66, 161; and Puerto Rico's migration law, 69–71
Socialist Party (Puerto Rico), 162, 185
Spanish-American War, 2
statehood (Puerto Rico), 44, 46
Stimson, Henry L., 39
Sugar industry (Puerto Rico), 162–63, 199–200
Sugar Trust, 162
Swope, Guy J., 40

The Puerto Rican Journey, 58, 82
Tió, Salvador, 52
Tobin, Maurice J., 78, 79–80, 81
Torres, Eulalio, 178, 181–82, 183
Torres González, Roamé, 123, 126
tourism in Puerto Rico, 114–19; hotel registrations, 116 table 3, 117 table 4. *See also* Air transportation in Puerto Rico
Transnationalism, 6; and study of Puerto Rican migration, 6–8, 10, 21–22
Travel Aid Society, 120, 209
Treaty of Paris, 13, 40
Truman, Harry, 44, 112
Tugwell, Redford G., 28, 37, 166, 168
Tydings, Millard, 17, 47, 181; Puerto Rico independence bill(s), 17, 163, 167
Tydings-McDuffie Act, 16, 163, 218n55

unincorporated territory (Puerto Rico), 2, 9, 10, 13, 14, 16, 17, 198, 212
University of Puerto Rico (UPR), 124, 135
U.S. agriculture: and agribusiness, 78; and alien/foreign labor, 74, 188, 192, 193–94, 195, 196; and migratory workers, 75, 190, 191–92
U.S. citizenship in Puerto Rico, 2, 8, 18–19; exclusion of Puerto Ricans from, 13–14; grant of, 13, 15, 17, 124; and migration, 2, 9, 13, 15–16, 18, 32, 43, 59, 73, 74, 79, 85, 90

U.S. Civil Rights Commission, report on Puerto Ricans in the U.S., 146–47, 211

U.S. empire studies, 10–11, 27; and Puerto Rican migration, 10–12

U.S. Employment Service (USES), 42, 76, 77, 78, 80, 195, 196, 199

U.S. government: and Puerto Rican migration, 34, 41, 45–46, 50, 89–90

U.S. government in Puerto Rico, 17; Americanization policy, 19, 123–24; colonialism, 17, 186; colonial policies, 13, 29; and Puerto Rican migration, 9, 10, 18, 36, 37, 38

U.S. House Committee on Insular Affairs, 165–67, 168, 169; 1945 report, 45

U.S. Senate Committee on Territories and Insular Affairs, 47; 1943 report on Puerto Rico, 45

U.S. Senate Committee on Territories and Insular Possessions, 43

U.S. sugar industry, 160, 161–62, 164; and Puerto Rico, 24, 162; sugar beet producers, 162, 164, 165, 189–90

U.S. Tariff Commission, 46–47. *See also* Dorfman Report

Valdés, Dennis, 164, 177, 184

Vega, Antonio, 178

Villaronga, Mariano, 62, 126, 133–35, 136, 137, 138

Wagner-Peyser Act, 80–82, 199

War Manpower Commission (WMC), 37, 42

Welfare Council of New York City, 33, 50, 56

WIPR, 139, 142, 144

Yager, Arthur, 35

GLOBAL LATIN/O AMERICAS
FREDERICK LUIS ALDAMA AND LOURDES TORRES, SERIES EDITORS

This new series focuses on the Latino experience in its totality as set within a global dimension. The series will showcase the variety and vitality of the presence and significant influence of Latinos in the shaping of the culture, history, politics and policies, and language of the Americas—and beyond. We welcome scholarship regarding the arts, literature, philosophy, popular culture, history, politics, law, history, and language studies, among others. Books in the series will draw from scholars from around the world.

Sponsored Migration: The State and Puerto Rican Postwar Migration to the United States
EDGARDO MELÉNDEZ

La Verdad: An International Dialogue on Hip Hop Latinidades
EDITED BY MELISSA CASTILLO-GARSOW AND JASON NICHOLS

www.ingramcontent.com/pod-product-compliance
Lightning Source LLC
Chambersburg PA
CBHW021138230426
43667CB00005B/169